PRACTICAL APPROACHES TO
DEVELOPMENT PLANNING:
KOREA'S SECOND FIVE-YEAR PLAN

PRACTICAL APPROACHES TO
DEVELOPMENT PLANNING:

KOREA'S SECOND FIVE-YEAR PLAN

EDITED BY IRMA ADELMAN

THE JOHNS HOPKINS PRESS, BALTIMORE

This volume, which is intended especially for development planners, describes a planning experience of high technical caliber and considerable real success: the formulation of the Second Five-Year Development Plan (1967–1971) of the Republic of Korea. The book itself is the outgrowth of a conference held in St. Charles, Illinois, in June, 1968, under the auspices of the Ford Foundation–supported Council for Intersocietal Studies of Northwestern University. Although the conference proceedings focused primarily on the technical work underlying the plan, penetrating analyses of the role that economic planning has played in South Korea's economic and political development are included, along with significant discussions of the practical measures taken in the implementation of the plan.

I am indebted, first of all, to the Council of Intersocietal Studies of Northwestern University, whose generosity in sponsoring the conference made this volume possible, and to the individual contributors for their patience with my sometimes drastic editing. I am grateful to Joyce Nussbaum and Dilys Rennie for their invaluable editorial assistance, and to Molly Fabian and Shirley Kettler for their help with the organization of the conference and for typing the manuscript through its many versions.

A planning process is the result of interaction among many people and many institutions. I would like to thank all individuals who were involved in the planning process, whether in plan formulation, data gathering and refining, or design of plan implementation. Those most directly involved are, of course, represented in the volume. In addition, however, Kay Auerbach and Donald Dembovsky of the AID mission, Professor Han Kee Chun of Yonsey University, Director Kim D. Soo of the Bank of Korea, Director Woo of the Economic Planning Board, Deputy Prime Ministers Chan Key Young and Choong Hoon Park of the government of Korea, Dr. P. Boucherie of the German advisory group, Dr. J. Johnson of the Nathan advisory group, Professors John Gurley, Edward Shaw, and Ronald McKinnon of Stanford University, Professors Hugh Patrick, Gustav Ranis, and John Fei of Yale University, and Professor and

Mrs. Richard Musgrave of Harvard University all made valuable contributions to various aspects of the planning effort.

It has been a great privilege to be involved with the formulation of
Korea's Second Five-Year Plan. The experience has been singularly
rewarding from both a professional and human point of view.

IRMA ADELMAN

Northwestern University
Evanston, Illinois

FOREWORD

There is a growing awareness among us that the planning in Korea has played an important role in formulating the rational development strategies for the period of the Second Five-Year Economic Development Plan. As recent performance has demonstrated, the plan has been successfully translated into operationally meaningful action programs and we think they have been implemented rather effectively. We are convinced that they will continue to be so carried out in the future.

In my view, this book is extremely valuable to those who are actually engaged in decision making, for, aside from its presentation of rigorous analytical tools, the book contains one of the most successful experiences about the practical application of high-powered planning techniques. We think the lessons we have learned over the last few years can contribute very much to a deeper understanding and to an improvement of development planning in general.

Moreover, since we intend to undertake the formulation of the Third Five-Year Plan next year, this book will serve as an invaluable guide.

I, on behalf of the Government of Korea, should like to take this opportunity to congratulate the group of people who organized and participated in the Conference on Korea's planning. In particular, we wish to thank Professor Irma Adelman for her effort in organizing the Conference and in publishing the proceedings.

CHOONG HOON PARK

September 3, 1968   *Deputy Prime Minister*
and
Minister, Economic Planning Board

CONTENTS

ix

CONTRIBUTORS

Irma Adelman received her Ph.D. from the University of California Berkeley and is currently a Professor of Economics at Northwestern University. Mrs. Adelman was a consultant to the Agency for International Development and to the government of Korea on technical aspects of development planning and has taken an active part in formulating the Second Five-Year Plan.

Among her major publications are: *Theories of Economic Growth and Development*, Stanford University Press, 1961; *The Theory and Design of Economic Development* (with Erik Thorbecke), The Johns Hopkins Press, 1966; and *Society, Politics, and Economic Development—A Quantitative Approach* (with Cynthia Taft Morris), The Johns Hopkins Press, 1967; and numerous articles in the professional journals.

David C. Cole was Senior Economic Advisor U.S. AID Mission to Korea during the formulation of the Second Five-Year Plan. Currently he is economic advisor to the government of Indonesia with the Harvard University Development Advisory Service.

Mr. Cole received his Ph.D. in Economics at the University of Michigan and published *The Growth and Financing of Manufacturing in the Philippines*, University of the Philippines, 1962. Forthcoming is *Korean Development: The Interplay of Politics and Economics*, with Princeton Lyman.

S. Kanesa-Thasan graduated from the University of Ceylon having earned his B.A. in Economics. Presently he is Assistant Chief of the Far Eastern Division of the International Monetary Fund and has had several articles published in the I.M.F. Staff Papers and other economic journals.

David Kendrick received his Ph.D. at Massachusetts Institute of Technology and is presently an Assistant Professor in the Department of Economics at Harvard University. Among his major publications are *Programming Investment in the Process Industries*, M.I.T. Press; and *Mathematical Methods in Economic Planning*, forthcoming.

Kim Mahn Je, Associate Professor of Economics at Sogang College, Seoul, Korea, earned his Ph.D. at the University of Missouri. During the Second Five-Year Plan he was program advisor at the U.S. Operations Mission to Korea. Major publications include "A Stabilization Model for Korea" (with Roger Norton); and "A Statistical Model for Monetary Management: The Case of Korea, 1956–67" (with Duck Woo Nam), presented at the Second Far Eastern Meeting of the Econometric Society, Tokyo, June, 1967; and the Third Far Eastern Meeting of the Econometric Society, June, 1968, respectively.

Paul W. Kuznets received his Ph.D. from Yale University. Among his recent publications are "Financial Determinants of Manufacturing Inventory Behavior, A Quarterly Study Based on United States Estimates: 1957–1961," *Yale Economic Essays* (Fall 1964), pp. 331–69; and *Capital Movements* (Proceedings of a Conference held by the International Economic Association), St. Martin's Press, 1967, assisted J. H. Adler, editor.

Mr. Kuznets is presently an Assistant Professor at Indiana University and a research associate, Economic Growth Center, Yale University.

Lee Hee Il earned his M.A. in Economics at Korea University, in Seoul, Korea. He is presently Director of the Economic Planning Bureau of the government of Korea. During the formulation of the Second Five-Year Plan, Mr. Lee was Chief of the Investment Program Division of the Planning Board.

Lee Kee Jung acted as Assistant Section Chief of the Over-all Programming Section, Economic Planning Bureau, during the formulation of the Second Five-Year Plan. He is currently a second-year graduate student in the Department of Economics, Northwestern University and earned his B.Sc. at the Seoul National University, Korea.

Roger D. Norton is a Ph.D. candidate at The Johns Hopkins University and an economist for the Agency for International Development. During the formulation of the Second Five-Year Plan he was Assistant Economic Advisor to the U.S. Operations Mission to Korea, Seoul.

Mr. Norton delivered two papers at the 2nd Far Eastern Econometric Society Meetings, Tokyo, June, 1967: "The Korean Input-Output Planning Model" (with Lee Kee Jung) and "A Stabilization Model for Korea" (with Kim Mahn Je).

Alan M. Strout, an industrial economist for the Agency for International Development during the formulation of the Second Five-Year Plan, is presently Chief of the Program Policy Division of the agency. Mr. Strout earned his Ph.D. at the University of Chicago and has published in the *American Economic Review*, September, 1966, "Foreign Assistance and Economic Development." He also presented a paper on *Savings, Imports, and Capital Productivity in Developing Countries*, to the First World Congress of the Econometric Society, Rome, September, 1965.

Lance J. Taylor is presently a Research Economist for the ODEPLAN-MIT Research Project in economic development, Santiago, Chile.

Among his major publications are "Development Patterns: A Simulation Study" forthcoming in *Quarterly Journal of Economics*, and "Development Patterns: Among Countries and Over Time" (with H. B. Chenery) forthcoming in *Review of Economics and Statistics*.

Mr. Taylor received his Ph.D. from Harvard University.

Larry E. Westphal received his Ph.D. from Harvard University and is at present an Assistant Professor at Princeton University. Mr. Westphal in cooperation with H. B. Chenery presented a paper entitled "Economics of Scale and Investment over Time," which will be published in the forthcoming *International Economic Association Volume* from Conference on Public Economics held at Biarritz, France, 1966.

Marshall K. Wood is the Director, Economic Programming Center, National Planning Association; and consultant, U.S. National Bureau of Standards. During the Second Five-Year Plan he was consultant to the Economic Planning Board of the government of Korea and to the Bank of Korea.

His major publications include *PARM—An Economic Programming Model*, Management Science, Vol. II; No. 7, May 1965; and *Design for an Interregional Economic Programming System*, 4th U.N. Conference on Input-Output Techniques, January, 1968. Mr. Wood received his M.B.A. from Harvard University.

OFFICIAL KOREAN EXCHANGE RATES

	Effective date	Rate, *won* or *hwan*/dollar
Hwan per dollar	5/ 1/51	25
	11/10/51	60
	8/28/53	60
	12/15/53	180
	1/10/55	180
	8/15/55	500
	1/20/60	500
	2/23/60	650
	1/ 1/61	1000
	2/ 2/61	1300
Won per dollar	5/ 3/64	256.53
	3/31/65	264.00
	6/30/65	272.20
	12/31/65	272.60
	6/30/66	272.00
	12/31/66	272.00
	6/30/67	272.45
	12/31/67	275.00
	6/30/68	275.20
	9/30/68	about 280.00

Notes: 1. The currency was redenominated in *won* on June 10, 1962 at a ratio of 10 *hwan* per *won*.
2. Rates represent the won selling rate offered to customers by the Korean foreign exchange banks.
3. On May 3, 1964 the adoption of a unitary floating rate system was announced. Under this system the Bank of Korea posts daily buying and selling rates with an eye to the free market rate.

Sources: Bank of Korea, *Economic Statistics Yearbook*, 1968, and Bank of Korea, *Monthly Statistical Review*, various dates.

Part I

ECONOMIC PERSPECTIVE

Chapter 1

INTRODUCTION

Irma Adelman

In order to provide the reader with an overall perspective on this volume, the first section of this introduction will briefly discuss the political and economic history of the Republic of Korea. Following that, there will be a discussion of the several models described in these proceedings, their relationship to the plan and to each other, and the extent to which their predictions tend to converge. After a short section on some of the practical features of the actual planning process, the introduction closes with a short summary.

INTERACTION BETWEEN ECONOMIC AND POLITICAL DEVELOPMENT[1]

The synergistic effects of economic and political development are strikingly illustrated by the experiences of the Republic of Korea from its inception in 1948 to the present. Korea had been a Japanese colony, and after the Second World War, under the influence of the two victorious world powers, it was divided into two diametrically opposed political units. South Korea, which was staunchly anti-Communist, did not have a viable economy (Korean industry was concentrated in North Korea). In addition, strong Japanese domination during the colonial period left the Koreans with very few trained administrators. The threat of Communist invasion from the North eventually forced South Korea to rely on military and economic aid from the United States. South Korea's weak economic base and the political insecurity that resulted from the division of the country contributed greatly to the near-anarchy that characterized the nation in the late 1940s.

The Korean War, which started in 1950, wrought tremendous economic havoc upon the country and created a great deal of social upheaval as well, without creating either political unity or total disruption. The problem of political identity was not solved by the war; rather, this problem continued to contribute greatly to the negativism and frustration that was

---

[1] The discussion in this section draws upon the forthcoming book on Korea by David Cole and Princeton Lyman. See also Chapter 2, below.

3

characteristic of postwar Korean politics. Throughout the 1950s Syngman Rhee continued in power, and his government became increasingly autocratic. Meanwhile, largely as a result of the American presence, a whole new generation was being exposed to Western democratic values and Western democratic institutions through the greatly revamped and expanded Korean educational system.

As a result of the contrast between the dictatorial structure of the Rhee regime and the democratic ideals of Korean youth, a clash was almost inevitable. In 1960 a national uprising, led by the nation's college students, overthrew the Rhee government. The new leaders dismantled Rhee's strong presidential system, set up parliamentary rule, and allowed freedom of speech and press. In less than a year, however, there was a split in the party in power, which virtually paralyzed the operation of the government.

The subsequent military coup of 1961 brought into power a nationalistic- and future-oriented leadership that mobilized the nation for economic modernization; simultaneously, there was very strong pressure from the highly vocal intellectual segment of the population for greater democratization. After the military regime was transformed into a civilian government, in 1963, the government moved increasingly toward the recognition that economic development was the key to its own political success, as well as to the establishment of a stable Republic of Korea. It saw economic development as the means for overcoming negativism and frustration in South Korea, and saw that a strong program of economic development, coupled with an increasing trend toward political liberalization, would improve its political status among students and intellectuals.

With the emergence of a political leadership committed to economic development, the nation's economy moved ahead rapidly after 1963. The economic progress was all the more remarkable in view of the country's earlier economic history. The story of the 1950s and early 1960s had been one of overall economic stagnation. After an initial period of recovery from the Korean War, per capita GNP remained stationary from 1958 to 1963 despite massive United States assistance. In addition, the country was in a state of chronic inflation, which became significantly worse between 1961 and 1963 as a result of attempts by the military regime to increase capital formation and to decrease the country's dependence on foreign aid through a very high rate of monetary expansion. A number of economic planning programs were sidetracked because of political developments. The official First Five-Year Plan was formally adopted in 1962 but was immediately attacked by the business and academic communities, as well as by the political opposition. The poor harvests of 1962 and 1963 relegated the original First Plan to practical oblivion.

A revision of the First Five-Year Plan, which amounted to a drastic and rather arbitrary scaling down of targets, was completed in 1964, but it was largely ignored. Instead, the government's economic efforts turned primarily toward economic stabilization. The major policy efforts in 1964 and 1965 were devoted to curbing the rate of inflation by means of fiscal and monetary restraint, by promoting exports and establishing import-substitute industries by means of devaluation and import liberalization, and by progressively expanding the role of the price system to achieve more efficient resource allocation by loosening direct controls. The stabilization efforts met with substantial success, as did the export drive, and policy attention again shifted toward emphasis on economic growth. Work on the Second Five-Year Plan started in 1965; the plan was approved by the President of South Korea in August of 1966 and went into effect in January, 1967.

Events in South Korea since 1963 show how economic and political development can be mutually reinforcing. The phenomenal rate of growth of GNP—9½ percent per year in real terms between 1963 and 1966—helped create a new image for the government, thereby permitting the government to give in to pressures from students and intellectuals for greater democratization. It became possible to liberalize controls over the press, to ease the severe restrictions on student political activities, and to encourage a functioning opposition. At the same time, the trend toward relaxation of government controls over the economy was accelerated.

The Second Five-Year Plan stressed balance between supply and demand in each sector of the economy and it selected an overall growth target consistent with both the availability of foreign and domestic savings and the supply of foreign exchange. For this reason, increasingly greater reliance could be placed on market mechanisms. The period of formulation and implementation of the Second Five-Year Plan, therefore, witnessed considerable loosening of traditional controls over the economy in both foreign trade and in banking.

The development of the planning process triggered a thorough review of the South Korean economy. As a result, a number of reforms were initiated that were prerequisite for the successful implementation of the plan that ultimately emerged. The revaluation of the exchange rate in 1964, combined with a 40 percent average annual rate of growth of exports, permitted the import liberalization program to be expanded. This program not only imparted a substantial impetus to investment but also eliminated one of the traditional sources of corruption (import licensing) on which so many fortunes had been built during the 1950s. Another source of perennial corruption was virtually eliminated by an interest-rate reform in 1965 that doubled interest rates on savings deposits. By increasing the volume of savings flowing through the banking system, the interest-rate reform allowed the government to free the banking system from some of its more severe controls, as well as from its dependence on nonmarket rationing devices for the allocation of loans.

Finally, the distribution of the real burden for financing the development program was made considerably more equitable by greatly increasing the efficiency of tax collection and by the overall success of the government's policies in reducing the rate of inflation from about 23 percent to 6 percent annually. When it is recognized that these economic gains were achieved in the context of a sustained growth rate that was close to 10 percent per year in real terms, the value of the planning process emerges quite clearly. The impact of the political situation upon economic growth is illustrated by the fact that, without a strong leadership commitment to economic development, no viable economic plan could have been adopted, and the necessary pre-plan steps would not have been taken. It is equally significant that this economic success gained a large measure of broadly based political support for the government, thereby contributing to political stability and facilitating the democratization of the regime.

PLANNING MODELS AND METHODOLOGY

In its original formulation, the formal planning methodology involved a two-prong approach.[2] A macroeconometric growth model was to be used to select a growth rate consistent with the supply of foreign and domestic savings and foreign exchange. Given the growth rate, a sectoral annual input-output model, disaggregated at the 43 x 43 sector level, was to be employed to assure the balance of demand and supply in each sector and to set minimal levels of investment. The sectoral model was to rely on some macroeconomically derived parameters, such as aggregate private consumption and imports, for the exogenous estimates of final demand. No programming models were to be formulated, primarily because of the unavailability of high-speed computers in Korea at that time.

Three separate attempts were made to estimate a macroeconomic model (Adelman, 88, 89),[3] each based on partial revisions of the national income accounts, but all resulted in unrealistic parameter estimates by international standards. Primary emphasis was therefore shifted to the formulation of the sectoral model, described in Chapter 5 of this book, which was used not only in its originally intended role as a consistency check, and as a means for investment program specification, but also to determine the overall dimensions of the development program (Adelman, 90). Only after a thorough revision of the national income accounts was it possible to estimate an adequate macroeconometric model, which is reproduced in

---

[2] See I. Adelman, "Consultant Report," October, 1965, USOM/K (mimeo.).
[3] See the numbered bibliography at the end of this volume.

Chapter 4 of this book. This model was particularly useful as the technical basis for the annual development programs linked in with the Second Five-Year Plan. In addition, a mixed integer programming model (see Chapter 6), which was developed too late for use in the original version of the Second Five-Year Plan, has recently been employed to check the optimality of two important import-substitute investment decisions. It is anticipated that this model will be utilized more fully in investigating trade-offs between export-oriented and import-substitution–oriented development patterns, a question likely to become increasingly important for the Third Five-Year Plan (see Chapter 3).

The longer-run, more flexible, and more aggregative optimizing analysis represented in the nonlinear model of Chapter 8 has not yet been used in planning. As its properties become better understood, it is hoped that a model of this nature can become useful in setting 15- to 20-year goals into which the Five-Year Plans can be phased.

The Second Five-Year Plan was national in scope and contained no regional parameters. The increasing dualism of the Korean economy, however, is giving rise to pressures for regional redistribution of income. The Third Five-Year Plan will therefore include a program for regional decentralization of industry. The regional model in Chapter 7 has been developed to provide a technical background for this effort.

The conclusions of the several planning models have served as cross-checks on each other. Indeed, there appears to be an amazing degree of consistency among their policy conclusions. For example, both the macroeconometric model and the mixed integer programming model indicate that Korea is moving from a regime in which growth has been savings constrained toward one in which growth will be constrained by foreign-exchange availability. This conclusion, which has important policy implications, is reinforced by the work represented in the Strout paper (Chapter 12 of this book) and by the more intuitive speculations in the Kuznets paper (Chapter 3).

The ranking of sectors by comparative advantage obtained from simple calculations of capital-output, labor-output, value added, and foreign-exchange content ratios (see Chapter 5) corresponds closely to the rankings obtained from the mixed integer programming model. Both computations indicate the desirability of concentrating investment in light manufacturing and in the low capital-output skill-intensive branches of heavy manufacturing. Similarly, both the programming model (Chapter 6) and the sectoral model (Chapter 5) indicate the desirability of undertaking construction of both a petrochemical plant and an iron and steel complex, with the former given the higher priority.

The macroeconometric model (Chapter 4) reinforces the observation by Kuznets (Chapter 3) that there has been underinvestment in agriculture in recent years and that, despite the impressive growth of output, this sector requires explicit policy attention in the future. The need to emphasize investment in physical overhead capital in the near future is apparent both from the sectoral model and from the macroeconometric model.

With respect to monetary and fiscal policy, the macroeconometric model and the analyses of Kanesa-Thasan (Chapter 10) and Kuznets (Chapter 3) suggest the continued need for substantial restraint in the expansion of the money supply. Similarly, the desirability of a further 20 percent devaluation of the exchange rate is indicated by the shadow price of foreign exchange in the programming model and by the parametric calculations of the macroeconometric model. This conclusion is reinforced by the reflections of Kuznets.

All the models tend to support the expectation that, with continued intelligent monetary, fiscal, and foreign trade policies, a 10 percent growth rate of GNP is a reasonable goal for the duration of Korea's Second Five-Year Plan.

SIDELIGHTS ON THE PLANNING PROCESS

Of what practical use were the planning models in the formation of South Korea's development program? Before planning work was actually begun, the planning division was deluged with project proposals amounting to about ten times the value the plan would ultimately support. The problem of selection was greatly complicated by the fact that each proposal contained a demand projection (see Chapter 9 of this book) that could not be checked against independent data. The use of the sectoral model produced more or less realistic investment and output demand estimates for each sector, which could then be applied to screening the investment suggestions for the Second Five-Year Plan.

The sectoral model also indicated several sectors, mostly in light manufacturing, in which investment was needed but in which too few project proposals had been submitted. The plan assumed that appropriate investment would take place in these sectors; meanwhile, relevant project proposals were solicited by the planning commission. This same model also helped to settle the debate on the desirability of two large import-substitute investments (a petrochemical plant and an iron and steel complex) and it helped indicate the scale of investment, particularly in physical overhead capital, that would have to be undertaken.

In addition, the planning process required a thorough review of the entire economy and the collection of a detailed, up-to-date mass of economic data. The resultant overview of the economy has provided the government with a basis for rational policy decisions in the economic sphere.

Among these policy decisions is the periodic revision of the plan that is required by the constant changes in exogenous conditions. The Second Five-Year Plan document explicitly provided that annual "overall resource budgets" would be constructed that would incorporate reviews of progress sector by sector, allocate the overall government budget, and devise monetary, fiscal, and trade policies in a manner consistent with the plan's longer-run goals. Since the plan was formulated, two such budgets have been constructed, each of which has incorporated substantial changes from the plan's sectoral configuration. These alterations have been generally accepted without discrediting the plan, a result that may be due in part to the fact that the changes instituted upward revisions in overall growth targets.

Another interesting function of the planning process was the creation of a series of industry committees to aid in the development of up-to-date detailed technological and demand information. These committees, composed of engineers, business experts, economists, ministry officials, and technical experts, soon transcended their original technical function and became vehicles for consensus building for plan formulation and implementation. They also served to disseminate information pertaining to industrial implementation and to industrial prospects, thus performing the "indicative planning" function so necessary for plan implementation in a mixed (public-private) economy.

The manner in which these committees have served in the planning process is worthy of note. By feeding information from the sectoral model solutions to the members of the committees and by getting the members' detailed criticisms and comments, the planners were able to get, in effect, a man-computer dialogue that assisted the understanding of the implications of both the economic data and the model results. This process was greatly facilitated by the input-output framework of the model, which provided an easily understood language and focus for planner-committee communications.

The use of industry committees—by its very nature—made the plan construction essentially a public process. This fact, coupled with the recognition that the planning process was essentially technical in nature, indicated to the business and intellectual communities the basic intellectual honesty and competence of the plan. This conviction served to gain general public acceptance for the plan and to make its implementation considerably more simple.

SUMMARY

The South Korean planning experience has been extraordinary in a number of ways. First of all, it offers an important example of the mutual reinforcement of economic and political development. This observation tends to confirm the result obtained in cross-national studies: that leadership commitment to economic development is the most critical noneconomic factor in governing the pace of economic development once the major social bottlenecks to development have been overcome.[4]

Second, the gap between planning theory and (as taught in universities throughout the world) the planning procedure utilized in the formulation of South Korea's Second Five-Year Plan was much smaller than usual. Not only were sophisticated econometric input-output and programming models constructed to assist in the formulation of the plan, a number of their results were used in the plan itself.

Third, the evolution of administrative and institutional mechanisms for planning and plan implementation was strongly influenced by the formal planning technology, and vice versa.

Fourth, the requirements of the planning process led to a vast improvement in the country's data base, which, in turn, led to improved planning models.

Last, but not least, the plan appears to be successful. The very high growth rate of the South Korean economy has been maintained, the rate of inflation has decreased, and bottlenecks that were anticipated before the plan was adopted have been much less severe than one would have expected in the absence of planning. Furthermore, the implementation of several reforms in 1966, in anticipation of the plan, helped raise the rate of growth of GNP in that year to an abnormally high value while still permitting a substantial degree of monetary stability.

Much of South Korea's economic success is attributed, by an International Monetary Fund observer, to the country's balanced growth process (see Chapter 11). This was the result of using an investment planning approach that tests for both the mutual consistency of growth rates in all sectors of the economy and the consistency of overall growth targets with domestic and foreign-finance and foreign-exchange availabilities.

The achievements of the plan are all the more remarkable when it is realized that—in only nine months—the South Korean planning effort moved from an almost academic exercise, without hard data, to a status of general government participation and public support, with one of the best data bases in the underdeveloped world. The entire effort was achieved with a handful of young, energetic government officials and a small group of Korean academicians and foreign advisors as prime movers.

---

[4] Irma Adelman and C. T. Morris, *Society, Politics, and Economic Development: A Quantitative Approach* (Baltimore: The Johns Hopkins Press, 1967).

Chapter 2

THE PATTERN AND SIGNIFICANCE OF
ECONOMIC PLANNING IN KOREA

David C. Cole and
Young Woo Nam

Economic planning is a politico-economic process which draws together the techniques of economic analysis and the forces of consensus building, decision making, and action taking that are the heart of the political process. The literature on planning is full of admonitions against a one-sided approach because economic analysis, no matter how good, has little impact on a country's development unless it can be transformed into effective policies and actions. Conversely, strong policies and government efforts that are based upon bad analysis or bad judgments about the future are likely to be very harmful. The Korean experience attests to the interdependence of the political and economic facets of planning. A series of planning attempts were sidetracked because the political conditions were inimical to serious consideration, much less adoption and implementation, of the plans. Eventually, in 1962, a plan was formally accepted, but it was subjected to serious criticism as being mainly a political device rather than a technically sound economic program. Finally, when an analytically competent plan was supported by an appropriate political environment, not only were the economic decisions of the government and the private sector influenced significantly but also the legitimacy of the government was strengthened and the antagonism of some alienated groups toward the government was mitigated.

The first efforts at planning in Korea were begun during the Korean War by the foreign assistance agencies that were trying to assess the best patterns and the potential costs of rehabilitating the Korean economy. The main result of this work was a program prepared by Robert R. Nathan and Associates for the United Nations Korean Reconstruction Agency.[1] This program was never formally adopted or even recognized by the Korean government, mainly for political reasons. Nonetheless, because no other similar planning work was undertaken for several years,

---

[1] Robert R. Nathan and Associates, *An Economic Programme for Korean Reconstruction*, prepared for the United Nations Reconstruction Agency, March, 1954.

the Nathan Plan provided the only overall perspective of the Korean economy's possible growth path during the riehabilitaton period.[2]

Eventually in 1958 a second planning effort was initiated by the newly established Economic Development Council of the Korean government. This was to be a seven-year plan which would be divided into a three-year and a four-year phase. The plan for the first phase, covering the years 1960–62, was formulated in 1959 and approved by the cabinet in January, 1960.[3] Three months later the Rhee government was overthrown and the plan was set aside.

In the following year, a new five-year plan was prepared by the Economic Development Council, but it suffered the same fate as the three-year plan.[4] The draft was completed just prior to the military coup of May, 1961, and was not acceptable to the new government which assumed power after the coup. It did, however, provide the basis for a third planning attempt which was finally carried through to completion and approved in late 1961 as the First Five-Year Economic Plan, 1962–66.

As a result of criticism leveled against this plan, and the poor performance of the economy in 1962, it was decided in 1963 to revise the growth targets and investment program downward. This revision was completed in 1964 but was never given much consideration, because the government was concerned with the more immediate problems of financial stabilization. In time the revised version of the First Five-Year Plan was forgotten altogether because the overall performance of the economy from 1963 onward was approaching or exceeding the so-called "over-ambitious" patterns of the original plan.

The Second Five-Year Economic Development Plan was prepared in 1965 and 1966 and was approved by the President in August, 1966. This basic program has since been supplemented and modified by annual plans, called Overall Resource Budgets (ORB's), prepared each year since 1967. These represent a major extension of the planning activities in Korea and the achievement of a degree of relevance for the planning process which had not previously been attained.

In the following discussion we will review Korea's experience with planning, in terms of who did the planning, how the plans were formulated, what the main lines of strategy were in the several plans, and finally the impact of the planning in both economic and political terms.

[2] There was a five-year program worked up by the Korean government at the time the Nathan team was working on its program, but it was mainly a compendium of possible investment projects.

[3] Joe Won Lee, "Planning Efforts for Economic Development," in Joseph S. Chung, ed., *Patterns of Economic Development: Korea* (The Korea Research and Publication, Inc., 1966), pp. I–11.

[4] Lee, *ibid.*, has appropriately labeled the three-year plan, 1960–63, and this first version of the five-year plan, 1962–66, as the "abortive plans."

Who Did the Planning?

The early planning work in Korea was done mainly by foreigners—the Nathan team and others associated with the United Nations and United States assistance programs—because there were very few Koreans with any experience in this area. In the second round of planning activity, from 1959 through 1961, Koreans played the major role, with only limited help from foreign technicians or advisors. A number of Koreans, who had recently completed training programs abroad, especially in the United States, were drawn into the staff of the Economic Development Council and the Ministry of Reconstruction where the planning work was concentrated, and these people were given the main responsibility for preparing the three-year plan and the first version of the five-year plan. There was an advisory team from the University of Oregon attached to the Economic Development Council at this time, but, according to its own summary report, the team played a very limited role.[5]

After the military coup, the Supreme Council for National Reconstruction, which had assumed all legislative, executive, and judicial powers, took an active interest in the planning work. It transformed the Economic Development Council into the Economic Planning Board, combining the planning, budgeting, and foreign assistance administering functions and charged the planning group with revising the draft Five-Year Plan to conform to some new guidelines laid down by the Supreme Council.[6] The revised plan was drafted over several months, again mainly by Korean staff of the Economic Planning Board. It was then reviewed by various Korean advisory groups during the last quarter of 1961 and finally approved by the Supreme Council.

Several groups of foreign experts undertook to review the plan and, as already noted, were quite critical. As a result of these criticisms, and the continuing irrelevance of planning for current policy decisions, many of the leading planners left the government or shifted to other positions and a new, younger group assumed responsibility for planning. When it was time to begin work on the Second Plan, a number of foreign advisory groups were drawn into the planning work to help the still relatively inexperienced Korean planners. In 1964 the U.S. Agency for International Development contracted with Robert Nathan Associates to provide a second team of planning experts. In contrast with the earlier Nathan

[5] The Oregon Advisory Group in Korea, A Report on the University of Oregon Advisory Mission to the Korean Economic Development Council, 1959–1961 (School of Business Administration, Univ. of Oregon, Eugene, 1961). This report contains a summary of the Three-Year Economic Development Plan, issued by the Economic Development Council, Jan. 25, 1960.

[6] Arthur D. Little, Inc. "Economic Development Planning in Korea, Report of the Arthur D. Little Reconnaissance Survey," May, 1962.

group, this one was to work with and for the Korean government—specifically the Economic Planning Board (EPB)—and was to help them prepare the Second Plan. In addition to the Nathan Group, there was an economic and technical advisory team of the German government which was attached to the EPB, and it assisted with the planning work. Also the United States AID mission took a very active and direct interest in the Korean government's planning from 1965 onward and, in contrast to the normal pattern of relationships, functioned as a planning advisory group. The AID mission and the Nathan team brought a number of experts in various aspects of planning to Korea in 1965 and 1966, who further contributed to the formulation of the Second Plan.[7] Finally several teams were brought in to develop programs for particular sectors. These included an AID-supported study of the power industry and a World Bank-supported study of transportation.[8] Thus there was much more participation of foreigners in the preparation of materials for and the formulation of the Second Five-Year Plan than there had been in any of Korea's previous planning efforts, except the original Nathan Plan which was a purely foreign product.

This broadening of involvement in the planning process for the Second Plan was also true among Koreans. The various ministries of the government were not only asked to propose projects for inclusion in the investment program, but their representatives participated in the deliberations on development strategy and planning methodology. Staff from the ministries and government-owned development banks made up the group of ten industry committees which were responsible for assessing the existing structure of production, estimating the future patterns of development, and reviewing the projects proposed for their industries.[9] A number of academic and research groups made studies of topics which were relevant to planning.[10] Finally a number of special interest groups and representa-

---

[7] These experts included, in approximate chronological order, Edward S. Shaw, John G. Gurley, and Hugh T. Patrick on the development of financial institutions and policies; Irma Adelman on planning models and conceptual approaches to planning; Richard A. Musgrave on tax and fiscal policy; Peggy B. Musgrave on foreign trade policy; Edward Hollander and Edgar McVoy on manpower planning; and Alan Strout on planning models.

[8] Korea Electric Co., *Korea Electric Power Survey*, 2 vols., prepared in 1965 by the Electric Power Industry Survey Team; and Ministry of Transportation, *Korea Transportation Survey*, Draft Report (Korea, 1966).

[9] No private enterprise representatives were included in these industry committees (as had been the pattern in France) because it was feared by the government that they would frequently take advantage of privileged information that they might obtain from the deliberations of the industry committees.

[10] These included Professor Kee Chun Han's study of "The Predicative Ability of the Korean Input-Output Tables," and the Korean Development Association's long-term projections in "Korean Economy in the 1980's."

tives of the public were consulted periodically, over the roughly eighteen months during which the Second Plan was being prepared, to obtain their views on national priorities and the approaches being contemplated by the government.

HOW THE PLANS WERE FORMULATED

The main considerations of planning methodology in Korea included the amount and kind of policy guidance given to the planners by higher political authority, the types of planning models used, the criteria for selecting investment projects or economic policies for inclusion in the plan, and what attempts that were made to see that the plans were internally consistent.

The Nathan Plan was prepared for the United Nations Reconstruction Agency and was attuned to the policy guidance of that agency more than to the desires of the Korean government or the people. Despite efforts by the Nathan team to elicit guidance and cooperation from the Koreans, Synghman Rhee never agreed to the undertaking and did nothing to encourage support for it.[11] The general guidelines given by the United Nations General Assembly to UNKRA (United Nations Korean Reconstruction Agency) were to restore the pre-war consumption levels and to achieve a viable self-supporting economy.[12] These were interpreted to mean that the per capita consumption levels of 1949–50 should be met by the end of the reconstruction program, that domestic savings should be sufficient to finance a level of investment which would maintain the growth rate of output at least equal to the rate of population increase, and that exports would be sufficient to pay for the imports that the country required.

The most critical dimension of the Nathan Plan related to the time period within which these goals could be achieved. Their report claims that after "various trial patterns were analyzed, . . . it appears that a programme of the size . . . proposed should take about five years to accomplish."[13] As it turned out, the combination of goals, assumptions, and time period were not a feasible configuration. Some parts were

[11] Joe Won Lee, "Planning Efforts for Economic Development," attributed President Rhee's chilly reception to the facts that Rhee was not consulted on the project beforehand, and also that Robert Nathan was associated with the Democratic party in the United States. Shortly after the Nathan team arrived in Korea, in the fall of 1952, the Republican party won the elections in the United States, and President Rhee, who reportedly identified more with the Republicans than the Democrats, apparently concluded that it would not help to elicit more assistance from the new administration in the U.S. if Korea's reconstruction program was openly based on the Nathan team's studies.
[12] Nathan Associates, *An Economic Programme for Korean Reconstruction*, pp. 77–80.
[13] *Ibid.*, pp. 76–77.

achieved within the prescribed five years, but others were not, and the economy was far from self-supporting by 1958–59. Whether a more realistic combination would have been devised if the Korean leaders had participated more actively in setting the guidelines for the program is difficult to say, but it seems clear that the main lines were heavily influenced by a desire to show how the objectives of UNKRA could be met within a reasonable time period. The Koreans for their part never felt bound by or committed to the Nathan Plan because they had not participated in its formulation.

The criteria for selecting investment in the Nathan Plan were primarily oriented toward demand and import substitution. As their report stated, refined calculations based on relative yields of all alternative investment opportunities were impractical. Instead by taking account of the resource pattern and the target year requirements for final products, and then assuming that there were fairly rigid limits on the attainable volume of exports which could finance the minimum needed imports, that pattern of investment was developed which would permit Korea to "produce at home the kinds and quantities of final products it consumes," as far as this was economically feasible.[14]

The methodology of the three-year plan formulated by the new Economic Development Council in 1959, and of the first version of the five-year plan completed in the spring of 1961 is not well documented. Both of these plans were prepared hastily and by a relatively small group with little publicity or effort to gain broadened participation. It is doubtful that the three-year plan received much positive policy guidance from the President, considering his previous anti-planning biases. The main reason given for formulating the plan was that "the recent trend in reductions in foreign aid requires a reappraisal of . . . economic policies and emphasizes the need for long-range planning."[15] The aim of the plan was "to achieve economic self-sufficiency as rapidly as possible through efficient use of domestic human and physical resources in conjunction with foreign economic aid."[16] These propositions suggest that the plan was directly influenced by foreign aid considerations and perhaps directed as much at justifying continuation of aid inflows as with programming investment.

According to Lee, the three-year plan used a planning model with the level of employment and labor productivity as the strategic variables for determining potential growth of output.[17] Increased employment was

---

[14] *Ibid.*, p. 105.

[15] Economic Development Council, Three-Year Economic Development Plan, Outline dated Jan. 25, 1960, in Univ. of Oregon. A Report on the Univ. of Oregon Advisory Mission to the Korean Economic Development Council, 1959–61.

[16] *Ibid.*

[17] Joe Won Lee, "Planning Efforts for Economic Development," pp. I–11.

one of the main targets, along with increased productivity and improvement of the trade balance.

The main lines of policy and the investment program were formulated by six consultative committees consisting of academics and private technicians who reviewed the proposals of the technical staff of the Economic Development Council. There were no clear criteria for selecting investment projects, and information on proposed projects was often inadequate. Consequently the decisions on the investment program were based mainly on the judgment of the consulting committees.

At the time work was started on the Five-Year Plan, in the summer of 1960, the new government felt called upon to respond to a different set of pressures than those which had confronted the deposed Rhee government. Severe demands of the unemployed and students for increased employment opportunities prompted the Democratic party to try to formulate policies and programs which could meet these pressures. Accordingly the Party leadership prepared a set of instructions for the Economic Development Council to guide their work in the new plan. These instructions set the strategy of the plan to concentrate on certain key types of infrastructure, or overhead capital and to use labor-intensive methods of construction in so far as possible.

Except for this new element of policy guidance the planning procedure was similar to that of the Three-Year Plan. There was some concentration of the project program on selected areas or key industries, in what was then considered to represent an "unbalanced growth strategy." But the main innovation was the concept of a National Construction Service which would employ the recently graduated students and the unemployed common laborers and farmers in labor-intensive construction of roads, dams, irrigation works, and other key projects.

Soon after the military coup in May, 1961, the Supreme Council for National Reconstruction made clear its intention to manage the national economy in accordance with a fully articulated, comprehensive plan. It designated a Korean advisory group for economic planning and charged them with responsibility for formulating the guidelines of a new five-year plan.[18] The members of the group were drawn from academic circles, the Bank of Korea, the Korean Reconstruction Bank, and other government agencies. Within two months the guidelines were formulated, approved by the Supreme Council, and sent to the Ministry of Reconstruction, which shortly thereafter was transformed into the Economic Planning Board (EPB) headed by the Deputy Prime Minister.

[18] Supreme Council for National Reconstruction, *Overall Economic Reconstruction Plan* (draft) from 1962 to 1966, Appendix (Korea, 1961).

The guidelines for the new plan made use of the work done by the previous government, but the advisory group did not limit itself to setting out the main lines of strategy. Instead it spelled out in considerable detail the overall and sectoral growth targets, the components of expenditure on GNP, the targets for income distribution, and the balance of payments. These numerous targets and projections were set without much consideration of alternatives or their internal consistency because of the limited time and technical apparatus for so doing.

The main responsibilities of the planning staff in the EPB were to fill in the details within the guidelines that they had been given. This involved designating specific projects and scheduling them to fit the annual investment levels. For this purpose, sectoral and industrial capital-output ratios were estimated from past series and applied to the specified output targets to determine investment levels. There were no particular efficiency criteria for selecting among alternative investment projects so the planners were guided mainly by those industries which were classified as strategic, or key, industries by the Supreme Council. These included coal mining, an integrated steel mill, cement making, petroleum refining, fertilizer production, and transportation. To the extent that these key projects did not absorb the total projected investment resources, other projects were added, either from those proposed for the earlier Five-Year Plan or on the basis of new proposals from the ministries.

The planners then went on to specify in considerable detail whether individual projects were to be carried out by the government or the private sector and what would be the sources of financing. This practice later created serious problems because private entrepreneurs tended to assume that they would automatically receive financing if they were authorized to carry out a project listed in the plan.

There was no good basis for checking the consistency of the plan in either macro or micro terms. As a consequence, there were some seriously imbalanced elements, especially between savings and investment at the macro level. Also there was only limited coordination and cooperation among the various parts of the government in preparing the investment program. Essentially the planners had done their scheduling job for the Supreme Council and they had not built any bridges to other government agencies which would have facilitated implementation.

Within a year the First Five-Year Plan was sent back to the planners for substantial revision. They were given some overall guidance on lower growth targets and resource availabilities, but in the confusion of rapid inflation, poor agricultural yields, and the political pressures of an election campaign, it proved impossible to devise a generally acceptable set of principles for scaling down the investment program. Thus the revision of the First Five-Year Plan was finally done in a rough and arbitrary manner, after which it was largely ignored.

Preparation of the Second Plan extended over a longer period and was more thorough and open than it had been for any of the previous plans.[19] Consideration of alternative planning models was begun in the fall of 1964, nearly two years before the plan was finally completed. In the spring of 1965 some basic guidelines for the plan were prepared by the Economic Planning Board, approved by the Cabinet, and circulated throughout the government. These guidelines did not contain quantitative targets for the plan but indicated the preliminary thinking on plan goals, strategy, and priority investment areas, and called for the various ministries to submit project proposals consistent with the guidelines. These proposals were received in the summer of 1965 and started through a long and not too effective process of checking the project data and trying to calculate some comparative measures of return for evaluating the projects.

Concurrently, work was going ahead on the overall planning models. In October of 1965 Professor Adelman proposed a macroeconomic two-gap model that was based on the national income and product accounts. Estimates of the relationships were prepared, using the then available national accounts. The main results of these efforts were to demonstrate that the existing accounts apparently contained some serious distortions, and that they did not adequately reflect the structural changes which were occuring in the economy as a result of devaluation, export expansion, and relaxation of import controls. Even if the previous relations could have been accurately estimated, they would not have given a good basis for projecting future possibilities. It was decided therefore to postpone further work on the macro model until the national accounts could be revised and a series prepared in constant 1965 prices.

Some very rough macro projections were devised while waiting for the revised national accounts, but these were used only to illustrate some of the broad strategy choices among alternative export, import, savings, investment, and foreign assistance levels. Eventually when the revised accounts were completed, in preliminary form in the spring of 1966, they appeared to be more reliable for recent years than for the 1950s. This meant that they were suitable for reflecting base year levels and structure of output and income, but that they still were not reliable for fitting econometric relations in time series form. Thus it was necessary, even in the final formulation of the Second Plan, to estimate most of the macro-economic targets on a largely intuitive basis, giving heavy weight to the

[19] There is a brief section on preparation of the plan in the Appendix to the *Second Five-Year Economic Development Plan 1967–71* (Govt. of the Republic of Korea: July, 1966).

structural shifts which were then occurring, rather than to use a formal model based on longer-run trends and relations.

Because of the deficiencies in the time series data and, on the other hand, the availability of a recent and apparently reasonably accurate inter-industry or input-output table, the focus of formal model building shifted to the latter area. It was decided to build a dynamic inter-industry projection model for estimating sectoral investment and import requirements and testing the consistency of the overall development program. This model was implemented on a crash basis within six months and provided the unifying element in the planning process. It gave a conceptual framework for gathering data and estimates on various types of demand and sources of supply. It was particularly well suited to assessing some of the implications of alternative patterns of manufacturing production.

Policy guidance for the Second Plan was given initially in the basic guidelines which were approved by the Cabinet and the President. But these broad terms of reference were translated into more specific and operational guidance in a perhaps unique forum which was labeled "The Second Plan Deliberation Joint Meeting."[20] This group, which was chaired by the Vice Minister of the Economic Planning Board, brought together senior officials from the various ministries of the government, members of the Economic and Scientific Council, representatives of the Government Political Party (the DRP) and representatives of the United States Aid Mission, and the Nathan and German groups advising the Economic Planning Board. Thirty-one joint meetings were held in the final year of work to "discuss and review formulation of the plan." Generally presentations were made by the staff of the Economic Planning Board, and after hearing the comments of the various participants decisions were made by the Vice Minister of the EPB or referred to higher authority for resolution. Although the meetings were not open to the public, the substance of the presentations and the decisions was frequently made available to the press so that the public was kept informed as to its progress and direction.

Investment decisions in the Second Plan were largely dominated by demand considerations. There was an attempt to apply internal rate of return calculations to the agricultural investment projects proposed by the Ministry of Agriculture and Forestry, but this did not prove successful. The rate of return estimates were not sufficiently reliable to be convincing and continuing disagreement over the relative emphasis on upland or tideland reclamation projects was not resolved by the time the plan was completed. As a consequence the agriculture investment program was quite unspecific and the absence of a clear statement of strategy for agriculture, forestry, and fisheries made that the weakest part of the plan.

[20] *The Second Five-Year Economic Development Plan*, p. 180.

Investment in manufacturing was heavily influenced by estimates of the potential demand for exports and the derived demand for intermediate goods to supply the export industries. There were only a few proposed projects involving a significant increase in import substitution—an integrated iron and steel mill (left over from the First Plan), a petrochemical complex, and an aluminum reduction smelter. These were tentatively incorporated in the plan without any careful comparative assessment of benefit to the economy. The infrastructure investment programs were demand-oriented and the allocations for social overhead, including housing, education, and other government services, were arbitrary decisions based on a combined assessment of demand, existing deficiencies, and available resources.

In the area of politics, the Second Plan did not propose any major new directions but mainly reiterated the reorientation of policy which had been carried out in the preceding two years and the effects of which were becoming significant at the time the plan was being prepared. Because the effects were generally in the desired and expected directions, but, on the other hand, because it was still premature in most areas to determine whether the prospective response was of the desired order of magnitude, there was not yet a sufficient basis for modifying most of the policies at that time.

The overall consistency and feasibility of the Second Plan was tested in part by the inter-industry model which was most relevant for assessing the level and composition of industrial investment and imports, given the estimates of the growth of final demand. But the main questions of feasibility centered around the increases in savings—especially domestic savings— and in exports that were projected in the plan. These were areas in which exceptionally rapid increases had been experienced, but for relatively brief periods. The plan assumed that these high rates of increase would continue, whereas some critics believed the plan was too ambitious. With the benefit of several more years, during which the high export and savings growth have persisted, it now seems more certain that a structural change has taken place, but in 1956 it was a difficult judgment to make.

PLAN STRATEGIES AND TARGETS

As W. Arthur Lewis has suggested, there is no single unifying theme to a discussion of development strategies, but instead a judgment as to which issues are important in a particular setting.[21] The issues of strategy which have been of most concern in Korean planning since the end of the Korean War appear to have been:

a) the overall rate of growth,

[21] W. Arthur Lewis, *Development Planning, The Essentials of Economic Policy* (New York, 1966), p. 26.

b) the structure of industrial production and foreign trade,
c) the division between domestic and foreign savings and between various forms of domestic saving.

Target Growth Rates

Although there are in any given setting practical upper limits on the potential rate of growth, there is also a range over which the rate can be expected to vary depending upon the commitment of the populace to achieving high growth, the effectiveness of the economic policies of government, and the uncontrollable influences of weather, international politics, and similar factors. In selecting the target growth rates for planning purposes, the planners or policy-makers are likely to be most influenced by what they think is a reasonable upper limit and by the degree of commitment to growth which they either perceive or can hope to instill in the populace. Conceptions of a reasonable limit to growth are influenced in turn by recent performance, at least during what are considered to be favorable periods.

In the Korean plans there has been an alternating pattern of projecting continuation of past growth rates when those have been relatively high or of projecting sharp increases in the growth rate when the immediately previous record has been unfavorable. The Nathan Plan, coming right after the Korean War in which so much of the industrial capacity and infrastructure had been destroyed, proposed a very rapid but decelerating recovery with an implicit compound growth rate of 8.6 percent per annum. Given the limited information on previous performance of the economy and the fact that this was a reconstruction program concerned with rebuilding along previously established lines, which was believed to be easier than charting new paths of development, the high growth target did not at that time seem unreasonable. In fact it proved to be far above actual achievement. In the subsequent Three-Year Plan the target growth rate was set at 5.2 percent, which was about equal to the average growth rate of the preceding five years. Then, the First Five-Year Plan, prepared in the midst of the stagnation period, contained a target growth rate of 6 percent in its first version and 7.1 percent in the final version issued by the military government in January, 1962. This was roughly double the growth rate of the preceding three years and was much above the levels that the Korean economy had been able previously to sustain for more than one or two years. Thus it had to imply either major changes in policies, commitment, and performance or it simply represented wishful thinking. The government clearly intended the former, but was accused by its critics of the latter. Poor performance during the first year of the plan supported the critics and caused the scaling down of the plan to 5 percent growth target, but, as previously noted, this was subsequently set aside when the realized growth rate from 1963 on pushed up above the original 7 percent target. After experiencing several years of very high growth, the 7 percent growth target of the Second Five-Year Plan seemed relatively modest. In subsequent annual planning exercises the target has been raised to 10 percent,[22] which is only slightly above the average growth rate for the four years 1963–66. This move to a very high planning target was prompted in large part by experiencing the severe constraints of bottlenecks in key infrastructure areas, such as power and transportation, where it is not possible to fill the shortages with imports. The planners concluded it was necessary to assume the highest possible growth rates in planning for these sectors to avoid constraining the growth of the whole economy.

As the various plans have been drafted and revised over the past fifteen years, and the growth targets have been moved about in the range from 5 to 10 percent, there has been little disagreement over the desirability of striving for the highest practicable rates of growth. The arguments have been mainly over what was realistic, with the implied concern that too high targets would result in overinvestment in some areas and the release of inflationary forces. The planners have generally tended to advocate the higher growth targets while those concerned with financial policy have urged more caution.

The other direction in which growth targets have had relevance is in terms of Korea's relations with the suppliers of foreign assistance. The Nathan Plan was explicitly intended to contribute to agreement among the aid donors on the overall reconstruction objectives and related assistance needs. It failed to serve this purpose because the Korean government never accepted the plan or agreed to its general directions. The high, 7.1 percent, growth target of the First Five-Year Plan and the related level of investment were judged by one group to exceed by far the potential of the economy, and were in need of being scaled down.[23] Another group, doing an evaluation on behalf of the United States government, while acknowledging that the growth target seemed very high, went on to say that there was not sufficient information on the Korean economy to estimate a practicable rate of growth. As a result of these reports and other assessments, neither the United States nor the World Bank accepted the plan as a basis for determining appropriate levels of their assistance.[24]

[22] Economic Planning Board, *Overall Resources Budget*, 1968 (July, 1967).
[23] This assessment is reported in the Arthur D. Little draft report, *Economic Development Planning in Korea* (May, 1962), pp. iv–1.
[24] Charles Wolf, Jr., in his article "Economic Planning in Korea," in *Korean Affairs*, III (2), July, 1964, urged that "U.S. policies and programs should strongly support the Korean Plan and subsequent plans," p. 237.

More recently the World Bank has formed a consultative group on assistance to Korea and has been evaluating Korea's growth record and targets as a basis for determining assistance needs. In its initial assessments of the Second Five-Year Plan, the World Bank experts concluded that the growth targets were too ambitious and recommended that consideration be given to adjustments that would be necessary to scale down from a 7 percent to a 6 percent growth target.

In time, as Korea's actual growth continued to average near 10 percent in 1966 and 1967, the World Bank raised its sights and accepted 7 percent as near the lower rather than upper end of the feasible growth range, with the upper limit running up to 10–11 percent. The Bank has also become more inclined to accept the Korean estimates of the investment and external resource requirements to attain these higher rates of growth.

Industrial Structure

The main choices confronting Korean planners in the area of industrial structure have involved the division between agriculture and manufacturing, and within manufacturing, the relative emphasis on light and heavy industry. The latter choice also has been related to the split between labor-intensive and capital-intensive production, the degree of integration of the industrial structure vs. international specialization, and thus the questions of international trade patterns. There have been a number of shifts in the thinking of Korean policy-makers since the Korean War which have been reflected in the plan targets and strategies relating to industrial structure.

The Nathan Plan emphasized the expansion of primary production—agriculture, fisheries, and mining—to satisfy domestic demand and meet the minimum necessary export levels. That program projected extensive import substitution to meet consumption and investment demands and to bring the import level down to roughly 10 percent of GNP by the end of the plan period. This move toward a more closed economy was deemed necessary because of the apparently limited prospects for boosting the export ratio above 10 percent, and also because of the objective set for the Nathan Plan that the economy would be self-supporting by the terminal year, 1958. Thus the program involved a turning inward toward self-sufficiency as the only apparent means of achieving trade balance. These trade and production projections proved very wrong, in part because they were not accepted by the Korean government, which therefore did not implement the policies that might have contributed toward their realization, but also because the projections were unrealistic to start with.

One of the critical assumptions of the Nathan Plan was that rice production could be raised quickly and that, by substituting other grains for rice, there could be a large surplus of rice available for export. This increase in rice production and exports did not occur. Instead Korea has continued to be a sizable importer of grains into the 1960s and has only been able to export limited amounts of rice in years following exceptionally good harvests.

The other major hope for exports was minerals, which it was assumed would amount to nearly $70 million by 1958, or one-fourth of total exports. Minerals did prove to be the main export, but they were only valued at about $10 million in 1958, which was nearly two-thirds of total exports of $16.5 million. Even in the recent years when exports have expanded rapidly, the level of mineral exports has not exceeded $25 million, while the failure of total exports to expand during the 1950s along the lines suggested in the Nathan Plan should be attributed mainly to the unwillingness of the Korean government to implement the exchange rate and other policies which would have encouraged exports, it also seems clear, on the basis of the subsequent experience with exports during the 1960s, that Korea's comparative advantage is mainly in the area of light manufactured goods, not the agricultural and mining areas which the Nathan Plan suggested.

The proposals for broad import substitution in manufacturing also failed to materialize. This was probably fortunate for the long-run growth of the economy. The import substitution that did occur was largely at the final processing stages, which resulted in continued dependence on imports of raw materials and intermediate goods. Large raw material imports were inevitable, given Korea's limited natural resources, but the choice between imports or domestic production of intermediate goods was one of comparative cost. Many intermediate goods have significant economies of scale, so that to produce them in the limited quantities required to satisfy only the internal demands of the Korean market would have been very inefficient. The costs of such inefficiency would have fallen on the Korean consumer and would have been a high price to pay for achieving self-support. The availability of substantial foreign aid, beyond the period originally contemplated in the Nathan Plan, made it possible to continue imports of intermediate as well as capital goods (imports of finished consumer goods dropped practically to zero) and reduced premature investment in capital-intensive intermediate goods industries.

The Three-Year Plan followed many of the same lines as the Nathan Plan in the areas of industrial and trade structure, but it called for "progress toward" rather than "achievement of" a balance between exports and imports. The export targets were less ambitious, and recognition of the need for a continuing import surplus, including imports of grains to meet the food deficit, was very different from the earlier program. But, like the

Nathan Plan, the new plan called for major import substitution in key industries, such as chemicals, metals, machinery, and nitrogenous fertilizer, and projected an absolute decline in the import level of 8 percent between 1958 and 1962, despite a planned 22.6 percent increase in real GNP. This proposed pattern of investment reflected the Korean objections to excessive growth of consumption goods industries and the desire to build an integrated or balanced industrial structure, which was generally conceived of as an increasing share of capital goods in total manufacturing production. The Three-Year Plan stated: "It is hoped we can change the ratio between the production of capital goods and consumer goods from 25:75 in the base year (1958) to 35:65 in the target year (1962)."

With the First Five-Year Plan the emphasis began to shift away from a self-sufficient, or inward-looking, industrial structure. Although there was still concern about raising the relative output of capital goods, there was also a growing acceptance of the need for relatively high levels of imports and of the idea that the trade gap would have to be closed mainly by raising the export ratio. As stated in the plan:[25]

> The ultimate course of the Korean economy lies in industrialization. During the plan period, the period of preparation for industrialization, emphasis will be placed on development of power, coal, and other energy sources, increase in the earnings of farm households by raising agricultural productivity, expansion of key industrial facilities and adequate provision of social overhead capital, utilization of idle resources, some improvement in the balance of international payments, primarily through increased exports, and technological advancement.

Wolf, who was one of the advocates of this so-called "unbalanced growth strategy," has interpreted it as implying concentration on three key sectors: electric power, agriculture, and social overhead capital.[26] The expansion in these areas was to provide a basis of essential inputs for growth of industrial production which would be carried out mainly by the private sector.

The investment programs in electric power and related expansion of coal mining were effectively implemented so that the country had sufficient supplies of electricity and coal by 1964 for the first time since the end of World War II. Also the plans for expansion of agricultural production were effective. The targets for increased cultivated and irrigated areas, and application of fertilizer and pesticides were approximately met and the effects on agricultural output were of the magnitude that had been predicted.

[25] *Summary of the First Five-Year Economic Plan*, 1962–1966 (Republic of Korea, 1962), p. 29.
[26] Charles Wolf, Jr., "Economic Planning in Korea," pp. 230–31.

While there was provision in the First Five-Year Plan for a number of import substitute-type industrial investments, these were less important than in the previous plans. As a consequence the ratio of imports to GNP was projected as being about 20 percent in the terminal year, which was approximately the level in the base year. Also a rise in the import ratio was called for during the plan period to cover needed investment goods. Clearly this implied moving toward a more open, trade-oriented economy. Even so, the import projections proved conservative. Actual imports over the whole plan period were about 7 percent above the plan levels, and in the final year they were 45 percent higher than the plan.

The export projections seemed quite unrealistic at the time the First Plan was issued, and it is doubtful that the planners had much of an idea as to how the targets might be achieved. But the implementation of a series of export incentive measures, beginning in 1961 and continuing over the next several years, resulted in such spectacular growth of exports that by 1966 the realized export level of $250 million was nearly double the target level of $137.5 million. The composition of exports predicted in the plan followed the traditional assumption that agricultural and mineral products would predominate, but this too proved very inaccurate as manufactures accounted for over 60 percent of the total by 1966.

Thus while the First Five-Year Plan had anticipated at least the direction of some of the changes in industrial and trade structure, it clearly underestimated the extent of those changes and it did not contemplate many of the policies that were subsequently used to bring these changes about.

As the preparation of the Second Five-Year Plan was getting underway, the favorable results of these new policies were becoming apparent and as a consequence the questions that had to be answered in connection with industrial structure for the Second Plan were more in terms of how far the existing trends would or should be pursued and what marginal adjustments seemed appropriate, rather than what major shifts in direction or policy were needed. One set of proposals argued for continued expansion of exports and of agricultural production, but with increasing reliance on a rural-oriented industrial sector to supply the export commodities. This was intended to provide stronger linkages between the urban and rural populations and to improve the incomes of the rural inhabitants so that they could buy more of the rapidly growing industrial production.[27] The basic strategy of export-led industrial development was generally accepted, but the rural industry emphasis was not, in part out of concern that decentralized, small-scale producing facilities might be less efficient and

[27] J. C. H. Fei and Gustav Ranis, "Toward a Long-Run Development Strategy for Korea," Oct. 1, 1964 (mimeo.), p. 39.

therefore impair the competitiveness of Korean exports in world markets. Although there was a willingness to give at least equal, if not some preferential, treatment to smaller scale industry, there was a reluctance to try to push such industry out into the rural areas as Fei and Ranis proposed. Furthermore, there was a disposition to continue the agricultural programs of the First Plan, which seemed to be paying off. While recognizing that the output of the agricultural sector would grow less rapidly than that of manufacturing, it was expected that farm income would continue to rise at a satisfactory rate, that the shift of population from rural to urban areas was inevitable, and that rapid expansion of employment opportunities must occur in the cities.

The main questions concerning industrial structure for the Second Plan were (a) how rapidly could exports be increased; (b) whether the growth of demand for certain intermediate goods would be sufficient to justify building efficient-sized plants within Korea; and (c) whether to permit large-scale importation of machinery and equipment to support a rapid expansion of investment, or to try to divert some of this demand to the domestic machinery and capital goods industries.

The export alternatives were posed as a choice between target levels for commodity exports in 1971 of $500 million or $700 million. These implied compound annual growth rates of 19 and 26 percent from the 1965 level of $175 million. The Ministry of Commerce and Industry and others advocating high growth and rapid industrialization supported the high target. Those who were more concerned about financial stability and a balanced industrial structure argued for the lower target.[28] The target finally chosen for the plan was $550 million, or a growth rate of 21 percent. But this fiugre had hardly been agreed upon when current developments began to indicate that it was too conservative. As shown in Table 1, current account earnings were well above planned levels in 1966 and 1967, due mainly to the service earnings, but this led to increases in the export targets for 1971 to $750 million for commodities and $1,075 million for goods and services. Thus there has been a continuing process of raising export targets and increasing the support for export activities as the current export results have exceeded earlier expectations. The strategy decisions involved in the formulation of the Second Plan were just one stage in this process.

At the time the Second Plan was being prepared there were two major investment projects under consideration for which it was recognized that economies of scale were important and therefore that the prospective

---

[28] World Bank experts as late as the summer of 1966 were still suggesting that a $400 million target for 1971 was more reasonable.

TABLE 1.   ACTUAL AND PLANNED LEVELS OF EXPORTS AND IMPORTS, 1965–71

(*millions of US dollars*)

	1965	1966		1967		1968		1971	
	Ac- tual	Planned	Ac- tual	Planned	Ac- tual	Orig. plan	Revis. plan	Orig. plan	Revis. plan
Exports									
Goods and									
Services	290	395	455	462	643	524	787	719	1,075
Merchandise only	175	250	250	300	320	360	450	550	750
Imports									
Goods and									
Services	488	676	778	767	1,060	834	1,156	962	1,371
Merchandise only	420	587	680	655	909	705	993	804	

Sources: Actuals for 1965–67 are from the BOK Monthly Statistical Review. Planned estimates for 1966 and 1967 and the Original Plan estimates for 1968 and 1971 are from the *Second Five-Year Economic Development Plan, 1967–71*, pp. 202–3. The Revised Plan estimates for 1968 and for 1971 are from the *Overall Resources Budget: 1968*, Economic Planning Board, Aug. 1967.

rates of growth of demand were very significant. These were an integrated steel mill and a petrochemical complex. Not only was the overall growth rate of the economy of relevance but the growth and composition of exports and the decision on imported vs. domestic capital goods was likely to have a bearing on the appropriate scale of the steel and petrochemical projects. One further consideration was that, if these projects were to supply the export industries, they should be able to do so at world market prices. Because there was a predisposition against subsidizing these products, it was hoped that costs of production could be brought down to world market levels.

The decisions incorporated in the Second Plan on these two big industrial projects were reached after an analysis of the overall growth of industrial demand and of the investments required in the lighter industry sectors to sustain that growth. It was then concluded that the petrochemical complex should be undertaken in the early part of the plan period, both because it required less total investment and because sufficient demand for its output seemed likely. The steel mill would be built in the latter part of the Second Plan and would only come into production in the Third Plan period. This kind of confrontation of demand prospects, overall investment availabilities and the investment needs of other sectors was an essential feature of the decision making on industrial structure in the Second Plan and was made possible by the multisectoral framework within which the plan was formulated. The framework both required and provided a basis for the reconciliation of conflicting demands in order to arrive at a feasible overall program.

The third critical decision, on whether to protect the machinery industries, was dominated by the desire to maintain high rates of growth and
investment and to take advantage of the potential foreign capital which
would be available for financing the importation of machinery and equipment. Therefore, despite statements at various points in the Second Plan
about the importance of building up the machinery sectors, the investment
tentatively earmarked for them was not very large and much of it was
expected to go into electric and mechanical appliances for the export and
consumer markets rather than into the heavier machine tool industries.

In sum, the Second Plan decisions on industrial structure were dominated by the desire for high rates of growth and increased efficiency. By
capitalizing on the rapid growth of exports, which emanated mainly from
the less capital-intensive manufacturing industries, by delaying some of
the more capital-intensive projects until adequate demand for their output
was assured, and by relying heavily on imported machinery, the plan was
intended to keep the economy moving ahead strongly. Growth was in
fact so rapid in 1966 and 1967 that what had previously seemed to be
ample capacity in the infrastructure areas of power and transportation
proved to be seriously deficient. Early revisions of the Second Plan
involved major acceleration and expansion of investment in these two
sectors so that they would "not become more serious bottlenecks to
growth."[29]

Domestic Savings and Foreign Assistance

The prospects for increasing domestic savings and reducing dependence
on foreign assistance have been among the most controversial issues of
Korean planning. Throughout the post-war period the level of domestic
savings in relation to GNP has been low by comparison either with other
countries or with Korea's investment needs and targets. As a corollary,
the level of foreign assistance has been high. While most Koreans have
expressed a desire to redress this balance and the foreign assistance pro-
viders have supported this idea, there has been continuing disagreement
on the speed with which the shift should be brought about. There have
also been differences as to whether the shift would be achieved mainly by
pushing for higher domestic savings rates or accepting lower rates of
growth. The conflict is illustrated by a comparison of the macro-economic
projections of the Nathan Plan and the First and Second Five-Year Plans.
(See Table 2.)

All three of these plans postulated a very sudden increase in investment
at the beginning of the plan. The Nathan Plan was most extreme in that

[29] Economic Planning Board, *Overall Resources Budget: 1968* (August, 1967), p. 13.

TABLE 2. MARGINAL RATES OF INVESTMENT, DOMESTIC SAVINGS AND FOREIGN CAPITAL
INFLOW, AS PROJECTED IN THREE KOREAN PLANS

	Base year to year 1	Year 1 to year 2	2 to 3	3 to 4	4 to 5
Nathan Plan (1954 to 1958–59)					
1. Marginal rate of:					
a. Investment	.72	.12	.16	−.23	−1.00
b. Domestic saving	.45	.42	.46	.16	.20
c. Foreign capital inflow	.27	−.29	−.62	−.39	−1.20
2. Per annum growth of GNP	15%	10%	9%	5%	5%
First Five-Year Plan (1962–66)					
1. Marginal rate of:					
a. Investment	1.38	.68	.39	.14	.16
b. Domestic saving	.89	.64	.52	.25	.25
c. Foreign capital inflow	.48	.04	−.13	−.19	−.09
2. Per annum growth of GNP	2%	6%	7%	8%	8%
Second Five-Year Plan (1967–71)					
1. Marginal rate of:					
a. Investment	.54	.27	.27	.28	.23
b. Domestic saving	.27	.25	.34	.35	.33
c. Foreign capital inflow	.26	.02	−.07	−.07	−.09
2. Per annum growth of GNP	7%	7%	7%	7%	7%

Note: Base years were for the Nathan Plan, 1953–54; for the First Five-Year Plan, 1960;
for the Second Five-Year Plan, 1965.

it provided for an increase in investment equal to 72 percent of the growth
of GNP while GNP was assumed to grow at 15 percent. Thus the proposed
investment increase exceeded 10 percent of GNP, a very unrealistic target
given the conditions in the country at that time. The investment increase
projected in the early years of the First Five-Year Plan was also large
relative to the change in GNP, but because that latter change was relatively
small the investment target was less ambitious. The Second Plan assumed
a more modest initial increase in investment and a fairly steady marginal
increment thereafter, whereas the earlier plans contained sharply declining
marginal increments. Here again the Nathan Plan was extreme in that it
assumed investment in the final year would decline absolutely by an
amount equal to the rise in GNP.

The domestic savings projections of the first two plans were similar in
that they assumed very high marginal savings rates during the first half
of the plans and then a sharp tapering off in the last two years. In the
Second Plan the marginal savings rate was less high on average and was
expected to increase significantly in the later years of the plan. All three
plans had similar patterns of foreign capital inflow with a significant
increase in the first year and then an absolute decline at least after the
second year. The Nathan Plan assumed a precipitous drop in foreign
capital receipts in the final year.

A simple comparison of the three plans shows that the earlier expectations of dramatic change have become more cautious and conditioned by reality with the passage of time. The kinds of adjustments called for in the Nathan Plan were extreme, and some similar ones were repeated in the First Five-Year Plan. By the Second Plan there was greater awareness of comparative experience in other countries as well as in Korea. The limits of change in marginal savings and investment rates were better appreciated, but also the structural relationships in the Korean economy were less seriously out of balance than at the beginning of the earlier plans. There was also a recognition that Korea should expect to have a sizable net capital inflow for the foreseeable future, but that the sources of financing for the inflow would shift from mainly grant aid to public and private loans and equity investment.[30] For these several reasons the Second Plan projected smoother and more reasonable adjustment in the structure of domestic and foreign savings than had the earlier plans.

The extreme assumptions about the potential increases in savings and foreign capital during the early years of the plans provided the basis for planning comparable expansion of investment. By attempting to carry out these investment programs, despite the failure of domestic savings to grow as expected, the potential for severe inflation was created. It is therefore not surprising that prices rose rapidly during the first years of both the Nathan Plan and the First Five-Year Plan. The clearest example of this is found in the 1962–63 period when investment was expanded substantially, but still not as rapidly as planned. Foreign capital inflow also rose, but savings did not respond at anything like the contemplated rate. As a consequence inflationary forces were unleashed. Domestic credit was doubled in two years to finance a large budgetary deficit (despite the highest ratio of taxes to GNP in Korea's postwar experience), and foreign exchange reserves were severely drawn down. This experience led to the imposition of strong stabilization measures and postponement of planned investment in 1964–65. Thus the unrealistic projections of domestic savings, noted by Wolf and others,[31] contributed to financial instability and disruption of plan implementation.

THE IMPACT OF PLANNING

After nearly a decade and a half of planning activity in Korea what can be said about its impact on the effectiveness of government operations

[30] See Peggy Musgrave, "Trade Targets and Policies in Korea's Economic Development," Aug. 22, 1965 (mimeo.), p. 15.

[31] Charles Wolf, Jr., "Economic Planning in Korea," p. 235; and Nam Duck Woo, "Korea's Experience with Planning," in Lee Sang-eun, ed., *Report of International Conference on the Problem of Modernization in Asia* (Seoul: Asiatic Research Center, 1966), pp. 520–23.

and on relations between the government and the people? Beyond this can anything be concluded on the contribution of planning to the overall growth and efficiency of the economy?

The early planning efforts, including the Nathan Plan, the Three-Year Plan of 1959 and the first version of the Five-Year Plan, did little to raise the government's effectiveness. The Nathan Plan's main significance was that it introduced the concept of overall planning to Korea, but because the Korean government had not participated in the planning process and did not accept the plan as a guide for policies or investment, the concept remained quite abstract and irrelevant for government operations. If anything, the government leaders during this period (1953 to 1958) rejected the idea of overall planning and were not interested in trying to define longer-run economic objectives or an integrated set of policies. This probably reflected a belief on their part that they could retain more flexibility and achieve better results in negotiations with aid donors by proceeding on an *ad hoc* basis and avoiding the overall commitments and constraints of a plan. Clearly the Nathan Plan called for very forceful policy action by the Korean government and set ambitious targets of self-support which the Koreans were not prepared to accept. To have agreed to the plan would have exposed the government to serious political risks.

Despite the government's rejection of the Nathan Plan, there was still some tendency to judge the country's economic performance against the standards of the Plan and to attribute the failures manifested in continuing inflation, rising trade deficits, and declining growth rates to the absence of an overall plan. It was as a result of these views that the Korean government established the Economic Development Council under the Minister of Reconstruction and initiated its own planning efforts in 1958. But this too proved to be mainly an educational experience and was not effective in influencing government operations.

The group responsible for formulating the Three-Year Plan was too isolated from either the operational or policy-making levels of government to draw upon the experience or guidance of either level in trying to articulate a meaningful development program. Also the Korean planners had no experience and practically no outside assistance in their work. The overthrow of the government shortly after the plan was drafted meant there was never an opportunity to test its possible influence on the government. Still some government officials had at least been exposed to the ideas and problems of planning and had gained some experience in those areas.

Consequently, the formulation of the first and second versions of the First Five-Year Plan, under governments that openly espoused planning, showed somewhat more sophistication and the prospects for greater influence on government programs. The main reasons why these prospects were not fully realized was that the Supreme Council for National Reconstruction imposed what seemed to be very unrealistic targets on the planners and the resulting plan was severely criticized by both foreign and domestic analysts. This immediately cut the ground out from under the planners and reduced their influence in the government. The very poor performance of the economy during the first year of the plan, the subsequent inflation, and the time-consuming but fruitless efforts of the planners to scale-down the plan to satisfy the critics completely removed the planners from the main stream of decision making. The First Plan as such was hardly referred to until work was started on the Second Plan and also until it became apparent that a number of the seemingly too ambitious First-Plan targets were going to be exceeded.

Some aspects of the investment program of the First Five-Year Plan were influential and contributed to the subsequent growth of the economy. The emphasis on agriculture and infrastructure helped to remove serious bottlenecks and activate lagging sectors of the economy. These were also the areas in which government had primary responsibility (as in power and railroad transport) or was able to carry out more effective programs than the private sector had been able to do (e.g., fertilizer distribution). Other more questionable areas emphasized in the plan were either ignored, as with the steel mill, or postponed until the economy was better prepared to implement them (e.g., the fertilizer plants). Thus the investment program of the plan served only as a rough guide and investment decisions continued to be made on a case by case basis, often without the planners having much say in the final decision.

Although the First Five-Year Plan did not present a well-worked-out set of economic policies, it did imply a number of policy directions that were subsequently followed and provided the real impetus for Korea's rapid growth. These included the encouragement of exports and domestic savings and maintenance of realistic, market-oriented interest and exchange rates. While it is difficult to assess the importance of these policy suggestions in the plan in bringing about the actual implementation of the policies, and it would undoubtedly be misleading to attribute a significant role, it can at least be said that the tendencies expressed in the plan were not contrary to the policy directions followed, mainly after 1964.

By the time work began on the Second Plan in 1965, planning as such was definitely not a well-established or influential process in the Korean government. The First Plan had been discredited, its revision ignored and the planning staff was not significantly involved in the current major economic policy deliberations. It is therefore remarkable that within little more than a year the planning function and the planners became integral parts of the government's decision-making process. This can be attributed to the following factors: the quality of the statistical and analytical work that went into the preparation of planning models and projections; the leadership of the Vice Minister of the Economic Planning Board, Kim Hak Yul, in organizing the planning effort, and the active participation of many officials from all parts of the government; the support and involvement of the foreign aid agencies in plan formulation, rather than simply sitting in judgment on the completed plan; and finally the realization that the plan was likely to have some continuing influence on the budgetary and policy actions of the government. Because the various agencies of the government began to suspect that the planning might have such an influence, they took it more seriously and thereby contributed to its increased significance.

In the policy areas, the Second Plan largely confirmed the policy directions which were established while the plan was being formulated. These included measures for increasing public and private saving, limiting inflation, encouraging exports, and freeing-up controls on imports. As regards investment, the Second Plan began to face up to the possibilities and needs of high growth rates. But it did not consider or accept the possibility of very high growth (e.g., above 7 percent per year), partly because of the criticism of such high targets in the First Plan, and also because of continuing admonitions from the World Bank to hold the growth target of the Second Plan to 6 percent. As for the composition of investment, the planning process led to some deferring of large, capital-intensive investment projects and some squeezing of the investment recommended for transportation. Such cuts were understandably resisted by the ministries concerned, but because representatives of those ministries had participated extensively in the plan deliberations they were well aware of the overall resource constraints. Thus the total investment program of the Second Plan was accepted by the various parts of government without serious disagreement and became a meaningful guide for the government's capital budget and decisions on approval of foreign investments within Korea.

The weakest part of the Second Plan was its program for agriculture, which failed to define a comprehensive set of targets, to relate investments and policies to those targets, or to indicate the other kinds of inputs required to expand agricultural output. Consequently the agriculture program in the Second Plan was largely ignored and agricultural investment has subsequently been decided without reference to the plan.

Although it became obvious during the first year of the Second Plan period that the overall growth targets of the plan were too low and in particular that the investment programmed for the power and transportation sectors was grossly inadequate, this did not result in discrediting the planners and the planning process. If anything, it strengthened the conviction that more and better planning was needed. In part this was because the limitations of predictive accuracy had been clearly acknowledged in the Second Plan and procedures recommended for revising the investment program annually to take advantage of new information and meet changing conditions. Also the sectors where shortages became acute were those which would benefit most from good medium term demand projections. Finally in Korea it is probably easier to revise estimates of growth and investment up rather than down, without "losing face," because it attests to the conservatism of the planners.

On balance it seems fair to conclude that the Second Plan achieved an important influence on the Korean government and that the annual overall resource budgets which have been formulated since 1967 have so far provided a focal point for review and revision of policies, investment programs and projections of Korean economic growth. The Second Plan also for the first time had the effect of strengthening the political stature of the government, both at home and abroad. Where the Nathan Plan and the First Five-Year Plan had resulted in major disagreements with foreign aid donors and had exposed the government to criticism and embarrassment within Korea, the Second Plan elicited much more favorable reactions and thereby generated greater recognition and cooperation for the government.

When the Second Plan was made public in the summer of 1966, many of its provisions were already well known through advance publicity and press conferences by the officials of the Economic Planning Board. Thus there were no surprises in the plan, but it immediately attracted a great deal of attention and comment in the press and on television. The government organized an effective program to publicize the plan and to answer questions or criticisms of it. The President indicated his approval and commitment to carry out the plan which the cabinet had endorsed to him. Thus the government presented the plan to the public with a united front and an air of confidence.

The principal reactions to the plan by the initial reviewers, both domestic and foreign, were that it was honest and represented a relatively high degree of competence. The admission in the plan document of past errors of policy and statistical misrepresentation, and the projection of growth rates below those of the recent past were all taken as evidence of a new integrity in the government. While there were criticisms of various aspects of the plan, most critics first acknowledged the apparent sincerity and conscientiousness of the planning effort. A sample survey of the opinions of Korean professors and journalists conducted in late 1966 found that

80 percent expected some success from the Second Five-Year Plan.[32] No comparable survey was taken after the earlier plans were completed, but the fact that such a large proportion of traditionally skeptical and anti-government groups were favorably disposed toward the Second Plan and relatively confident about the benefits to be derived from it, was a noteworthy political achievement. There was even some tendency, in the glow of enthusiasm and confidence at the time the plan was made public in mid-1966, to talk as though the targets of 1971 had already been achieved. This was remarkable for a people who had previously been inclined to live from day to day and to view the future without hope. The obvious improvements in living conditions during the mid-1960s helped to change such attitudes, but the Second Plan marked a turning point in infusing the Korean people with a more optimistic conception of the future.

[32] Sung Chick Hong, *The Intellectual and Modernization — A Study of Korean Attitudes* (Seoul: Dachan Textbook Co., 1967).

KOREA'S FIVE-YEAR PLANS

P. W. Kuznets

Introduction

Plan evaluation, unlike plan description, is neither simple nor straight-forward. The most obvious way to evaluate a plan, given the benefit of hindsight, is to compare plan targets with the actual results. By itself, however, this procedure may easily produce misleading conclusions, for it fails to question the desirability of stated goals—to recognize that five-year economic plans are political as well as economic documents, with targets frequently set merely to satisfy the public or the donor countries' lending conditions. Plans may also be ambitious on the theory that a larger carrot will allow more vigorous use of the stick. Thus a modest plan with modest results may be rated higher than an ambitious plan with better results.

It must also be recognized that planning requires the projecting of variables and the forecasting of parameter values that are exogenously determined, such as agricultural output and foreign aid. Events that occur after the plan is framed may invalidate the plan or justify substantial revision even before the plan goes into effect.[1]

Ideally, then, evaluation requires that actual goals be distinguished from ostensible goals, and that the extent and accuracy of the data available at the time the plan was constructed be known, so that the analyst can determine the extent to which alternative plans might have approached the goals more fully, more quickly, or more economically. This type of evaluation, however, is highly speculative; it requires information which is virtually impossible to obtain and is, therefore, unlikely to yield useful results.

Perhaps a more fruitful approach is first to analyze the plan as a plan (i.e., *in vacuo*). Are the size and the timing of projected expenditures consistent with the expected amounts and timing of available resources? Are instruments consistent with goals? Are particular targets consistent

---

[1] This is one reason why Korean planning has featured the preparation of annual overall-resource budgets (ORBs) in recent years and why both basic structure and speed of adjustment to observed change should be considered in evaluating planning.

with each other? Is the time pattern of growth in savings, etc., a reasonable one? Inconsistencies may be the result of discrepancies between actual and ostensible goals as well as the result of deficiencies in planning. Since most plans are political documents, it may be possible to detect an unstated ordering of goals, implicit in such discrepancies, and one might then be able to assess the desirability of stated priorities.

The next step is to examine the realism of the plan. Recent experience in Korea, or in other countries in similar circumstances, may show, for example, that as income rises from very low levels it is difficult to restrain consumption, as may be required by the plan. This kind of information may be especially helpful when targets are compared with results.

In comparing targets and results, evaluation in terms of the plan's realism, while suggestive, is not, however, sufficient. A number of factors not considered in the plan are likely to have an important bearing on target achievement. Clearly, monetary, fiscal, and trade policies are important to the success of the plan, as are the planning mechanism, methods of plan implementation, and the relationship between the macro and micro aspects of the plan. What is required is knowledge of the planning and implementation processes, plus an understanding of how the course of economic events during the plan period is indirectly affected by policy action.

An attempt will be made in the discussion which follows to observe the procedure outlined above. Since the planning process has been fairly continuous and since economies of scale exist in plan evaluation (as elsewhere), the First Five-Year Plan will be considered in conjunction with the adjusted version of the plan,[2] the actual results, and the Second Five-Year Plan (SFYP).

THE FIRST FIVE-YEAR PLAN (FFYP)

FFYP's first chapter, on planning background, painted a grim picture of economic stagnation and corruption. Despite large-scale foreign aid, Korea, with a predominantly agricultural economy, had to import large quantities of food grains, and it had not been able to raise its extremely low living standards. Large-scale state enterprises were "irresponsibly and irrationally managed"; foreign-exchange rates, pegged at low levels, had led to overinvestment in industries that were highly dependent on imported raw materials. Little had been done to relieve a shortage of electric power, the most serious bottleneck for industrialization. Other constraints were caused by a severe shortage of capital and limited access to bank credit. Because of the wide gap between bank and curb-market interest rates,

---

[2] Referred to hereafter as the Revised FFYP (see Bibliography entry 115).

bankers were "arrogant lords meting out special favors." An unrealistic tax system, with prohibitively high rates and "arbitrary assessment by the subjective judgment of capricious tax officials," made "evasion prerequisite for staying in business." In such a situation, "many entrepreneurs went into unsavory league with politicians and bureaucrats seeking to amass easy fortunes. Business conditions were foul indeed. . . . Virtually all social evils were connected with the greed and maladministration of government officials. . . . The process of seeking illegal wealth became vicious as political instability grew."

While the new government's harsh indictment of the conditions which prevailed under earlier regimes could hardly have been unbiased, the indictment indicates some of the difficulties facing implementation of the new plan. It also explains why the government has coupled its economic development goals with the goal of "modernization," which, in the Korean context, requires nothing less than the restructuring of traditional values and behavior.[3]

The "gist of the first five-year economic plan" lies in the attempt to "build an industrial base principally through increased energy production" (124:24).[4] Self-sufficiency in food grains by 1966 was another major goal; the construction of social overhead capital that could be built through mobilization of idle resources was also to be emphasized. Finally, cement, chemical-fertilizer, synthetic fiber, and other import-substitute industries were to be expanded or created. These major objectives were to be achieved under a system that was characterized as "a form of 'guided capitalism' in which the principle of free enterprise will be observed, but in which the government will either directly participate in or indirectly render guidance to the basic industries and other important fields" (124:28).

In addition, the plan presents a detailed statement of sectoral output and investment targets and it provides a set of estimates for investment sources, resource allocation, output growth, and income distribution at highly aggregate levels.

Gross national product in the FFYP was to increase at an accelerating rate, with an average annual (compound) increase of 7.1 percent, mainly through a 51 percent rise in investment (see Appendix Tables 1, 2, and 7 at the end of this chapter). Consumption (especially government consumption), however, was to rise less rapidly. The lag in the growth of consumption is reflected in per capita data. GNP per capita was expected

---

[3] See, for example, Bibliography entry 48.

[4] The first number in parentheses refers to the number of the cited work in the Bibliography presented at the end of this volume; the second number indicates the page reference.

to rise 19.1 percent over the plan period, private consumption 11.1 percent, and government consumption only 5 percent.[5]

Estimates of GNP, available resources, and various breakdowns of consumption, investment, and saving given in the FFYP generally appear to be consistent. Private consumption was expected to rise by 45 percent between 1962 and 1966 (see Appendix Table 7), although the output of major consumption items, such as grains, was to increase more slowly, presumably to allow for the well-known low-income elasticities of the demand for food.[6] The plan shows a 5 percent fall in private consumption between 1960 and 1962, however, which does not seem realistic in a low-income country like Korea.

Because of concentration on industrial investment and the lumpiness of investment in major targets, the investment ratio was to rise from 20.1 percent of GNP in 1962 to 24.1 percent in 1964, before dropping back to 22.7 percent in 1966 (see Appendix Table 10). A marked concentration on the secondary sector, especially mining and manufacturing, is consistent with the plan's industrialization goals, but not necessarily with the goals of breaking the power bottleneck and achieving self-sufficiency in food grains. Insufficient information exists to determine the full impact of the investment program on the industrial structure, but published growth targets provided for a doubling of GNP originating in mining and manufacturing, and smaller increases in the primary and tertiary sectors.

The marginal capital output ratio of 4:1 implied by the projected increase in GNP, even with the lumpy investments and long gestation periods associated with power facilities and the iron and steel industries, suggests (according to evidence at the time of substantial excess capacity) that the estimate of capital requirements was too high.[7]

The government sector accounts for approximately one-third of the total investment and more than one-half of capital formation by source of funds, since the government acts as an intermediary between foreign savings and domestic investment.[8] The government share drops after

[5] Average consumption was equivalent to $56.00 in 1962 at the then overvalued *won* rate of 130 per U.S. dollar. Although cross-national comparisons based on official exchange rates are notoriously dangerous, the plan's reference to extremely low living standards was undoubtedly correct.

[6] Export and import programs, incidentally, show a marked drop in food imports and a 75 percent rise in food exports.

[7] For evidence of overcapacity, see Bibliography entry 122.

[8] The government's intermediary role, as exemplified in lending to large-scale (public and private) enterprises by the Korean Reconstruction Bank, has been one of the main instruments of control implicit in the "guided capitalism" which was to characterize the FFYP. A little under three-quarters of capital formation was to be financed with domestic currency. The domestic currency share drops after 1962, probably because of the heavy capital imports required by government-purchased and government-financed

1962–63, mainly reflecting the expected decline in the importance of foreign aid.

Of total government investment, one-half was to be allocated to manufacturing, of which four-fifths was to be invested in petroleum-refining, chemical-fertilizer, iron and steel, and heavy machinery and transport industries.

Although investment and output targets are spelled out in some detail in the FFYP, estimates for sources of funds are not. Since consumption was to absorb 96 percent of GNP in 1962, and investment ratios were on the order of 20 to 25 percent during the plan period, substantial foreign savings were required. No estimates of domestic savings are shown, although they can be derived as a residual (see Appendix Table 9). This calculation can be checked by estimating the proportion of investment to be financed domestically.[9]

The declining relative and absolute dependence on foreign savings is reflected in balance-of-payments projections that show deficits on current account of $310 million in 1962, declining to $247 million in 1966. The total deficit during the plan period was $1.4 billion, two-thirds of which was to be covered by "public donations," mainly in the form of U.S. supporting assistance and PL 480 imports. These estimates are supported by invisibles and by commodity import and export programs. Although up substantially from 1960, largely because of increasing requirements for machinery and transport equipment, annual import levels were to rise less than 10 percent during the plan period.

Estimates of population, labor force, and employment growth are all but neglected in the FFYP. The rate of population increase projected in the plan drops 0.04 of a percentage point per year, and it was expected that "population control measures will be required" (124). An 11 percent increase in the labor force and a 26 percent rise in employment are shown, which would reduce unemployment from 2.4 million in 1962 to 1.8 million in 1966. The derivation of these figures, however, is not shown, and little if any reference is made to them in the plan.[10]

Domestic savings were expected to more than quadruple during the plan period. To reach a domestic savings ratio of 13 percent by 1966, an incremental ratio of 41 percent was required. The estimates of whole-period

investment in power facilities, transport, and industries with long investment gestation periods.

[9] The proportion rises from 18 percent in 1962 to 57 percent in 1966, and is almost identical with the figures shown in the FFYP (124:34).

[10] Although there may be practical reasons for neglecting the labor force and employment in planning for labor-surplus countries like Korea, the literature on the development process in such countries in recent years suggests that neglect of a plan's employment consequences is not justified.

savings magnitudes may or may not be realistic, but the declining annual increments in domestic savings (see Appendix Table 9) are certainly unrealistic, as are the falling marginal ratios they suggest.[11]

The plan's fiscal targets show a sizable government deficit on current account in 1962, replaced by an even larger surplus by 1966 as taxes and other government income rose by about two-thirds. Current expenditure was expected to rise less than 10 percent, while the growing current account surplus was to be employed to finance substantial increases in capital expenditure. Thus the government was *not* to be responsible for the lagging growth of domestic savings. Estimates of the size and distribution of national income show a doubling of corporate savings between 1962 and 1966. The weak link is private noncorporate savings. Direct calculation of private income (employee compensation plus income from unincorporated enterprises and property) less private consumption reveals virtually no increase in private noncorporate savings after 1964. The level for 1966 is, in fact, lower than in 1964 and 1965.

The FFYP does not give sufficient information for properly evaluating the main demand projections and supply targets. Where supply and demand estimates are given, their accuracy or consistency cannot be assessed without knowledge of detailed intersectoral relationships of the sort provided by input-output tables.[12]

The accuracy or consistency of supply-and-demand relationships cannot be determined from analysis of the plan itself, but a limited attempt can be made to assess the feasibility of several of its output goals in terms of their investment allocations. The investment program in coal mining, for example, requires a total fixed capital expenditure of 113 billion *hwan* during the plan period. The increase in coal production expected between 1962 and 1966,[13] in 1961 wholesale prices, is estimated at almost 140 billion *hwan*.[14] Although a fairly large proportion of the outlay is to be in foreign currency, which would be undervalued at the official exchange rate, the implied marginal capital-output ratio of less than 1.0 seems quite low.[15]

---

[11] Marginal or incremental ratios drop from 64 percent in 1962–63 to 24 percent in 1965–66. This was noted at the time by Charles Wolf, Jr. (109).

[12] Input-output tables were constructed by the Bank of Korea (BOK) for the years 1960 and 1963 (130, 131, 132) but were not available to the planners in 1961. Even if they had been, introduction of new products or substitution among existing products would have rendered the 1960 relationships obsolete by 1966.

[13] Even growth is assumed, since annual investment outlays are distributed fairly equally throughout the period.

[14] These are really producers' selling prices, not wholesale prices, and as such are more desirable for present purposes (see 91). The currency was redenominated in 1962, and revalued at a ratio of 10 *hwan* per *won*.

[15] R. S. Eckaus and L. Lefeber (24) show a capital coefficients matrix for India, based on data derived by Vinod Prakash of the Indian Statistical Institute. The coefficient for mining and metals is 2.15.

A similar crude calculation can be made for the agricultural sector. Annual investment levels were expected to increase by 28.2 billion *won* between 1962 and 1966, while the value of output was to grow by 227.7 billion *hwan*. The implied incremental capital-output ratio is too low to be consistent with experience elsewhere. One can only conclude that insufficient investment was to be allocated to the coal mining and the agricultural sectors.

A more basic issue is the legitimacy of the goal of self-sufficiency in food grains. The extensive literature on "agricultural revolutions" and the recent argument over the merits of "balanced" versus "unbalanced growth" raise the point that sharp increases in agricultural productivity may be a necessary precondition for industrialization.[16] Unquestionably, however, emphasis in the FFYP has been on the industrial sector, not on agriculture. It has been said that "AID made a premature effort to industrialize Korea during the middle 1950's, before agricultural productivity was raised"—a statement that might apply equally to the FFYP.[17] On the other hand, with one of the world's highest man-land ratios, with limited opportunity for extending the area under cultivation, and with a somewhat unfavorable climate, Korea's long-run comparative advantage seems to lie elsewhere than in agriculture, and the resource cost of self-sufficiency in food grains might well be very high.

Broader questions than those of consistency and time pattern of savings growth should be considered in examining the plan's structure. Nothing is said of tax, foreign-exchange, trade, or monetary policies in the FFYP, all of which are obviously of crucial importance in implementing the plan. Although it is unnecessary to outline such policies in detail in a planning document, the whole planning process may be reduced to an exercise in futility if the policies required to implement the plan are not feasible. Second, the general description of the planning procedure (123:28) does not describe how macro and micro decisions were reconciled. The criteria employed in choosing particular projects are of major interest, and a brief discussion of such criteria would not have been out of place. In addition, because Korea has had to maintain a large military establishment, the relationship between defense budgets and the FFYP's economic targets is significant, but nothing is said of this in the plan document. Finally, the infrastructure, industrialization, and agricultural targets, when taken together, appear too ambitious—especially if they are judged at face value (109).

[16] In addition to the widely known issue of "balanced-unbalanced growth" associated with the work of Rosenstein-Rodan, Nurkse, and Hirschman, articles dealing with the Japanese experience, by Kazushi Ohkawa and Henry Rosovsky (71) and Gustav Ranis (76), are particularly instructive.

[17] Neil H. Jacoby (43:160).

BACKGROUND AND REVISION

During the years immediately preceding the beginning of the First Five-Year Plan, Korea was marked not only by political chaos but by economic stagnation.[18] (A summary of its economic conditions is presented in Table 1.) Perhaps the most striking condition was the low growth level of GNP—and the stagnation in per capita private consumption and government consumption which accompanied it. Investment, more than two-thirds of which was financed by foreign savings, was quite low. There was an encouraging increase in exports in 1961, but this was overwhelmed by a large and increasing import balance. What Table 1 does not show is the virtual stagnation of agriculture in the period 1958–60 and the below-average growth of the mining and manufacturing sectors.

The plan called for a 5.6 percent rise in GNP from the base year, 1960, to the first year, 1962, which does not seem overoptimistic in view of the 1959 and 1960 growth levels. Subsequent growth was to be more rapid. Structural changes embodied in the plan required a substantial growth in mining and manufacturing, so that, by 1966, GNP originating in these sectors would be equal to half the GNP originating in the primary sector.

The actual allocation of investment in 1959–61 was not too different from the investment programmed in the FFYP. The plan called for relatively more investment in both the primary and the secondary sectors, and relatively less investment in tertiary industries, than took place during 1959–61.

One must examine sources of financing and actual developments to see why the FFYP went awry during the first year of the plan period. First, although the plan called for only a modest increase in domestic savings (from 3.0 percent of GNP in 1959–61 to 3.7 percent in 1962), the actual increase was a miserable 2.2 percent (see Appendix Table 10). A second factor was the failure of government revenue to increase as expected.[19] Insofar as government budget surpluses can be used to finance domestic capital formation, or general government expenditure can be employed for investment purposes, the government's success in raising revenues

---

[18] Three years, 1959 to 1961, are taken for a comparison base because they include the plan's base year, 1960, and because a single-year base is likely to be unrepresentative, especially in predominantly agricultural countries. The 1960 rice crop, for example, was 4 percent below the 1959 level. With over 40 percent of income originating in agriculture, and rice production constituting approximately half of agricultural output, such variation can have a substantial influence on aggregate estimates.

[19] The plan called for the revenue ratio to rise to 16.5 percent of GNP in 1962, from 12.4 percent in 1959–61, and continuing increases thereafter, so that rather large current account deficits in 1962–63 might be converted into surpluses from 1964 on. Actual revenue ratios averaged less than 10 percent during the plan period (see Appendix Table 10).

TABLE 1. THE KOREAN ECONOMY: 1959–1961*

	1959	1960	1961	Whole period	%
1. Expenditure on GNP ('65 prices)	575.8	589.1	613.6	1,778.5	
2. Annual growth rates (%)	4.4	2.3	4.2		
3. Population (millions)ᵃ	24.3	25.0	25.7		
4. Private consumption	508.6	523.3	528.4	1,560.3	
5. Per capita GNP (won)	23,697	23,563	23,876		
6. Private C per capita (won)	20,930	20,932	20,560		
7. Industrial origin of GNP				1,778.5	100.0
Primary				756.2	42.5
Secondary				319.5	18.0
(Mining, manufacturing)				(261.7)	(14.7)
Tertiary				702.9	39.5
8. Investment by sectorᵇ				193.3	100.0
Primary				24.8	12.8
Secondary				59.1	30.6
(Mining, manufacturing)				(47.5)	(24.6)
Tertiary				109.4	56.6
9. Investment by purchaser	57.8	62.5	73.0	193.3	100.0
Government	18.3	16.2	19.3	53.9	27.9
Private	41.0	45.5	45.9	132.4	68.5
Increase in stocks	−1.5	0.8	7.7	7.0	3.6
10. Consumption by purchaser	578.4	594.4	598.2	1,771.0	100.0
Private	508.6	523.3	528.4	1,560.2	88.1
Government	69.8	71.1	69.8	210.8	11.9
11. Domestic saving (current prices)ᶜ	8.66	5.81	13.50	27.97	
12. GDCF (current prices)	23.72	26.80	38.79	89.31	
13. = 11/12 × 100					31.3
14. GNP in current prices	221.00	246.69	296.82	764.51	
15. Foreign saving/GNP × 100					8.7
16. Domestic S/GNP × 100					3.0
17. Government revenueᵈ	24.65	31.35	38.75	94.75	
18. Govt. rev/GNP × 100					12.4
19. Exports (current won prices)	5.88	8.22	15.76		
20. Imports (current won prices)	22.40	31.02	43.83		

* Unless otherwise indicated, all data in billions of won, valued in 1965 prices. From (128).
ᵃ Estimates, except for 1960, when a census was taken.
ᵇ Change in stocks allocated to primary sector (50%), mining and manufacturing (50%).
ᶜ GDCF less sum of net borrowing and transfers from the rest of the world.
ᵈ Current revenue less current transfers from the rest of the world.

and contributing its share of GNP can be crucial in holding down consumption and raising investment levels. Fiscal experience in Korea in the early 1960s has been marked by the conspicuous failure of the government to do this.

Foreign savings were to play a much more important role during the early plan years than they had in 1959–61.[20] Although the 1962 deficit

[20] Foreign savings had averaged 8.7 percent of GNP in 1959–61, and were to rise to a peak of 16 percent in 1962, before falling back in later years. In balance-of-payments terms, this meant that current account deficits, averaging around $230 million a year during 1959–61, were to rise to a little over $300 million per year in 1962–64. Deficits

was $18 million less than planned, the inadequacy of foreign savings, which might have been expected to be the main reason for inability to meet plan targets, was not an important cause of the failure to raise investment levels.

Difficulties in meeting investment targets were compounded by poor harvests in 1962 and 1963,[21] an increasing rate of inflation, and a poorly timed currency reform in mid-1962. The poor harvests were largely responsible for a two-and-a-half-fold jump in food imports from 1962 to 1963 and for the large increase in the balance-of-payments deficit during 1963. Prices, which had been fairly stable since 1957, started to rise in 1960, and, led by grains, they rose at an accelerated pace from early 1963.

The currency reform took place on June 10, 1962, when all *hwan* had to be turned in for the new *won* currency, at the rate of 10 *hwan* per *won*. A limited amount of *won* was to be made available for living expenses, and the rest was to be frozen and channeled into financing industrial investment, in order to bring out hoarded currency for development purposes, to prevent inflation, and to limit currency speculation. The immediate effect of the measure, however, was a sharp drop in output; enterprises that depended upon loans in the unorganized money market were starved for operating funds.[22] The reform has been described as "ill-conceived, ill-prepared, ill-timed, and therefore ill-fated" (94:45), a description that seems apt.

No explicit recognition is given in the plans to the possibility of poor crops or inflation; it is, of course, difficult to account for stochastic processes within a plan framework. Inflation, however, has been a regular feature of economic life in Korea since World War II. Despite the political and psychological reasons for failing to build price increases into a plan, this failure can—it is clear—distort projections of savings and other major plan elements. The combination of crop failures and inflation, the overoptimistic savings and revenue targets, the unrealistic estimate of ability to restrain private consumption, and the difficulties associated with the poorly timed currency reform made it obvious by 1963 that the plan would need major revision.

---

of this size had been incurred before, in 1957–58; the actual figures for 1962–64 were, on the average, close to target levels (1962: $292 million; 1963: $403 million; 1964: $221 million).

[21] The 1962 rice crop was the smallest since 1957, and more than 10 percent below the 1961 crop. The summer-grain harvest of 1963 was unbelievably poor, less than a third of the 1962 harvest.

[22] Manufacturing output, for instance, fell 8 percent between May and July of 1962 before recovering to earlier levels (aided partly by a seasonal pattern which calls for higher output in autumn).

An adjusted version of the plan (the Revised FFYP) was published in March, 1964 (115). Adjustment consisted of converting 1961 prices to 1962 prices,[23] replacing 1962 estimates with 1962 results, and revising the 1964–66 targets. Justification for the modification included the food grain shortage, resulting from poor harvests; the sharp increase in consumption between 1961 and 1962; and increasing prices and decreasing foreign-exchange holdings. In addition, a number of defects in the FFYP were listed, particularly the failure to consider the necessity of repaying foreign loans, insufficient attention to the importance of public finance, neglect of intersectoral and interproject relationships, and inadequacies of supporting measures and supply-demand scheduling.

The keynote of the revision is the statement that "Rome was not built in a day" (115:2)—an attitude that is evident in the scaling down of GNP growth targets in the Revised FFYP (see Appendix Table 1), in a sharp downward revision of government consumption (see Appendix Table 8), and in reductions in domestic savings, government revenue, and investment ratios (see Appendix Table 10).[24] The planned growth of mining and manufacturing also was sharply reduced (see Appendix Table 5). The greater austerity of the Revised FFYP *vis-à-vis* the FFYP (see Appendix Table 4) is partly illusory inasmuch as base-year consumption was badly underestimated in the FFYP. The estimated increase, nevertheless, was quite modest.

COMPARISON OF PLANNED AND ACTUAL PERFORMANCE

Comparison of the FFYP, the Revised FFYP, and actual progress indicates that the revision was unduly pessimistic. Annual GNP growth rates, with the exception of 1965, were substantially above those envisioned in the FFYP, with the result that growth during the plan period exceeded the targets in both plans. Population increased no more than had been estimated in the Revised FFYP,[25] so that actual increases in GNP per capita and in private consumption per capita were higher than expected. Despite statements that consumption must be restricted (115:26, 41–42), government consumption also increased more than was planned (see Appendix Table 8). If, however, levels rather than growth rates are considered, public-sector expenditure was in fact marked by austerity. Both

---

[23] The wholesale price index rose 9.4 percent between 1961 and 1962.

[24] The major impact of reduced investment was to be felt in transport, communications, and other service-sector projects (especially in housing, which is reflected in a general way in Appendix Table 6, and in mining and manufacturing, where plans for an integrated steel mill and expansion of machinery industries were dropped).

[25] The population estimates were lower in the Revised FFYP than in the FFYP; this was the only instance of a revised estimate which was more optimistic than the original.

plans called for government consumption higher than the 11 percent that actually took place.[26]

The relative importance of both the primary and tertiary sectors declined between 1962 and 1966 (see Appendix Table 5). Comparison of planned and actual changes in sectoral balance is impossible, however, because the data in the FFYP are incomplete, and the Revised FFYP employs gross values that are not comparable with the value-added data in the national accounts. The sectoral investment distribution shows relatively more investment in tertiary industries than was planned under the Revised FFYP, and less investment in agriculture and the nonmining, nonmanufacturing component of the secondary sector (i.e., power). Because the Revised FFYP called for the greatest reduction in tertiary sector investment, especially housing, the results may constitute evidence of difficulties that were met in restraining such investment.

The actual growth of investment is most impressive; it increased more than two and a half times between 1962 and 1966, compared with the Revised FFYP target of 32 percent, but less than the increase called for in the FFYP. This fact, coupled with the fact that the GNP growth rate was higher than the FFYP target rate, confirms the earlier conclusion that the marginal capital coefficients implicit in the FFYP output and investment targets were too high.

Examination of investment by type of purchaser (see Appendix Table 7) and source of finance (Appendix Table 9) reveals that both domestic savings and private investment played a larger role than planned.[27] Domestic savings constituted 51 percent of total savings during 1962–66— a larger share than was expected in either plan, which occurred largely because of sharp increases between 1962 and 1963 and again between 1965 and 1966. Sources of the first increase are difficult to locate. Price increases in 1963 averaged less than those in 1960 and 1961, but they were still large enough to discourage saving at the prevailing interest rates—as can

[26] Nineteen percent of the total in the FFYP, 17 percent in the Revised FFYP.

[27] Another comparison problem arises in comparing actual investment with Revised FFYP type-of-purchaser categories because the private-government split in the Revised FFYP refers to source of funds, not type of purchaser, and therefore gives too much weight to government investment. If comparison is made between actual and FFYP targets, however, one finds that the government's share was less than 25 percent, instead of a planned share of almost one-third of total investment. The Revised FFYP asserts that "there has been a reduction in the number of public projects as a means of further fostering the growth of free enterprise" (115:13). Given the earlier formulation of "guided capitalism" and government participation in the FFYP, which was later followed by a statement in the Revised FFYP that "the private sector will play a greater role in the development of the Korean economy" (115:6), one suspects either a change in economic philosophy between 1962 and 1964 or, more likely, an attempt to put the best face on evidence of inability to expand the public sector.

be seen in the failure of commercial bank deposits to increase between 1962 and 1963 and, more generally, in the very minor increase in the money supply. Much of the early increase in domestic savings probably took place in the unorganized money market.

The sharp rise in 1966 can be traced directly to the stabilization program, marked by sharp increases in deposit rates at the end of September, 1965, which resulted in a doubling of savings deposits at commercial banks between 1965 and 1966. The domestic supply situation also was favorable, since an increase in exports of $75 million was more than offset by the $253 million increase in imports. Harvests were good in 1966 and price increases were below average. There was, in addition, evidence of growing income inequality and increasing foreign remittances (especially from Vietnam).[28]

Investment and domestic savings ratios were below those implicit in the FFYP but above those implied in the Revised FFYP. Actual government revenue ratios, however, were well below the targets for both plans.[29] What are the reasons for this failure to increase revenues?

In late 1965, Richard Musgrave, noting a decline in domestic revenues from 1962 to 1965, found a declining indirect tax ratio, because an increasingly unrealistic exchange rate was eroding customs duties while internal commodity taxes were held down by undervaluation of imports and price controls—and, in the liquor tax, by a unit rather than an *ad valorem* base. The corporation tax was weakened by loopholes that provided a wide range of special privileges; the profits of public corporations, for example, were exempt, and the dividends of closely held corporations (the predominant type in Korea) were exempt from individual income taxes. Also, although nothing is said (as in the FFYP) of the corruption and inequity that marked enforcement, Professor Musgrave noted that "vigorous measures to improve administration are essential" (104:29).

There were some signs of improvement in public revenue toward the very end of the plan period. General government expenditures, which had been restricted in 1963–64 as part of the price stabilization program, increased sharply in 1965–66. Growth in the relative size of the public

---

[28] A large portion of the remittances have reportedly been placed with commercial banks in the form of installment deposits.

[29] One can argue that revenue ratios should include nontax as well as tax revenues, and that a figure which excludes income from government enterprises and other current transfers is biased downward. In Korea—unlike most other countries—government and quasi-government corporations are included with the private, not the public, sector. In the absence of consolidated accounts, this omission has tended to understate current revenues on the order of 5 to 10 percent in recent years. Even if these items are included, the actual revenue ratio rises only to 12.2 percent during the plan period, still well below plan targets.

sector was accompanied by a rise in capital, relative to current expenditure, and by modest positive savings as improvements in tax collection caused government revenue to rise more rapidly than expenditure.

Encouraging signs of economic progress were by no means limited to government revenues during the closing years of the FFYP. In 1966, for example, GNP rose by more than 13 percent. Gross domestic capital formation exceeded 20 percent of GNP (see Appendix Table 10), and the increase in fixed capital formation between 1964 and 1966 accounted for more than half of the rise in GNP between these two years. The growth of domestic savings also was encouraging. Declining grant assistance was offset by the rapid growth of commercial credit and the beginnings of direct foreign investment. The normalization treaty with Japan, signed in late 1965, provided for $200 million of "soft" loans and at least $300 million in commercial credits during the next decade.

A sharp increase in exports,[30] of which a large and rising proportion has been manufactured commodities, has been coincident with rapid growth of the manufacturing sector.[31] Part of this growth is due to new invest-ment, part to increasing utilization of capacity. The transport, construc-tion, and utilities sectors grew at least as rapidly as manufacturing from 1964 to 1966. Progress in these sectors allowed manufacturing output to grow without restriction from inadequate social overhead capital. In agriculture—unlike the 1962–63 period, there were bumper crops in 1964 and 1966, and in 1965 only a slight decline from 1964 levels.

Thus, by the time the results of the rice harvest in the autumn of 1966 became known, the First Plan appeared to be a success. Although not all FFYP targets were met, overall growth had been more rapid than expected; this, and more detailed results, was confirmed by mid-1967 as final figures for 1966 became available.

Comparison of the plan targets and the actual results raises a number of questions that deserve attention. In particular, why did the revised plan yield worse forecasts than the earlier version of the same plan? Were the increases in agricultural output and domestic savings underestimated and was the growth of manufacturing overestimated? Was there evidence that projection errors influenced policy, or that policies would have been different had projections been more accurate?

A combination of public opinion and change in the short-term outlook probably was the factor most responsible for the poorer performance of

[30] In 1965, exports of goods and services, valued at 1965 *won* prices, rose 40 percent over 1964 levels, and 53 percent from 1965 to 1966.
[31] The average rate of annual increase in manufacturing output rose from 12 percent in 1962–64 to 19 percent in 1965–66.

the Revised FFYP *vis-à-vis* the FFYP as a guide to what actually happened. Inasmuch as the years immediately preceding the beginning of the FFYP were years of little or no growth, the plan appeared overambitious to many critics. Their criticism seemed justified toward the end of 1963, when two bad crop years and the accompanying inflation increased doubts that targets could be met. The Revised FFYP was a response to such criticism, and, as an extrapolation of recent poor performance, proved to be an even worse predictor of the rapid progress made during the last two years of the plan period.

A possible explanation for the underestimate of the increase in agricultural output lies in the poor rice harvest of 1962 and the disastrous summer grains crops of 1963. Growth from this low base was bound to be more impressive than expected. Clearly, the underestimated growth of the domestic savings–GNP ratio (see Appendix Table 10) was a result of the stabilization program and its success in curbing inflation and raising real rates of return on savings deposits. This could hardly have been anticipated at the time either the FFYP or the Revised FFYP was framed. The growth of manufactures was less than the FFYP projections but more than the Revised FFYP targets. Discrepancies between actual results and FFYP overestimates can be explained, at least in part, by the dropping of plans for constructing an integrated steel mill and expanding the machinery industries; and the underestimate of the Revised FFYP was undoubtedly due to the unforeseen increase in manufactured exports, which began in 1963 and had a major impact on manufacturing output by 1965 and 1966.

Answers to the other questions are necessarily speculative. For example, the overestimate of manufacturing growth in the FFYP, insofar as it was due to difficulties of implementing import-substitute projects (e.g., the integrated steel mill and the machinery plants), may have turned planners toward the export promotion campaign during the later years of the plan. More accurate estimates of supply and demand for food grains might have led either to more agricultural investment or to an earlier decision to switch from grains to cash crops. On the other hand—as David Cole and Young Woo Nam have noted in Ch. 2 of this book—the Revised FFYP was largely ignored because its provisions were felt to be irrelevant for current policy. If so, projection errors—and even the possibility of more accurate projection—had little or no effect on policy. One lesson certainly learned from experience during the First Plan period, however, was that the effects of unexpected change would have to be incorporated in the five-year plans if the plans were to continue to be relevant to current policy decisions over time. This lesson was embodied in the annual overall resources budgets of the next (Second) plan.

THE SECOND FIVE-YEAR PLAN AND AFTER

The Second Five-Year Plan (SFYP), for the period 1967–71, was released in mid-1966 (126). The SFYP is essentially a medium-term plan, presented as the next stage in meeting long-range goals.[32] The SFYP called for annual overall resources budgets (ORBs), which were to be the basic instrument for translating plans into action (126:171–72). These ORBs have been constructed to review past performance, to set goals, and to coordinate budget, trade, stabilization, and other programs so that they will be consistent with SFYP goals as modified in the ORB itself (112, 113).

Unlike the FFYP, the SFYP and the ORBs have been prepared with the aid of aggregate and sectoral models based on the Bank of Korea's 1960 and 1963 input-output tables (more recently, an updated I–O table, employing 1965 prices, has been used in the planning). A number of engineering and technical feasibility studies also were used in preparing the SFYP and the ORBs. The effects of fuller information and experience are seen in franker discussions of policy-oriented problems, the presentation of demand as well as supply projections, and a statistical presentation that is more pertinent than that in the FFYP or the Revised FFYP and that requires fewer calculations by the reader. There is, also—unlike earlier plans—a brief description of the criteria employed in project selection, a discussion of implementation and administration, and a review of how the plan was prepared (126:81–82, 167–81). The SFYP is a more sophisticated document than the FFYP in practically all important aspects.

"The basic objective of the Second Plan is 'to promote the modernization of the industrial structure and to build the foundations for a self-supporting economy' " (126:33). Thus basic objectives are virtually the same as those of the earlier plans. Major SFYP targets include the following: self-sufficiency in food production; increased output of the chemical, machinery, and iron and steel industries; export expansion and further import substitution; encouragement of family planning and higher employment levels; substantial income growth, with special emphasis on increasing farmers' productivity and incomes through diversification; and improvement of manpower resources by promotion of scientific and management skills (126:33–34). "Key strategies" to be pursued to achieve these targets include rapid export expansion, increased capital mobilization, efficient manpower utilization, and continuing financial stability (126:15).

Growth of GNP during the SFYP period is to be at an even annual rate of 7 percent (see Appendix Table 2). This growth target is slightly below the FFYP target because of more capital-intensive investment and

[32] A second SFYP, the five-year plan for the development of science and technology (SFYPST), also was published in mid-1966 (2).

less utilization of excess capacity than during the FFYP period (126:40). A steady 0.1 percent per year decline in the population growth is envisioned with "continuous and rigorous implementation of family planning" (126:42). Increases in per capita output are expected to be slightly above FFYP levels but well below actual increases; increases in per capita private consumption are close to actual and FFYP levels, and lie between them. Employment and labor force estimates show that the unemployment rate is to drop from 7.4 percent to 5 percent (126:37, 188–89).[33]

The SFYP provides for a further decline in the relative importance of agriculture and for a continued increase in the relative growth of mining and manufacturing (see Appendix Table 5). There is also a continued attempt to raise the primary and reduce the tertiary shares of investment.[34]

The planned increase in investment, though above the Revised FFYP rates, is below both FFYP and actual 1962–66 levels. The aggregate capital coefficient of 2.9:1 is considerably below the 4.0:1 coefficient implicit in the FFYP but slightly above that which actually prevailed during 1962–65 (126:44, 50). The marginal domestic savings ratio (32 percent) is also below the 41 percent of the FFYP. The government's share of total investment is higher than in either FFYP targets or actual experience, but private investment is to grow faster than government investment, as it did during the FFYP period (see Appendix Table 7). The government's share of total consumption also is higher than it was during 1962–66, and is to rise more rapidly than private consumption during the plan period (see Appendix Table 8). Continued increase in the reliance on domestic savings, and increases in investment and domestic savings ratios, mark the SFYP as well, although initial-year estimates in each case are below actual 1966 levels (see Appendix Tables 9 and 10). The most ambitious proposal is the planned increase in government revenue ratios, which are to rise sharply from 1967 to 1968 (before leveling off) and which reflect plans for improvements in tax administration and expansion of the tax base (126:53).

Perhaps the most striking change reflected in these aggregates is the attempt to expand the public sector role. This is also reflected in the dis-

---

[33] The SFYP 1965 base year figures (which were probably drawn from the economically active population survey for 1965 [116]) yield a much lower unemployment rate than the FFYP estimate of 18 percent.

[34] Comparisons of industrial structure, and of the sectoral distribution of investment as well, are made difficult by subsequent revision of the 1965 national account data used in the SFYP and by differences in SFYP and FFYP format. For example, GNP originating in the secondary sector is not shown in the SFYP, so that output of the construction and power industries is presumably included in the tertiary sector. Also, the sectoral distribution of investment is given only for the whole period, and annual figures are not provided.

cussion of savings, where it is noted that "by far the most dramatic increase will occur in the government sector" (126:43). One reason for expanding the public sector might be increased emphasis on investment in social overhead capital, which generally requires public rather than private outlays. On the other hand, with the exception of a statement that "health, education, housing, urban and regional planning, and the development of science and technology will be given greater emphasis during the Second Plan," I can find no evidence of intent to allocate relatively more investment to social overhead capital in the Second Plan (126:114).[35] Another possible reason is that intended tax reforms were expected to have an adverse effect on private saving, so that savings ratios would decline at some point in the course of the SFYP. But there is no evidence of this; the estimates, in fact, show a steady increase.

Government investment has thus far been limited to the infrastructure, agriculture, and basic industries in which minimum investment requirements are too large to be financed by local entrepreneurs; private investment, in contrast, dominates most manufacturing and service activities. Government intervention is seen not in ownership but, rather, in control of access to credit, import licensing, the benefits accorded to successful exporters, and, occasionally, in the imposition of price ceilings on consumer necessities—all of which have been somewhat relaxed. More important are the many instruments available to the government to ensure that entrepreneurs will behave in a manner consistent with its economic goals.

The SFYP was prepared before the growth during 1965–66 was seen, although at the time of publication the question of the realism of target levels had already arisen. In the plan's preface, Chang Key-Young[36] noted that "my fellow countrymen criticize the Plan objectives as being too conservative. On the other hand, our friends from abroad observed that the Plan targets were too ambitious." (126) When the final figures for 1966 became available and revealed that GNP had increased 13.4 percent over the previous year's level, Mr. Chang's fellow countrymen seemed to be correct, and targets were raised in the 1967 and 1968 ORBs.[37] Out-

[35] Only crude calculation is possible since it is not at all obvious which published investment categories represent social overhead capital as opposed to other types of capital; but if one accepts the SFYP category "social overhead and other services" as representing what is generally considered to be social overhead, the proportion of investment allocated to expanding social overhead actually drops in the SFYP. It is 53.0 percent (126:85), calculated by combining tertiary sector investment with the non-mining and manufacturing portion of secondary sector investment (see Appendix Table 6). If these last two categories are again combined to obtain actual investment during the First Plan period in social overhead facilities, the FFYP proportion was 55.6 percent.

[36] Then Deputy Prime Minister and chief of the Economic Planning Board.

[37] The 1968 ORB projects a 10 percent annual growth rate for the 1968–71 period, so that GNP is to be 26 percent higher in 1971 than was originally estimated in the SFYP.

put of all sectors, especially social overhead and services, is expected to rise above the original target levels. There was also talk in 1967 of meeting plan targets in three and a half years rather than five years, and of reaching a commodity export level of $1 billion by 1971 (compared with the $550 million shown in the SFYP).[38]

Like the SFYP, the 1968 ORB (published in August, 1967) had to be released before the latest full year's developments were known. Recent information indicates that, as a result of a prolonged drought in 1967, agricultural production dropped 6 percent.[39] In spite of power and water shortages and transport bottlenecks, industrial production rose 26 percent. Preliminary estimates show an increase in GNP of 8.9 percent above 1966 levels. A more rapid rise in consumption expenditures resulted in a sharp drop in the marginal savings ratio, from 31 percent in 1966 to 5 percent in 1967. Thus economic growth in 1967, though above original SFYP targets, evidently was somewhat disappointing. More recently, the attack on President Park by the North Koreans and an increasing number of border incidents have turned public energies to defense measures and have raised fears that economic development may be slowed or interrupted by military requirements.[40] Considering the sharp changes in outlook each spring since 1966, following new information on the economy during the previous year, one can only conclude that the course of events has magnified the importance of short-range planning.

Continuing Policy Problems

A number of basic problems which affect economic growth were apparent in the Korean economy before the FFYP was written. Some of these, particularly those summarized under the title "modernization," will take generations to overcome. Other problems are more immediately susceptible to solution, and sufficient time has now passed that the policies employed to deal with them can be evaluated. Among the more important problems in this last group have been those associated with agriculture, employment, sources and uses of savings, and trade.

Agriculture

Self-sufficiency in food grains production has been a major target in all the plans. However, not only was self-sufficiency *not* achieved, demand

[38] This last projection has been attributed to the Ministry of Commerce and Industry (MCI), the government agency in charge of export promotion.

[39] This last projection also has been attributed to the Ministry of Commerce and Industry.

[40] Evidence of this is seen in plans to arm 2.5 million reservists, and in the first supplementary budget, where some 27 percent of the proposed expenditure has been set aside for defense projects.

was underestimated.[41] SFYP food grains targets are above the FFYP and Revised FFYP target levels but slightly less than actual 1962–66 performance. Recently there has been evidence of a slowdown in agricultural development programs.[42]

The fragmentation of holdings that followed land reform after World War II, especially because the new small holders have been unable to obtain credit on reasonable terms, has certainly contributed to the slowdown. The government's response has not been to increase credit substantially, but to raise the maximum for the legal holding size. Another factor is a possibly inefficient distribution system—"possibly" because almost nothing is known of private marketing channels for domestic agricultural products in Korea. A third factor—revealed in April, 1968—was that farmers' incomes rose only 8 percent (in 1956 prices) between 1960 and 1966, making it difficult to mobilize savings for agricultural investment.[43]

In mid-April, the Agriculture and Forestry Minister, Kim Yung-Joon, announced that the production and demand estimates for food grains shown in the SFYP were unrealistic, and that sluggish implementation of

[41] Actual output of rice and other grains exceeded the FFYP and Revised FFYP targets, but the net export balance in rice in 1959–61 practically disappeared during 1962–66, while imports of other grains, cereals, and cereal preparations rose sharply in 1962–66 over 1959–61 levels.

[42] Domestic fertilizer production has risen dramatically since 1961, but, if domestic supply as a whole is considered, the growth of this important input has not been very impressive. Comparisons of fertilizer consumption and yields for major grains in Korea, China (Taiwan), and Japan indicate that consumption of nitrogen, phosphates, and potassium in 1964–65 was generally much lower in Korea than in the other two countries (134). Yield levels, even after incorporation of the latest upward revisions in Korean production estimates, show rice output per unit land area during 1964–65 was less than two-thirds that in Japan, barley less than 60 percent, and wheat less than 50 percent of Japanese levels (134, 136). Calculations of potential output, in which Korean cultivated areas are multiplied by Japanese and Taiwanese productivity levels, show potential output of the major grains for the 1964–65 period of 42.3 million *suk* (Taiwanese productivity levels) to 63.6 million *suk* (Japanese productivity levels). (The *suk* is a Korean measure of volume: for rice, 1 *suk* = 144 kilograms; for wheat, 1 *suk* = 100 kilograms; for barley, 1 *suk* = 141 kilograms.) Actual Korean output was 38.6 million *suk*. Climate and soil conditions are different among the three countries, and various adverse factors may be as important in determining relative performance as differences in fertilizer inputs, but the findings suggest an unexploited potential for raising Korean agricultural productivity.

[43] In fact, if the NACF (National Association of Cooperative Federations) index of prices paid by farmers is used to deflate the MAF (Ministry of Agriculture and Forestry) data on average farm household income, real farm income actually declined from 1962 to 1966 (even though 1962 was marked by a poor rice harvest and 1966 by bumper crops). The national accounts, on the other hand, show that value added in agriculture (and fisheries) rose 40 percent from 1960 to 1966, while BOK and EPB data on the rural and farm population show increases on the order of 8 percent during the same period. The picture is somewhat confused, to say the least.

irrigation and seed-grain projects necessitated readjustment of the esti-mates.[44] Although a more recent statement by Minister Kim indicates that self-sufficiency in food grains might be achieved by 1971, recent events have inspired doubts about the feasibility of this target.

Employment and Manpower

One of the four key strategies listed in the SFYP is "efficient manpower utilization" (126:15). Regular collection of labor force data in Korea did not begin until the end of 1962, but most observers would agree that unemployment and underemployment have been quite high. The FFYP shows a very high but declining level of unemployment; the Revised FFYP shows lower labor force and unemployment estimates. Given large estimation errors, wide seasonal swings in employment, and the fact that unemployment is a residual condition of unclear meaning in a context of widespread underemployment, one should probably ignore the evidence of unemployment and instead, examine actual and SFYP employment estimates.

The data in Table 2 can be used to calculate percentage increases in actual output (value added) per worker from 1963 to 1966 and the increases implicit in SFYP estimates for the period 1965–67.

	Total labor force	Mining and manufacturing	All other
Actual 1963–66 (%)	20.6	2.1	25.3
Estimated 1965–71 (%)	23.3	14.0	19.2

The plan's employment estimates are based on the labor coefficients associated with particular types of output and on assumptions about rates of change in labor productivity. One would expect productivity to rise much more rapidly in mining and manufacturing than in other sectors, and that SFYP estimates would show more rapid increase than the actual 1963–66 performance. Although estimates for 1963–66 are undoubtedly biased upward because of the unusually poor 1963 summer grains harvest (while the 1966 harvests were unusually good), the results are disturbing. Annual productivity is expected to increase only half as much during the

[44] Although 1967 grain imports were the highest since 1963, the 1.66 million tons projected in the adjusted estimates for 1968 are, to the best of my knowledge, an all-time record. Other government statements at the beginning of the year, urging that output of cash crops (mushrooms, raw silk, etc.) be stressed during the SFYP period, suggest a shift in emphasis from food grains toward a type of production that makes more sense in the Korean context.

TABLE 2.   EMPLOYMENT, HOURS WORKED, VALUE ADDED

Actual	Total[a] hours worked	GNP	Min. & mfg.[a] hours worked	Value added: min. & mfg.	All other[a] hours worked	Value added: all other
1963	377,406	693.03	37,311	123.49	340,095	549.54
1966	413,007	913.82	53,692	181.43	359,315	732.39
percent change	9.4	31.9	43.9	46.9	5.6	33.3

SFYP	Total employ.	GNP	Min. & mfg. employ.	Value added: min. & mfg.	All other employ.	Value added: all other
1965	8,522	779.4	786	168.9	7,736	610.5
1971	10,371	1,169.7	1,283	314.2	9,088	855.5
percent change	21.7	50.1	63.2	86.0	17.5	40.1

Sources: (128, 110). Units: employment and hours worked, 1,000's; GNP and value added, billions of won ('65 prices).
[a] Average of hours worked during four quarterly survey weeks.

1965–71 period as it did in 1963–66, and increases in the mining and manufacturing sectors are again below those in other sectors.

Although its educational system is unusually extensive for a country at Korea's level of development, the SFYP shows an increasing shortage of technicians and a growing imbalance between supply and demand for particular skills. Wage data are too unreliable to use for testing supply-demand estimates, but hearsay evidence suggests that wage differentials for skilled workers have increased sharply during the past few years.

The problems of education and the need for improving the quality of technical manpower have been amply recognized in the SFYP (126:129–30, 132–33, 159–60). They are, briefly, excessive classroom size and inadequately trained teachers, the still pervasive influence of the Confucian ethic on educational values, and excessively rigid governmental control.[45] Although the first problem could conceivably be solved in the near future, the other two difficulties are more resistant to change. Also, there is a serious "brain drain" problem.[46]

[45] These assertions are more fully documented in an unpublished paper, "Population, Education, and Labor Force in Korea—A Preliminary Survey," dated March 31, 1967, and written by the author. Copies are available on request.

[46] More than 6,000 students have received Ministry of Education approval to study abroad in the period 1953 through 1966, and an untold number have undoubtedly gone without such approval (120:31). Many of these students have not returned to Korea.

Savings

Three of the four key strategies listed in the SFYP (i.e., rapid export expansion, increased capital mobilization, and continued financial stability) are directly or indirectly associated with savings and with policies designed to influence saving (126:15). This emphasis is natural inasmuch as savings and investment levels were quite low until recently, and domestic saving was even lower.[47] Recent success in increasing public and private savings was noted earlier.

The Office of National Tax Administration was established in March, 1966, to improve revenue collection by the central government. Administrative improvements were mainly responsible for an increase of more than 50 percent in the central government's direct and indirect tax revenues between fiscal year 1965 and fiscal year 1966 (111:36), and further improvement should come with "modernization" of public administration.[48] Insofar as inflation can be restrained, as private disposable income increases, and as income inequality grows, private savings should continue to increase. Remittances from Vietnam, however, cannot be expected to remain a major factor in savings.

Before 1963, government borrowing from the BOK was a major source of increase in the money supply. The austerity budgets of 1963–64 reduced the inflationary impact of the government's overdrafts with the central bank, while increased emphasis on indirect controls and credit ceilings marked the government's stabilization efforts in subsequent years. More recently, a rapid rise in net foreign-exchange credits has threatened to sabotage stabilization policies.[49]

[47] A United Nations Economic Commission for Asia and the Far East study (for 1963–64) found Korea, along with Pakistan and Ceylon, among the lowest countries in the region when ranked by domestic savings ratios (133). Another study (by Chenery and Strout) of savings, investment, and trade criteria to be met in achieving an adequate rate of self-sustaining growth covered thirty-one countries during the 1957–62 period and listed Korea as one of five countries which failed to meet the investment criteria (16). The investment criteria specified that investment grow more rapidly than the target growth rate (5 percent per year) during "Phase I" (defined as the period in which growth is limited by absorptive capacity, investment, and saving) and be sufficient to sustain the target growth rate thereafter. Absorptive capacity (measured in terms of maximum previous growth in investment) in Korea, as in most of the other countries, was sufficient. Export growth and the marginal propensity to save also were sufficient to meet the trade and savings criteria, although the average savings ratio was notably low.

[48] Koh (96:123) summarizes the major weaknesses of administration as follows: particularistic personnel practices, paucity of expertise, pervasive feelings of insecurity, subservience to political power, and excessive formalism. Such weaknesses are not overcome quickly or easily.

[49] The net purchases of foreign exchange by BOK doubled in 1965, almost quadrupled in 1966, and almost doubled again in 1967. By the end of 1967, BOK purchases (less

The burden of the government policy to offset monetary expansion generated by foreign borrowing has fallen on private domestic bank loans. Money supply ceilings were supplemented in late 1966 by an increase in reserve requirements to 45 and 50 percent on new deposits. As a result, net lending to the private sector was no higher at the end of 1967 than at the end of 1965, and actually fell between the end of 1965 and the end of 1966.[50]

Some price stability has been achieved, but the credit policies employed to achieve this stability require further examination. At issue is the obvious conflict between policies that encourage foreign borrowing and those that are designed to increase domestic savings. No one can deny that capital is a scarce (if not *the* scarce) resource in Korea, that foreign borrowing should be encouraged for this reason, and that some form of governmental repayment guarantee is needed to obtain foreign loans. Similarly, it is obvious that the increase in bank deposit rates that marked stabilization efforts in 1965 was required to mobilize domestic savings. Success in raising the level of domestic savings, however, has been offset by the failure to use the savings for investment purposes, since private investment is frustrated by credit restrictions that are employed to counter the inflationary effects of foreign borrowing. Credit restriction is evident not only in loan ceilings but also in very high reserve requirements on new deposits and in the practice of requiring commercial banks to purchase government bonds. The 100 percent guarantees and a much lower loan rate abroad than at home make foreign borrowing exceedingly attractive to both lender and borrower.

---

deposits of foreign organizations) accounted for 78 billion *won* of a total money supply of 120 billion *won* (129). These purchases for the most part represent short- and medium-term foreign commercial loans that have been supported by BOK (more recently by Korea Exchange Bank) guarantees.

[50] The picture is obscured by the government's annual year-end credit squeeze, which chokes off credit to meet money supply targets and is followed by a bulge in new loans (or possibly in renewals of old loans) during the first quarter of the next year. Despite such seasonal swings, there is no question that private borrowing from the banking system has been severely restricted.

Other, more direct techniques have been used to limit price increases, such as the release of government grain stocks when grain prices rose, liberalization of cement imports after the domestic prices rose, and suspension of butcher-shop licenses when owners raised meat prices. The success of these different policy instruments is seen in decreasing annual rates of inflation. The implicit GNP deflator rose 33 percent between 1963 and 1964, only 8 percent between 1964 and 1965, and 13 percent between 1965 and 1966. From December, 1966, to December, 1967, the Seoul consumer price index increased 12 percent, the wholesale price index 7 percent. These figures may be too low, since the implicit GNP deflator showed greater price increases between 1965 and 1966 than either the Seoul CPI or the WPI. Clearly, though, the rate of inflation in recent years has been well below that which prevailed earlier.

Foreign Trade

The government's desire to reduce dependence on foreign savings, based on the downward trend in aid levels that began around 1957 and is expected to continue, has resulted in an export promotion drive and in moderately restrictive import policies, which are, however, less severe than the earlier policies. In 1967, a well-publicized switch in tariff structure from a so-called negative to a positive list was heralded as a major step in the direction of trade liberalization.[51] Although the scissors of export promotion and import restriction has made stabilization policies more difficult, the government clearly hopes to use export promotion to close the trade gap and to end Korea's dependence on foreign savings.

Exports have been encouraged by tax advantages and import-linkage privileges, as well as by granting exporters easy access to credit on favorable terms. In fact, immense pressure has been put on producers to achieve export targets; and negative incentives (threats to cut off access to credit or necessary raw material imports) also have been used in the drive for "export first." Many Korean producers find that they must take losses on exports to make profits on output for the home market.[52]

The "export first" program has been quite successful thus far. Future success probably will depend more upon the domestic supply situation than upon foreign demand, since Korea is still relatively small in most of its export markets and has ample scope for further diversification by item and by country. The main export bottlenecks are (1) high-cost domestic production, which has been encouraged by tariff protection and must be offset in practice by export subsidies, and (2) the resultant price structure, which discourages exports. Devaluation, which has recently been suggested, cannot provide a simple solution for the disincentive effects of domestic inflation and lagging exchange rates, since in Korea the import content of exports is very high.

In addition to increasingly higher domestic price levels, two other developments may limit Korea's export potential. The first is a policy that, by encouraging imports of capital goods, has retarded the growth of the Korean machinery industry. Because the machine tool industries

[51] A commodity that is not listed under the negative list system cannot be imported; under a positive list system, it must be listed to be prohibited. The added barriers that are placed in the way of restriction by the change from negative to positive lists can—and have been—overcome by using broader commodity categories in the positive list.

[52] As a result, stories have occasionally appeared in recent years about an unusual practice which might be called "inverted smuggling." Exporters have been caught shipping dirt or sand out of the country under false bills of lading, instead of nylon bags or more conventional export items. The nylon bags probably were sold in domestic markets, at higher prices than they would have fetched abroad, and the sand packages were intended to satisfy officials that exporters' commitments had been fulfilled.

are in many ways central to the industrialization process, the long-run consequences of this policy may be quite serious (36). The second development may be an increase in the prices of intermediate goods that is likely to follow completion of the import-substitute projects of the SFYP. It is likely that the "infant industry" argument will be used to raise barriers against competing imports, but the inevitable increase in materials' prices could only make Korean exports less competitive in international markets.

Three criteria can be used to evaluate export promotion policies: (1) Does export provide the exporting economy with the benefits of economies of scale? (2) Where labor is unemployed or underemployed, do export industries offer more employment than other types of industry? (3) Are resource costs per dollar of net foreign-exchange earnings minimized?

Because economies of scale and the existence of strong forward and backward linkages usually are associated with manufacturing, and because manufactures' share in Korea's exports is large and is rising, Korea undoubtedly scores well on the basis of the first criterion. Employment has risen much more rapidly in manufacturing than in other sectors of the economy (see Table 2), and the growth of manufactures has been tied closely to the increase in exports. Korea should do well according to the second criterion, too. Performance as measured by the third criterion, however, may well be suboptimal. When the opportunity costs—represented by cheap credit, favored access to imported materials, tax preference, and the other subsidies given exporters—are added to conventional costs, total resource costs per unit value of exports may be quite high.

If resource costs can be decreased and net foreign-exchange earnings per unit value of exports increased, resources have been wasted in export promotion. I suspect that this has occurred—that it has occurred because little attention has been paid to the economic values associated with exports and because little is known of the actual cost of export subsidies or the opportunity costs associated with the current policies. The drive for "export first" has obscured the purpose and the costs of exports. Perhaps when the novelty of the export push wears off, there may be an opportunity to apply the traditional economic calculus.

Conclusion

At the end of this analysis of Korea's five-year plans, a few comments should be made about the significance of the subject and about what has and has not been attempted.

Five-year plans are politico-economic documents that present the government's economic goals, reveal its assessment of the problems to be overcome, and illustrate the consistency and imagination of the planners.

Political stability, social structure, and involvement in wars—to say nothing of location, climate, cultural heritage, and a large number of economic factors—are explanatory variables infinitely more important than the existence and the nature of planning documents. Such plans must be considered in the context of their time and with reference to the policies employed to implement them.

For these reasons the first step of the analysis—the essentially sterile exercise of examining the plans as plans, to check consistency and coverage—was followed by a comparison of plan targets and recent experience to evaluate the realism and the ambition of the planning. The third step, which began with the identification of discrepancies between targets and results, devolved into a general examination of economic problems and the policies designed to deal with them. The analysis in this last section tended to be critical, partly because of a tendency—shared by the author—to take Korea's overall economic success for granted, and partly because the more interesting and important problems usually are those that have yet to be solved.

Conspicuous by their absence from the analysis was consideration of the planning process itself, consideration of the nature and the validity of the economic model that was inherent in the plans, and consideration of the machinery that was employed to translate the plans into action. An evaluation of the role of United States aid, its effectiveness, and the influence of donor interests on recipients' behavior also is lacking. A number of these topics are to be covered in the papers that follow, and my fellow authors will undoubtedly shed light on some of the problems that should have been discussed but were ignored, or that deserve more and better attention than they were given here.

CHAPTER 3 APPENDIX

TABLE 1. EXPENDITURE ON GNP

(*billion* [*hwan*] *won*)

	1962(A)	1966(B)	(B)/(A) × 100
1. First Five-Year Plan (FFYP)[a]	2,453	3,269	133
2. Revised FFYP[b]	281.5	340.2	121
3. Actual[c]	635	914	144
	1967(A)	1971(B)	
4. Second Five-Year Plan (SFYP)[d]	892	1,170	131

Unless otherwise indicated sources used are as follows:

[a] Republic of Korea (ROK), *Summary of First Five-Year Economic Plan, 1962–1966*, May, 1962. Units: billion *hwan*, 1961 prices.

[b] ROK, *First Five-Year Economic Development Plan* (*1962–1966*), *Adjusted Version*, March, 1964. Units: billion *won* (1 *won* = 10 *hwan*), 1962 prices.

[c] Bank of Korea (BOK), "Revision of National Accounts, 1953–1965 and Actual Estimates for 1966," *Monthly Statistical Review*, July, 1967 (Korean version). Units: billion *won*, 1965 prices.

[d] ROK, *The Second Five-Year Economic Development Plan* (*1967–1971*), July, 1966. Units: billion *won*, 1965 prices.

TABLE 2. GNP: ANNUAL GROWTH RATES (%)

(*billion* [*hwan*] *won*)

	1962	1963	1964	1965	1966	Average (compound)
1. FFYP[a]	5.7	6.4	7.3	7.8	8.3	7.1
2. Revised FFYP	2.8	4.4	5.0	5.0	5.0	4.8
3. Actual[b]	3.5	9.1	8.3	7.4	13.4	9.4
	1967	1968	1969	1970	1971	
4. SFYP	7.0	7.0	7.0	7.0	7.0	7.0

[a] *Revised FFYP*, p. 17.

[b] BOK, *Korean National Income Statistics* (Korean), Nov., 1967, p. 213.

TABLE 3. TOTAL POPULATION AND ANNUAL GROWTH RATES

(billion [hwan] won)

	1961	1962	1963	1964	1965	1966	Average (compound)
1. FFYP (millions)	25.4	26.1	26.9	27.6	28.4	29.2	
Growth rate	—	2.88	2.85	2.82	2.78	2.74	2.8
2. Revised FFYP (1,000's)		26,136	26,867	27,592	28,307	29,016	
Growth rate		2.88	2.80	2.70	2.60	2.50	2.6
	1960					1966	
3. Actual (1,000's)[a]	24,989					29,208	
Growth rate							2.6
	1966	1967	1968	1969	1970	1971	
4. SFYP (1,000's)	29,086	29,784	30,469	31,139	31,793	32,429	
Growth rate		2.4	2.3	2.2	2.1	2.0	2.2

[a] Economic Planning Board (EPB), *Economic Survey, 1967*, p. 158. Census data in each year.

67

TABLE 4. OUTPUT AND PRIVATE CONSUMPTION PER CAPITA

	1962 (A)	1966 (B)	(B)/(A) × 100
1. FFYP			
(1) GNP[a]	2,453	3,269	
(2) Private C[a]	1,897	2,358	
(3) Population[b]	26.1	29.2	
(4) (1)/(3)	93,984	111,952	119.1
(5) (2)/(3)	72,682	80,753	111.1
2. Revised FFYP			
(1) GNP[a]	281.5	340.2	
(2) Private C[a]	227.6	262.1	
(3) Population[b]	26.1	29.0	
(4) (1)/(3)	10,785	11,731	108.8
(5) (2)/(3)	8,720	9,038	103.6
3. Actual			
(1) GNP[a]	635	914	
(2) Private C[a]	569	717	
(3) Population[b]	26.4[d]	29.2	
(4) (1)/(3)	24,053	31,301	130.1
(5) (2)/(3)	21,553	24,555	113.9

	1967 (A)	1971 (B)	
4. SFYP			
(1) GNP[a]	892	1,170	
(2) Private C[a]	693	849	
(3) Population[c]	29,784	32,429	
(4) (1)/(3)	29,949	36,078	120.5
(5) (2)/(3)	23,268	26,180	112.5

[a] Billions.
[b] Millions.
[c] Thousands.
[d] Estimate for 1962 based on 1955 and 1960 census results: EPB, *Korea Statistical Year-book, 1967.*

(billion [hwan] won)

	1962 (A)		1963		1964		1965		1966 (B)		(B)/(A) × 100
	Amt.	%	Amt.	%	Amt.	%	Amt.	%	Amt.	%	
1. FFYP[a]											
Primary	910.0	—	960.4	—	1,013.7	—	1,071.6	—	1,137.7	—	131.6
Secondary	(317.9)	—	(362.9)	—	(424.2)	—	(486.9)	—	(573.6)	—	199.3
Tertiary											124.4
2. Revised FFYP[b]											
Primary	94.0	33.4	96.6	32.9	100.3	32.5	104.1	32.1	108.0	31.7	114.9
Secondary	58.4	20.8	63.8	21.7	70.9	23.0	78.7	24.3	87.6	25.8	150.0
(Min., Mfg.)	(42.8)	(15.2)	(46.8)	(15.9)	(52.1)	(16.9)	(58.0)	(17.9)	(64.9)	(19.1)	(151.6)
Tertiary	129.1	45.8	133.5	45.4	137.4	44.5	141.2	43.6	144.6	42.5	112.0
Total	281.5	100.0	293.9	100.0	308.6	100.0	324.0	100.0	340.2	100.0	120.9
3. Actual											
Primary	252.37	39.7	270.56	39.1	314.31	41.9	311.63	38.7	345.91	37.9	137.1
Secondary	129.60	20.4	150.37	21.7	159.51	21.3	194.36	24.0	227.36	24.8	175.4
(Min., Mfg.)	(106.00)	(16.7)	(123.49)	(17.8)	(130.14)	(17.4)	(157.54)	(19.5)	(181.43)	(19.8)	(171.2)
Tertiary	253.00	39.9	272.10	39.2	276.48	36.8	299.86	37.3	340.55	37.3	134.6
Total	634.97	100.0	693.03	100.0	750.31	100.0	805.85	100.0	913.82	100.0	143.9

	1967 (A)		1968		1969		1970		1971 (B)		
	Amt.	%	Amt.	%	Amt.	%	Amt.	%	Amt.	%	
4. SFYP[c]											
Primary	326.82	36.6	343.16	36.0	360.32	35.3	378.34	34.6	397.26	34.0	121.6
(Min., Mfg.)	209.11	(23.4)	231.51	(24.2)	256.30	(25.1)	283.75	(26.0)	314.16	(26.8)	(150.2)
Tertiary	356.41	40.0	380.13	39.8	405.02	39.6	431.06	39.4	458.25	39.2	128.6
Total	892.34	100.0	954.80	100.0	1,021.64	100.0	1,093.15	100.0	1,169.67	100.0	131.1

* Output of agriculture, forestry, and fishing are included in the primary sector. The secondary sector includes mining and quarrying, manufacturing, construction, and electric industries. GNP originating in all other industries is included in the tertiary sector.

[a] There is no breakdown of GNP by sector of origin in the FFYP. Sectoral growth targets are shown, however (p. 30), as is value added in primary industry (p. 76) and in the manufacturing sector (p. 82). Figures shown for secondary sector include manufacturing only.

[b] Revised FFYP, pp. 10, 89. Figures given are gross (duplicated) output, not value added, which tends to overstate the net contribution of the secondary and tertiary sectors.

[c] The secondary sector data given in the Revised FFYP and actual results include output of the construction and electric industries as well as mining and manufacturing production. There are no estimates in the SFYP for the secondary sector.

TABLE 6. SECTORAL INVESTMENT DISTRIBUTION

(billion [hwan] won)

	1962 Amt.	1962 %	1963 Amt.	1963 %	1964 Amt.	1964 %	1965 Amt.	1965 %	1966 Amt.	1966 %	Whole period Amt.[a]	Whole period %
1. FFYP												
Primary	—	19.3								16.6	552.9	17.2
Secondary	—	30.3								35.1	1,092.9	34.0
(Min., Mfg.)	(148.0)	—	(194.8)		(234.0)		(242.6)		(256.7)	—	(1,076.1)	(33.5)
Tertiary	—	50.4								48.3	1,568.7	48.8
Total		100.0								100.0	3,214.5	100.0
2. Revised FFYP[b]												
Primary	3.8	8.7	8.4	16.1	8.9	16.7	10.2	18.5	10.9	19.1	42.2	16.1
Secondary	11.3	25.9	22.6	43.2	25.4	47.7	25.3	45.9	27.6	48.0	112.2	42.9
(Min., Mfg.)	(6.8)	(15.6)	(15.6)	(29.8)	(19.1)	(35.8)	(15.8)	(28.7)	(18.9)	(32.9)	(76.2)	(29.1)
Tertiary	28.5	65.4	21.3	40.7	19.0	35.6	19.6	35.6	18.9	32.9	107.3	41.0
Total	43.6	100.0	52.3	100.0	53.3	100.0	55.1	100.0	57.4	100.0	261.7	100.0
3. Actual[c]												
Primary	3.69	4.7	25.94	18.9	21.20	18.5	14.09	11.9	31.53	15.2	96.45	14.7
Secondary	27.46	35.2	56.82	41.4	42.45	37.1	35.81	30.2	83.66	40.3	246.20	37.6
(Min., Mfg.)	(15.48)	(19.8)	(41.18)	(30.0)	(33.83)	(29.6)	(32.27)	(27.2)	(72.11)	(34.8)	(194.87)	(29.7)
Tertiary	46.84	60.1	54.51	39.7	50.76	44.4	68.58	57.9	92.11	44.5	312.88	47.7
Total	77.99	100.0	137.27	100.0	114.41	100.0	118.48	100.0	207.38	100.0	655.53	100.0
4. SFYP												
Primary											159.9	16.3
Secondary[d]											468.2	47.8
(Min., Mfg.)											(301.0)	(30.7)
Tertiary											351.9	35.9
Total											980.0	100.0

[a] Calculated by applying published distribution (%) to published hwan total for GDCF. Power generation is considered a tertiary activity in the FFYP (p. 33).

[b] The Revised FFYP estimates include adjustments for 1964–66 only. The data for 1962 represent actual results then available, while those for 1963

[c] Published data are for fixed capital formation only. Inventory change arbitrarily assigned to agriculture (50%) and mining-manufacturing (50%).

[d] Includes investment targets for mining and manufacturing plus electric power, public works and other construction works (does not include investment in housing of 74.9 billion won).

70

TABLE 7. INVESTMENT BY TYPE OF PURCHASER

(*billion* [*hwan*] *won*)

	1962(A)	1963	1964	1965	1966(B)	(B)/(A) × 100
1. FFYP						
Govt.	152.1	227.1	257.1	236.4	249.1	151
Pvt.	341.0	372.7	416.6	471.9	494.5	145
Total	493.1	599.8	673.7	704.3	743.6	151
2. Revised FFYP[a]						
Govt.	—	29.2	26.8	29.0	27.5	
Pvt.	—	23.2	26.5	26.1	30.0	
Total	43.6	52.4	53.3	55.1	57.5	132
3. Actual						
Govt.	25.40	29.12	20.70	25.79	42.05	166
Pvt.	58.65	76.83	72.63	91.85	148.58	253
Increase in stocks	−6.06	31.32	21.08	0.84	16.75	
Total	77.99	137.27	114.41	118.48	207.38	266
	1967(A)	1968	1969	1970	1971(B)	
4. SFYP						
Govt.	71.93	73.75	78.50	86.69	90.22	125
Pvt.	87.88	103.04	116.53	128.75	142.78	162
Total	159.81	176.79	195.03	215.44	233.00	146

[a] Investment by source of funds, not—as in other estimates—by types of purchaser. Investment by type of purchaser is not shown in the *Revised FFYP*.

TABLE 8. CONSUMPTION BY TYPE OF PURCHASER

(*billion* [*hwan*] *won*)

	1962(A)	1963	1964	1965	1966(B)	(B)/(A) × 100
1. FFYP						
Pvt.	1,896.5	1,951.9	2,039.0	2,178.0	2,357.6	124
Govt.	465.8	467.6	472.4	478.3	488.5	105
Total	2,362.3	2,419.5	2,511.4	2,656.3	2,846.1	121
2. Revised FFYP						
Pvt.	227.6	238.7	241.5	251.6	262.1	115.2
Govt.	48.1	50.5	48.6	48.8	50.1	104.3
Total	275.7	289.2	290.1	300.4	312.2	113
3. Actual						
Pvt.	568.96	587.74	620.44	669.08	716.99	126
Govt.	70.44	73.84	71.18	76.02	84.76	120
Total	639.40	661.58	691.62	745.10	801.75	125
	1967(A)	1968	1969	1970	1971(B)	
4. SFYP						
Pvt.	693.02	722.09	760.75	802.58	848.86	122
Govt.	120.64	138.14	142.72	147.48	152.41	126
Total	813.66	860.23	903.47	950.06	1,001.27	123

71

TABLE 9. SOURCES OF FINANCING DOMESTIC INVESTMENT (GDCF)

(*billion* [*hwan*] *won*)

	1962	1963	1964	1965	1966	Whole period	Increase (1966/1962)
1. FFYP[a]							
A. Domestic saving	9.0	19.0	28.9	36.2	42.3	135.4	4.7 ✕
B. Total investment	49.3	60.0	67.4	70.4	74.4	321.5	1.5 ✕
A/B (%)	18.3	31.7	42.9	51.4	56.9	42.1	
2. Revised FFYP							
A. Domestic S	5.8	4.7	18.5	23.7	27.9	80.6	4.8 ✕
B. Total I	43.6	52.3	53.3	55.1	57.5	261.8	1.3 ✕
A/B (%)	13.3	9.0	34.7	43.0	48.5	30.8	
3. Actual[b]							
A. Domestic S[c]	7.8	37.3	52.0	65.8	135.5	298.4	9.4 ✕[d]
B. Total I	45.5	89.7	101.2	118.5	223.1	578.0	2.7 ✕[d]
A/B (%)	17.1	41.6	51.4	55.5	60.7	51.6	
	1967	**1968**	**1969**	**1970**	**1971**		
4. SFYP							
A. Domestic S	78.68	94.57	118.17	143.09	168.40	602.91	2.1 ✕
B. Total I	159.81	176.79	195.03	215.44	233.00	980.07	1.5 ✕
A/B (%)	49.2	53.5	60.6	66.4	72.3	61.5	

[a] *Revised FFYP*, p. 18.

[b] Current, not 1965 prices.

[c] Domestic savings calculated as a residual (GDCF less the sum of net borrowing and net transfers from the rest of the world). Estimates of domestic savings and domestic savings as a proportion of total saving (i.e., GDCF) shown here are very close to those shown in the EPB's *Economic Survey, 1967* (pp. 107–8).

[d] Estimates based on deflated GDCF and deflated domestic savings, using the implicit deflator for GDCF to deflate domestic savings. Estimated domestic savings in 1965 prices were: 1962, 13.4 billion *won*; 1963, 57.1; 1964, 58.8; 1965, 65.8; 1966, 125.9.

TABLE 10. INVESTMENT, DOMESTIC SAVINGS, AND GOVERNMENT REVENUE RATIOS

(billion [hwan] won)

	1962	1963	1964	1965	1966	Whole period
1. FFYP						
(1) GDCF	493.1	599.8	673.7	704.3	743.5	3,215.0
(2) Dom. saving	90	190	289	362	423	1,354
(3) Govt. revenues[a]	404.4	463.2	528.7	596.7	660.1	2,653.1
(4) GNP	2,453	2,610	2,800	3,019	3,269	14,151
(1)/(4) × 100	20.1	23.0	24.1	23.3	22.7	22.7
(2)/(4) × 100	3.7	7.3	10.3	12.0	19.9	9.6
(3)/(4) × 100	16.5	17.7	18.9	19.8	20.2	18.7
2. Revised FFYP						
(1) GDCF	43.6	52.3	53.3	55.1	57.5	261.8
(2) Dom. S.	5.8	4.7	18.5	23.7	27.9	80.6
(3) Govt. rev.[b]	36.5	44.6	49.9	52.2	54.5	237.7
(4) GNP	281.5	293.9	308.6	324.0	340.2	1,548.2
(1)/(4) × 100	15.5	17.8	17.3	17.0	16.9	16.9
(2)/(4) × 100	2.1	1.6	6.0	7.3	8.2	5.2
(3)/(4) × 100	13.0	15.2	16.2	16.1	16.0	15.4
3. Actual (current prices)						
(1) GDCF	45.5	89.7	101.2	118.5	223.1	578.0
(2) Dom. S.	7.8	37.3	52.0	65.8	135.5	298.4
(3) Govt. rev.[c]	38.2	44.0	52.1	70.3	111.5	316.1
(4) GNP	349.0	488.0	696.8	805.9	1,032.0	3,371.7
(1)/(4) × 100	13.0	18.3	14.5	14.7	21.6	17.1
(2)/(4) × 100	2.2	7.6	7.5	8.2	13.1	8.9
(3)/(4) × 100	10.9	9.0	7.5	8.7	10.8	9.4
	1967	1968	1969	1970	1971	
4. SFYP						
(1) GDCF	159.8	176.8	195.0	215.4	233.0	980.1
(2) Dom. S.	78.7	94.6	118.2	143.1	168.4	602.9
(3) Govt. rev.[d]	107.9	126.8	138.6	150.0	161.6	684.9
(4) GNP	892.3	954.8	1,021.6	1,093.2	1,169.7	5,131.6
(1)/(4) × 100	17.9	19.8	19.1	19.7	19.9	19.1
(2)/(4) × 100	8.8	10.6	11.6	13.1	14.4	11.7
(3)/(4) × 100	12.1	14.2	13.6	13.7	13.8	13.3

[a] Current revenues.

[b] Includes taxes, surplus of enterprises, and non-enterprise current transfer.

[c] From EPB, Economic Survey, 1966, p. 104; Economic Survey, 1967, p. 37. A second set of figures from the national accounts, which is higher mainly because it includes income from government enterprises and other current transfers from households and non-profit institutions (i.e., various fees, stamp taxes, etc.) is as follows:

1962	1963	1964	1965	1966	Whole period	Ratio: Govt. rev./GNP
48.4	57.5	69.8	93.9	140.5	410.1	12.2

[d] General government tax and non-tax revenue (1965 prices).

Part II

PLANNING MODELS

AN ECONOMETRIC MODEL OF THE
KOREAN ECONOMY (1956-66)

Irma Adelman and
Kim Mahn Je

I. BACKGROUND AND INTRODUCTION

Preparation of Korea's Second Five-Year Plan, covering the period 1967–71, was initiated in early 1965 with an attempt to design a suitable macro model for estimating the overall growth of output, savings, investment, and imports and exports. At the same time, information on all potential investment projects was solicited.

It soon became apparent, however, that the traditional type of macro model, based on the national product accounts, would not provide a satisfactory basis for planning because the national income and product accounts were found to be seriously distorted in critical areas. Preparation of input-output tables for 1960 and 1963 indicated that manufacturing production in the national income accounts was understated by roughly 30 percent for both those years. New techniques for estimating crop production showed that the previous output estimates for major grains were from 30 to 50 percent too low. An exchange rate that was overvalued in varying degrees prior to 1964 gave unrealistic values for exports, imports, and foreign savings, which in turn caused an understatement of domestic private savings, a residual in the accounts.

Attempts were made to correct these distortions and defects and to reestimate the model, but there was not sufficient time to carry out a thorough revision of the accounts, and the "patching" of the data was not sufficient to improve the validity of the model. In some cases, short-cut adjustments, based on extrapolations of the 1960 and 1963 input-output tables, helped improve the "fit" of regressions in the macro model, but this did not increase our confidence in their reliability.

It was not until the revised set of national income accounts (prepared by the Bank of Korea in November, 1967) became available that a reasonable macroeconometric model could be estimated. Since its estimation, the model has been used to help formulate the 1968 overall resources budget (ORB). It is anticipated that greater reliance will be placed upon the aggregative model in future planning work.

The present model portrays the Korean economy as a set of inter-related processes involving production, savings, investment, and foreign trade. Based upon conditions in Korea during the period 1956–66, it was designed primarily for the annual macroeconomic projections that underlie the formulation of the annual plans (the ORBs).

The analytical framework of the model combines Gurley and Shaw's theory of finance with Chenery's "two gap" approach. The model emphasizes the roles of financial intermediation and price level changes in determining Korea's economic growth. The model does not merely examine possible gaps between aggregate real savings and investment, imports and exports, and aggregate production and aggregate demand, it also introduces financial intermediation variables that affect the allocation of real resources to particular uses. Fiscal and monetary policies alike are allowed to influence the real sectors significantly.

An increase in the efficiency of financial intermediation brings about increased efficiency in the allocation of savings to investment, as well as rises in overall savings and investment levels. Because private savings are related in the model to after-tax income, tax policy directly influences the marginal savings propensity of the private sector. Increases in private savings are transmitted to investment primarily through the lending of real savings, channeled through cash balances and time deposits. The availability of lendable real savings in liquid form in turn affects the desired level of real investment.

Another powerful financial intermediation technique in the model is the transformation of real savings into investment by the use of the government's fiscal power. The government can "borrow" private savings in the form of taxes, and can either finance real investment directly or lend the proceeds to private investors through the investment and loan portion of its budget.[1]

The price effects incorporated in the model reflect agricultural price policy and the effects of variations in the overall price level. Changes in relative prices in favor of agriculture bring about forced savings that result in increases in investment. A rise in the wholesale price or a fall in the exchange rate both raise desired imports and thereby increase the trade gap.

The model attempts to answer three questions. (1) Given the government's growth targets, are there sufficient potential savings (both domestic and foreign) to finance investment requirements? (2) Which sets of mone-

---

[1] It should be noted that intermediation in the form of government loans and investment does not create money or time deposits, although government loans create bank loans in government banks. When the government practices deficit financing through the issuance of money, it competes directly with potential investors for claims on private savings.

tary and fiscal policies must be adopted to avoid bottlenecks in the financial intermediation process? (3) In the short run, if disequilibria arise between the *ex ante* total available supply of goods and services (i.e., the domestic supply of goods and services plus imports minus exports) and the *ex ante* total final demand (i.e., consumption and investment demands), which combination of policies and targets appears to be optimal for minimizing net foreign capital inflows? In short, the model attempts to provide a tool that can assist planners by simulating alternative growth paths and the effects of alternative monetary and fiscal policies.

Section II of this paper presents the structural equations of the model. Next, the model is used to analyze Korea's economic growth process during the past decade. We find that in this period the primary stimulus to growth came from a buoyant aggregate demand, led by the export sector. The major constraint upon growth was provided by the economy's domestic savings potential. Section IV of the paper is devoted to a discussion of the dynamic multipliers of changes in policy variables. The paper concludes with a comparison of alternative development strategies.

II. Estimation of the Structural Equations

This section is devoted primarily to the derivation of structural equations to describe Korean growth. Least square methods were used to estimate the equations because experience with such models has indicated that the additional improvement due to using less biased statistical techniques is frequently less than the extra computational burden.

The basic data, provided by the Bank of Korea National Income Division, are based on the 1967 revisions of accounts. The period chosen was 1956 to 1966 as it was felt that the degree of war ravage and postwar dislocation of the Korean economy would distort any model that attempted to include earlier years. All values, unless otherwise specified, are in billions of *won* at 1965 prices.

Our previous experience with estimating structural equations for Korea has indicated that the best-fitting equations tend to underpredict changes of the most recent years. In view of the planning orientation of this model, however, it was desirable that variables and statistical procedures be chosen so as to predict recent conditions and likely future changes more accurately than earlier conditions. Therefore a weighting scheme was applied that emphasizes the most recent observations. In particular, the weight associated with year s, w_s, was set equal to

$$w_s = 0.96^{1966-s} \qquad s = t - 1956^*$$

where t is calendar time in years.

---

* Other weighting schemes were tried (e.g., $w_s = 0.99^{1966-s}$; $w_s = 0.97^{1966-s}$), and the present scheme was selected after examining the autocorrelation of residuals, the

The logical ordering of the model is largely recursive, except for some blocks of equations that are interdependent. The complete model consists of fourteen statistical equations and twelve identities. The system includes twenty-six endogenous variables, five exogenous policy variables, and thirteen other exogenous and predetermined variables.

Five groups of structural equations were estimated: production functions, consumption functions, investment equations, import demand equations, and some tax and monetary equations. The equations are used primarily in evaluating internally consistent dynamic multipliers; the functions are discussed briefly below.

Production Functions

Production was disaggregated into four sectoral functions, covering the primary, mining and manufacturing, social overhead, and service sectors respectively. In each sector the growth of output was assumed to be a function of the growth of the capital stock, implying strictly complementary production functions of the Leontief type in which labor inputs are not scarce. This latter assumption appears justified in the Korean context.[2]

An apparent limitation of the estimated production functions is the omission of variables describing fluctuations in the rate of utilization of capacity. In the primary and the mining and manufacturing sectors, the estimated equations allow for variations in capacity utilization induced by variations in weather conditions and by the availability of imported raw materials. The production functions in the social overhead and service sectors, on the other hand, have not taken account of capacity utilization. In Korea, it is quite reasonable to assume full-capacity operation in the social overhead sector in view of the continuing shortages of transportation, water, and electricity services over this period.

Production function of the primary sector. Output in this sector was assumed to be a function of the beginning-of-year capital stock and weather conditions. Specifically,

$$V^a = 192.08 + 9.183\ D^w + 1.812\ K^a \qquad R^2 = 0.963 \qquad (1)$$
$$(9.342)^* \quad (3.016) \qquad (0.152)$$

residuals for 1965 and 1966, and the plausibility of the regression coefficients. By all criteria, the chosen weights performed best. The regression equations with different weighting schemes are presented for comparison in Appendix B to this paper.

It should be noted that in weighted regression one minimizes the *weighted* sum of the squared residuals from the regression equation. A weight is therefore applied not only to the dependent and independent variables in each equation, but also to the constant term.

[2] In addition, any other type of production function would have been virtually impossible to estimate because of the incompleteness of employment data and the inaccuracy of other relevant data (such as information on labor shares in national income).

* The number in parentheses under each coefficient is its standard error.

In this equation,

V^a = value added in agriculture, forestry, and fishing
K^a = beginning-of-year capital stock in the primary sector
D^w = a dummy variable, describing weather conditions, that takes values of $-1, 0,$ and $+1$ for unfavorable, neutral, and favorable weather conditions.

The estimated function indicates that the marginal capital-output ratio in the primary sector is about $\dfrac{1}{1.812} = 0.55$, an estimate that accords quite well with the results of recent cross-sectional analyses.

Production function for mining and manufacturing. Mining and manufacturing production was assumed to be a function of two types of scarce resources, capital stock and imports of intermediate raw materials. As in the primary sector, fixed-input proportions were assumed. The estimated function is:

$$V^m = -2.723 + 0.931\ K^m + 0.329\ M^i \qquad R^2 = 0.985 \qquad (2)$$
$$(6.701) \quad (0.066) \quad (0.102)$$

V^m = value added in mining and manufacturing
K^m = beginning-of-year capital stock in mining and manufacturing
M^i = import of intermediate goods in billion *won*, converted at 1965 exchange rate of 265 *won* per U.S. dollar (SITC nos. 0 except 04, 1, 2, 3, 4, 5, 6, 8, and 9)

The net marginal capital-output ratio for this sector was found to be about 1.10. This estimate is approximately the same as the engineering estimates of 1965, which place the incremental gross capital to value-added ratio between 1.4 and 1.5.

Production function for social overhead. Growth of output in this sector was assumed to be related to the capital stock at the beginning of the previous year. Thus,

$$V^o = 5.341 + 0.338\ K^o_{t-1} \qquad R^2 = 0.973 \qquad (3)$$
$$(1.870) \quad (0.019)$$

V^o = value added in electricity, water, sanitary service, transportation, storage, and communications
K^o_{t-1} = beginning-of-year capital stock in the social overhead sector in the prior year.

The marginal capital-output ratio in equation 3 was estimated to be 2.96, which is quite low in comparison with engineering estimates for new capacity in this sector. Part of the reason for the low historical estimate of the capital-output ratio is that, over the entire sample period, the rate of capacity utilization in this sector was considerably above normal levels.

Over much of the period, electricity was rationed and electrical capacity was generated privately. In addition, the average age of railroad rolling stock was quite high.

Production function for services. Production in the services sector was related to capital stock at the beginning of the year. We have this as:

$$V^s = 138.48 + 0.636 \ K^s \qquad R^2 = 0.946 \qquad (4)$$
$$(11.270) \quad (0.050)$$

V^s = value added in construction, wholesale and retail trades, banking and insurance, ownership of dwellings, public administration, defense, education, and other services

K^s = start-of-year capital stock in the service sector.

The marginal capital-output ratio in services is estimated to be 1.57, which is in line with cross-sectional estimates.

Consumption

Consumption expenditures were disaggregated into food and nonfood private consumption and government consumption. Because Korea has experienced a large long-term shift in the relationship between food and nonfood consumption, this disaggregation of private consumption appeared worthwhile. Similarly, separate treatment of government consumption was called for because variations in the government's current expenditures have been influenced by factors that are generally different from those that affect private consumption.

Food consumption. Food consumption was related to after-tax income and to the terms of trade that applied to agriculture. The estimated function is:

$$C^f = 164.27 + 0.334 \ (V - T) - 17.813 \ PI^g/PI^w \qquad R^2 = 0.979 \qquad (5)$$
$$(21.722) \quad (0.017) \qquad\qquad (6.663)$$

C^f = food consumption
V = GNP
T = domestic taxes deflated by the wholesale price index
$\qquad$ (1965 = 100)

PI^g/PI^w = ratio of the grain price index (1960 = 100) to the wholesale price index (1965 = 100).

As might be expected, the price elasticity of food with respect to an increase in relative prices is negative, and approximately 0.15. The marginal propensity to consume food from disposable income is approximately 0.334.

Nonfood consumption. Consumption expenditures on nonfood items were related to after-tax GNP and to the ratio of the grain price index to the wholesale price index. Real liquid asset variables were tried in this function, but they turned out to be relatively insignificant. Specifically,

$$C^{nf} = 2.816 + 0.385 \ (V - T) + 4.473 \ PI^g/PI^w \qquad R^2 = 0.933 \quad (6)$$
$$\phantom{C^{nf} = } (45.368) \quad (0.037) \qquad\quad (13.916)$$

C^{nf} = nonfood consumption
V = GNP
T = domestic taxes deflated by the wholesale price index
  (1965 = 100).

As expected, the marginal propensity to consume nonfood items is larger than that for food items, and varies positively with increases in the relative price of agricultural commodities. The elasticity is 0.05.

Government consumption. Government consumption was related to tax revenue intake. Thus,

$$C^g = 55.257 + 0.285 \ T \qquad R^2 = 0.946 \qquad\qquad (7)$$
$$ (1.721) \quad (0.023)$$

C^g = government consumption
T = domestic taxes deflated by the wholesale price index (1965 = 100).

Investment Equations

These equations describe how the desired level of investment is determined in each sector. They reflect the interaction between the process of financial intermediation, on the one hand, and the process of adjustment of actual capacity to desired capacity levels, on the other. Thus all the investment demand equations estimated are of the "accelerator" type and all include some financial variables.

Gross fixed-capital formation was disaggregated into the same four sectors that are used for production functions: primary, mining and manufacturing, social overhead, and service. Changes in inventories were taken as exogenous because of the very poor statistical fits obtained.

Gross fixed investment in the primary sector. The primary sector's investment levels have fluctuated rather erratically in the past and therefore were difficult to estimate. Desired investment levels in this sector were assumed to be a function of past changes in agricultural production and of the availability of financing, as represented by governmental noncon-sumption expenditures. Specifically,

$$I^a = -3.944 + 0.329\ GL + 0.111\ (V^a_{t-2} - V^a_{t-3}) \qquad R^2 = 0.877 \quad (8)$$
$$ (3.600) \quad (0.083) \qquad\quad (0.050)$$

I^a = gross fixed investment in the primary sector
V^a = value added in the primary sector
GL = government nonconsumption expenditures, deflated by the whole-sale price index (1965 = 100).

The primary sector's response to its demand appears to be sluggish and delayed, and the availability of financing seems to be more important. The investment accelerator coefficient for agriculture is 0.11, and the marginal capital-output ratio estimated from the agricultural production function is 0.55. Thus it would appear that, if no stimulating effects of the avail-ability of government financing are assumed, the simultaneous operation of the investment and the production functions would result either in capital shallowing or serious capacity bottlenecks in agriculture. The low investment accelerator in this sector is not surprising in view of the recent deterioration in the terms of trade for agriculture and declining per capita farm income.

Gross fixed investment in mining and manufacturing. Gross fixed-capital formation in mining and manufacturing has been explained by reference to a capacity form of the accelerator relationship and to the availability of financing. The levels of private real liquid assets and government noncon-sumption expenditures were used as indicators of the availability of invest-ment finance. Government loans and investment accounts were included in the financial variable because, in the past, government loans—mostly in the form of U.S. AID counterpart funds—have played an important role in financing capital formation in this sector. Thus,

$$I^m_t = -42.258 + 1.126\ V^m_{t-1} - 0.786\ K^m_{t-1} \qquad\qquad (9)$$
$$ (2.149) \quad\ (0.070) \qquad\quad (0.058)$$
$$\qquad\qquad + 0.240\ (\overline{MS} + \overline{TD} + GL)_t \qquad R^2 = 0.995$$
$$\qquad\qquad (0.029)$$

I^m = gross fixed investment in mining and manufacturing sector
V^m = value added in mining and manufacturing sector
K^m = capital stock in mining and manufacturing sector
$\overline{MS}$ = money supply outstanding, deflated by the wholesale price index (1965 = 100)
$\overline{TD}$ = time deposits outstanding, deflated by the wholesale price index (1965 = 100)
GL = government nonconsumption expenditures, deflated by the whole-sale price index (1965 = 100).

The investment accelerator coefficient in this sector is 1.43, which is roughly 20 percent higher than the net marginal capital-output ratio estimated from the production function. The simultaneous operation of investment function 9 and production function 2 when financial incentives are taken into account is indicative of a tendency toward capital deepening and/or the buildup of excess capacity in mining and manufacturing.

Gross fixed investment in social overhead. Gross fixed investment in social overhead was assumed to be a function of the derived demand generated by the growth of the entire economy and of the availability of government finance. The accelerator relationship was assumed to be of the capacity type. We have this as:

$$I^o = -225.01 - 1.071\ K^o_{t-1} + 0.537\ V_{t-2} + 0.193\ GL \qquad (10)$$
$$\quad\ \ (61.460) \quad (0.299) \qquad (0.157) \qquad (0.520)$$

$$R^2 = 0.920$$

I^o = gross fixed investment in the social overhead sector
K^o = capital stock in the social overhead sector
V = GNP
GL = government nonconsumption expenditures, deflated by the wholesale price index (1965 = 100).

The investment accelerator coefficient in this sector is approximately 0.54 with respect to GNP and 10.56 with respect to "own" output. This high accelerator ratio indicates a tendency to catch up with underinvestment in the past in physical overhead capital. The marginal capital-output ratios implicit in the investment function are more nearly akin to the engineering estimates than the ratios estimated in the production function.

Gross fixed investment in the service sector. For this sector, too, investment demand was assumed to be derived from changes in economic conditions in the economy as a whole. Hence gross fixed investment in the service sector was made a function of changes in GNP in the prior year and real liquid assets outstanding. The estimated function is:

$$I^s = 4.811 + 0.235\ (\overline{MS} + \overline{TD}) + 0.230\ (V_{t-1} - V_{t-2}) \qquad (11)$$
$$\quad\ \ (2.938) \quad (0.033) \qquad\qquad (0.051)$$

$$R^2 = 0.940$$

I^s = gross fixed investment in service sector
V = GNP
$\overline{MS}$ = money supply outstanding, deflated by the wholesale price index (1965 = 100)
$\overline{TD}$ = time deposits outstanding, deflated by the wholesale price index (1965 = 100).

The accelerator coefficient for services with respect to GNP is 0.23, and with respect to "own" output it is 0.65. This accelerator value is considerably lower than the 1.7 marginal capital-output ratio estimated from the production function, indicating a tendency to underinvest in this sector relative to long-run capital requirements.

Import Demand Equations

Three categories of import functions were estimated, namely, imports of machinery and equipment (SITC 7), all other imports (including intermediate raw materials), and imports of intermediate raw materials.

Imports of machinery and equipment. Imports of machinery and equipment were made a function of gross fixed-capital formation and of the balance-of-payments deficit. Because almost all capital goods have been financed either by grants or by loans from abroad, the availability of foreign financing represented by the import-export gap can be presumed to be an important determinant of such imports.

$$M^k = -17.386 + 0.220\ I - 0.205\ (X - M) \qquad R^2 = 0.983 \qquad (12)$$
$$\quad\ (2.596) \quad\ (0.014) \quad\ (0.034)$$

M^k = imports of machinery and equipment (SITC = 7)
I = gross fixed investment
X = exports of goods and services
M = imports of goods and services.

All other imports. All other imports, that is, imports of goods and services (except capital goods), are related to the levels of nonagricultural value added as well as to the relative price of foreign and domestic goods. In the past, this category of imports has consisted predominantly of industrial raw materials. In recent years, the rapid rise in manufacturing has brought about a faster increase in raw material imports.

$$M^{nk} = 40.467 + 0.421\ V^n - 1.302\ PI^m/PI^w \qquad R^2 = 0.898 \qquad (13)$$
$$\quad\ (21.935) \quad (0.054) \quad\ (0.354)$$

M^{nk} = import of goods and services other than machinery
V^n = value added exclusive of agriculture
PI^m = implicit import deflator (1965 = 100)
PI^w = wholesale price index (1965 = 100).

Imports of intermediate raw materials. Because the availability of imported intermediate inputs is a determinant of production in mining and manufacturing, it was necessary to define a function for intermediate imports. Therefore, imports of intermediate raw materials were assumed to be a function of the value added in the nonagricultural sector and of the relative prices of foreign and domestic goods.

$$M^i \; = \; 26.049 \; + \; 0.333 \; V^n \; - \; 0.966 \; PI^m/PI^w \qquad R^2 = 0.883 \quad (14)$$
$$ (18.964) \quad (0.046) \qquad (0.306)$$

M^i = imports of intermediate raw materials
V^n = value added exclusive of agriculture
PI^m = implicit import deflator (1960 = 100)
PI^w = wholesale price index (1960 = 100).

Definitions and Identities

In addition to the usual accounting identities that express consumption, investment, and imports as the sum of their component parts, the model includes definitions of gross national product from both the originating industry and expenditure sides, and definitions of capital stock in each industry. The capital stock at the start of the period is expressed as the sum of depreciated capital stock at the beginning of the previous period and gross capital formation during the period. Three equilibrium conditions also are incorporated into the system: (1) a balance-of-payments condition, which states that the difference between imports and exports of goods and services is represented by net foreign capital inflows; (2) a savings-investment constraint, which specifies that the difference between gross domestic savings and investment consists of net foreign capital inflows; and (3) a requirement that aggregate demand equal aggregate supply, which implies that GNP estimated from the industrial origin side must equal GNP estimated from the expenditure side. These constraints and equilibrium conditions are listed below.

$$C = C^{nf} + C^f + C^g \tag{15}$$

$$I = I^a + I^m + I^o + I^s + I^i \qquad (I^i = \text{inventory investment}) \tag{16}$$

$$M = M^{nk} + M^k \tag{17}$$

$$V = C + I + X - M + V^f \qquad (V^f = \text{net factor income} \tag{18}$$
$$\text{from abroad)}$$

$$V = V^a + V^m + V^o + V^s + V^f \tag{19}$$

$$K^a_t = 0.97 \; K^a_{t-1} + I^a_t \qquad (K^a_{1953} = 0) \tag{20}$$

$$K^m_t = 0.94 \; K^m_{t-1} + I^m_t \qquad (K^m_{1953} = 0) \tag{21}$$

$$K_t^o = 0.85 \ K_{t-1}^o + I_t^o \qquad\qquad (K_{1953}^o = 0) \qquad\qquad (22)$$

$$K_t^s = 0.97 \ K_{t-1}^s + I_t^s \qquad\qquad (K_{1953}^s = 0) \qquad\qquad (23)$$

$$M = X + F + V^f \qquad\qquad (F \text{ is net foreign capital inflow}) \quad (24)$$

$$S = V - C = I + X - M + V^f \qquad\qquad\qquad (25)$$

$$C + I + X - M + V^f = V^a + V^m + V^o + V^s + V^f \qquad\qquad (26)$$

III. Performance of the Model, 1956–66

One way to test the descriptive validity of an econometric model is to compare the predicted values of the endogenous variables with the values actually observed during a sample period. In Tables 1 to 4 the estimated and the actual values of the endogenous variables are listed side by side. Two kinds of estimates are given: in one kind the predetermined and exogenous variables are at their actual levels (called "regression estimates") and, in the other kind, the estimated values of the current and lagged endogenous variables are substituted for their observed values in the solution of the simultaneous equations (called "dynamic estimates"). These latter estimates provide a more stringent test of the performance of the model economy, for they tend to reveal systematic biases arising from cumulation of estimation errors caused by the simultaneous and dynamic structure of the model.

The equation system presented above is not internally consistent inasmuch as it offers two alternative approaches to the estimation of GNP. GNP could be estimated from the production side by using production functions 1 to 4, investment functions 9 to 11, the definitions of GNP by industrial origin, 19, and the definitions of each industry's capital stock, 20 to 23. However, the desired levels of aggregate production and gross investment, when estimated in this manner, will not necessarily be consistent with either aggregate demand (as estimated from the expenditure side of GNP) or the desired supply of domestic savings forthcoming at that level of GNP.

Alternatively, one could estimate GNP from the expenditure side by using all the equations except the definition of GNP, 19. With this approach, however, there is no guarantee that the generated aggregate demand could be satisfied by domestic production plus imports.

The following procedure therefore was adopted in the dynamic forecasts. Equations 24, 25, and 26, which express the *ex post* equality between realized imports and exports, between realized savings and investment (both adjusted for foreign capital inflows), and between realized aggregate demand for goods and services and aggregate production, were replaced by *ex ante* inequalities. These state that:

$$S^* \leq I^* + X - M^* + V^f \tag{24'}$$

$$M^* \leq X + F + V^f \tag{25'}$$

$$C^* + I^* + X - M^* + V^f \leq 1.15\,(V^{a*} + V^{m*} + V^{o*} + V^{s*} + V^f) \tag{26'}$$

The model was then solved in an iterative fashion. First, the aggregate supply was calculated from equations 1 to 4 and definition 19, with V^f exogenous. Then desired investment levels were estimated from equations 8 to 11 and definition 16. Next, using the calculated value of GNP from definition 19, consumption functions 5 to 7, the calculated value of investment from the previous step, and import equations 12, 13, and 17, we performed the savings-investment test implied in 24'. If 24' was satisfied, we proceeded to the next step; otherwise, total gross investment and total consumption were set equal to their actual levels and were allocated to their constituent components in proportion to their calculated values.

The balance-of-payments test implied in 25' was performed next, with either actual or calculated investment, depending upon the results of the savings-investment test. If 25' was satisfied, we proceeded to the next step; otherwise, the value of total imports was set equal to the actual level and imports were allocated between M^k and M^{nk} in proportion to their regression estimates.

We next solved for GNP from definition 18, and performed test 26'. If the test was satisfied, we accepted the calculated value of GNP from the expenditure side. If it was not, we set GNP equal to 1.15 ($V^{a*} + V^{o*} + V^{s*} + V^{m*} + V^f$). We also performed balance-of-payments test 25' once more, with the value of GNP calculated in the previous step, replacing calculated M^* by actual M if the test failed, and recalculating GNP from 18. Note that if both the balance-of-payments test and the savings-investment test failed, calculated GNP was set equal to actual GNP with this procedure.

A few words concerning the assumptions about the adjustment process implicit in the algorithm sketched above may be in order. In general, when an *ex ante* inequality arises between the savings-investment gap and the import-export gap, adjustments to equate the two must occur *ex post*. If the savings-investment gap is the larger of the two, these adjustments may take the form of extra imports, less investment, fewer exports, or lower

---

* The asterisks indicate the desired levels of the variables as calculated from the appropriate statistical functions.

consumption levels than were desired on the basis of the behavioral relationships. The particular adjustment mechanism one chooses is critical
to the economy's performance, the most effective adjustment from the
point of view of growth being reductions in consumption and the least
effective adjustment being suboptimal performance in the foreign trade
section.

Similarly, if the import-export gap is the larger of the two, the process
of adjustment can involve extra consumption, greater investment, fewer
imports or greater exports. Of these, increased investment in import or
export industries provides the most efficient adjustment mechanism, and
increased consumption is the least effective.

Finally, if aggregate demand exceeds aggregate supply, adjustment can
take the form of more intensive utilization of productive capacity, price
increases, or commodity rationing coupled with price controls. If aggregate
supply exceeds aggregate demand, the result can be unintended inventory accumulation, greater excess capacity, more consumption, lower
price levels, import reductions, or export expansion.

The adjustment process implicit in the computational algorithm was
designed to reflect the process that actually took place. Typically, the
savings-investment gap was dominant in Korea during the sample period.
Generally, the adjustment process entailed both an upward revision in
savings and a downward revision in investment, with actual investment
being roughly two-thirds of desired investment. Thus the adjustment
process appears to have been fairly efficient from the point of view of
growth. By the same token, because aggregate demand usually was at
least as large as "full capacity" output, adjustments among them took
the form of an inflation and growth combination.

Comparison of the estimated and actual values in Tables 1 to 4 indicates
that the model economy reproduces the time paths of all the endogenous
variables quite faithfully. There is little evidence of any systematic bias
in the model.

As is evident from Table 5, the most binding constraint upon Korea's
growth in this period was its savings rate. Capacity bottlenecks do not
appear to have placed severe limitations upon Korea's growth during
this period inasmuch as aggregate demand always fell within 15 percent
of aggregate supply. The balance-of-payments constraint was binding
in 1958–60 and 1964–65, but even during these years it was—on the
average—less binding than the savings-investment constraint. A reasonable interpretation of Korea's economic growth during this period would
therefore appear to be that it was propelled by aggregate demand (particularly exports) and was limited primarily by the availability of financial
resources for investment purposes.

TABLE 1. VALUE ADDED

(in billion won)

| | Agriculture | | | Manufacturing | | | Overheads | | | Services | | | Net factor income |
Year	Actual[b]	Regression equation	Dynamic model	Actual[c]	Regression equation	Dynamic model	Actual	Regression equation	Dynamic model	Actual	Regression equation	Dynamic from model	Dynamic from model abroad
1956	213.23	204.11	231.87	61.45	46.30	41.30	15.17	10.27	12.02	184.24	174.98	198.79	7.38
1957	230.57	221.69	240.64	69.13	60.36	64.10	15.92	12.46	14.37	199.52	185.91	199.44	7.59
1958	246.26	232.71	252.75	74.42	73.16	60.49	18.08	16.11	13.96	205.34	196.34	216.90	7.59
1959	243.66	231.98	250.30	81.33	81.18	65.80	20.83	18.69	19.21	222.27	206.70	232.78	7.75
1960	243.97	241.31	246.92	88.81	92.08	71.00	22.90	21.63	23.31	226.01	219.29	240.46	7.38
1961	268.53	270.62	274.94	91.64	97.76	71.51	23.15	23.04	27.76	224.50	233.07	251.17	5.79
1962	252.37	265.32	259.31	106.00	110.82	84.17	26.30	26.56	30.58	234.82	244.38	254.06	6.48
1963	270.56	284.19	277.04	123.49	122.67	100.46	30.57	32.14	32.83	261.62	260.53	265.75	6.79
1964	314.31	309.27	311.36	130.14	133.15	114.04	35.62	40.18	35.48	263.71	276.94	282.89	6.53
1965	311.63	306.98	305.00	157.54	151.16	152.82	42.40	43.25	41.30	286.63	293.40	299.09	7.65
1966	345.91	346.43	362.89	181.43	183.06	167.04	49.91	47.22	46.81	323.49	314.76	333.74	13.08

TOTAL GROSS NATIONAL PRODUCT

Year	Actual[d]	Regression equation	Dynamic model
1956	480.47	443.04	491.37
1957	522.73	488.01	526.14
1958	551.69	525.91	551.69[a]
1959	575.84	546.30	575.84[a]
1960	589.07	581.69	589.07[a]
1961	613.61	630.28	631.18
1962	634.97	653.56	634.61
1963	693.03	706.32	682.87
1964	750.31	766.07	750.31
1965	805.85	802.44	805.85[a]
1966	913.82	904.55	923.55[a]

[a] Set equal to actual because both savings-investment and import-export restraints were binding.
[b] 1954 = 219.10, 1955 = 224.06.
[c] 1954 = 43.02, 1955 = 52.50.
[d] 1954 = 447.36, 1955 = 474.54.

TABLE 2. GROSS FIXED CAPITAL FORMATION

(in billion won)

Year	Agriculture			Manufacturing			Overheads			Services		
	Actual	Regression equation	Dynamic model	Actual	Regression equation	Dynamic model	Actual	Regression equation	Dynamic model	Actual	Regression equation	Dynamic model
1956	5.07	6.38	7.03	18.17	20.25	22.31	10.40	5.84	3.13	19.13	18.43	20.31
1957	6.48	4.33	9.03	20.56	19.83	0.25	15.88	23.41	18.10	18.39	13.74	33.93
1958	5.35	1.58	4.06	18.17	17.72	9.51	15.21	5.96	19.11	19.06	24.97	25.11
1959	5.99	3.70	2.85	13.60	12.37	9.95	16.62	17.92	20.85	23.08	25.49	25.64
1960	6.97	7.28	6.41	16.15	11.52	12.35	13.20	15.17	20.67	25.39	24.38	22.28
1961	8.35	7.52	7.26	14.23	15.39	15.41	20.44	30.57	20.71	22.24	22.75	21.92
1962	6.72	10.86	10.45	18.51	18.79	18.52	28.40	27.63	19.10	30.42	31.91	35.96
1963	10.28	12.72	13.10	25.52	27.07	22.61	38.63	33.21	31.17	31.52	30.59	26.48
1964	10.66	8.33	8.35	23.29	33.25	26.10	26.97	27.67	26.16	32.41	35.14	32.72
1965	13.67	15.70	14.76	31.95	31.52	31.57	31.16	31.46	33.59	40.86	37.63	37.72
1966	23.16	21.57	19.01	63.73	63.46	69.24	56.52	56.27	58.34	47.22	47.73	44.23

TOTAL OF GOVERNMENT AND PRIVATE SECTORS

Year	Actual	Regression equation	Dynamic model
1956	52.77	50.90	52.77[a]
1957	61.31	61.31	61.31[a]
1958	57.79	50.23	57.79[a]
1959	59.29	59.48	59.29[a]
1960	61.71	58.35	61.71[a]
1961	65.26	76.23	65.26[a]
1962	84.05	89.19	84.04
1963	105.95	103.59	93.36
1964	93.33	104.39	93.33[a]
1965	117.64	116.31	117.64[a]
1966	190.63	189.03	190.63[a]

[a] Set equal to actual because savings-investment constraint was binding.

92

TABLE 3. CONSUMPTION

(in billion won)

Year	Private — Food			Private — Non-Food			Private — Total			Government — Total		
	Actual	Regression equation	Dynamic model	Actual	Regression equation	Dynamic model	Actual	Regression equation	Dynamic model	Actual	Regression equation	Dynamic model
1956	264.77	267.38	261.25	180.08	190.68	187.00	444.85	458.07	448.25	65.73	62.33	62.33
1957	270.35	278.67	273.68	200.97	202.76	198.83	471.32	481.43	472.51	66.34	65.15	65.15
1958	295.89	291.58	285.20	190.16	209.02	203.53	486.05	500.60	488.73	70.52	67.84	67.84
1959	306.12	302.18	298.44	202.43	212.75	209.14	508.55	514.92	507.58	69.84	70.81	70.81
1960	300.01	303.25	305.03	223.29	218.01	218.23	523.30	521.26	523.26	71.13	71.17	71.17
1961	306.70	317.89	301.77	221.68	240.08	225.32	528.38	557.97	527.09	69.84	71.13	71.13
1962	317.31	312.26	312.39	251.65	231.85	231.16	568.96	544.12	543.55	70.44	74.53	74.53
1963	314.66	319.67	316.67	273.08	258.87	254.27	587.74	578.54	570.94	73.84	73.51	73.51
1964	350.83	345.18	341.34	269.61	283.24	279.13	620.44	628.42	620.47	71.18	71.15	71.15
1965	370.97	366.67	370.51	298.11	297.48	299.53	669.08	664.15	670.04	76.02	75.06	75.06
1966	389.45	392.73	391.91	327.54	325.98	325.27	716.99	718.71	717.18	84.76	84.57	84.57

TOTAL PRIVATE AND GOVERNMENT SECTORS

Year	Actual	Regression equation	Dynamic model
1956	510.58	520.40	510.58[a]
1957	537.66	546.58	537.66[a]
1958	556.57	568.43	556.57[a]
1959	578.39	585.73	578.39[a]
1960	594.43	592.43	594.43[a]
1961	598.22	629.10	598.22[a]
1962	639.40	618.65	618.08
1963	661.58	652.05	644.45
1964	691.62	699.57	691.62[a]
1965	745.10	739.21	745.10[a]
1966	801.75	803.28	801.75[a]

[a] Set equal to actual because savings-investment constraint was binding.

TABLE 4. IMPORTS

(in billion won)

Date	Capital goods			Non-capital goods			Total			Intermediate goods		
	Actual	Regression equation	Dynamic model	Actual	Regression equation	Dynamic model	Actual	Regression equation	Dynamic model	Actual	Regression equation	Dynamic model
1956	11.36	13.68	11.66	93.21	85.80	82.01	104.57	99.48	93.67	82.83	65.27	62.22
1957	11.25	18.75	18.24	112.48	104.93	102.08	123.73	123.68	120.32	83.74	79.95	77.64
1958	9.73	13.84	13.26	97.31	101.49	93.78	107.04	115.33	107.04[a]	77.02	77.68	71.66
1959	11.07	9.64	7.69	76.59	98.42	79.97	87.66	108.06	87.66[a]	64.73	75.96	61.64
1960	10.63	11.98	11.04	89.80	97.34	89.39	100.43	109.32	100.43[a]	74.98	75.42	69.20
1961	11.17	8.97	5.57	79.92	63.49	68.17	91.09	72.46	73.74	64.16	50.33	53.95
1962	18.43	18.25	12.70	101.77	88.42	86.53	120.20	106.67	99.23	82.36	69.60	68.02
1963	30.62	29.28	21.84	122.57	118.24	111.79	153.19	147.52	133.63	87.40	92.54	87.37
1964	18.35	16.56	15.74	95.69	130.11	98.30	114.04	146.67	114.04[a]	42.35	81.61	77.73
1965	19.30	20.89	19.32	109.63	118.54	109.61	128.93	139.43	128.93[a]	88.67	94.26	87.09
1966	45.18	45.13	42.72	159.47	154.81	151.92	204.65	199.94	194.91	127.62	112.70	120.33

[a] Set equal to actual because import-export constraint was binding.

94

TABLE 5. BINDING CONSTRAINTS—DYNAMIC SOLUTION

Year	Savings–investment surplus	Export–import surplus	Demand–supply surplus
1956	−46.48	10.90	58.05
1957	− 5.03	3.41	32.97
1958	−16.14	− 5.44	0.00
1959	− 2.83	−12.85	0.00
1960	− 3.16	− 4.44	0.00
1961	−30.98	12.45	13.03
1962	0.00	15.56	− 6.39
1963	0.00	20.90	−26.03
1964	− 0.73	−10.50	0.00
1965	− 1.38	−28.82	0.00
1966	−35.27	1.51	26.60

IV. DYNAMIC MULTIPLIERS OF MAJOR POLICY INSTRUMENTS

In order to evaluate the effects of major policy variables on the system, dynamic multipliers have been calculated for changes in money and time deposits, the government's investment budget, taxes, and agricultural terms of trade. Before we discuss the multipliers, however, it should be recalled that the model focuses on the analysis of *ex ante* disequilibria between aggregate demand and aggregate supply. Thus partial dynamic multipliers, calculated for such policies as increasing the money supply, have an impact either upon aggregate demand or aggregate supply, or upon both, revealing the possibilities for *ex ante* inequalities between the two factors. In the real world, such gaps would be closed by price level changes, by adjustments in real aggregate demand or supply, or by both measures, so that equilibrium in nominal value would always be assured *ex post*.

The calculated multipliers indicate the time path of responses implicit in the model to a one-year unit increase in each exogenous variable. That is to say, a *gedanken* experiment was performed in which each exogenous variable was raised by one unit in year 0 and was returned to its initial level thereafter. In the calculation of these multipliers the *impact* effect of each change was allowed to manifest itself even if it violated equilibrium conditions 24', 25', or 26'. However, subsequent induced rounds in, say, investment were not allowed to take place unless 24' and 25' were in fact satisfied.

Each multiplier is discussed briefly below, and the calculated multipliers on aggregate demand and aggregate supply are graphed in Figures 1 to 4 for a five-year period, beyond which their impact is truncated.

Multiplier of changes in money and time deposits. The reaction of the model economy to increases in credit is very Schumpeterian in nature and consistent with the Gurlay-Shaw theory of finance. According to the

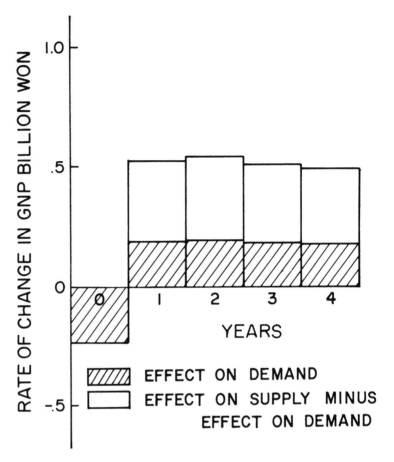

FIGURE 1. IMPACT OF A ONE BILLION WON INCREASE IN TAXES.

model, an increase in money and time deposits initially augments desired capital formation, particularly in the mining and manufacturing sectors. At the same time, the increase in investment raises aggregate demand through the multiplier mechanism. Time lags, however, prevent the increase in investment from resulting in a greater aggregate supply of goods and services until the following year. Thus the impact effect of an increase in the supply of money and time deposits is inflationary. In subsequent years, however, the productive capacity generated by the increased investment raises aggregate supply potential by more than the increases in aggregate demand, so that the ultimate effect of enlarging the money supply is deflationary.

It should be noted that, in keeping with the conventions we have

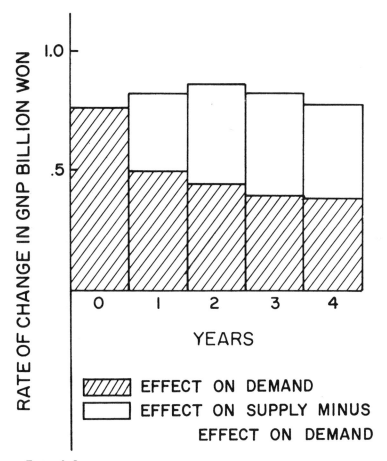

FIGURE 2. IMPACT OF A ONE BILLION WON INCREASE IN GOVERNMENT LENDING.

adopted, secondary accelerator-induced rounds in investment were not allowed to manifest themselves because they required increased supplies of savings and foreign exchange. Although the former could, in principle, occur, the latter cannot, because exports are exogenous to the model.

Multiplier of changes in the government investment budget. The impact of increases in government investments and loans is very similar to that of increases in money. Increases in both cases augment investment and have an initial inflationary effect, which is more than compensated for by increases in potential productive capacity. The impact of increases in government loans appears to be greater than that of increases in the money supply, and it affects the production structure of the economy differently in that it substantially increases the share of agriculture.

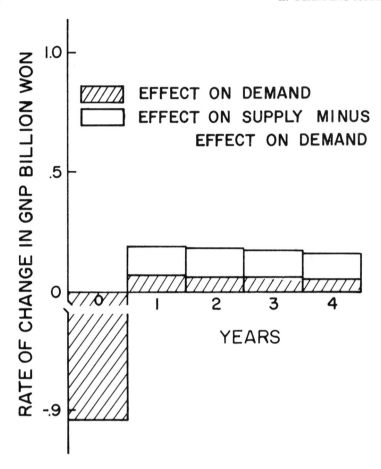

FIGURE 3. IMPACT OF A ONE PERCENTAGE POINT INCREASE IN AGRICULTURAL PRICES.

Multiplier of increases in taxes. The government influences aggregate demand in the model in three major ways: (1) by increasing tax levies, it reduces private consumption expenditures; (2) by financing higher government consumption, it raises GNP; and (3) by increasing the loan and investment portion of the government budget, it raises overall investment.[3] An increase in tax revenues also brings about additional savings by reducing private consumption and by increasing government savings, because the government's marginal propensity to consume out of taxes is less than that of the private sector. The increase in savings, in turn, creates more

[3] During the sample period, $GL = 8.599 + 0.550\,T \qquad R^2 = 0.780.$
$\qquad\qquad\qquad\qquad\quad (7.365) \quad (0.098)$

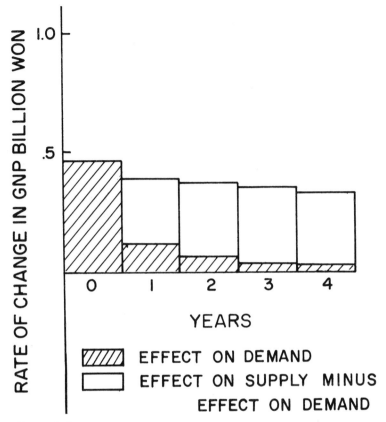

FIGURE 4. IMPACT OF A ONE BILLION WON INCREASE IN MONEY AND TIME DEPOSITS.

money and time deposits,[4] which finances additional capital formation. Thus, initially, a larger tax revenue directly reduces private consumption demand and increases investment financed by bank money and through the government budget. In subsequent periods the aggregate supply potential rises because of the additional investment during the initial period. Initially, a larger tax revenue reduces aggregate demand; thereafter, aggregate demand rises with investment, but to a lesser extent than aggregate supply, so that the overall effect of tax increases is very deflationary.

Multiplier of changes in relative agricultural prices. A change in the terms of trade in favor of agriculture affects both food and nonfood private consumption. Since, however, desired food consumption decreases more

[4] During the sample period, $MS + TD = 26.989 + 0.491\ S$ $R^2 = 0.813.$
$\qquad\qquad\qquad\qquad\quad\ (10.923)\quad (0.079)$

than desired nonfood consumption increases, aggregate demand declines and therefore the domestic savings potential rises. The increment in savings is channeled to the banking sector to finance an increase in investment that generates greater aggregate supply. Thus an improvement in the terms of trade of agriculture puts pressure on the urban sector to generate forced savings, and is therefore deflationary.

V. ALTERNATIVE DEVELOPMENT STRATEGIES FOR KOREA

The present model is designed primarily for planning purposes and should be used as a decision-making model for comparing alternative policy strategies. In this section, the strategies designed to minimize external capital requirements for specified GNP and sectoral target growth rates are compared under various assumptions pertaining to the future course of the policy variables. The model has eight classes of targets and policy variables, which are considered in various combinations (these are listed in Table 6).

TABLE 6.   ALTERNATIVE PLANNING STRATEGIES

Strategies	Case I	Case II	Case III
(1) GNP growth rate	10.0	10.0	7.0
(% per annum)			
(2) Sectoral output growth rate			
(% per annum)			
(a) Primary sector	5.0	6.3	5.0
(b) Mining and manufacturing	19.0	19.2	10.7
(c) Social overhead	20.0	14.1	9.7
(d) Services	6.1	6.0	5.3
(e) Factor income from abroad	30.0	21.3	20.0

(3) Policy Mixes	Taxes	Government investment budget	Money and time deposits	Exports	Agriculture price[a]	Foreign exchange rate[b]
Program (1)	Medium	Medium	Medium	High	Medium	Medium
Program (2)	"	"	"	"	"	No change
Program (3)	"	"	"	Medium	"	Medium
Program (4)	"	"	"	"	"	No change
Program (5)	"	"	"	"	"	Low
Program (6)	High	High	"	High	"	Medium
Program (7)	Medium	Medium	Low	"	"	No change
Program (8)	"	"	Medium	"	High	Medium
Program (9)	High	Low	Low	"	"	No change

Note: Case I is derived from the revised Second Five-Year Plan in *1969 Overall Resources Budget,* Case II is the consistent targets estimated by the *Sectoral Model,* and Case III is the original Second Five-Year Plan.

[a] Agriculture price is the ratio of grain prices to general wholesale prices, PI^g/PI^w.

[b] The foreign exchange rate variable is the ratio of the implicit import deflator to the wholesale price index.

To determine the combined effects of the above-listed strategies upon requirements for foreign capital inflows, two different sets of reduced-form equations have been formulated. One set is derived from the expenditure side of GNP and is based upon investment functions 8 to 11; the savings and foreign-trade gaps that correspond to this system are denoted F^{s1} and F^{t1}. The second set is derived from the investment requirements implicit in production functions 1 to 4, and reflects investment needs derived from "engineering based" estimates of capital requirements derived by differentiating the production functions. The savings and trade gaps calculated by the latter approach are denoted F^{s2} and F^{t2}. In deriving equations F^{s2} and F^{t2}, we raised the marginal capital-output ratio in the social overhead sector to 8.5, rather than kept it at its production function estimate of approximately 3.0, in order to correspond more closely to engineering estimates for new capital in this sector. The reduced-form equations for estimating each of these four gaps are as follows.

$$
\begin{aligned}
F^{s1} = V - C - I' = &-142.886 + .434\,T + 13.340\,PI^g/PI^w \\
&- 0.858GL - 0.535\,(\overline{MS} + \overline{TD}) - 0.125\,V_0^a(1 + r^a)^{t-3}r^a \\
&- 1.614V_0^m(1 + r^m)^{t-3}r^m - V_0(1 + r)^{t-3} \\
&[2.505r + 0.259r^2 - 0.281\,(1 + r)^3]
\end{aligned}
\tag{27}
$$

$$
\begin{aligned}
F^{s2} = V - C - I^2 = &-222.343 + 0.434T + 13.340\,PI^g/PI^w \\
&+ 0.281V_0(1 + r)^t - 0.541V_0^a(1 + r^a)^t r^a - 1.042V_0^m(1 + r^m)^t r^m \\
&- 1.578V_0^s - 9.461V_0^o(1 + r^o)^{t+1}r^o
\end{aligned}
\tag{28}
$$

$$
\begin{aligned}
F^{t1} = M' - X - V^f = &9.492 + 0.211GL + 0.132(\overline{MS} + \overline{TD}) \\
&- 1.638\,PI^m/PI^w - 0.258X + 0.031V_0^a(1 + r^a)^{t-3}r^a \\
&+ 0.397V_0^m(1 + r^m)^{t-3}r^m + 0.530V_0^n(1 + r^n)^t \\
&+ V_0 r(1 + r)^{t-3}(0.616 + 0.064r) - V_0^f(1 + r^f)^t
\end{aligned}
\tag{29}
$$

$$
\begin{aligned}
F^{t2} = M^2 - X - V^f = &29.032 - 1.638\,PI^m/PI^w - 0.258X \\
&+ 0.133V_0^a(1 + r^a)^t r^a + 0.256V_0^m(1 + r^m)^t r^m \\
&+ 0.388V_0^s(1 + r^s)^t r^s + 2.327V_0^o(1 + r^o)^{t+1}r^o \\
&+ 0.530V_0^n(1 + r^n)^t - V_0^f(1 + r^f)^t
\end{aligned}
\tag{30}
$$

Tables 7 and 8 show the projected net capital inflows required under various assumptions about future policies and targets. Table 7 presents prospective foreign-capital needs, assuming the exercise of only a minimal domestic restraint. Under this assumption, the required capital inflow is equal to the maximum of F^{s1}, F^{t1}, F^{s2}, or F^{t2}. Projections derived on this basis indicate that, with a 10 percent GNP growth rate, the savings gap dominates during the first two years, in most cases, and then the import gap becomes dominant. With a 7 percent GNP growth rate, on the other hand, the savings-investment constraint is effective at least until 1971.

TABLE 7. MAXIMUM FOREIGN CAPITAL REQUIREMENTS TO SUPPORT ASSUMED GROWTH RATES

Year/Identification	Case I.1, I.2	Case I.3	Case I.4	Case I.5	Case I.6	Case I.7	Case I.8	Case I.9	Case II.1	Case II.9	Case III.1	Case III.9
1968	189[a]	189[a]	189[a]	189[a]	191[a]	183[a]	188[a]	167[a]	180[a]	159[a]	137[b]	126[b]
1969	202[a]	202[a]	182[a]	200[b]	204[a]	191[a]	199[a]	168[a]	190[a]	155[a]	143[b]	124[b]
1970	217[a]	244[b]	220[b]	257[b]	219[a]	199[a]	213[a]	171[a]	202[b]	168[b]	149[b]	121[b]
1971	234[a]	292[b]	261[b]	308[b]	236[a]	208[a]	229[a]	179[b]	224[b]	180[b]	149[b]	107[b]
1972	225[a]	343[b]	305[b]	361[b]	258[a]	220[a]	249[a]	185[b]	244[b]	188[b]	136[a]	85[b]

[a] Foreign capital requirements are determined from the savings-investment constraint using investment functions 8–11 to determine investment (F^{s1}).

[b] Foreign capital requirements are determined for the import-export constraint using import functions 12–13 and investment functions 8–11—(F^{t1}).

TABLE 8. MINIMUM FOREIGN CAPITAL REQUIREMENTS TO SUPPORT ASSUMED GROWTH RATES

Year/Identification	Cases I.1, I.4, I.6, I.7, I.8	Case I.3	Case I.5	Cases I.9, I.2	Cases II.1, II.4, II.6, II.7, II.8	Case II.3	Case II.5	Cases II.9, II.2	Cases III.1, III.4, III.6, III.7, III.8	Case III.3	Case III.5	Cases III.9, III.2
1968	122	131	136	113	107	116	121	99	77	86	91	77
1969	145	171	180	128	126	153	162	110	76	102	112	86
1970	171	214	227	147	148	191	205	124	75	118	131	95
1971	190	261	277	159	162	234	250	132	61	133	149	102
1972	205	312	330	167	173	281	299	136	40	147	165	109

Note: All foreign capital requirements determined from the import-export constraint using production-function based investment functions (F^{t2}).

Foreign-capital requirements, based on the assumption that restrictive policies are adopted to keep desired investment at levels dictated by engineering considerations, are listed in Table 8.

Comparison of Tables 7 and 8 reveals that foreign-capital requirements are almost twice as large when desired investment is determined from the

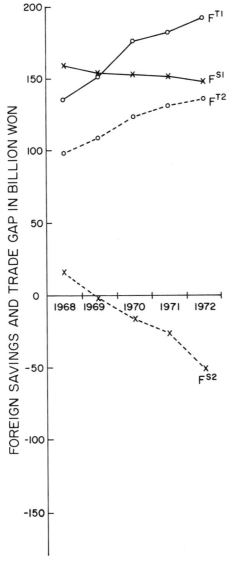

FIGURE 5. PROSPECTIVE FOREIGN CAPITAL REQUIREMENTS, ASSUMING A 10 PERCENT GROWTH RATE IN GNP (CASE II.9).

behavioral investment functions as when it is determined from engineering relationships. When investment is maintained at the minimum level consistent with growth, the amount of foreign exchange required to finance imports greatly exceeds the amount of foreign savings needed to finance investment.

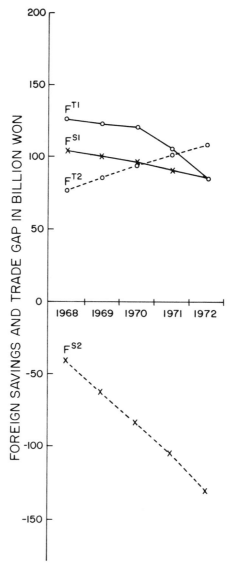

FIGURE 6. PROSPECTIVE FOREIGN CAPITAL REQUIREMENTS, ASSUMING A 7 PERCENT GROWTH RATE IN GNP (CASE III.9).

The optimal mix of policies is shown in Program 9 of Table 6. This strategy assumes that (1) taxes are raised to the maximum feasible level, reducing the need for foreign savings by decreasing domestic consumption; (2) government lending for investment purposes is not increased, thereby maintaining investment and both gaps at approximately the "engineering" levels; (3) increases in the money supply are minimized, restraining investment; (4) high export targets are met; (5) the terms of trade of agriculture are improved in order to force additional savings from the urban sector; and (6) the exchange rate is devalued in order to stimulate import substitution and reduce imports.

The prospective foreign-capital requirements during the period 1968–72, assuming a 10 percent GNP growth rate and a structure of production corresponding to the structure calculated in the sectoral model, are depicted in Figure 5. The corresponding information for a 7 percent growth rate is portrayed in Figure 6. Of course, a 7 percent growth rate is considerably easier to achieve with anticipated foreign-capital inflows than a 10 percent growth rate. The graph indicates that a 10 percent GNP growth rate can be maintained with a reasonable foreign-capital inflow only if (1) investment can be lowered substantially below its "excited" level, to something corresponding more nearly to engineering require-ments, and (2) further import substitution is effected in order to reduce the dominant trade gap. It should be noted, however, that the real effort implied in the pursuit of these policies is substantial, because monetary, fiscal, pricing, and foreign-exchange policies have already been assumed to be optimal.

CHAPTER 4 APPENDIX A

TABLE A-1.   VALUES OF EXOGENOUS VARIABLES DURING SAMPLE PERIOD

(*in billion won*)

Year	T	$(\overline{MS}+\overline{TD})$	GL	PI^m/PI^w	PI^g/PI^w	X	I^i	D^w
1956	24.74	31.40	26.32	52.00	2.77	9.79	4.52	−1.00
1957	34.77	32.27	23.69	45.00	2.73	13.30	26.60	0.00
1958	43.97	44.43	20.97	52.00	2.39	16.85	19.93	0.00
1959	54.41	59.69	17.54	63.00	2.05	19.53	−1.43	−1.00
1960	55.72	59.68	29.09	68.00	2.21	23.49	0.77	−1.00
1961	55.53	63.43	36.06	94.00	2.42	32.64	7.69	1.00
1962	67.43	91.35	45.32	87.00	2.35	36.71	−6.06	−1.00
1963	63.88	88.84	42.74	77.00	3.09	39.44	31.32	0.00
1964	55.60	72.28	43.16	93.00	2.89	48.75	21.08	1.00
1965	69.27	83.65	54.06	100.00	2.47	68.61	0.84	−1.00
1966	102.56	128.35	63.35	96.00	2.41	104.49	16.75	1.00

TABLE A-2.   VALUES OF VARIABLES DURING SAMPLE PERIOD

(*in billion won*)

Year	K^a	K^m	K^o	K^e
1954	4.04	7.07	7.05	17.12
1955	7.37	13.37	16.30	37.79
1956	11.68	26.18	24.01	57.33
1957	16.40	42.78	30.81	74.74
1958	22.38	60.78	42.06	90.89
1959	27.06	75.30	50.06	107.22
1960	32.24	84.38	59.17	127.09
1961	38.24	95.47	63.50	148.66
1962	45.45	103.97	74.41	166.44
1963	50.80	116.24	91.65	191.87
1964	59.56	134.79	116.53	217.63
1965	68.43	149.99	126.02	243.51
1966	80.05	172.94	138.28	277.07

TABLE A–3. ALTERNATIVE ASSUMPTIONS CONCERNING FUTURE VALUES OF EXOGENOUS
POLICY VARIABLES

(*in billion won*)

Variable/Year	1968	1969	1970	1971	1972
1. Taxes					
High	162.94	190.78	223.38	255.82	299.72
Medium	145.30	169.53	197.84	226.09	264.07
Low	130.78	150.37	172.84	196.36	225.81
High[a]	154.70	176.20	200.67	223.55	254.77
Medium[a]	137.95	156.57	177.73	197.57	224.47
Low[a]	124.16	138.87	155.27	171.59	191.94
2. Government loans					
High	97.76	114.47	134.03	153.49	179.83
Medium	87.18	101.72	118.70	135.65	158.44
Low	78.47	90.22	103.70	117.82	135.49
High[a]	92.82	105.72	120.40	134.13	152.86
Medium[a]	82.77	93.94	106.64	118.54	134.68
Low[a]	74.50	83.32	93.16	102.96	115.17
3. Ratio of agricultural index to general price index					
High	2.58	2.68	2.78	2.88	2.98
Medium	2.48	2.48	2.48	2.48	2.48
Low	2.38	2.28	2.18	2.08	1.98
4. Money and time deposits					
High	238.78	286.54	343.85	412.62	495.14
Medium	218.88	240.77	264.85	291.13	320.24
Low	208.93	219.38	230.35	241.87	253.96
High[a]	226.84	258.71	293.09	334.12	380.90
Medium[a]	212.91	227.81	244.11	261.20	279.48
Low[a]	206.94	215.22	223.83	232.01	241.29
5. Ratio of import price index to general price index					
High	87.00	84.47	82.01	79.62	77.30
Medium	84.54	79.76	75.24	70.98	66.96
Low	81.46	74.05	67.33	61.20	55.64
No change	89.86	89.86	89.86	89.86	89.86
6. Total exports					
High	160.19	189.14	219.76	260.70	309.29
Medium	153.07	168.37	185.21	203.73	224.10

[a] Figures are based on 7% GNP growth.

1. $V^a = 203.02 + 1.610\ K^a + 10.153\ D^w$ $R^2 =$
    $\quad\quad (6.675)\quad (.141)\quad\quad\quad (3.554)$
    $V^a = 196.30 + 1.741\ K^a + 9.637\ D^w$ $R^2 =$
    $\quad\quad (8.520)\quad (.149)\quad\quad\quad (3.306)$

2. $V^m = -7.582 + .718\ K^m + .536\ M^i$ $R^2 =$
    $\quad\quad (8.155)\quad (.043)\quad\quad (.144)$
    $V^m = -3.440 + .787\ K^m + .399\ M^i$ $R^2 =$
    $\quad\quad (7.041)\quad (.058)\quad\quad (.107)$

3. $V^o = 8.025 + .306\ K^o_{t-1}$ $R^2 =$
    $\quad\quad (1.122)\quad (.016)$
    $V^o = 6.353 + .327\ K^o_{t-1}$ $R^2 =$
    $\quad\quad (1.567)\quad (.017)$

4. $V^s = 152.99 + .563\ K^s$ $R^2 =$
    $\quad\quad (6.211)\quad (.037)$
    $V^s = 145.22 + .604\ K^s$ $R^2 =$
    $\quad\quad (9.323)\quad (.045)$

5. $C^f = 169.55 + .344\ (V - T) - 22.541\ PI^g/PI^w$ $R^2 =$
    $\quad\quad (18.716)\quad (.018)\quad\quad\quad (6.531)$
    $C^f = 164.81 + .338\ (V - T) - 19.175\ PI^g/PI^w$ $R^2 =$
    $\quad\quad (20.024)\quad (.017)\quad\quad\quad (6.625)$

6. $C^{nf} = -21.669 + .407\ (V - T) + 7.909\ PI^g/PI^w$ $R^2 =$
    $\quad\quad (41.118)\quad (.039)\quad\quad\quad (14.348)$
    $C^{nf} = -7.315 + .392\ (V - T) + 6.431\ PI^g/PI^w$ $R^2 =$
    $\quad\quad (4.312)\quad (.037)\quad\quad\quad (14.267)$

7. $C^g = 58.061 + .240\ T$ $R^2 =$
    $\quad\quad (1.763)\quad (.029)$
    $C^g = 55.888 + .276\ T$ $R^2 =$
    $\quad\quad (1.823)\quad (.026)$

8. $I^a = -1.358 + .267\ GL + .093\ (V^a_{t-2} - V^a_{t-3})$ $R^2 =$
    $\quad\quad (2.179)\quad (.060)\quad\quad (.051)$
    $I^a = -2.812 + .301\ GL + .111\ (V^a_{t-2} - V^a_{t-3})$ $R^2 =$
    $\quad\quad (2.982)\quad (.072)\quad\quad (.050)$

9. $I^m = -39.763 + 1.087\ V^m_{t-1} - .732\ K^m_{t-1} + .211\ (\overline{MS} + \overline{TD} + GL)$ $R^2 =$
    $\quad\quad (3.214)\quad (.082)\quad\quad (.064)\quad\quad (.045)$
    $I^m = -41.652 + 1.119\ V^m_{t-1} - .777\ K^m_{t-1} + .235\ (\overline{MS} + \overline{TD} + GL)$ $R^2 =$
    $\quad\quad (2.426)\quad (.073)\quad\quad (.060)\quad\quad (.034)$

10. $I^o = -114.25 + .275\ V_{t-2} - .529\ K^o_{t-1} + .385\ GL$ $R^2 =$
    $\quad\quad (74.561)\quad (.184)\quad\quad (.449)\quad (.391)$
    $I^o = -191.15 + .456\ V_{t-2} - .925\ K^o_{t-1} + .309\ GL$ $R^2 =$
    $\quad\quad (68.287)\quad (.172)\quad\quad (.360)\quad (.492)$

11. $I^s = 5.617 + .250\ (\overline{MS} + \overline{TD}) + .165\ (V_{t-1} - V_{t-2})$ $R^2 =$
    $\quad\quad (2.565)\quad (.038)\quad\quad\quad (.061)$
    $I^s = 4.697 + .242\ (\overline{MS} + \overline{TD}) + .215\ (V_{t-1} - V_{t-2})$ $R^2 =$
    $\quad\quad (2.772)\quad (.035)\quad\quad\quad (.061)$

12. $M^k = -13.803 + .246\ I - .125\ (X - M)$ $R^2 =$
    $\quad\quad (3.829)\quad (.021)\quad\quad (.043)$
    $M^k = -16.473 + .229\ I - .181\ (X - M)$ $R^2 =$
    $\quad\quad (3.090)\quad (.016)\quad\quad (.039)$

13. $M^{nk} = 42.433 + .363\ V^n - 1.025\ PI^m/PI^w$ $R^2 =$
    $\quad\quad (16.504)\quad (.072)\quad\quad (.328)$
    $M^{nk} = 38.600 + .399\ V^n - 1.163\ PI^m/PI^w$ $R^2 =$
    $\quad\quad (19.044)\quad (.058)\quad\quad (.335)$

14. $M^i = 38.232 + .262\ V^n - .743\ PI^m/PI^w$ $R^2 =$
    $\quad\quad (13.502)\quad (.059)\quad\quad (.268)$
    $M^i = 29.049 + .310\ V^n - .876\ PI^m/PI^w$ $R^2 =$
    $\quad\quad (16.193)\quad (.050)\quad\quad (.285)$

$GL = 2.612 + .595\ T$ $R^2 =$
$\quad\quad (8.075)\quad (.134)$
$GL = 4.638 + .593\ T$ $R^2 =$
$\quad\quad (7.806)\quad (.110)$

$MS + TD = 19.112 + .517\ S$ $R^2 =$
$\quad\quad\quad (14.221)\quad (.136)$
$MS + TD = 25.609 + .494\ S$ $R^2 =$
$\quad\quad\quad (11.844)\quad (.092)$

$T = -33.213 + .139\ V$ $R^2 =$
$\quad\quad (14.855)\quad (.022)$
$T = -33.280 + .139\ V$ $R^2 =$
$\quad\quad (17.912)\quad (.024)$

* Each equation is listed first unweighted, then weighted with $W_s = .97^{1966-s}$.

THE KOREAN SECTORAL MODEL

Irma Adelman, David C. Cole,
Roger Norton, Lee Kee Jung

I. BACKGROUND

Early in the preparation of Korea's Second Five-Year Plan a sectoral or interindustry model was proposed for testing the consistency and feasibility of the overall development program.[1] The model was originally intended for use in conjunction with a macro-economic growth model designed to estimate overall rates of growth of output, investment, savings, exports and imports, and was to serve as a bridge between the macro estimates and sectoral investment programs arising from project proposals. The sectoral model could also be used to derive a minimal although not necessarily optimal, investment program.

As the work on the plan proceeded, it became increasingly clear that the statistical base for the macro-model was inadequate and that more reliance should, if possible, be placed on the more statistically sound sectoral model to project such macro-economic variables as investment and imports. In addition, rapid structural changes were occurring in exports and savings, rendering questionable the validity of projections on the basis of past time series and vitiating one of the potentially significant contributions of the macro-model. The export and savings targets had to be founded more on guesswork than on scientific estimates.

At the same time, the analysis of investment projects was floundering because the numerous proposals, far exceeding the potentially available investment resources, were poorly prepared and generally unrealistic in their demand projections. There was an urgent need for guidance in esti-

---

The work of implementing the model for the Second Five-Year Plan was carried out by an army of government officials and academic advisors. In particular, we would like to mention Director Wooh Youn-Hwi of the Economic Planning Board, who supervised the work; Alan M. Strout and Marshall K. Wood, who have given helpful advice; Professor Han Kee Choon of Yonsei University, who performed predictive tests on the input-output tables; and Nam Young Woo, Kim Mahn Je, Lee Hee Il, Donald Dembowski, and Kay Auerbach, who devoted great effort to implementing the model.

[1] Irma Adelman, "A Resource and Material Balance Model for Sectoral Planning in Korea," unpublished paper dated October 27, 1965.

mating the probable growth and structure of demand in order to establish industrial priorities and check demand estimates.

Thus the need for a sectoral model became increasingly apparent and an all out effort was made to assemble a working version of the model in six months. Although not without significant defects, the result was probably the best planning framework possible, given the limitations of time and statistics. The model provided a systematic framework for organizing the information needed for planning and for confronting some of the basic choices of plan strategy. It was used to derive macro-estimates and to guide investment choices for the Second Plan, and this to a degree that had not originally been envisaged but which proved necessary because of the weakness of alternative means. Subsequently, as the macro-models have been improved and better information has become available on industrial demand and on supply and cost prospects, the sectoral model has reverted toward its original role as a test of consistency.

II. Structure of the Model

The Korean sectoral model was originally designed to test the consistency of a development program based on targets derived from the macro-model and to indicate total investment requirements and the appropriate sectoral allocation of investment. The model was subsequently modified to concentrate on investment needs in the mining and manufacturing sectors and to compare the effects of several alternative patterns of import substitution and export expansion.

The initial formulation of the model divided the economy into forty-three sectors. Two types of variables were distinguished. Endogenous variables represent production, investment, and—for selected industries— import activities in each sector of the economy, and exogenous variables specify the economic and technological constraints: (1) the limits upon the availability of primary resources (labor, capital, essential imports, and foreign exchange) at the start of each planning period or (2) the sectoral goals for consumption, exports, and—for selected industries— investment and imports.

Five types of constraints were included in the model. The first constraints, physical-balance equations, specify that—for each sector— the total amount of product available from production, imports, and opening inventories must equal its total use in intermediate production, investment, exports, final consumption, and stockpiling activities.

The second set of constraints provides a check on imbalances in the relationship of output to capacity. In particular, these constraints state that, for the given time period, domestic production in each sector is limited by the available capacity. Available capacity is defined as initial capacity at the start of the plan plus the net investment planned for all plan years prior to that for which the computation is carried out. This procedure allows for the possibility of lags in the rate at which investment can be used to increase capacity in each year of the planning period.

The third set of constraints deals with possible labor supply inequalities; that is, it specifies that the sum of labor of a given skill demanded for production or capacity-incrementing activities cannot exceed the availability of that grade of labor during the period.

The balance-of-payments constraints provide the fourth set of limitations for each time period. They specify that the total *won* value of imports must be equal to the sum of the *won* value of exports, the net foreign-capital commitments available for the period, and the accumulated balance-of-payments surplus. This total value of imports may be demanded for direct consumption, intermediate production, or capacity-incrementing purposes.

The fifth and last set of constraints involves savings and investment; it differs from the other constraints in the model in that it represents a behavioral rather than a technological limitation on the system. The number of *won* used for investment is limited to the funds available for this purpose from domestic savings and from foreign sources. This requirement, of course, is always satisfied *ex post*, because savings is merely the accounting difference between GNP and consumption—but, when, as in this model, savings are calculated from a savings function, it becomes a behavioral constraint. It is important to note that the model's actual savings ratio, *ex post*, need not be equal to the average *ex ante*, propensity to save that is assumed in this constraint.

As work on the model progressed, several structural changes were made. The labor constraints were discarded because Korea has a relatively large supply of skilled labor and substantial unemplopment or underemployment of skilled workers. The model was too crude a device to identify the highly specialized skills that might be in short supply. Only a single-total employment equation was retained to estimate the potential employment effects of various programs.

For fixed investment, a division was made between investment in mining and manufacturing and investment destined for all other sectors. The former was endogenous to the model whereas the latter was determined exogenously and was included in the estimates of final demand. This change reduced the number of sectors for which capital coefficients were used, and, in particular, it excluded those sectors—such as agriculture, trade, and services—where capital coefficients are likely to be

most unreliable or unstable. It also helped focus attention on the consequences for mining and manufacturing investment of changes in assumptions about various elements of final demand.

Imports were also divided into endogenous and exogenous components.
The former included noncompetitive intermediate and capital goods, and
competitive imports were estimated outside the model and incorporated
into the final-demand calculations. It would have been desirable to have
all imports endogenous, but the computations for testing alternative
assumptions about import substitution were greatly simplified by including
competitive imports as a negative element of final demand.

The model originally provided for a constraint on the minimum size
of plant in selected sectors, but this constraint was not employed. A mathematical statement of the final form of the model is given in Section IV
of this paper.

III. Process of Solution

A technique of successive approximations was employed to estimate
investment requirements for each sector. After policy targets and forecasts
were made for each plan year (up to 1971) of exports, consumption requirements, exogenous investment, competitive imports, and inventory change
for each sector, the physical-balance equations were solved, under the
assumption that capacity remains unchanged at its pre-plan level. The
solution for this set of equations gave a first approximation of the production requirements in each year of the plan.

Then the capacity constraints were converted into equalities. After
allowance for depreciation and the normal rate of capacity utilization, an
estimate of cumulative investment requirements over the plan period was
obtained by comparing existing capacity with that required to meet production needs. These calculated investment requirements were introduced
into the physical-balance equations and the system was solved again for
the production requirements over the entire planning horizon. The newly
computed production requirements were then reintroduced into the
capacity constraints, and this entire process was repeated until the solutions for the two sets of equations converged.

Once convergence was obtained, the extent to which the labor supply
inequalities were not satisfied indicated manpower training requirements.
Nonsatisfaction of the fourth set of constraints was indicative of balance-
of-payments difficulties, and nonsatisfaction of the savings-investment
constraints reflected an investment program that was too ambitious relative to Korea's financial resources. It should be noted that, since the
model does not incorporate any of the real-life possibilities for substitution
between resources, it tends to overstate the degree of inconsistency of the

projects incorporated in any development plan. It therefore makes for conservative planning.

IV. Mathematical Foundation of the Model

Total Use: Total Availability Equalities

These restrictions specify that, for each sector, domestic production must make up the difference between the amount of product available from imports and opening inventories and the requirements for intermediate production, investment, exports, final consumption, and stockpiling. The constraints (for all j) can be expressed as:

$$X_j + M_j = \sum_i a_{ij}X_i + \Delta K_j^n + Y_j \tag{1}$$

a_{ij} = the coefficients of the input-output matrix, which represent the *won* value of domestic inputs from the ith sector required to produce a *won*'s worth of output of the jth industry

X_j = total domestic production in the jth sector

ΔK_j^n = capital goods required for endogenous investment from domestic production in the jth sector

Y_j = the amount of exogenously specified final demand for the output of the jth sector. It consists of the sum of private and public consumption, exogenous investment, exports, and changes in inventories.

M_j = total imports of the jth commodity.

Required Expansion of Capacity in Mining and Manufacturing

These constraints state that required capacity increases in the jth sector must make up the discrepancy between capacity available for use at the start of the period and capacity required for production at a normal rate of capacity utilization. Virtually all public investment falls in the primary and tertiary sectors; so only the secondary sector investment is endogenous in the model. Formally, one can state this constraint as follows for all j with a one-period gestation lag for inventories:

$$I_{jt}^1 = \max{(0, u_j X_{jt+1} - (1 - \delta_j)K_{jt})} \tag{2'}$$

I_{jt}^1 = gross increases in capacity required in period t in the jth sector, in *won*'s worth of output; j ranges over sectors with a one-period gestation lag

$K_{j,t}$ = capacity in the jth sector available for production in tth period, in *won*'s worth of output

u_j = inverse of the rate of utilization of capacity in the jth sector

δ_j = annual rate of capacity depreciation in industry j.

For sectors with a two-period gestation lag the analogous equation becomes:

$$I^2_{jt} = \max(0, u_j X_{t+2} - (1 - \delta^2_j)K_{jt}) \qquad (2'')$$

I^2_{jt} = gross increases in capacity required in period t in sectors j with a two-period gestation lag, measured in *won*'s worth of output.

Domestic Production of Capital Goods for Investment in Mining and Manufacturing

These equations convert required increases in capacity, measured in output terms, into investment requirements by producing sectors. Because of the division of sectors into categories with different gestation lags for investment, two sets of capital coefficients were distinguished. One set, b^1_{ij}, contains coefficients that apply to the first year, and the second set, b^2_{ij}, contains coefficients that apply to the second year. The equation can be written as:

$$\Delta K^n_{jt} = \sum_i b^1_{ij}(I^1_{it} + I^2_{it}) + \sum_i b^2_{ij}(I^1_{it} + I^2_{i,t-1}) \qquad (3)$$

b^1_{ij} = domestic purchases from the construction sectors (13 and 33) for capital formation in section i

b^2_{ij} = domestic purchases from the machinery and transportation sectors (29, 30, 31, and 39) for capacity expansion in sector i.

As we explained in the previous section, equations 1 to 3 were solved iteratively to approximate convergence, with ΔK^n_{jt} initially set equal to zero. In each iteration the solution proceeded forward in time, with year 1 values solved first, then year 2, and so on. After approximate convergence of equations 1 to 3, the remaining equations were solved to evaluate the financial and employment implications of each program.

Balance-of-payments constraint. For each time period the total *won* value of imports must be equal to the sum of the *won* value of exports, the net foreign-capital commitments available for the period, and the accumulated balance-of-payments surplus. That is:

$$\sum_j M^c_j + \sum_i \sum_j m_{ij}X_j + \sum_j m^1_j(I^1_{jt} + I^2_{j,t-1}) + \sum_j M^n_j$$

$$= \sum_j E_j + F_t + S_{\beta t} \qquad (4)$$

M_{ij} = *won* value of noncompetitive imports of industry i required to produce one *won*'s worth of output in the jth sector. Various rates of import substitution were assumed over time to alter these coefficients. Note, however, that if the m_{ij} are reduced, the corresponding a_{ij} must be increased by the same amount.

$m_j^1 =$ *won* value of noncompetitive imports required to increment capacity by one *won* in the jth sector

$M_j^c =$ competitive final-demand imports in sector j

$M_j^n =$ noncompetitive final-demand imports in sector j. These include imports for exogenously specified capital function.

$S_{\beta t} =$ change in the foreign-exchange surplus carried over from the previous period

$F_t =$ net foreign-capital commitments upon which the economy can draw during the period

$E_j =$ exports of sector j.

Savings-investment constraint. This constraint differs from the other constraints in the model because it represents a behavioral rather than a technological limitation upon the system. It expresses the requirement that the number of *won* used for investment shall not exceed the funds available for this purpose from domestic savings and foreign sources. This requirement is always satisfied *ex post*, since savings are calculated as a residual. It becomes a behavioral constraint, however, when savings are calculated from a savings function, as done here, rather than as the accounting difference between GNP and consumption. Mathematically, this constraint can be written as:

$$\sum_j \Delta K_j^n + \sum_j m_j^1(I_{jt}^1 + I_{j,t-1}^2) + \sum_j \Delta K_j^x$$

$$\leq S_0 + S_1 \Delta \text{GNP} + F_t - S_{\beta t} \qquad (5)$$

$\Delta K_j^x =$ amount of product of industry j required for exogenous investment. This output includes both domestically produced and imported capital goods.

$S_0 =$ savings level in the base year

$S_1 =$ marginal propensity to save out of GNP

$\Delta \text{GNP} =$ change in GNP since the base year.

The employment function. To evaluate the employment effect of each development strategy, we forecast total employment as:

$$N_t = \sum_j X_{j0} n_{j0} + \sum_j (X_{jt} - X_{j0}) n_j^m \qquad (6)$$

$N_t =$ total employment

$n_{j0} =$ average employment-output ratio for sector j in the base year

$n_j^m =$ marginal employment-output ratio for years 0 to t for sector j.

Equations 1 to 6 constitute the model as it was used in formulating Korea's Second Five-Year Economic Development Plan. The constraint equations (4 to 6) were not made a part of the formal solution in order to avoid linear programming computations; rather, conditional forecasts were made without reference to the constraints and then checks were made: to see which sets of solutions satisfied the foreign-exchange availability and total savings limits and to evaluate the employment effect of the program. Of course, only those variants that are feasible from a savings and balance-of-payments point of view were presented as alternatives for consideration by policy-makers.

V. DEVELOPMENT OF THE DATA

Two types of data were prepared for the sectoral model: parameters and exogenous variables. The former represent the structural relationships in the economy (input-output ratios, depreciation rates, etc.) and the latter are projections of various economic quantities, such as exports, investment in agriculture, and services that are considered planning targets.

Parameters

The parameters include input-output ratios, capital coefficients, initial productive capacity, rates of utilization of capacity, depreciation rates, gestation lags for construction, competitive import to output ratios, stock change to output ratios, noncompetitive import-input coefficients, and labor use coefficients.

Input-output coefficients. The Bank of Korea input-output studies provided the basis for the input coefficients, and these studies culminated in two sets of input-output tables of the Korean economy, for 1960 and 1963. A modified version of the 1963 coefficients was used in the model.

The initial modification was conversion of the coefficients into 1965 prices. For this purpose the Bank of Korea converted its wholesale price indices to conform to the input-output commodity groupings.

The second modification, to account for expected changes in technology, was replacement of the Bank of Korea's 1965 price coefficients with independently developed coefficients for electricity, fertilizer, textiles, basic iron and steel, primary steel products, and petroleum and coal products. A new fertilizer production function for 1967–71 was calculated from data compiled by "industry committees," composed of engineers and economists from all existing and proposed plants and from the fertilizer supply-demand program. With three large new fertilizer plants commencing production in 1967, using production methods different from those of the existing plants, it was particularly important to develop new production coefficients for this sector. New coefficients for fertilizer use in agriculture were developed by an agricultural working group.

Industry committees also designed 1969–71 production functions for basic iron and steel and for primary steel products, and new coefficients for fiber use in textile production. The Korea Electric Company provided statistics on the generation of electric power and on electric power use by industry in 1965. The latter were revised to reflect expected 1969–71 conditions in the petroleum products, iron and steel, steel products, fertilizer, and nonferrous metals sectors. In the nonferrous metals sector, the revision took account of a proposed aluminum refining plant.

From the preliminary solution of the model, it was apparent that the 1963 petroleum and coal products use ratios were considerably out of date by 1965. Instead of retaining the 1963 ratios, subsequent runs of the model allowed for the rapid trend toward substitution of domestically produced petroleum products. The noncompetitive import-input coefficients from the 1963 table were combined with the domestic coefficients to give new domestic ratios that represented total use of petroleum and coal products. These synthesized coefficients subsequently "predicted" the 1965 output of petroleum and coal products very accurately.

The lack of a petroleum products production function for Korea was temporarily compensated by using the 1955 Japanese production function. In further work with the planning model, a Korean production function will be developed.

Capital coefficients. The information on capital costs that was used in the model culminated from a long series of attempts to develop accurate data. Although unsuccessful, the first few attempts proved instructive; so they are briefly recounted here, and the method is then described in some detail.

Over the past decade, a large file of technical information on Korean industry has been accumulated in the form of supporting data for foreign and domestic loan applications. These data were tabulated and analyzed, but they contained a great many inconsistencies, stemming from three primary causes. (1) Many of the data on capital costs concerned the rehabilitation of plants that were partially destroyed during the war. (2) Many of the loans were for plant expansion, and, because plant expansion is designed to relieve specific production bottlenecks, the capital-to-increased-output ratios were often quite different from ratios for entirely new plants. (3) The bases for estimating the new capacity created by the projects were unclear; that is, assumptions concerning the average number of working hours per day and product prices often were not stated. In addition, much of the information in these files was from the 1954–60 period, when a great deal of very old machinery was in use, when prices were severely distorted, and when the exchange rate was unrealistic.

With the assistance of the Korean Reconstruction Bank, a mail sample survey of firms' investment and production costs was conducted in January and February, 1966. The sample was confined to firms that had undertaken capital expenditures in the past five years, and the information on capital expenditures was to be correlated with increased capacity to obtain marginal capital coefficients. (The value of existing capital stock, which is used to obtain average capital coefficients, was not requested in the questionnaire.) In the responses, the information on current operating costs proved much more reliable than the information that was needed for capital coefficients. The data on both capacity and capital expenditures were weak, in spite of detailed definitions of the basis for computing capacity. (A cross-check on the capacity responses was added to the questionnaire as a query on the rate of utilization of capacity.) Additional problems arose in deflating investment expenditures spread over several years and in calculating capacity change when the product composition changed.

After these disappointing results from plant-by-plant data had been obtained, existing time series on the value of capital stock by industry were checked by Professor Kee Choon Han of Yonsei University. These data had not been investigated previously because of the widespread conviction that they contained serious inaccuracies, due mainly to the variable depreciation and appreciation policies followed by the reporting firms. Unfortunately, simple consistency tests on the capital-output ratios derived from these data revealed serious inaccuracies.

Subsequently, the focus of investigation was returned to the individual plant data, this time concentrating on very recent expenditures on new buildings and equipment. The starting point was a small sample of data (for about forty firms) provided by the Korean Reconstruction Bank from its loan-application files. These applications had three desirable properties: (1) all were written within the past year; (2) all concerned projects for which the value of proposed new capital was greater than the value of existing capital; and (3) existing capital and expected new capacity were appraised by the Korean Reconstruction Bank's technicians, who used consistent appraisal techniques. The capital to capacity ratios inherent in these project analyses were tested and were proved to be much more reliable indicators of recent trends than the capital stock survey data.

The remaining problem—How to expand the size of the sample?—was solved with data the industry committees had begun to compile. Their profiles of some two hundred manufacturing and mining plants provided detailed data on production costs, fixed assets, capacity, and output.

The profiled fixed-asset data are to some extent subject to the evaluation problems mentioned above, but the data are of higher quality than other capital data for two reasons. (1) The sample firms are, generally, among the most modern in their sectors, and thus their equipment tends to be recently acquired and their bookkeeping more accurate than that of the average firm; (2) the industry committees' members, often very familiar with the sampled firms, frequently corrected the firms' data submissions and supplied data from their own files.

Two other advantages of the profile data are: (1) the modernity of the sampled firms means that the data provide a good indication of future cost and technology trends in their respective industries, and (2) the basis for calculating capacity was well defined in the profile, and the committee members' familiarity with the firms provided a check on the accuracy of the figures.

In computing marginal capital coefficients, estimates are needed of the value of future capacity expansion by subsector, and truly marginal capital coefficients are therefore almost never made. Marginal coefficients were approximated for this plan, however, by a roundabout procedure. First, the profile data were aggregated into average sectoral capital coefficients by using the Bank of Korea's 1965 subsector output data as approximations to relative capacity sizes. Then preliminary projections of the growth of output through 1971 were made with the sectoral model, which used these average coefficients. The industry committees subdivided these estimates into estimates of subsector outputs through 1971, which reflected the technicians' knowledge of the present state of each industry and their expectations of the relative growth in the subsectors of each industry. The subsector growth of output estimates were then used as approximations of changes in capacity for reaggregating the capital coefficients. The revised coefficients (i.e., marginal coefficients) were then used for the second solution of the model. These marginal coefficients are listed in Table 1.

Initial capacity. In connection with the planning effort, the existing industrial capacity surveys underwent review and revision. In February the Korean Reconstruction Bank conducted a survey of end-of-1965 productive capacity, based on a somewhat revised methodology. Because the measurement of capacity is always difficult, the new features of the KRB survey are mentioned only briefly.

First, the output potential of all machinery and equipment that worked less than a specified number of days per year was excluded from the computation of full-capacity output in order to overcome the upward bias in former estimates of capacity, a bias caused by inclusion of the potential output of obsolete machinery.

Second, the full-capacity working schedule was more carefully defined

TABLE 1. 1965 KOREAN CAPITAL COEFFICIENTS

(in end-of-1965 purchasers' prices)

from (i sector) / to (j sector)	Sector 33 Const.	Imported mach.	Sector 29	Sector 30	Sector 31	Sector 13	Sector 39	Total
5. Coal	.46698	.26061	.02867	.13199	.07928	.00244	.08750	1.05747
6. Other minerals	.18213	.03570	.09017	.01293	.03016	.00164	.00880	.36155
7. Processed foods	.10278	.04094	.11271	.01730	.00260	.00377	.00509	.28521
8. Beverages & tobacco	.14353	.03681	.02033	.00843	.00435	.00230	.01383	.22960
9. Fibre spinning	.30177[a]	.92074	.01756	.00327	.00497	.00074	.03818	1.28724[a]
10. Textile fabrics	.09757	.19975	.05358	.00323	.00274	.00022	.00693	.36402
11. Finished textile products	.07562	.05544	.02374	.00524	.00101	.00157	.00182	.16443
12. Lumber & plywood	.03474	.09515	.00979	.00463	.00958	.00036	.00115	.15540[b]
13. Wood products & furniture	.17901	.16111	.00358	.00597	.00597	.00239	.00179	.35980
14. Paper products	.08478	.25677	.01366	.01947	.00527	—	.00911	.38901
15. Printing & publishing	.02047	.17222	.01967	.00194	—	—	.00319	.21749
16. Leather & leather products	.03324	.02252	.00016	.01610	.00219	.00019	.00089	.07537
17. Rubber products	.03664	.09027	.01608	.00745	.00187	.00314	.00422	.15967
18. Basic chemicals	.29623	.51207	.05878	.02470	.00923	.00260	.01823	.92186
19. Intermediate chemicals	.15797	.21720	.08166	.04609	.01213	.00469	.02296	.54269
20. Finished chemical products	.03581	.12529	.00779	.00802	.00020	.00038	.00477	.18226
21. Chemical fertilizer	.20365	1.16715	.00573	.00127	.03425	.00731	.01074	1.43013
22. Petroleum & coal products	.03398	.31700	.00266	—	.04152	.00122	.00980	.40618
23. Cement	.23561	.87893	.13608	.06782	.00282	.00478	.07187	1.39791
24. Other ceramic, clay & stone products	.29915	.33270	.03814	.03661	.00595	.00372	.00770	.72397
25. Iron & steel	.56785	.18667	.01593	.07489	.01097	.00162	.00526	.86318
26. Steel products	.07511	.26544	.08694	.00777	.00288	.00018	.00738	.44566
27. Nonferrous metals & primary products	.51138	.19428	.02578	.10881	.00245	.00156	.00584	.85009
28. Finished metal products	.05461	.15356	.05452	.01130	.00088	.00201	.00242	.27927
29. Nonelectrical machinery	.15215	.22035	.10799	.00992	.00509	.00454	.00685	.50688
30. Electrical machinery	.04324	.10975	.01992	.01552	.00124	.00179	.01763	.20908
31. Transport equipment	.14479	.11051	.01628	.00428	.00602	.04789	.00586	.33564
32. Miscellaneous manufacturing	.09030	.07372	.01163	.02260	.00367	.00025	.00170	.20386
	.23443	.71528	.01364	.00254	.00386	.00057	.02966	1.00000

a For the model calculations, the sector 9 capital coefficients were lowered to the following:

b This sector was recently revised to the figures shown.

120

for each industry, on the basis of the "normal" number of working hours per day and days per month for each industry. "Normal" here means the number of hours per month beyond which, if it were required to work a plant a greater number of hours per month for an extended period, either an entrepreneur would expand his plant or competitors would enter the industry and the entrepreneur would revert to the normal schedule. This definition attempts to make operational both the economic profit-maximizing definition of the optimal work schedule and the concepts of sociological and technical forces that influence a plant's work schedule.

Third, a separate measure of capacity was applied to cottage industries, where available labor supply, rather than plant and equipment, is generally the primary constraint on production. Full-capacity monthly output for cottage industries was defined as the output of the month during which the highest number of assistants was employed by the cottage entrepreneur.[2] The results of this revised survey were used in conjunction with the Bank of Korea's 1965 output estimates and with the average rate utilization of capacity in order to obtain the capital stock figure for the end of 1965, as used in the sectoral model.

Depreciation rates, gestation lags, and rates of utilization. To obtain data on depreciation rates, the Economic Planning Board again found it necessary to break new ground. The prevailing depreciation procedures were based either on the Korean tax laws or on the U.S. Commerce Department depreciation guidelines established in the early 1940s. For the model, however, it was desirable to have depreciation rates that were based on actual economic lifetimes. The EPB therefore called together an *ad hoc* working group to estimate the economic lifetimes of buildings and (separately) machinery for each profile subsector under present conditions. In making these estimates the working group took account of the fact that some industries have a high proportion of very old equipment and will face increased pressure for modernization because of international competition. After these estimates were compiled, the reciprocals of the numbers were taken as annual depreciation rates.

The same working group estimated the construction period (gestation lag) for each sector. This period was defined as extending from the first disbursement of construction funds to the commencement of normal production operations.

Rates of utilization of capacity during the plan period were arbitrarily set at 80 or 90 percent. These high rates were chosen to safeguard against recommending expansion in industries with idle capacity.

---

[2] Seasonalities of supply or demand were taken into account in computing twelve-month capacity from this one-month-capacity output.

TABLE 2. EMPLOYMENT COEFFICIENTS (1965 PRICES)

(*Unit: Man-years per million won of output*)

Sector	Average 1960	Average 1963	Marginal 1965	1960 1965	1963 1965
1. Rice, barley, & wheat	22.4731	19.5454	n.a.	—	—
2. Other agriculture	22.9322	15.6321	n.a.	—	—
3. Forestry	29.9272	30.9994	n.a.	—	—
4. Fishery	17.7940	17.2044	n.a.	—	—
5. Coal	3.6339	3.2361	2.3349	1.556	1.386
6. Other minerals	4.1252	3.8011	2.4917	1.656	1.526
7. Processed foods	0.6414	1.1169	0.7665	0.837	1.457
8. Beverages & tobacco	0.8859	0.8794	0.3039	2.915	2.894
9. Fibre spinning	1.0931	1.4115	1.0937	0.999	1.291
10. Textile fabrics	2.1177	1.9274	1.2514	1.692	1.540
11. Finished textile products	2.6095	1.6417	1.6819	1.552	0.976
12. Lumber & plywood	1.2377	0.8560	0.5151	2.403	1.662
13. Wood products & furniture	3.1963	3.0595	2.4344	1.313	1.257
14. Paper products	1.6059	0.9506	0.4068	3.948	2.337
15. Printing & publishing	1.5342	1.7198	—	—	—
16. Leather & leather products	1.5874	1.5027	0.2407	6.595	6.243
17. Rubber products	1.6166	1.5913	1.1637	1.389	1.367
18. Basic chemicals	1.2286	0.8860	0.7054	1.742	1.256
19. Intermediate chemicals	0.8717	0.8341	0.7373	1.182	1.131
20. Finished chemical products	1.4406	0.7926	0.5633	2.557	1.407
21. Chemical fertilizer	1.3900	0.3975	0.1997	6.960	1.990
22. Petroleum & coal products	1.6301	1.0727	0.1085[a]	15.024[a]	9.887[a]
23. Cement	0.5373	0.4243	0.2315	2.321	1.833
24. Other ceramic, clay, & stone	0.4135	3.0918	2.7128	0.152	1.140
25. Iron & steel	0.8049	0.5346	0.2011	4.002	2.658
26. Steel products	0.9754	0.7900	0.4109	2.374	1.923
27. Nonferrous metals	0.9660	0.8213	0.3710	2.604	2.214
28. Finished metal products	1.6562	1.8805	1.4208	1.166	1.324
29. Nonelectrical machinery	4.2645	2.4449	1.9057	2.238	1.283
30. Electrical machinery	2.8569	1.7163	1.1940	2.393	1.437
31. Transport equipment	2.5701	2.0548	1.3393	1.919	1.534
32. Miscellaneous manufacturing	1.0998	1.8523	n.a.	—	—
33. Building & maintenance	7.1088	2.4500	n.a.	—	—
34. Other construction	2.4086	3.2863	n.a.	—	—
35. Electricity	5.0838	1.0209	n.a.	—	—
36. Banking, insurance	1.0727	0.8575	n.a.	—	—
37. Water & sanitary	0.6810	4.6452	n.a.	—	—
38. Communication	4.9230	3.0170	n.a.	—	—
39. Transportation & storage	5.0445	4.5412	n.a.	—	—
40. Trade	9.3933	5.9005	n.a.	—	—
41. Other services	5.4487	5.1122	n.a.	—	—
Weighted average (weighted with 1965 output)			1.05626	1.89219	1.68519

[a] The marked discrepancy between the profile and the other coefficients in sector 22 arises because the profile figure is for the petroleum refining industry and the 1960 and 1963 figures represent almost solely the coal briquette making industry. Sector 22 is excluded from the weighted average.

Import-input ratios. Estimates of the rate of substitution of domestic products for competitive imports were provided by another *ad hoc* working group. As noted earlier, these rates were expressed in the form of changing sectoral ratios of imports to output, and the ratios were converted to import levels in the course of the preliminary solution of the model. The

EPB then studied further the possibilities of import substitution and drafted a revised set of competitive import projections before performing the second solution of the model. Data for noncompetitive imports were obtained by using the noncompetitive import-input coefficients in the Bank of Korea's 1963 input-output table. The 1963 coefficients, converted to 1965 prices, were for the first solution, assumed constant over time. The industry committees studied the first-solution results and recommended lowering the noncompetitive import figures, in some cases, to account for known import substitution since 1963 and for future substitution that was definitely anticipated. These recommendations were cast in the form of new noncompetitive import-input coefficients for the subsequent solutions.

Labor input coefficients. The Bank of Korea obtained average labor input coefficients for each industry in 1965 from a small sample survey conducted specifically for that purpose. The marginal coefficients were taken from the industry committees' profile information. A rough check on the marginal coefficients, made by comparing them with the sectoral time trends of the labor coefficients established by the 1960 and 1963 input-output tables, showed that they are of the correct order of magnitude. The coefficients are shown in Table 2.

Final-Demand Projections

Along with the development of the coefficients describing the structure of the Korean economy, detailed projections were prepared of private consumption, government consumption, investment in various sectors, competitive imports, and exports. In projecting final demands, the planning-time horizon was considered in order to avoid the danger that the specified capital expansion will be sufficient only to achieve the target-year final-demand goals and will not provide the foundation for further growth at the same annual rate. This phenomenon is sometimes referred to as "consumption of capital" in order to meet consumption goals. A five-year horizon can be made satisfactory either by specifying end-of-period capital stocks or by specifying that final demand continue to grow at the same average annual rate for, say, two years beyond the target year. The latter device was chosen, and projections of final demand were carried through 1973.

First, in order to project private consumption by commodity group, expenditure elasticities were calculated for a detailed list of commodities.[3]

---

[3] The elasticities, β^k, were computed as follows for the kth commodity:

$$\beta^k = \frac{\Delta c^k}{c^k} \cdot \frac{E}{\Delta E}$$

$$= \frac{\Delta c^k}{\Delta E} \cdot \frac{E}{c^k} = b^k \frac{E}{c^k}$$

TABLE 3. EXPENDITURE ELASTICITIES OF DEMAND

Sector	Elasticities			TM	BM
	1963	1964	Average		
1. Rice, barley, & wheat	0.67591	0.64797	0.66194	0.5474	5.5784
2. Other agriculture	0.67018	0.71502	0.69260	0.4147	18.1645
3. Forestry	0.45762	0.41577	0.43669	1.2919	11.0611
4. Fishery	1.27386	1.11992	1.19689	1.3628	12.6710
5. Coal				12.6591	6.8600
6. Other minerals	0.25343	0.13949	0.19645	7.5107	8.5594
7. Processed food	1.06256	1.09822	1.08039	0.8766	14.7325
8. Beverages & tobacco	0.95276	0.94444	0.94860	0.8017	9.0796
9. Fibre spinning	0.20913	0.22649	0.21781	0.0143	7.4563
10. Textile fabrics	1.02158	0.98036	1.00097	0.2718	12.1437
11. Finished textile products	1.45473	1.39700	1.42586	0.0957	6.8445
12. Wood products. & furniture	1.58916	1.67087	1.63002	0.2597	21.0093
13. Paper products				2.4752	13.0693
14. Printing & publishing	1.52266	1.51856	1.52061	0.4500	5.5941
15. Leather & leather products	1.79878	1.72083	1.75981	0.2969	5.8182
16. Rubber products	0.67286	0.61699	0.64492	1.9810	16.3281
17. Finished chemical products	1.05589	1.23158	1.14373	1.7043	17.7955
18. Petroleum & coal products	0.84785	0.75427	0.80106	3.2454	8.7868
19. Other ceramic, clay, & stone	0.80827	0.66644	0.73785	4.9829	12.7774
20. Finished metal products	1.03379	0.96034	0.99706	1.3925	12.8020
21. Nonelectrical machinery	1.05118	0.92771	0.98944	0.4984	13.1007
22. Electrical machinery	2.33415	2.49245	2.41330	1.1094	13.5275
23. Transport equipment	1.63553	1.44592	1.54072	2.6602	10.5502
24. Miscellaneous manufacturing	1.35326	1.19786	1.27556	0.4352	18.1338
25. Electricity	0.91731	0.92467	0.92099	—	—
26. Communication	2.05312	2.06805	2.06058	—	—
27. Transportation & storage	1.29322	1.26614	1.27968	—	—
28. Other services	1.43986	1.56535	1.50261	—	—

These expenditure elasticities were calculated from 1963 and 1964 cross-section household-budget survey data compiled by the Bureau of Statistics of the EPB and the Ministry of Agriculture and Forestry.[4] Elasticities were calculated separately for urban and rural consumers, aggregated by the use of consumption expenditure weights, and applied to alternative targets for the growth of total private consumption.

This series of calculations was made for both the 1963 and the 1964 data, and averages of the sectoral elasticities for the two years were taken

where β^k is estimated by least squares from $c^k = a + b^k E$. In the above, c^k is the private consumption expenditure for the kth commodity and E is the total private consumption expenditure. This procedure is equivalent to the more usual method of estimating demand elasticities from the logarithmic equation:

$$ln\ c^k = a + \beta^k\ ln\ E$$

The commodity elasticities were then aggregated into urban and rural sectoral elasticities, and the rural and urban elasticities were then combined for each sector by weighting by the appropriate consumption expenditures.

[4] The data are collected quarterly for rural areas by the Ministry of Agriculture and Forestry and quarterly for urban areas by the Bureau of Statistics of the Economic Planning Board.

for projection purposes. The 1963 and 1964 elasticities are presented in Table 3. The differences between rural and urban consumption behavior are illustrated by the elasticities for 1964, shown in Table 4. Levels of consumption for some new commodities, such as petrochemical products, were estimated independently, with consideration of expected changes in future behavior.

Estimated total private consumption expenditures for each year of the plan period were calculated in the context of the macro model on the basis of high and low estimates of the rate of consumption growth. The estimates derived by this method were converted from purchasers' prices to producers' prices with the aid of estimates of business and trade margins provided by the Bank of Korea. (See Table 3 for the ratios of transport cost $[TM]$ and trade cost $[BM]$ to total delivered production costs by commodity.) Due to the lack of private consumption data for 1965, the 1963 I–0 consumption estimates by sector (converted to 1965 prices) formed the basis for the projections of consumption expenditures. These projections were made as follows.

$$c_t^i = \left[\beta^i \cdot \left(\frac{E_t}{E_0} - 1 \right) + 1 \right] c_0^i \qquad (7)$$

c_t^i = private consumption expenditures on ith sector commodities in year t

c_0^i = private consumption expenditures in ith sector in 1963

β^i = private expenditure elasticity for ith sector goods

E_0 = total private consumption expenditure in 1963

E_t = total private consumption expenditure in year t.

Prediction of government consumption expenditures required the tabulation and classification of several volumes of 1965 budget data and proposed 1966 budget data from various government ministries. The data were initially classified by the Final-Demand Working Group into four categories: defense expenditures, general government expenditures, special account expenditures, and local government expenditures. The categories were then classified into commodity groups. After patterns for government consumption of the different commodity groups were calculated, discussions were held with government officials to determine whether the patterns were misleading, and, if so, whether the 1965 or the 1966 budget more accurately reflected long-term trends. When guidelines were established for each commodity group, projections were made for each year through 1973.

Export projections were based on two possible overall target figures for commodity exports, since the model was designed to test the consistency

TABLE 4.   SELECTED RURAL AND URBAN DEMAND ELASTICITIES, 1964

Commodity	Expenditure elasticities	
	Rural	Urban
Rice	1.04864	0.73913
Barley	−0.09777	0.01593
Cereals	0.36615	0.53139
Flour	n.a.	−0.05658
Pulses	1.74212	n.a.
Potatoes	0.17637	n.a.
Other crop production	−1.39035	n.a.
Vegetables	0.49253	1.14563
Beef	1.62475	1.61756
Livestock	1.90403	n.a.
Fishery products	0.86794	1.26352
Processed food	1.03005	n.a.
Processed marine products	n.a.	1.20069
Eggs	n.a.	1.70343
Salt	0.67877	0.76137
Milk product	n.a.	1.22540
Red pepper	0.58300	n.a.
Laver, etc.	n.a.	1.52165
Fruits	n.a.	1.63796
Seasoning	n.a.	1.14136
Liquor	0.95808	n.a.
Other seasoning		1.15908
Tobacco	0.73882	n.a.
Refreshment	n.a.	1.54529
Pastries & candies	1.15254	1.37700
Dining out	0.46777	n.a.
Basic furniture		1.97473
Other furniture	1.10519	3.02729
Electrical appliances	n.a.	2.89070
Building expenditure	0.95902	n.a.
Tableware	n.a.	1.23094
Other household effects	1.49519	
Charcoal	n.a.	−0.12772
Briquettes	n.a.	0.82400
Fuel & light	0.57965	n.a.
Clothing	1.32829	n.a.
Match & candle	n.a.	0.01179
Footwear	0.81599[a]	1.65208[a]
Personal adornment	1.03732	1.15451
Education expenditure	2.37361	n.a.
Parasol, ring, wristwatch	n.a.	1.42088
Toilet & hygiene expenditure	0.84739	2.36074
Medicine	1.46832	1.37588
Communication	1.09477	2.19585
Transportation	n.a.	1.47275
Clinic fees	n.a.	1.44209
Social expenses	1.69917	n.a.
Haircut, hairdo, bath	n.a.	1.08220
Cosmetic, soap, etc.	n.a.	1.05913
Tuition	n.a.	1.75579
Printing & publishing	n.a.	1.53079
Stationery	n.a.	1.06941
Movie	n.a.	1.42279
Other manufactured products	n.a.	2.14853
Wedding & mourning practice	0.94528	n.a.

[a] In urban areas, leather footwear only; in rural areas, all footwear.

and feasibility of the plan targets. An export-import committee elaborated the basic target figures into a fine breakdown of commodities.

In the breakdown of the basic target figures, much attention was paid to the analysis of the world market situation for export items that were expected to exceed $1 million. In addition to the high and low target figures, a third set of predictions, similar to the original figures in annual totals bur of lighter stress on manufactured and primary exports, also was developed. This third set was adopted as the target projections, after the model was solved separately for each of the three sets of projections.

Prediction of exports by regression of past trends on variables representing world market demands was not feasible because of the extremely rapid growth of Korean exports between 1960 and 1965 (40 to 50 percent per year).

Investment in the agriculture, fishery, public works, and service sectors also was regarded as part of the target program. Because the investment in these sectors is the largest part of total investment in every year of the plan period, several alternative estimates were prepared for testing. Working groups for each sector prepared investment programs, and the investment expenditures were classified by type of capital good for use in the model. The sectoral programs were compiled and alternative totals, by type of capital good, were calculated for each year through 1973.

Recently, a new method of projecting exogenous investment was developed for some sectors, based on regression of categories of capital formation on categories of income in the national accounts, and it helps tie the macro and the sectoral models closer together.

Predictive Ability of Model

During the early stage of the data development, some tests on predictive ability of the model were performed by Professor Kee Choon Han of Yonsei University.[5] These tests were performed with the Bank of Koreas' 1960 and 1963 input-output coefficients, not with the actual coefficients used for the model's five-year-plan projections, and therefore the tests should be regarded as general tests of the input-output method rather than specific tests of the coefficients used in the five-year plan.

The tests consisted of "forecasting" 1960 and 1963 sectoral outputs with 1963 and 1960 I-0 tables, respectively. Final demands for each year were assumed as given, and the actual sectoral outputs were compared with forecasts by the "final-demand blow-up" method and by the "GNP

[5] See Kee Choon Han, "The Predictive Ability of the Korean Input-Output Tables" (preliminary paper), August 15, 1966 (mimeo.); Alan M. Strout, "Tests of Korean 1963 I-0 Tables," February 25, 1966 (mimeo.); and Alan M. Strout, "Price Adjustments to the 1960 Input-Output Tables," February 15, 1966 (mimeo.).

blow-up" method. In the final-demand blow-up, the ratio of each sector's final-demand output to its total output was assumed constant over time; in the GNP blow-up, the ratio of each sector's output to total GNP was assumed constant.

These tests closely approximated the conditions of the actual plan forecasting, for, although future final demands are not known, target levels are given for the application of the consistency model. Thus Professor Han's tests showed how well the I–0 model measured the total and sectoral output required to meet the final-demand targets.

The results of the tests are summarized in Table 5. The matrix $(I - A + M)^{-1}$ was used for the I–0 projections.

It is clear from the comparisons in Table 5 that the I–0 method is superior in accuracy, especially for individual sectors. In actual forecasting, many of the high individual-sector errors due to anticipation of major technological changes were no doubt reduced through forecasts of changes in the input-output coefficients.

This margin of superiority of the I–0 method is greater than the margin generally reported for advanced countries.[6] This margin may well be due to the relative stability of engineering-based relationships compared to more aggregate economic relationships in a period of rapid economic development.

Implementation of the model. The Korean model was implemented in two stages. In the first stage a single set of exogenous final-demand projections was used, along with the structural coefficients for 1963—in 1965 prices—to make a straightforward projection of total output, investment, and imports through the Second Plan period. This projection resulted in excessively high levels for all three totals, indicating the need for a general scaling down. Information from the first run was then used as a guide in adjusting both the exogenous demands and the coefficients to reflect known or expected changes in the economy and to move toward a feasible solution.

In the second stage, six sets of exogenous projections were used, reflecting different patterns of import substitution and export expansion as well as different levels of private consumption and exogenous investment. There were eleven different assumptions altogether, which should have been tried independently of each other, but, to limit the computational demands, they were combined into six cases that reflected mutually consistent assumptions (see Table 6). The results of these six cases were then compared, particularly in terms of the ratios of investment to growth of

---

[6] See, for example, C. F. Christ, "A Review of Input-Output Analysis," in *Input-Output Analysis: An Appraisal*, 1955; and Michio Hatanaka, *Testing the Workability of Input-Output Analysis* (Princeton, Princeton University Press, 1960).

TABLE 5.   ERRORS IN VARIOUS PROJECTION METHODS

	I–O	GNP	Final demand
I. Projecting 1963 output			
Weighted absolute average error	10.5%	24.7%	19.3%
Weighted algebraic average error	−3.0%	−4.0%	3.6%
Coefficient of variation[a]	0.1589	0.2959	0.3337
II. Projecting 1960 output			
Weighted absolute average error	11.2%	19.9%	16.9%
Weighted algebraic average error	3.2%	13.9%	4.8%
Coefficient of variation[a]	0.1480	0.3342	0.2838

[a] Defined as

$$\frac{(\Sigma \, d_i^2/n)^{\frac{1}{2}}}{\Sigma \, X_i/n}$$

where

X_i = actual output of sector i
$d_i = X_i - \hat{X}_i$
n = number of sectors

(The weighted average algebraic error can be taken as a measure of the error in predicting total output.)

TABLE 6.   COMBINATIONS OF ALTERNATIVE ASSUMPTIONS

I. List of alternatives for each variable
  A. Imports
    A. Low import substitution—$846 million of imports in 1971
    B. Build steel complex—$794 million
    C. Build petrochemical complex—$816 million
    D. Build steel and petrochemical complex—$694 million
  B. Exports
    1. Primary products and textiles—$550 million of exports in 1971
    2. Low export—$465 million
    3. Diversified manufacturing goods—$542 million
  C. Changes in exogenous investment
    α High
    β Low
  D. Personal consumption
    H. High
    L. Low

II. Combinations of all variables considered in constructing the basic plan

Variant	Imports	Exports	Exogenous investment	Personal consumption
1	C	1	β	L
2	C	1	α	H
3	C	3	α	H
4	A	1	α	H
5	D	2	α	L
6	B	3	β	L

output and to employment for the plan period as a whole. The case that was chosen as the basic guide for the plan was the one that produced the best composite results under those two criteria. No elaborate weighting system, as between output and employment, was used for this selection because the results were not considered sufficiently precise. However, the selected case (variant 3) ranked highest in terms of employment and second highest on output per unit of investment, and its assumptions were those most closely consistent with the planners' preconceptions (see Table 7).

The most interesting parts of the model-implementation process involved the adjustment of the input-output coefficients and the related consideration of alternative paths of import substitution. On the basis of the first-run solution, the industry committees were asked to estimate the changes that might occur in the composition of output from their respective sectors and the degree to which domestic production might be expanded or initiated to take the place of competitive or noncompetitive imports. They also were asked to reassess each sector's input structure, especially as a consequence of starting new types of production.

The initial response of most committees was to postulate a high degree of substitution for imports of domestically manufactured goods, which resulted in an almost complete elimination of dependence on imports, except for basic raw materials not found in Korea. The committees, reminded of the limitations on the amount of investment that could be made in the next five years, were given the general guideline that they should consider substitution only in areas where the cost of domestic products would not exceed the cost of comparable imports. There was also some divergence of views between the supplying and the using sectors; the specialists responsible for a supplying sector would propose domestic production of a particular commodity but those responsible for the using sector would be opposed to this, either on the grounds of inferior quality or higher cost for the domestic product. The fact that many manufacturing sectors were exporting an increasing share of their products caused the industry specialists to be particularly concerned about

TABLE 7. COMPARISON OF ALTERNATIVE PLANS

Variant	Capital per unit of output increase	Employment per unit of output increase	Balance of payments (in $)
1	2.97	.550	266
2	2.81	.589	266
3	2.77	.606	274
4	2.70	.524	296
5	2.91	.545	229
6	2.82	.556	282

the cost and quality of intermediate inputs. This served as a check on overambitious programs of import substitution.

Impact of the model on the investment program. At the time of the plan's construction, two major undertakings were being considered: a petrochemical complex and an integrated steel mill. Each undertaking would absorb about 10 percent of the prospective total investment in manufacturing during the period of the Second Plan and it appeared doubtful that both major investments could or should be undertaken concurrently. It was decided to test the alternatives in the context of the full model by examining four different patterns of import substitution, corresponding to building neither project, building both of them, or building one or the other.

The solution of the model indicated that the best results, both in terms of growth of output and employment, were associated with construction of the petrochemical complex. On the other hand—even without the assumption of significant import substitution for steel—it appeared that the projected growth of demand for steel and steel products over the five-year period would be sufficient to absorb the production of a minimum-size (500,000 ton) steel plant by the end of the Second Plan. Thus the conclusion, as presented in the plan documents, was to proceed first with construction of the petrochemical complex, in the early years of the Second Plan, and to build the steel mill in the later years—if further analysis corroborated the demand projections and if the mill could be fitted within the total investment program.

In addition to influencing the planned timing of the petrochemical and steel projects, the sectoral model had other types of impact on the final investment program of the plan. Probably most important was the indication it gave of the potential growth of demand for the products of different sectors. These, in turn, could be translated into demands for particular commodities by disaggregating from the 43-sector to the 270-sector coefficients and by making some assumptions about the growth of the major using sectors, final demands, and import substitutes. As has been mentioned, demand analysis was the weakest part of the project proposals, and the sectoral model not only provided guidance in this area but forced a systematic consideration of the assumptions underlying any particular set of demand projections.

Another significant contribution of the sectoral model was its indication of various sectors for which either project proposals were insufficient or adequate investment funds had not been earmarked. Quite naturally, the project proposals that had been submitted to or devised by the planning authorities tended to be the larger-scale, relatively capital-intensive projects. A preliminary program of investment projects in mining and manufacturing, which had been prepared independently of the sectoral model, was about 30 percent smaller than the program indicated by the model and was weighted significantly toward heavy industry. A number of light industries, such as food processing, finished textiles, leather products, and printing and publishing, had been largely overlooked.

After comparing the project program and the sectoral model investment program, it was decided to reapportion the total investment by allocating more money to manufacturing, by earmarking allocations for a number of sectors for which there were no project proposals, and by cutting back on the programmed amounts for some of the heavy industry sectors. The result was an investment program that was better balanced and more feasible. Many of the industries that were neglected in the project program are those in which the government has little direct involvement, either as a sponsor or financer of the projects. If investment were undertaken by the private sector in response to growing demand and if corresponding cutbacks were not made in the investments more directly controlled by the government, total investment expenditures could become excessive.

Subsequent applications of the model. Since the formulation of the Second Five-Year Plan, the sectoral model has been modified to reflect some obvious structural changes in the economy and has been used to explore the feasibility and the implications of higher growth rates, as well as changes in the composition of final demand. The results of runs with the modified model have been used in preparing the overall resources budgets for 1968 and 1969.

The original version of the sectoral model, it was found, underestimated the demands for power and transportation because the coefficients used for these sectors in the 1963 input-output tables reflected supply constraints rather than normal demand. As the supplies expanded in subsequent years and various rationing devices were removed, the demands shifted upward.

A second modification of the model was the introduction of revised import coefficients that reflected the rapidly changing import levels and patterns after 1965. These shifts have been due to the relaxation of import controls, the greater availability of external financing for imports, and the heavy import demands of the rapidly growing export industries.

Because the Korean economy has continued to expand more rapidly than originally planned and because the composition of final demand has been changing, the overall resources budgets have had to reflect these changes and have had to propose modifications in the plan targets and investment programs. As one element in the preparation of these annual budgets, the sectoral model has been rerun with higher levels of demand for consumption, exports, and investment, approximating 8, 10, and 12 percent compound annual GNP growth rates. The resulting demands for total investment and imports have been compared with savings and foreign-exchange availability estimates (obtained from a macro model) to assess the feasibility of the higher growth rates. After such comparisons, the combination of final-demand and import estimates that seemed most feasible and most nearly consistent with the targets of the policy-makers was chosen as the basis for the annual plan.

Some appreciation of the extent to which the sectoral growth-rate estimates have been changed since the Second Plan was formulated can be gained by comparing the results of the sectoral model run adopted for the 1969 overall resources budget with the growth rates projected in the original plan. To simplify the comparison, the original forty-three sectors can be consolidated into fourteen sectors and related to the growth rates in the preceding years, 1960 to 1965.

The Second Plan targets involved a decline from previous growth rates but the 1969 ORB projections involve a substantial increase. This change reflects, in part, the great growth of total output in 1966 and the continuing expansion of all sectors (except agriculture) in 1967. With these developments, the new projections of growth through 1971 have tended to restore the growth rate in five sectors to the 1960–65 levels—in agriculture, mining, food and tobacco, cement and ceramics, and machinery. In six other sectors (forestry and fisheries; wood, paper, leather, and rubber products; iron and steel and related products; construction; electricity; and transportation and communication) the new projections indicate sharply increased rates in comparison with the original plan and the past record. Several other sectors show mixed patterns.

TABLE 8. COMPOUND ANNUAL—GROWTH RATES

	Actual	Second Plan	1969 ORB
	1960/65	1965/71	1965/71
1. Agriculture	8.3	5.8	8.9
2. Forestry, fishery	4.8	12.0	14.5
3. Coal, other minerals	16.8	7.2	13.6
4. Food, beverage, tobacco	9.7	7.8	11.1
5. Textile goods	13.4	11.7	16.2
6. Wood, paper, leather, rubber	12.1	11.2	19.5
7. Chemical goods	14.0	17.0	16.0
8. Fertilizer, coal goods, petroleum	33.0	15.0	20.0
9. Cement, stone, ceramic	20.0	13.5	22.0
10. Iron, steel, metal goods	13.3	15.9	23.0
11. Machinery transport. equipment	25.0	13.9	29.0
12. Building construction	13.5	13.4	21.0
13. Elect. transpt. communication	13.8	9.7	20.0
14. Banking, trade services		7.0	
Total Growth Rate	11.0	9.3	14.2

The most significant implication of these new projections is the critical importance of rapid expansion in the output of construction materials and public utilities to meet the demands of rapid growth in the other sectors. Because it is very difficult to import or substitute for the services of the public utility sector, it is essential that these outputs be in adequate supply.

The growth elasticity (the ratio of the sectoral to overall output growth rate) for the public utility sector was 1.25 between 1960 and 1965 but was estimated at only 1.0 in the original version of the Second Plan. In the 1969 ORB, however, it is revised to 1.4, reflecting both the new use-coefficients and changing patterns of demand. To fail to anticipate such changes, and the needs of higher overall growth, would undoubtedly slow the progress of the whole economy.

Another continuing use of the sectoral model is its overseer function on progress in implementing the investment program. Each year the new projections of the sectoral output and investment requirements over the forthcoming five years are matched against the estimates of existing capacity, investment in process of construction, and projects under consideration—to see whether bottlenecks or surpluses are likely and may require corrective action by the government.

These consequences of the model, along with the systematic framework it provides for partial or overall analysis of the economy, appear to have more than justified the effort that went into its preparation. And several other benefits may be noted. First, many data were generated that are useful for project analysis, such as typical production and investment costs in all branches of manufacturing and mining. Second, the disaggregated census information underlying the construction of each new input-output table, and the results of the computations performed with it in the framework of a sectoral model, provide very valuable independent cross-checks upon the validity of the national income statistics.

Finally, the sectoral model seemed to offer a common ground or basis for communication between the engineer and the economist and between the operating official and the planner. It bridged the gap between the very aggregative terms of the national product accounts and the specifics of proposed projects, so that the technician (and the economist) could see where a particular program or industry fit into a somewhat wider plan. This factor contributed greatly to eliciting broader participation in the planning process.

CHAPTER 5 APPENDIX:
IMPLEMENTATION OF THE KOREAN SECTORAL MODEL

Marshall K. Wood,
David E. Labovitz

During 1967 the Korean sectoral model (described in the preceding portion of this chapter) has been revised and extended in a number of ways. The sectoral classification of the model has been expanded to incorporate 110 domestic producing sectors and 34 noncompetitive import sectors, plus four value-added and seven final-demand columns. The input-output coefficients have been completely revised, based on a balanced 1965 transactions table. The computational model has been reformulated as a sequential economic programming system, with an annual time-recursive macro structure and a "triangular" sequence of activities within each year. This sequential programming system has been implemented in a form that is suitable for hand computation, using desk calculators or abacuses, together with printed worksheets. Implementation of the model for computer calculation is in progress. Further extensions, to provide regional detail and to reflect interregional trading and migration relationships, are contemplated.

Early in 1966 the U.S. National Bureau of Standards was asked to prepare an improved sectoral model. The interindustry portion of the 270 sector 1963 coefficient table, the basic data for this model, was furnished by the Bank of Korea on punched cards, with separate coefficients for domestic and imported products. The cards contained many errors, however, mainly due to transcribing and punching errors, and to correct these errors and to rebalance the table, the 1963 transactions were reconstructed and checked against the published data. This difficult and time-consuming task was complicated by the fact that the division between purchases of domestic and imported products was not published. (Large differential price changes between domestic and imported goods made this a critical deficiency of the data.)

The first sectoral model computations, made about mid-1966, used estimated 1965 input coefficients that were derived by price adjusting the 1963 input coefficients. Each coefficient in the interindustry portion of the table was multiplied by the 1965 to 1963 price index of the producing sector and divided by the price index of the consuming sector. This procedure for updating an input coefficient matrix is often used because of its relative simplicity. It always gives inconsistent results, however, because only one set of relative prices is consistent with the implicit technical coefficients of any input-output table. If relative prices change, the implicit technical coefficients also must change. Generally, it is assumed that the discrepancies can be absorbed in the value-added components, and for small relative price changes this is not an unreasonable assumption. However, Korea experienced large and highly variable price changes between 1963 and 1965 (see Figure A-1), and the assumption therefore was open to serious question. Further analysis showed the assumption that discrepancies could be absorbed in the value-added components was indeed untenable. When the input-output table was constructed, the implicit value-added component was negative for 43 of the 270 sectors, and the value-added ratios averaged 5 percentage points lower than those for 1963. This suggested a bias in the price indices.

The Bank of Korea staff then reviewed the price indices and produced a considerably different set, using data from a number of additional sources and allowing more adequately for major shifts in the weights of the component commodities between 1963 and 1965. When these price indices were applied to the I-O coefficient matrix, the discrepancies between the implicit 1965 and the actual 1963 value-added ratios, though still large, were considerably reduced. Evidence of a consistent bias between finished products and raw materials had also diminished. However, a number of sectors had implicit negative value-added ratios in 1965.

To determine whether these imputed 1965 value-added estimates were reasonable, the Bank of Korea was asked to make independent estimates of the 1965 value-added components by sector, based on the monthly small-sample data they collect for preparing the national accounts. This was done in the form of indices of change between 1963 and 1965, which were to be applied in some cases to individual sectors and in other cases to groups of sectors. These indices of change were applied to the corrected 1963 value-added components to construct estimates of the 1965 value-added components. However, the aggregate value-added resulting from the process was nearly 20 percent lower than the revised GNP, so little use could be made of these indices.

Further revisions and extensions of the sectoral model were made at the National Planning Association, starting in the summer of 1967. There were many large differences between the first and the second sets of BOK sectoral price indices, and large discrepancies between the imputed value-added ratios and the "actual" value-added ratios. It was thought that these discrepancies resulted primarily from errors in the price indices or other systematic factors, and that accurate estimates could be made by using mathematical procedures to adjust the observations. Initial plans were to use a procedure substantially equivalent to Richard Stone's "RAS procedure" for reflecting technological change.[1] However, analysis and

---

[1] Richard N. Stone (ed.), *A Programme for Growth*, Vol. 3: *Input-Output Relationships, 1954-1956* (5 vols.; Cambridge, Mass.: The M.I.T. Press, 1963), pp. 27-41.

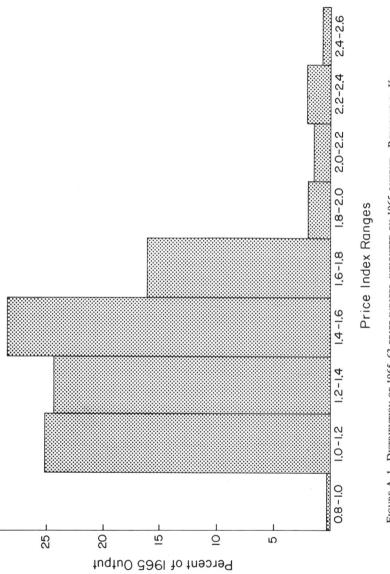

FIGURE A–1. DISTRIBUTION OF 1965–63 PRICE INDICES, WEIGHTED BY 1965 OUTPUT—REPUBLIC OF KOREA.

careful examination of the data proved that such an adjustment would be unsatisfactory. This led to a detailed examination of the model that began with the control totals and was extended to a detailed examination and revision of almost all the large individual cells of the table.

This examination caused revision of much of the data. The BOK produced new output estimates, based on the 1966 census, and the benchmark revisions of the national accounts were made. The use of these data changed the 1965 output estimates by approximately the ratio of the revised 1966 output estimates over the original 1966 output estimates. These output changes (restricted by balance constraints on the individual rows) greatly reduced the discrepancies in the interindustry portion of the table. Most of the remaining inconsistencies were resolved by reestimating the large coefficients from the 1966 census input data.

After an approximate balance of the rows was achieved, the columns were roughly balanced. This was an iterative process, with repeated alternations between row and column adjustments, which resulted in further revisions of the output estimates. In all cases, care was taken to maintain a reasonable time-series relationship between the 1965 output estimates and the deflated 1963 and 1966 output estimates.

Other minor adjustments were made to produce a fully balanced 110 sector input-output table for 1965 that was consistent with the control totals of the revised national accounts. Coefficients from this table have been used as the basis for a sequential programming system.

Reformulation of the model as a sequential programming system. The sectoral model that was presented earlier has been reformulated in the framework of a sequential economic programming system.[2] Sequential economic programming, a man-machine system, depends on human participation for the formulation of problems, the interpretation and analysis of results, and value judgments about the consequences of all proposed programs. This kind of system reflects a circular interdependence among goals, instrumentalities, and means, which is resolved in the model through explicit time lags and dynamic feedback relationships. The model projects sequentially from the present, in incremental annual stages, and each annual projection builds on the terminal status of the preceding year. The model simulates the behavior of decentralized decision-makers in an economy in which a substantial amount of purposive central direction and control is superimposed on a free market system. The model also is designed to assist decision-making about actions that are directed toward

---

[2] This name denotes a family of economic programming models that was developed by the National Planning Association and is now being adapted to several different substantive problems.

medium-term goals—by estimating the ramifications of implementing, in various combinations, proposed programs.

The basic distinguishing characteristic of the sequential programming system is its time- and activity-sequential structure. Historical time series and initial status data at the beginning of the first year are supplied exogenously. The decisions and economic activities of the first period are simulated, based on these data and on other exogenous policy and program stipulations for the first period. The simulation for the first period also constructs new initial status data for the second period, and updates the historical time series to provide a quasi-historical time series up to the beginning of the second period. This process is then repeated for each year in turn. There is no limit to the number of successive periods that can be projected (although the projections for more distant future periods obviously will be progressively lower in reliability).

For each year, activities are considered in a sequence so chosen that the primary determinants of demand against each activity either precede it in the computational sequence in the current period or precede it temporally.

If the input-output relationships in the production model are expressed in matrix form—as in a conventional input-output transactions table—we are free to permute any row and column without changing the basic relationships, provided the row and column permutations are identical. To achieve a sequential relationship, these permutations must be made so that they result in concentrating the transactions on or below the principal diagonal—so that the cells above the diagonal either are zero or very small. A computer algorithm has been developed to accomplish this.

The effect of this procedure is to order the activities so that the principal consumers of each commodity or service precede the producer in the computation sequence. Application of this algorithm to the 110 production sectors of the Korean input-output table for 1965 gives the following:

Percent determined by final demand and prior sectors	≥ 98	≥ 96	≥ 94	≥ 92	≥ 90	≥ 88	≥ 87
Number of sectors	31	48	62	73	91	98	110

Use of this triangular sequence permits a computational procedure that solves the system sequentially for each variable in turn, with only one unknown in each equation.

This sequential structure permits great freedom in designing the sub-models for specific activities. Any appropriate algebraic form or logical procedure may be used within the submodels for individual activities; one need not restrict himself to linear forms, as usually is necessary for working with the conventionally formulated types of large models in which simultaneous multivariate relationships are used. In this framework, it is also relatively easy to change the structure of individual subprogram modules without doing violence to the system's macro structure and to work with systems involving hundreds or thousands of variables. These are essential features for a large system, which can be created only gradually, on an incremental basis, and which must be continually modified, in an evolutionary fashion, if it is to be useful.

As each production activity is considered in turn, a series of sequential operations is performed, which leads to the simulation of the relevant production and investment decisions for the period.

Implementation of the sequential programming model. The sequential economic programming system has been implemented for Korea as a hand-computation procedure, suitable for use with abacuses or desk calculators. The initial model is quite similar in function to the sectoral model described earlier by Professor Adelman and her associates.

Implementation as a computer model is in process at the National Planning Association, using a small IBM 1130 computer. Later, it will probably be programmed for a larger computer to be installed in Seoul. Although initially implemented at the national level only, it is formulated and programmed so as to be easily expandable into an interregional model.

The most important substantive differences between the new model and the original sectoral model are (1) the great increase in level of detail and internal consistency of the current input coefficients and (2) the increased number and proportional coverage of the capital coefficients and the associated endogenous investment activities. The new model incorporates 112 domestic production activities, 94 endogenous investment activities, and 38 noncompetitive import rows.[3] These basic technological data are used to project—for each year of a program—the levels of industrial capacity, output, and imports that are consistent with the stipulated patterns of growth of final demand, import quotas, investment programs, and expected technological changes in input requirements.

The system operates sequentially, beginning with the base year, 1965. For each year's computation, and for each activity presented in the model, a projected time series of activity levels is generated. In the case of exogenous activities, these time series are constructed directly from the stipulations for the program under examination. For endogenous activities, the time series are based upon data and computations for previous years and

---

[3] All the current input coefficients are derived from a balanced 1965 input-output transactions table, as described in this appendix.

consist of time-series projections of the levels of operation or output of those activities. For investment activities, for example, these time series pertain to planned or expected capacity increments.

The computation for each year consists of reestimating the projected time series so as to incorporate (1) actual (computed) rather than anticipated (extrapolated) activity levels for the year in question and (2) improved estimates of future activity levels. Thus the sequential programming system is employed as a device for synthesizing technological and demand relationships among activities and for projecting—for all years of the program interval—a set of balanced and mutually consistent time series of activity levels for the individual economic activities represented in the model. These activity time series are then summarized and displayed, so as to facilitate analysis of the feasibility of the program and evaluation of alternative programs.

For each endogenous activity, each year's computations consist of three logically distinct operations.

First, an estimate is made of the total demand against the activity for current production. This estimate is based upon the levels of other activities (both endogenous and exogenous), together with technological coefficients that permit the computation from these activity levels of the corresponding input requirements for the product produced by the activity under consideration. The relevant technological coefficients may be adjusted for each "using" activity so as to reflect changes in production processes and product use, as well as changes in planned programs of import substitution. The production level for the activity under consideration is then set equal to the difference between the total demand for its product by other activities and the current availability of that product from inventory and competitive imports, net of the activity's production input requirements for its own product and for the stipulated (or generated) stock accumulation for the current period.[4]

Second, parallel to the computation for the current year, corresponding estimates are made of anticipated activity levels for each subsequent year, up to a stipulated horizon. This extrapolation involves the replacement of current estimates of future activity levels with improved estimates that are based upon corresponding estimates in other activities of future demand for the activity's product. As in the computation for the current

---

[4] Activity levels are constrained, of course, to be nonnegative, as production processes are not reversible. However, because competitive imports and minimum inventory levels are stipulated exogenously as part of the program being examined, no capacity constraints are imposed upon production levels. Instead, over- or under-utilization of capacity is used (as described below) to generate capacity adjustments through the expansion or retirement of capacity.

period, future-demand estimates reflect not only the anticipated activity levels of other activities but also the changes in technology that may be expected during successive periods.

Third, given an updated estimate of future production levels for the activity under consideration, a consistent program of capacity expansion is computed in accordance with stipulated capacity utilization objectives. The data for this computation consist of an activity-capacity time series, adjusted for retirements during the current period and for expected retirements during succeeding periods.

Within each year's computation, endogenous activities are carried out in triangular sequence (as described above). This procedure ensures that 80 to 90 percent (or more) of the total demand for each activity's product can be determined with certainty when an estimate of total demand for a particular product is required. The remaining demand, which cannot be determined with certainty until all activity levels are known for the current year, is then estimated on the basis of estimated activity levels for activities that come later in the computational sequence. This so-called upper-triangular demand is based upon activity levels that have been extrapolated from historical and quasi-historical time-series data for the activities in question.[5]

Changing technology and input and import substitution are implemented by mixing the base-year input coefficients (from the estimated 1965 input-output table) with balanced vectors of technological-change coefficients. Each vector of base-year input coefficients adds to unity; each vector of technological-change coefficients adds algebraically to zero. Thus any mixture of these vectors adds to unity, as is required for consistency in an input-output–based model. The mix proportions and the technological-change coefficients would be derived primarily from industry-committee studies. For each activity affected, the 1965 capacity that has been associated with modern technology, as well as the modern capacity expected for various future years, was estimated (in most cases for 1971).[6] The proportions of modern and traditional capacity are computed in the model (as a consequence of the investment decisions described earlier) for each year of the projection period. The technological-change coefficients are then applied to the computed proportions of modern capacity in each

[5] To support the computation of these upper-triangular demand increments, the time series of activity levels must be extrapolated for the full program interval before the computation is begun. However, because these extrapolated activity levels are used only for the computation of the relatively less important upper-triangular demand increments, the quality of the extrapolation procedure is not of critical importance to the success of the sequential economic programming technique.

[6] Modern capacity has been defined, arbitrarily, as capacity constructed since 1960.

year for estimating the change in input coefficients associated with the expected change in the proportion of modern to total capacity.[7]

Final demands for personal consumption, government consumption, and exports are stipulated exogenously, as in the sectoral model. The availability of competitive imports is stipulated in commodity detail, in a manner consistent with import-substitution targets. This forces domestic production (and investment) to provide the remaining quantities that are needed for each commodity, as generated in the model. Alternatively, it would be possible to stipulate investment in import-substitution industries, to impose a capacity constraint, and to derive competitive imports as a residual. Noncompetitive imports are generated by the model, separately for each of 38 commodity groups, as defined at the two-digit level of the Korean Standard Trade Classification.

The extension of this system to multiple regions will involve the replication of these processes for each region, as each activity is considered in turn within the triangular sequence. One or more interregional trade algorithms must then be introduced to allocate demand from consuming region to producing region. The method by which interregional demand is allocated determines the effective demand and hence the capacity utilization in the producing region—and thus indirectly influences the geographic allocation of investment. This interregional feedback process will be most important with respect to activities that are primarily residentiary in character. Investment decisions on major plants that are designed to produce for a national and/or an export market will normally be made exogenously, but these decisions will be influenced by their effect upon other residentiary activities, infrastructure investment, and local employment and income generation, direct and indirect. We hope to undertake the regional elaboration of the system as soon as the national version is adequately tested.

---

[7] When technological change is induced by import substitution, the technological change in the consuming industry can be related to the growth of domestic capacity in the industry that produces the material. In other cases the technological change is related to the proportion of modern capacity in the consuming industry, the result of investment (both for capacity expansion and for replacement of retired capacity) by the consuming industry. A variety of other endogenous variables, or combinations thereof, may — if desired — be used to control the phased incorporation of technological changes.

MULTISECTORAL PROJECT ANALYSIS EMPLOYING MIXED INTEGER PROGRAMMING

Larry E. Westphal

I. Introduction

The coordination of investment is one of the central tasks of development policy in Korea. At the project level, investment planning in most developing economies is typically carried out through the analysis of individual projects that are considered, more or less, in isolation from one another. The application of benefit-cost investment criteria is unwarranted, however, if industries are linked by intermediate products and if future product prices depend upon the set of projects selected for investment. If there are significant economies of scale, future product prices will certainly depend on the projects selected. Thus, one must rely on planning procedures that consider these sectors simultaneously, in order to reflect accurately the interdependence of the profitability of the several projects.

All projects do not equally influence the course of relative prices in the near future. The decision to build a large steel mill, for example, has much greater impact on the future price structure of the Korean economy than the decision to build a textile plant. A project must be examined in a general-equilibrium setting if it would require a large fraction of the investment budget and would result in a major change in relative prices. This is often the case when economies of scale are present.

The effects of economies of scale in one sector upon the optimal allocation of investment funds among other sectors have been discussed in terms of "external economies."[1] To date, there has been no operational means by which the external economies arising from a particular project

The author is indebted to Hollis B. Chenery, David C. Cole, and David A. Kendrick for many valuable suggestions offered during the course of this study. Computer time and research facilities were provided by the Project for Quantitative Research in Economic Development, at Harvard University, through Contract CSD–1543 from the Agency for International Development. The study was completed while the author held fellowships from the Ford Foundation and the Richard D. Irwin Foundation. I thank these organizations for making the study possible. Naturally, the responsibility for all statements and conclusions in this paper rests solely with the author.
[1] See Scitovsky (82).

can be satisfactorily included in a partial analysis of that project's benefits and costs. It therefore is necessary to turn to general-equilibrium analysis, where scarce resources are simultaneously allocated among sectors, so that there is no need to associate benefits and costs with particular investment projects.

This paper presents a dynamic, multisectoral optimizing model for investment planning. The model incorporates the effects of both economies of scale and interdependence among sectors within a framework that is appropriate for examination of the costs and benefits of large investment projects. External economies are internalized in the model as resources are simultaneously allocated to all sectors of the economy.

Dynamic input-output models usually are specified at a level of aggregation that is much higher than the level of the individual plant or project.[2] However, because investment decisions are made at the project level, a practical model must focus upon projects. To be operational, in the sense that solutions can be computed, the model must focus upon a small subset of specific projects. The projects that are most usefully singled out for detailed attention within a multisectoral framework are those that, through the competition for scarce investment resources or input-output relationships, are likely to have the greatest impact on the welfare gains from investment in the rest of the economy. Factors that are relevant to the investment decisions for these projects should be specified in considerable detail in the model, and details of the remainder of the economy be included only to the extent they ensure that competing demands by all sectors for scarce resources are adequately reflected.

The present model, which takes the latter approach, is applied to planning the timing of investment in a petrochemical plant and an integrated iron and steel mill in Korea, both of which are under serious consideration for the Second Five-Year Plan. The economies of scale in the construction of these plants and the cost of their construction (either project would require more than 5 percent of the budget for manufacturing investment in the SFYP) give rise to a strong argument in favor of analyzing the merits of each project within a multisectoral framework.

The model is described in section II, and some solutions are analyzed in section III. The Conclusion discusses the model's usefulness in determining the extent to which the construction of either plant would contribute to Korea's development goals.

II. The Model

Except for the inclusion of economies of scale and the treatment of import substitution, the model resembles those of Chenery and Kret-

---

[2] Consider, for example, the Korean sectoral planning model (117) that was used in formulating the SFYP.

schmer (14), Manne (58), Bruno (9), Eckaus and Parikh (23), and Chenery and MacEwan (15). Like the first four models, the Korean model emphasizes the choice between domestic production and imports to satisfy endogenously and exogenously generated demands; like the last two models, it also focuses on the optimal savings problem, though over a shorter period of time. The model is formulated as a dynamic input-output model with inequality constraints, import alternatives, and foreign-capital inflows. As a mixed-integer programming model, it draws on the work of Chenery and Westphal (18).

Economies of scale in capacity construction in the petrochemical and steel sectors are included by means of fixed-charge cost functions. The cost of capacity is typically related to the scale of the plant through the equation: Total cost $= a(\Delta c)^b$, where a is a constant, Δc is the scale of plant, and b is the elasticity of total cost with respect to scale. In the construction of petrochemical plants and integrated steel mills, b has been found to range between 0.6 and 0.8.[3] To obtain a solvable model, the constant elasticity cost function has been approximated by a fixed-charge cost function of the form: Total cost $= B^a\delta + B\Delta c$, where B^a is a fixed charge that is incurred only if capacity is built and B is the unit cost of construction. δ is equal to zero if a plant is not constructed, and is equal to 1 if a plant, regardless of size, is built. The fixed-charge cost function closely approximates the constant elasticity cost function over a wide range of plant sizes.[4]

The Korean model is linear except for the specification of fixed-charge capacity-cost functions in the two sectors noted above. Consequently, linear programming cannot be used to obtain solutions, and recourse is made to mixed-integer programming techniques.[5] A "branch and bound" mixed-integer programming solution algorithm, developed by Davis, Kendrick, and Weitzman (20), has been used to compute solutions.

Treatment of Production and Import Substitution

The sectors in the model are divided into "traditional" sectors and import-substituting "complexes."[6] The fifteen traditional sectors cover all production in the economy that competed with imports in 1966. The relevant input-output data and investment cost figures are based on

---

[3] See Haldi and Whitcomb (33) and Ramseyer (75).
[4] Haldi (32) was the first to use this approximation in a multisectoral programming model designed for illustrative purposes.
[5] See Dantzig (19:545) for the formulation of a fixed-charge cost function in mixed integer–continuous variable form.
[6] Hereafter the petrochemical plant and the integrated steel mill will often be referred to as "complexes."

historical statistics that have been modified to reflect structural changes thought to have occurred by the end of 1966.[7]

The two projects that have been singled out for special attention are largely import-substituting investments. The product mix and the technology assumed for each plant were predetermined on the basis of engineering studies.[8] No petrochemicals (plastics, synthetic fibers, or synthetic rubber), at any stage of production, are currently produced in Korea. There are, on the other hand, facilities for producing iron and crude steel and for processing light steel sheets and bars for use in construction. But the Korean steel industry is unbalanced: the bulk of pig iron production goes into castings, so that the tonnage of crude steel production is less than half that of iron, and most of the steel production is based on the use of scrap. The integrated steel mill is proposed to redress the imbalance between pig iron and crude steel production and to introduce the production of more specialized steel products and heavier forms of rolled products.

Since the integrated steel mill involves import substitution and the expansion of an already existing (albeit incompletely rationalized) industry, three classes of unfinished ferrous metal products have been distinguished: traditional iron and crude steel, traditional steel products, and formerly noncompetitive iron, crude steel, and steel products.[9] The model includes sectors that produce traditional iron and crude steel and traditional steel products by the existing techniques, and it distinguishes three production activities for the integrated mill: iron and crude steel, steel products, and the provision of formerly noncompetitive iron, crude steel, and steel products. Since the model embodies alternative means of producing traditional iron and crude steel and traditional steel products, there are nineteen production activities but only seventeen commodities.

Three sectoral categories have been distinguished in the model: commodity, capacity, and production. Commodity 17 is nontraditional iron, crude steel, and steel products; capacity sector 17 is integrated mill; and production activities 17, 18, and 19 correspond to the production in the integrated mill of iron and crude steel, steel products, and formerly noncompetitive iron, crude steel, and steel products, respectively. For the fifteen traditional sectors and for petrochemicals, the three classifica-

---

[7] The derivation of the structural parameters used in the model is discussed in Westphal (86).

[8] See Westphal (86) for the project feasibility studies employed in specifying the parameters for the two complexes.

[9] Iron and crude steel are distinguished from steel products since the former may be imported to produce the latter, and even if both are domestically produced, the proper balance between the two is not *a priori* determinant.

TABLE 1. SECTOR CLASSIFICATION IN THE MODEL

I. Traditional sectors
    1. Agriculture, Forestry, and Fishery (1, 2, 3, 4)
    2. Coal and Other Minerals, Coal Products (5, 6, 32210/270, 32990/270)
  *3. Processed Foods, Beverages, Tobacco, Forestry Products, Printing and Publishing (7, 8, 12, 13, 14, 15)
    4. Fiber Spinning (9)
    5. Textile Fabrics and Products (10, 11)
    6. Leather and Rubber Products, Miscellaneous Light Manufactured Products (16, 17, 32)
    7. Chemicals (18, 19, 20)
    8. Fertilizer (21)
    9. Petroleum Fuels and Lubricants (32300/270)
 *10. Cement and Earthen Products, Construction (23, 24, 33, 34)
  11. Iron and Crude Steel (25)
  12. Steel Products (26)
  13. Finished Metal Products, Non-ferrous Metals (27, 28)
 *14. Machinery and Transport Equipment (29, 30, 31)
  15. Electricity, Water, Commerce, Transport and Services (35, 36, 37, 38, 39, 40, 41)

II. Import substituting complexes
  16. Petrochemicals Complex (Includes all stages of petrochemicals processing up to and including the production of plastic resins, synthetic rubber polymers, and synthetic fiber intermediates prior to conversion to filament.)
  17. Integrated Iron and Steel Mill (Includes both traditional iron and crude steel and steel products, and formerly non-competitive types of iron and crude steel and steel products.)
    Corresponding to capacity sector 17 are three production activities:
  17. Iron and crude steel produced in the integrated mill
  18. Steel products produced in the integrated mill
  19. Provision of non-traditional iron, crude steel, and steel products from the production of the integrated mill (corresponds to commodity class 17)

Notes: The numbers in parentheses appearing after each traditional sector are the numbers of the included sectors in the 43 sector aggregation scheme of the Bank of Korea (1963 Input-Output Table).

A "*" designates a sector which produces capital goods.

tion schemes coincide and the numerical designations are the same for each sector in each class. Thus, for example, sector 4 is fiber spinning in all three classification schemes (see Table 1 for the various numerical designations).

An outline of production activity is given in Chart 1, which shows, in tableau format, the input-output production functions for the nineteen production activities. From left to right, fifteen activities are shown for the traditional sectors, another activity for petrochemicals, and three activities for production in the integrated steel mill. (A_{ij} stands for input-output coefficients.) Production activity 19 takes iron, crude steel, and the steel products produced in the mill in fixed proportions and "transforms" them into nontraditional unfinished ferrous metal products. (Q_i determines the proportion of iron and crude steel [$i = 1$] and steel products [$i = 2$] needed for import-substituting production in the new mill.) Henceforth the elements in the production-activity tableau will be designated A_{ij}^*.

CHART 1. PRODUCTION ACTIVITY TABLEAU: THE A* MATRIX

From \ To	Traditional sectors	Iron and steel mill			
		Petro-chemicals	Iron & crude steel	Steel products	Non-traditional ferrous products
Traditional commodities	$1 - A_{1,1}$ —— $-A_{1,15}$	$-A_{1,16}$	$-A_{1,17}$	$-A_{1,18}$	0
	$-A_{i,j}$				0
			$1 - A_{11,17}$		$-Q_1$
				$1 - A_{12,18}$	$-Q_2$
					0
	$-A_{15,1}$ —— $1 - A_{15,15}$	$-A_{15,16}$	$-A_{15,17}$	$-A_{15,18}$	0
Petrochemicals	$-A_{16,1}$ —— $-A_{16,15}$	$1 - A_{16,16}$	0	0	0
Non-traditional iron & steel	$-A_{17,1}$ —— $-A_{17,15}$	0	0	0	1

Figure 1 indicates the major supply-and-demand relationships between production in the complexes and production in the traditional sectors.

Activities in the Model

The model is run over three periods of two years each: 1967–68, 1969–70, and 1971–72. Each period or cycle of activity is composed of seven sets of activities (the time subscript, t, is omitted except where needed for clarity):

1. Production, x_n
2. Increments to capacity, Δc_n
3. Imports, m_n
4. Exports, e_n
5. Foreign-exchange borrowing, b, and repayment, rp
6. Accumulation of foreign-exchange reserves, Δs^f
7. Consumption, cn^t.

All production and capacity creation is endogenous. The investment function for each of the complexes involves two variables: δ_n, the zero–one integer variable determining the fixed-charge cost of capacity creation and Δc_n, the amount of capacity created. A common capacity constraint is shared by the activities that represent production in the integrated steel mill.

Imports of all products (with the exception of overhead and services that are not traded) are endogenous, as are exports of petrochemicals. For computational simplicity, all other exports are determined exogenously by projections of export demand and commodity availability.

Foreign-exchange accumulation is specified relative to the initial level of foreign-exchange reserves in the economy. Income earned by Koreans who work abroad is exogenously determined and is important only in the foreign-exchange constraint. Exogenous foreign-capital inflows and net factor income from abroad are included in f_t. Government demands for goods and services, g_n, also are exogenous. The sum total of production activity in the model yields gross domestic product less direct employment of persons by the government and the household sectors.

All magnitudes in the model are measured in billions of Korean *won* (270 *won* = \$1). Capacity is stated in terms of the yearly output available from the normal operation of plant and equipment.

Constraints in the Model

The major constraints pertain to the use of capacity in each sector, the use of foreign exchange, and the availability of domestic savings. There are no labor constraints in the model. All variables and parameters are defined in the Glossary at the end of this chapter.

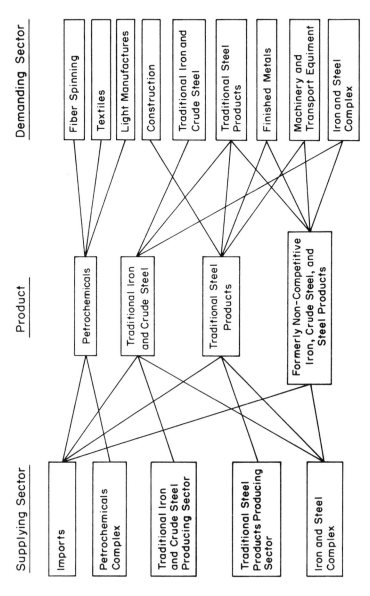

FIGURE 1. FLOW DIAGRAM FOR PETROCHEMICALS AND FERROUS METALS.

Commodity balance.

$$m_i + \sum_{j=1}^{19} A_{ij}^* x_j - \Delta k_i - cn_i = g_i + e_i \qquad i = 1, \cdots, 17 \qquad \text{(A)}$$

The first fifteen equations equate the supply and demand for the traditional sector outputs; the last two equations equate the supply and demand for the formerly noncompetitive goods produced in the two complexes. All production in the petrochemical complex is used for import substitution, and x_{19} gives the amount of the integrated mill's output that is devoted to import substitution.

Supply consists of domestic production and imports.[10] Demand is divided into five parts:

1. Intermediate demand for use in production, reflected through the input-output coefficients, A_{ij} and Q_i (see Chart 1)
2. Investment demand for capacity creation, Δk_i
3. Private consumption demands, cn_i
4. Exogenous demands for exports, e_i[11]
5. Exogenous demand on government account, g_i

Private consumption demand.

$$cn_{i,t} = (P_t/P_0)S_i^a + S_i\, cn_t^T \qquad i = 1, \ldots, 15 \qquad \text{(B1)}$$

$$\sum_{i=1}^{15} cn_{i,t} = cn_t^T \qquad \text{(B2)}$$

The demand for traditional commodities is determined by a set of marginal propensities to consume out of total consumption expenditure, S_i. The intercepts and slopes of these relationships can be varied to approximate any income demand elasticity. Since the demand elasticities from which the coefficients in equation B1 were derived pertain to per capita consumption, a correction for anticipated population changes is applied to the intercept term, S_i^a. P_t is the sum over the period of the population in each year of that period.

Demand for investment goods.

$$\Delta k_i = \sum_{j=1}^{17} B_{ij}\Delta c_j + \sum_{j=16}^{17} B_{ij}^a \delta_j + E_i\Delta c_i \qquad i = 1, \ldots, 15 \qquad \text{(C1)}$$

[10] Imports of overhead and services (sector 15) are excluded.
[11] Exports of overhead and services (sector 15) and nontraditional unfinished ferrous metal products (17) are not allowed, and exports of petrochemicals (16) are endogenous.

$$\Delta k_{16} = E_{16}\Delta x_{16} \tag{C2}$$

$$\Delta k_{17} = E_{17}\Delta x_{17} + E_{18}\Delta x_{18} \tag{C3}$$

$$\Delta k_{\text{hous.}} = B_{10,\text{hous.}} cn^T \tag{C4}$$

Input-capacity coefficients, B_{ij}, define the demand for investment use in terms of the gross additions to capacity in each sector, Δc_i. Stock accumulation is endogenous and is tied to the producing, rather than the using, sector.

Equation C1 defines the demand for the traditional sector outputs for use on investment account. Equations C2 and C3 define stock accumulation in the two complexes. Stock accumulation in the traditional sectors is defined as taking place when capacity is created; in the complexes, it is defined as occurring when output increases. The latter would seem to be the better specification, but the fact that the model is solved in a reduced form makes the former a more convenient formulation for the traditional sectors. In equation C4, gross investment in housing is related to total consumption expenditure by a regression based on the national income accounts. $B_{10,\text{hous.}}$ is the parameter in this relation.

Foreign exchange use.

$$\sum_{i=1}^{18} M_i^n x_i + \sum_{i=1}^{17} B_i^n \Delta c_i + \sum_{i=16}^{17} B_i^{na}\delta_i + \sum_{i=1}^{17} m_i + \Delta s^f$$

$$- b + rp \leq f + F\sum_{i=1}^{17} e_i \tag{D1}$$

$$\Delta s_1^f \geq 0 \tag{D2}$$

$$\Delta s_t^f \geq -\left(\sum_{u=1}^{t-1} \Delta s_u^f\right) \qquad t = 2, 3 \tag{D3}$$

The use of foreign exchange is restricted to the supply provided by exports plus net foreign-capital inflows and net factor incomes from abroad.[12] Demand for foreign exchange derives from the production of commodities and investment goods that require noncompetitive imports of intermediate goods, machinery, and the services of skilled technicians.

---

[12] The foreign exchange derived from exports is the sum of exports, measured in domestic prices and multiplied by a conversion factor, F, which translates domestic prices into f.o.b. export prices. A different conversion factor should be used for each sector's commodity, since freight, insurance, and tariff rates depend upon the sector as well as the destination of the exports. Unfortunately, data distinguishing between these prices at the sectoral level do not exist.

The other demand components are competitive imports and the net foreign-exchange accumulation of the period.[13]

Capacity constraints.

$$x_i - c_i^* \leq 0 \qquad i = 1, \ldots, 16 \tag{E1}$$

$$x_{17} + x_{18} - c_{17}^* \leq 0 \tag{E2}$$

$$x_{19} - x_{18} - x_{17} \leq 0 \tag{E3}$$

Output in each sector is prohibited from exceeding the available capacity to produce, c_i^*. In equation E3, the use of the output of the integrated steel mill to replace formerly noncompetitive imports is restricted to less than, or equal to, the output of the mill.[14]

Capacity determination.

$$c_{i,t}^* = 2(1 - D_i)^{2(t-1)}c_{i,1} + \sum_{s=1}^{t-1} 2\Delta c_{i,s} \qquad i = 1, \ldots, 17 \tag{F}$$

Capacity in any sector in period t is equal to last period's capacity less depreciation plus the capacity expansion due to last period's investment. Capacity as stated in terms of normal yearly output, c_i, must be multiplied by 2 to obtain the output actually possible over a two-year period, c_i^*. The gestation period between initial investment and usable capacity is assumed to be the length of the period in which the investment takes place (two years) so that gestation lags will be included without the necessity of distinguishing the lags for different capital goods inputs. This formulation assumes that when plants come on line, they are immediately capable of producing at full "normal" capacity.

Depreciation occurs only in the fifteen traditional sectors and is related to the capacity existing at the beginning of the planning period.[15] D_i is the yearly depreciation rate of capacity. The planning horizon is too short for a new plant to deteriorate or sufficiently obsolesce to cause normal output to decline.

Competitive import bounds.

$$m_i \leq \mu_i \qquad i = 1, \ldots, 14 \tag{G}$$

Competitive imports of the traditional sector's commodities are bounded

---

[13] A transformation is applied to $\Delta s'$ so that the transformed variable (the accumulated change in reserves) is always positive.

[14] In practice, this equation has been sufficient to ensure that $Q_1 x_{19} \leq x_{17}$ and $Q_2 x_{19} \leq x_{18}$.

[15] Recall that capacity in sectors 16 and 17 is initially zero.

from above by μ_i, which generally equals between 10 and 15 percent of total imports within the period. These bounds are introduced in place of nonlinear or step functions for production in the traditional sectors. Without the bounds and with constant costs, a sector's entire supply could be provided through imports. Bounds on competitive imports are used, rather than step functions or further disaggregation of the sectors, because of the lack of empirical knowledge that is necessary for specifying step production functions and the ever-present problem of computational capacity.[16]

Private consumption and savings bounds.

$$cn_t^T \geq (P_t/P_0)cn_0^T(1 + \epsilon)^{2t} \tag{H1}$$

$$\left.\begin{array}{l} -\sigma \displaystyle\sum_{j=1}^{18} V_j \Delta x_{j,t} + \displaystyle\sum_{j=1}^{17} B_j^T(\Delta c_{j,t} - \Delta c_{j,t-1}) + \displaystyle\sum_{j=16}^{17} B_j^{aT}\Delta\delta_{j,t} \\[2mm] + (\Delta k_{16,t} - \Delta k_{16,t-1}) + (\Delta k_{17,t} - \Delta k_{17,t-1}) + B_{10,\text{hous}}.\, \Delta cn_t^T \\[2mm] + (\Delta s_t^f - \Delta s_{t-1}^f) - \Delta b_t + \Delta rp_t + \Delta sl_{d.1,t} \leq \Delta f_t \end{array}\right\} \tag{H2}$$

These bounds—substitutes for a nonlinear objective function based on consumption—respectively place a floor under consumption in every period and a ceiling on the marginal propensity to save out of gross domestic product. The first constraint stipulates that per capita consumption must grow at a rate at least equal to ϵ. The second constraint holds the marginal savings propensity to less than σ. In H2 the first term determines the change in gross domestic product by means of the value-added coefficients, V_i. The next five terms define the change in investment and the remaining terms introduce a correction due to foreign-capital inflows and foreign-exchange accumulation, which is necessary to determine domestic savings.

Iron-and-steel complex bound.

$$\Delta x_i \geq 0 \qquad i = 17, 18 \tag{I}$$

This equation ensures that the composition of the output of the integrated mill will not change over time in a perverse fashion.

Integer constraints

$$\Delta c_{16} - Y_{16}\delta_{16} \leq 0 \tag{J1}$$

$$\delta_{16} = 1 \text{ if } \Delta c_{16} > 0; \quad \delta_{16} = 0 \text{ if } \Delta c_{16} = 0 \tag{J2}$$

---

[16] For interesting examples of models that use step production functions, see Nugent (70) and Adelman and Sparrow (1).

$$\Delta c_{17} - Y_{17}\delta_{17} \leq 0 \tag{J3}$$

$$\delta_{17} = 1 \text{ if } \Delta c_{17} > 0; \quad \delta_{17} = 0 \text{ if } \Delta c_{17} = 0 \tag{J4}$$

These constraints are used to obtain the desired fixed-charge cost functions for investment in the two complexes.

Terminal conditions and the objective function.

Terminal conditions in a dynamic planning model cannot be chosen independently of the objective function, and vice versa. It is a trite but true observation that the world, or in our case Korea, does not die with the final period of the model. The impact on the future of activity within the finite horizon of the planning model must, in some fashion, be included in the welfare function. The influence of future production upon plan-period activity, especially investment, also must be reflected. The usual procedure is to specify the amount and composition of investment in the terminal period of the model without a correction in the objective function. The Chenery-MacEwan model (15) uses a different approach, which is followed here.

Terminal growth constraint.

$$\sum_{i=1}^{16} V_i c_{i,4}^* + V_{17}^* c_{17,4}^* - (1+\gamma)^2 \left[\sum_{i=1}^{15} V_i c_{i,3}^* + \sum_{i=16}^{18} V_i x_{i,3} \right] \geq 0 \tag{K}$$

$$\left. \begin{array}{l} \displaystyle\sum_{i=1}^{16} V_i c_{i,4}^* + V_{17}^* c_{17,4}^* - (1+\gamma)^2 \left[\sum_{i=1}^{15} V_i c_{i,3}^* + \sum_{i=16}^{18} V_i x_{i,3} \right. \\[3ex] \left. - \Delta s_3^f + b_3 - rp_3 \right] \geq -f_4 + (1+\gamma)^2 f_3 \end{array} \right\} \tag{K'}$$

As in all models of this type, a constraint is required to assure that investment takes place in the terminal period of the planning horizon. Equation K provides for sufficient investment to assure a minimum post-terminal rate of growth of gross domestic product of not less than γ per annum. If full utilization of capacity in the post-terminal period is assumed, gross domestic product in that period will equal the sum of the value-added coefficients times the sectoral capacities available in the period (the first two terms in the equation). A feature of this specification, which is notable particularly in a model with economies of scale, is allowance for growth in output either from investment or from excess capacity in the terminal period in the sectors with economies of scale.

Equation K', which replaces K in some runs of the model, states that total sources (equal to gross domestic product plus foreign-capital inflow and net factor income from abroad less net foreign-exchange accumulation) must grow by at least γ percent. It is assumed that net foreign-capital borrowing and net foreign-exchange accumulation in the post-terminal period will be zero, as a matter of convenience. This slight change in the constraint's specification has the effect of keeping the model from using foreign-exchange accumulations for consumption in the terminal period without having to compensate for the increased consumption by additional investment.

Terminal capital stock bounds.

$$(1 + \gamma)^2 \phi_i x_{i,3} - c^*_{i,4} \geq 0 \qquad i = 1, \ldots, 14, 16 \tag{L1}$$

$$-(1 + \gamma)^2 x_{15,3} + c^*_{15,4} \geq 0 \tag{L2}$$

$$(1 + \gamma)^2 \phi_{17}(x_{17,3} + x_{18,3}) - c^*_{17,4} \geq 0 \tag{L3}$$

These constraints are necessary to avoid edge effects that would lead to terminal investment in one or, at most, only a few sectors. Placing upper bounds on the terminal capital stocks and relating them to the capital stock that would exist if all capital stocks were to grow at γ percent precludes this potential problem. The multiplicative factor in the upper bound constraints, ϕ_i, is always greater than 1.

It was necessary to use a lower bound on terminal investment in overhead and services to ensure an *a priori* appropriate amount of investment in that sector (see equation L2).

Terminal debt constraint.

$$\sum_{t=1}^{3} (1 + r)^{2(3-t)} b_t - \sum_{t=1}^{3} (1 + r)^{2(3-t)} r p_t \leq \tau \tag{M}$$

This equation reflects the fact that no underdeveloped country can obtain unlimited amounts of foreign capital at constant cost. τ is the maximum discounted value of debt that can remain in the terminal period. Interest charges on foreign borrowing are introduced by accumulating interest, at rate r, in the debt constraint.

The objective function.

$$\max W = \sum_{t=1}^{3} \frac{1 + (1 + \rho)^{-1}}{(1 + \rho)^{2(t-1)}} \frac{cn_t^T}{2} + \frac{1}{(1 + \rho)^6} \sum_{s=1}^{\infty} \frac{(1 + \gamma)^s}{(1 + \omega)^{s-1}} \frac{cn_3^T}{2}$$

The objective to be maximized is the discounted sum of consumption over an infinite horizon. The first term in the function includes consumption during the plan period, which enters the objective function discounted at rate ρ to the first year of the plan period. The awkward appearance of the term is due to the use of a one-year discount factor to discount consumption occurring in periods of two years.

The second expression is the value of post-terminal consumption that can be obtained by virtue of the terminal capital stocks. The terminal growth constraint can be interpreted as an injunction that the economy embark on a growth path along which consumption grows at rate γ, starting from the level of consumption achieved in the terminal period. Post-terminal consumption is assumed to grow at this rate and is discounted relative to the immediate post-terminal year. The rate of discount ω may differ from the plan-period rate of discount because of a nation's willingness to endure sacrifice for a short period to achieve a high plateau from which to initiate a path of constant growth.

The large weight on terminal consumption in the objective function has been rationalized in terms of giving post-terminal consumption value in the welfare function. This procedure, by indirectly giving value to the terminal capital stocks, eliminates the need to put terminal capital stocks directly into the welfare function.

Summary. Constraints A through J4 are repeated for each period of the plan. The objective function is maximized, subject to constraints A through M, and the additional condition that all variables be nonnegative.[17] Chart 2 is a tableau of the activities and constraints in each period of the model.

The Data

The structural parameter values actually used in the model are based on data similar to those used in the Korean sectoral planning model (117). Table 2 presents the values of some of the major parameters. It should be noted that the capital cost of the two complexes is dominated by the foreign-exchange component and that the return from building either complex is a large saving of foreign exchange due to lower requirements for noncompetitive imports.

III. Use of the Model in Project Analysis

Investment in either complex is characterized by lumpiness (i.e., a high proportion of the total economy-wide investment is required to build a single plant) and by increasing returns. The issues related to economies of scale involve the question of how much excess capacity should be permitted when the plant comes on line. By overbuilding capacity when plant con-

---

[17] As presented here, however, Δs^f may be negative.

CHART 2.   ONE PERIOD TABLEAU OF THE MODEL

No. of activities	15	1	1	1	1	15	1	1	1	1	15
Activity vector	x_t	$x_{16,t}$	$x_{17,t}$	$x_{18,t}$	$x_{19,t}$	Δc_t	$\Delta c_{16,t}$	$\Delta c_{17,t}$	$\delta_{16,t}$	$\delta_{17,t}$	m_t
Commodity balance:											
Traditional	$I - A$	$-A_{16}^c$	$-A_{17}^c$	$-A_{18}^c$	$-Q$	$-B - E$	$-B_{16}^c$	$-B_{17}^c$	$-B_{16}^a$	$-B_{17}^a$	$+I$
Petrochemical	$-A_{16}^r$	$1 + **$									
Steel mill	$-A_{17}^r$		$-E_{17}$	$-E_{18}$	$+1$						
Foreign exchange constraint	$+M^n$	$+M_{16}^n$	$+M_{17}^n$	$+M_{18}^n$		$+B^n$	$+B_{16}^n$	$+B_{17}^n$	$+B_{16}^{na}$	$+B_{17}^{na}$	$+L$
Exchange accumulation bound											
Capacity constraint:											
Traditional	$+I$										
Petrochemical		$+1$									
Steel mill											
Import bounds			$+1$	$+1$							$+I$
Consumption bound											
Savings bound	$-\sigma V$	$-\sigma V_{16}§$	$-\sigma V_{17}§$	$-\sigma V_{18}§$	-1	$+B^T$	$+B_{16}^T$	$+B_{17}^T$	$+B_{16}^{aT}$	$+B_{17}^{aT}$	
Steel mill bounds			$+1$ $+1$	$+1$							
Integer constraints:											
Petrochemical									Y_{16}		
Steel mill							-1		1	Y_{17}	
Terminal debt constraint								-1		1	

Activity vector	$m_{16,t}$	$m_{17,t}$	$e_{16,t}$	b_t	rp_t	Δs_t^f	cn_t	RHS	No. of Rows
(No. of activities)	1	1	1	1	1	1	1		
Commodity balance:									
Traditional							$-S$	$= (P_t/P_o)S^a + e_t + g_t$	15
Petrochemical	+1		-1					$\geq -E_{16}x_{16,t-1}$	1
Steel mill		+1						$\geq -E_{17}x_{17,t-1} - E_{18}x_{18,t-1}$	1
Foreign exchange constraint	+1	+1	$-F$	-1	+1	+1		$\leq f_t + F\sum_i e_{i,t}$	1
Exchange accumulation bound						+1		$\geq -\sum_{u=1}^{t-1}\Delta s_u^f$	1
Capacity constraint:									
Traditional								$\leq c_t^*$	15
Petrochemical								$\leq c_{16,t}^*$	1
Steel mill								$\leq c_{17,t}^*$	1
Import bounds								$\geq \mu_t$ ($\mu_{15,t}=0$)	15
Consumption bound							1	$\geq (P_t/P_o)cn_o^T (1+\epsilon)^{2t}$	1
Savings bound								††	1
Steel mill bounds				-1	+1	+1	$B_{10,hous.}$	≥ 0	1
								$\geq x_{17,t-1}$	1
								$\geq x_{18,t-1}$	1
Integer constraints:									
Petrochemical								≥ 0	1
								$= 1$ or 0	1
Steel mill								≥ 0	1
								$= 1$ or 0	1
Terminal debt constraint				$+(1+r)^{\dagger}$	$-(1+r)^{\dagger}$			$\leq \tau - \sum_{u\neq t}(1+r)^{2(3-w)}(b_u - rp_u)$	1

Note: To simplify the presentation of this tableau, vectors and constraints relating to the sectors have been decomposed into the fifteen traditional sectors, petrochemicals, and relevant steel mill sectors. Letters without super- or subscripts (other than those generally employed) denote the traditional sectors, self-explanatory special superscripts and subscripts are used to denote non-traditional sectors; "r" indicates row; "c" column.

**: $-A_{16,16} - E_{16}$. §: Includes $+E_{16}$, $+E_{17}$, $+E_{18}$ respectively. †: $2(3 - t)$.

††: $\Delta f_t + \Delta s_{t-1}^f + B^T\Delta c_{t-1} + B_{16}^T\Delta c_{16,t-1} + B_{17}^T\Delta c_{17,t-1} + B_{16}^{aT}\delta_{16,t-1} + B_{17}^{aT}\delta_{17,t-1} + B_{10,hous.}cn_{t-1}^T$
$-\Delta sl_{d.1,t} - \sigma Vx_{t-1} - \sigma V_{16,t-1}^{\$} - \sigma V_{17,t-1}^{\$} - \sigma V_{18,t-1}^{\$} - b_{t-1} + rp_{t-1}$.

TABLE 2. SUMMARY INFORMATION—KOREAN PLANNING MODEL

									Sectors									
	1	2	3	4	5	6	7	8	9	10	11	12	13	14	15	16	17	18
Input-output coefficients (A_{ij})																		
1. Agriculture	.09	.03	.24	.36	.01	.02	.03	.03		.02	.06	.01	.07	.01	.02		.09	.01
2. Mining		.17	.01	.01		.01	.01	.06		.04	.01		.01	.03	.04	.01		
3. Food		.01	.13	.01		.04	.05			.10								
4. Fiber spinning				.05	.37	.03									.01			
5. Textiles	.01	.01			.10	.05	.01	.01							.02			
6. Light manufacturing		.01	.01	.01	.01	.09	.06	.01					.01		.02			
7. Chemicals	.01	.03	.01		.01	.06		.08	.01	.01			.01		.02	.05		
8. Fertilizer	.06									.13								
9. Petroleum	.03	.01	.01				.01			.02								
10. Construction & cement		.01				.01	.02			.13	.05		.01	.02	.02		.04	.01
11. Iron & steel				.01	.01		.02			.05	.14	.36	.01	.01	.02		.03	.40
12. Steel products				.08	.09	.03	.01	.02		.04	.02	.07	.02	.02	.02		.21	.11
13. Finished metal products		.01		.16	.04	.01	.17			.03	.01	.03	.03	.01	.01		.01	.02
14. Machinery		.03	.01			.14				.12	.01	.01	.13	.08			.01	.01
15. Overhead & service	.03	.18	.12			.07	.17	.16	.04	.12	.06	.09	.12	.12	.12	.15	.11	.12
16. Petrochemicals																		
17. Iron-steel complex																		
Non-competitive imports (M_i^n)	.77	.01	.09	.01	.01	.11	.17	.01	.43	.02	.01	.10	.08	.06	.01	.12	.23	.09
Value-added coefficients (V_i)	.28	.48	.34	.29	.35	.30	.43	.59	.47	.37	.34	.09	.15	.08	.70	.59	.26	.21
Consumption demand (S_i)			.18		.10	.04	.02		.01	.03[c]			.01	.01	.33			
Capital/output (B_i^T, B_i^{aT})	1.17	.97	.40	.73	.39	.29	.47	1.89	.93	.80	.95	.52	.78	.50	1.54	1.84[a]	.95[b]	.95[b]
Imported mach./output (B_i^r)	.20	.19	.10	.44	.15	.09	.21	1.46	.67	.40	.19	.27	.21	.20	.39	1.53	.72	.72
Capital/value added (B_i^T/V_i, B_i^{aT}/V_i)	1.54	2.04	1.16	2.25	1.11	.96	1.11	3.17	1.95	2.15	3.69	2.48	2.26	1.68	2.21	3.12	3.65	4.52

Notes: All coefficients have been rounded to the nearest 100th. Totals may not reconcile due to rounding. $Q_1 = .18$; $Q_2 = .82$.

[a] Based on a petrochemicals complex of size 25 million won, double the planned size.

[b] Based on an iron and steel complex of size 44 billion won, the planned size.

[c] Includes induced investment in housing.

162

struction exhibits increasing returns, it is possible to decrease average unit costs. When, however, investment also is lumpy, overbuilding requires large amounts of investment resources, obtained either through increased domestic savings or foreign-capital inflows or at the sacrifice of capacity expansion elsewhere. Consequently, the questions to be asked in determining the optimality of lumpy investment in decreasing cost industries largely concern the resulting adjustments that must be made in the rest of the economy. Can the plant be financed without requiring a major reduction of investment elsewhere (e.g., by increased foreign borrowing)? If so, will its return be high enough to repay the cost expended in its construction? If not, are the returns from the investment sufficient to compensate for the large sacrifice of capacity elsewhere in the economy?

Where lumpiness and economies of scale are combined in the investment cost for a single plant, the return to the concentration of investment in that plant and in related industries (related through supply and demand) over a short period of time is high. If enough investment resources can be mustered, a large plant with low unit capacity costs can be built and immediately utilized due to the simultaneous investment in the suppliers of its intermediate inputs and the users of its output. If, however, the plant is financed through the reduction of investment in other sectors (particularly its related industries), potential domestic demand for the output of the plant must fall. In this case either a smaller plant must be built, with less reduction of investment in the rest of the economy, or greater excess capacity must be experienced when the plant comes on line. Both alternatives mean greater costs of production in the plant and lower profits, at least in the first few periods of its operation.

An alternative to creating overcapacity is to delay construction of the plant and to build up demand for its products, temporarily satisfied by imports. Then, when the plant comes on line, the demand for its output already exists—with less need for a large concentration of investment in the plant and the related industries. If the cost of importing the plant's output greatly exceeds domestic production costs, however, this pattern may be less attractive than the simultaneous concentration of investment in the related sectors or building up excess capacity in the supply-and-demand sectors prior to the plant's coming on line.

Finally, although available capacity is desirable in demand sectors when the plant comes on line, it is much less essential in the supply sectors, since the required intermediate goods can simply be imported. Then other imports must be cut back, or exports expanded, at the expense of providing capacity in the export industries (if we assume full-capacity production and unchanged foreign-exchange reserves).

The preceding discussion need not imply that production is constant or increases in every sector. Intermediate products can be obtained by cutting back production in other sectors that require the same intermediate goods, as sometimes occurs either through the death of old and inefficient industries or through a lack of sufficient planning.

In determining the optimality of investment in projects that require large amounts of investment resources, such as petrochemicals and iron and steel, it is necessary to determine whether investment in these industries will be at the expense of investment elsewhere and whether such expense is justified. It is justified if the foreign-exchange potentially no longer needed for imports of petrochemicals or nontraditional iron and steel can be used to permit a more rapid growth of supply in other sectors.

In summary, four determinations must be made:

1. What happens to the level of total investment if a complex is built?
2. What happens to investment in the using and the supplying industries related to the complex?
3. What is the effect on the size of the complex that is built and on its utilization?
4. How is the growth of supply in the rest of the economy affected?

The last point emphasizes supply rather than production because, in a trading world, the supply of goods and services is most relevant to welfare determination.

The answers to these four questions can be provided only by a multisectoral intertemporal model of the kind formulated above. In fact, the issues are suggested by the dynamic general-equilibrium system from which such a model is derived.

The economy's accommodation to investment in the two complexes is best explored by examining alternative solutions to a given specification, one in which the investment patterns in the complexes are varied. We can omit the third period from the description of the pattern because investment in this period was not optimal in any of the solutions obtained by the model; nor is the construction of more than one plant in each nontraditional sector ever optimal. Thus there are nine possible patterns of investment that are relevant, of which we shall consider only the patterns generated by the solution algorithm. The solution for each pattern is the optimal solution, given the pattern of investment in the complexes.

Analysis of Alternative Solutions

The model has been solved under a variety of assumptions about the availability of foreign capital, the required post-terminal growth rate, and the parameter values in the objective function. As might be expected, the optimality of building either complex was found to be most sensitive to the assumed amount and timing of foreign-capital inflows throughout the period.

The solutions to the model exhibit very high growth rates of gross domestic production (rates as high as 13 percent per annum are not unusual), largely because of the low unit cost of capacity in many sectors, coupled with the absence of capacity absorption limits or decreasing returns to investment activity as a whole.[18] In addition, the high value of consumption in the terminal period usually causes investment to approach its upper bound in the first two periods, and consumption growth therefore is near its lower bound.

As indicated in Table 3, the model yields a ranking of sectors by comparative costs: fiber spinning, fertilizer, petroleum, traditional iron and crude steel and steel products, finished metals, and machinery and transport equipment have high costs. Production in the complexes also ranks high in comparative cost. Consumer goods and intermediates to consumer-goods production have low comparative costs. The availability of foreign exchange determines which products are imported.[19]

We begin by examining alternative solutions to two specifications of the model. In both specifications the in-plan discount rate, ρ, has been set at zero (reflecting the desire of the Korean government for investment now, consumption later); the post-plan discount rate, ω, is 25 percent; and the minimum growth rate of per capita consumption is 2 percent.[20] In the first specification, foreign-capital inflows are exogenous—the borrowing and repayment activities are deleted from the model; in the second specification, foreign-capital inflows are endogenously determined on the basis of the interest rate on borrowing and the productivity of foreign exchange.

The treatment of foreign-capital inflows as exogenous is, admittedly, unrealistic, but in early experiments with the model such treatment had the virtue of simplifying interpretation. The Korean government has some control over the amount and the timing of foreign-capital inflows; one instrument of its control is the licensing of projects, since the foreign-exchange cost of large projects is generally financed abroad.[21] This aspect

[18] The incremental capital-output ratio in the model runs about 2.1, which is close to that for Korea over the past six years. Real growth in the Korean economy has exceeded 10 percent recently.

[19] For reasonable assumptions for the foreign-capital inflow, the shadow exchange rate between *won* and U.S. dollars, is between 405 to 324 *won* per dollar in the first period and 390 to 270 *won* per dollar in the last, depending upon the exact specification of the model. The first set of limits is for the borrowing specification (discussed below), the second is for the nonborrowing specification.

[20] $\phi_i = 1.1$ for all sectors.

[21] Roughly 70 percent of the total cost of both the integrated steel mill and the petrochemical plant will be financed by foreign capital.

TABLE 3.   SECTOR RANKING BY COMPARATIVE ADVANTAGE[a]

| | Commodity shadow price divided by shadow foreign exchange rate | |
	Exogenous foreign[b] capital	Long run[c]
Low cost		
Chemicals[d]	.87	.79
Food, wood products	.89	.81
Agriculture	.95	.85
Light manufacturing	.86	.85
Textiles	.97	.93
Medium cost		
Petroleum	1.00	1.10
Machinery	1.00	1.12
Construction, cement	1.00	1.13
Overhead, services	n.c.	1.18
Mining	1.00	1.18
Fiber spinning	1.13	1.18
High cost		
Finished metal products	1.00	1.33
Steel products	1.00	1.56
Petrochemicals	1.00	1.56
Non-traditional steel	1.00	1.73
Iron and steel	1.00	1.82
Fertilizer	1.00	1.84

Note: n.c. indicates value not computed.

[a] Shadow prices may be interpreted as marginal revenue products in the mixed integer programming model used here, but they are relative to the pattern of investment in the complexes. See Westphal (86), Section 3.3.4.

[b] Prices are from the nonborrowing specification in which agricultural growth is unlimited, third period.

[c] Prices taken from a single period model which gives the composition of output and the relative prices along an approximation to the asymptotic balanced growth path of the mixed integer programming model. See Westphal (86), Section 5.4.

[d] Chemicals include animal and vegetable oils, dyestuffs, explosives, paint, drugs and cosmetics, with some basic chemicals.

of the country's control over foreign-capital inflows is best reflected in the borrowing activity incorporated in the second specification of the model, although even in this specification the magnitude of foreign-capital inflows is not directly related to the construction of the plants.

It is worthwhile to look at solutions in which borrowing is not permitted and foreign-capital inflows are exogenous. The contrast between the optimal solutions when borrowing is permitted and when foreign-capital inflows are exogenous illustrates the conditions under which it is profitable to build one or both complexes.

Capacity expansion paths with exogenous foreign-capital inflows. For this specification, the foreign-capital inflow plus net factor income from abroad, f_t, is 180 billion *won* per year in each period.[22] The terminal growth

[22] On the basis of discussions with David Cole, it appears this is unrealistically high.

constraint related to gross domestic product is used, and the required post-terminal growth rate is 13 percent (the average growth rate during the plan period). The marginal savings propensity is unbounded; that is, constraint H2 is omitted.

The amount of investment in this specification is bounded from above in the first two periods by the consumption requirement constraint and by the fixed amount of foreign-capital inflow, and bounded from below in the terminal period by the terminal growth constraint. In all solutions to this specification, due to the high welfare value of terminal consumption, investment in each period is at its upper bound regardless of its composition. Consequently, capacity expansion in the complexes takes place at the cost of growth in the traditional sectors' capacity. This is strikingly illustrated in Table 4, which presents selected details for four alternative solutions (corresponding to four patterns of investment in the complexes) to this specification.

The welfare values of the four patterns differ by virtue of differences in consumption in the terminal period. Solution A is the optimal solution, having the greatest terminal consumption.[23] The level of investment is almost the same for all patterns in the first period, but it varies in the second and third periods because of two factors: variations in the composition of investment in the first two periods and in foreign-exchange reserve accumulation in the second period.

The composition of investment within a period determines the incremental capital-output ratio and, together with the level of investment, establishes the upper bound to the growth of gross domestic product from the current period to the next. Because the growth of domestic savings is limited by the growth of gross domestic product, the growth of investment depends upon the composition of investment in prior periods. Thus the effects of a suboptimal composition of investment in one period are compounded through time by a lower growth rate of investment. The pattern of investment in the complexes in a given period not only influences investment in the traditional sectors in that period but has a profound impact on the future course of total investment.

A comparison of solutions A, B, and C illustrates the determinants of the accumulation of foreign-exchange reserves in period two (1969–70). As more import-substituting investment takes place in the first period,

---

[23] This solution also demonstrates the need for constraining the marginal propensity to save. Over the three periods it is -0.16, 0.72, and -0.19, respectively—reflecting a mobility of resources between investment and consumption that probably does not exist in a real economy. Its erratic behavior is due to the valuation of terminal consumption and the bounds on investment in each period. Most optimal savings models behave in a similar fashion, unless constrained (see Eckaus and Parikh [23: chap. 5]).

TABLE 4.   ALTERNATIVE SOLUTIONS: NON-BORROWING SPECIFICATION[a]

	Solution			
	A[b]	B	C	D
Period of investment				
Petrochemicals	n.p.	1	1	2
Steel mill	n.p.	n.p.	1	1
Period	Average yearly gross domestic product			
1967/68	982	979	979	n.c.
1969/70	1280	1252	1268	n.c.
1971/72	1807 (13.8)	1712	1653	n.c.
	Average yearly consumption			
1967/68	765	765	765	765
1969/70	833	833	833	833
1971/72	1445 (12.4)	1410	1389	1417
	Average yearly investment			
1967/68	326	323	323	n.c.
1969/70	510	464	409	n.c.
1971/72	472 (13.8)	433	416	n.c.
	Total imports minus exports—yearly average			
1967/68	180	180	180	180
1969/70	149	135	64	175
1971/72	211	245	256	182
Sector	Terminal capacity			
1	823 (12.7)	755	719	775
2	60 (13.5)	40	40	59
3	457 (16.3)	439	378	438
4	87 (14.1)	85	63	85
5	267 (18.4)	262	205	262
6	134 (25.0)	131	127	131
7	77 (22.0)	76	73	78
8	19 (31.0)	19	19	19
9	39 (03.8)	42	43	40
10	352 (19.8)	274	265	285
11	6 (01.5)	6	6	6
12	23 (05.8)	21	21	21
13	21 (06.6)	22	22	22
14	143 (21.0)	132	123	139
15	831 (15.9)	808	781	819
16	0	75	75	75
17	0	0	55	66

Notes: n.c.—Not computed. n.p.—Plant not constructed during plan.
[a] All magnitudes in billions of won.
[b] The numbers in parentheses are compound growth rates for 1966 to 1972 for solution A.

through the construction of the complexes, less foreign exchange is needed to support production in the second period, thereby releasing foreign exchange for reserve accumulation. The increase in foreign-exchange reserve accumulation in period two (moving from solution A to B and then from B to C) is equal to the foreign-exchange savings permitted by the construction of, first, the petrochemical plant and then, in addition, the integrated steel mill. The accumulated reserves are used to increase consumption in the terminal period through competitive imports. More foreign exchange is required in the second period in solution D because of less import substitution in the first period and the foreign-exchange cost of the petrochemical plant's construction in that period.

We now turn to the composition of the capital stocks in period three. In solution B, a petrochemical plant is constructed in the first period. Comparison of the capacity levels of the third period for solution B with the levels for solution A, during which plan period neither complex was built, very clearly shows that the cost of building the petrochemical plant was a decline in the capacity of its using sectors and the consumer-goods industries. Consequently, the profit from building the plant has been restricted, because it cannot be utilized as completely as it would have been had its construction not been responsible for a decline in capacity expansion in the rest of the economy.

In solution C, both complexes are constructed in the first period, and there is a further cutback in the capacity of the using sectors of both plants and in the consumption goods industries. In solution D, the construction of the petrochemical plant is postponed to the second period and the integrated mill is built in the first. Of the four solutions, D is the second best; delayed construction of the petrochemical facility permits construction of greater capacity in the using sectors of both complexes, and capacity in the major supplier of the integrated mill can be expanded. Consequently, a larger mill is constructed; the largest permissible petrochemical plant always is built because there is no bound on its exports (in this specification only) and because excess terminal capacity in petrochemicals contributes to the terminal growth requirement. Terminal consumption in solution D falls short of that in solution A because less foreign exchange can be passed into the terminal period when the petrochemical complex is built in the second period.

There appear, then, to be three causes for the absence of investment in the complex sectors in the optimal solution for this specification. First, investment in either complex leads to a higher incremental capital-output ratio that reduces the growth of domestic savings and therefore, that of gross domestic product and consumption. Second, the demand for the output of the complexes is diminished by reductions of investment in their using sectors when the complexes are built. As a result, the plants cannot be sufficiently utilized to justify their construction. Third, construction of the plants is possible only if capacity expansion in the consumption goods industries is limited. This fact alone is insignificant, except when it is coupled with the additional result that the savings in foreign exchange, which results from building the plants, does not permit sufficiently high imports of consumption goods to offset the decline in their domestic production.[24]

Alternative capacity expansion paths in the case of more flexible foreign-exchange inflows. Whereas the alternative solutions to the first specification demonstrate the adjustments required to permit investment in the increasing returns sectors when investment in each period is fixed, the various solutions to the borrowing specification indicate an alternative adjustment: increasing the level of investment in periods when complexes are built.

Because investment is equal to domestic savings plus the gap between imports and exports, permitting flexible foreign-exchange inflows through borrowing gives the model greater discretion over the amount of investment in any given period. This choice is present in only a single direction in the first specification: foreign-exchange reserves can be accumulated for future use.

Tables 5 and 6 present selected information from the solutions for alternative patterns of investments in the complexes for the borrowing specification.[25] In this specification, the total sources terminal growth constraint (equation K′) is used, and the required post-terminal growth rate is 10 percent. The limit on discounted total borrowing less repayment is equal to the six-year foreign-capital inflow (plus net factor income from abroad) in the first specification, 1,080 billion *won*.[26] The rate of interest on foreign capital is 5 percent per annum. The upper limit to the marginal propensity to save, σ, is 0.30.[27]

Solution *A* for this specification is devoid of investment in either complex. Relative to the optimal solution in which both complexes are constructed in the second period, this investment pattern results in a loss of

---

[24] Alternative runs were made in which the post-terminal growth rate, γ, ranged from 7 to 16 percent; no change in the optimal pattern of investment in the complexes occurred. Alternative runs also were made with exogenous foreign-capital inflows (180 billion *won*/year) in which ρ ranged upward to 0.25 and the weight on post-terminal consumption was reduced to zero without investment in the complexes becoming profitable. The highest discount rates on consumption yielded gross domestic product growth rates of 9 percent. The complexes remained unprofitable even if the foreign-capital inflow was reduced to 45 billion *won* in each year. However, if the foreign-capital inflows were assumed to fall over time (starting at 450 billion *won* per annum and falling to 45 billion) investment in the petrochemical complex proved optimal.

[25] $f_t = 0$ for $t = 1, \ldots, 4$. For convenience, net factor income from abroad is assumed to be zero.

[26] This means that, after repayment, less foreign exchange is available from abroad for imports, because interest charges are accumulated in the debt constraint.

[27] Too much importance should not be attached to the fact that more than a single parameter is changed from one specification to the next; experiments not reported here indicate that the influence of reasonable changes in ρ, ω, γ, ϕ, and in the form of equation k on the optimal pattern of investment in the complexes is nil. Furthermore, decreasing σ reduces the profitability of the complexes.

slightly more than 2 percent in the optimum value of the welfare function. This pattern also is less attractive than the others enumerated in the table, all of which involve the construction of a plant in at least one of the complex sectors.

Examination of the five solutions to this specification indicates that the paths of gross domestic product and consumption are much less sensitive to the pattern of investment in the complexes when borrowing is permitted than when borrowing is absent. The path of the gap between imports and exports displays the most sensitivity to changes in the pattern of investment. Of all the determinants of this gap, competitive imports and noncompetitive imports of capital goods display the greatest variability inasmuch as borrowing is timed to accommodate the construction of the complexes.

The petrochemical complex costs about 47.2 billion *won* on an annual basis (for the size of plant constructed in these solutions) and the integrated steel mill costs approximately 30.7 billion *won*, again on an annual basis. Moving from solution *A* to solution *B*, where a petrochemical complex is constructed in the initial period, we see that borrowing increases in the first period by 31 billion *won* (annual basis), so that two-thirds of the cost of the plant is financed by an increase in the foreign-capital inflow. The higher inflow in period one is offset by a reduction in borrowing in the second period and by increased debt repayment in the third, so that total investment over the plan period is about the same in both solutions. The part of the plant's financing that is not provided for by increased borrowing is obtained by a reduction in investment in the traditional sectors. Noncompetitive imports of capital goods in the first period increase between the two solutions by the full amount of the increase in borrowing that is used to finance the foreign-exchange component of the petrochemical plant; and competitive imports bear the brunt of the reduction of net foreign-capital inflows in the latter two periods. The reduction of competitive imports is possible because of import substitution in petrochemicals.

This same pattern of accommodation to investment in the complexes is repeated in solutions *C* through *E*. The level of investment rises in the period of a complex's construction (relative to the situation in which a complex is not built in that period) and subsequently falls as competitive imports are cut back, along with borrowing in the following periods.[28] In

---

[28] Complete import substitution in some solutions for the borrowing specification (see solutions *D* and *E*) is due to a fundamental property of the model. If the economy can grow rapidly enough, foreign exchange becomes the only scarce resource, and, under this condition, competitive imports are not profitable unless there is an absolute limit to domestic supply or unless more foreign exchange is required to produce the commodity than to import it.

TABLE 5. ALTERNATIVE SOLUTIONS: BORROWING SPECIFICATION NATIONAL INCOME ACCOUNTS*

Solution	Petro-chemicals	Steel mill	W	GDP	C^T	I	E	M	M^1	M^2	M^3	M-E
A 1967/68	n.p.	n.p.	21,024	982	765	311	102	268	65	92	112	166
1969/70				1,258	944	541	179	492	91	150	251	313
1971/72				1,757	1,279	373	280	275	136	73	66	-5
B 1967/68	1	n.p.	21,409	981	765	341	102	299	64	124	110	197
1969/70				1,263	948	535	179	485	92	151	242	306
1971/72				1,788	1,306	347	280	248	137	71	40	-34
C 1967/68	2	n.p.	21,434	981	765	306	102	264	65	89	111	162
1969/70				1,265	948	573	179	521	93	188	240	344
1971/72				1,790	1,306	347	280	249	137	71	40	-34
D 1967/68	2	1	21,442	980	765	324	102	283	64	109	109	181
1969/70				1,255	942	584	179	537	95	191	250	358
1971/72				1,787	1,309	305	280	210	146	64	0	-72
E 1967/68	2	2	21,468	980	765	295	102	263	65	88	110	161
1969/70				1,264	949	607	179	558	91	214	253	379
1971/72				1,789	1,310	306	280	211	147	147	0	-71

Notes: *All national income accounts are yearly averages for the period in billions of won. "n.p." indicates no plant built in plan period.
Column headings are:

W —objective value
GDP—gross domestic product
C^T —consumption
I —investment
E —exports
M —total imports
M^1 —non-competitive imports for production
M^2 —non-competitive investment goods imports
M^3 —competitive imports

172

short, the timing of foreign-capital inflows responds to that of investment in the complexes, but total plan-period investment displays little variability. The increased borrowing necessary to finance the rise in investment is repaid with the foreign exchange saved through import substitution for petrochemicals and/or nontraditional iron and steel. Because the timing of investment no longer is as rigidly set as it was in the basic specification, construction of both complexes in the second period is the optimal pattern. Of the total investment in the second period in solution E (the optimal solution), almost 13 percent goes into the two complexes. They account for 6.50 percent of total investment over the plan period although together they account for only 2.25 percent of gross domestic product in the terminal period.

Foreign capital worth 379 billion *won* on an annual basis, or $1.4 billion, is needed to finance investment in the second period. Although it is highly doubtful that Korea will receive such a large inflow of foreign capital (plus net factor income from abroad) in 1969 or 1970, she has sufficient foreign-exchange reserves to permit a wedge this size to be driven between imports and exports. Investment in the second period (in the solutions) rises as high as 607 billion *won* (annual basis) even though the marginal propensity to save is limited to 0.30. This high level of investment is possible because of large foreign-capital inflows, and is profitable because of the high terminal consumption it provides.

Table 6 presents details of the capacity expansion paths for the solutions to the borrowing specification. Except for sectors 6, 10, 11, and 12, there are only marginal differences between the solutions with regard to the paths of commodity supply and production in each sector. In particular, production and total supply in the major consumption goods sectors are almost the same for each solution in each period. Since total investment can be increased to accommodate investment in the complex sectors, there is no need to sacrifice consumption to finance either a petrochemical plant or an integrated steel mill.

The differences between the solutions in the production and total supply of sector 10's output are related to differences in the amount of terminal investment. Terminal investment is not the same in all solutions because repayment of debt is a substitute for investment in the terminal growth constraint, and, as we have observed, the level of repayment in the terminal period of the solutions depends upon whether and when the complexes are built. The differences in sectors 11 and 12 are related to the timing of investment in the integrated steel mill, which produces a substitute for the output of these sectors.

Investment in sector 6 (light manufactures) is sensitive to the pattern of investment in the complex sectors. When there is investment in either

TABLE 6. CAPACITY AND SUPPLY: BORROWING SPECIFICATION[a]

									Sector								
	1	2	3	4	5	6	7	8	9	10	11	12	13	14	15	16	17
Average annual capacity																	
1967–68	473	54	246	55	137	62	42	25	22	158	7	26	27	73	444	0	0
1969–70																	
Solution A	546	47	304	50	164	106	76	22	42	302	6	34	24	107	573	0	0
B	547	47	303	49	163	69	51	22	43	294	6	23	24	105	547	58	0
C	549	47	305	51	165	87	51	22	43	296	6	34	24	110	577	0	0
D	544	47	302	49	162	55	49	22	43	300	6	33	24	107	574	0	73
E	549	47	306	51	165	87	51	22	42	302	6	23	24	107	577	0	0
1971–72																	
Solution A	773	81	411	127	246	125	72	50	61	310	23	41	59	156	804	0	0
B	779	79	416	128	250	126	75	50	63	291	6	39	58	159	785	58	0
C	780	80	417	128	250	127	75	50	63	292	6	40	58	159	786	59	0
D	776	82	413	129	250	126	75	50	64	297	6	40	57	155	788	59	73
E	777	82	414	129	250	127	75	50	65	298	6	40	57	155	789	59	78
Average annual imports minus excess capacity																	
1967–68																	
Solution A	8	-3	-18	-3	-33	0	-4	5	10	28	5	-3	2	24	-3	17	13
B	8	-3	-18	-3	-33	-1	-5	5	10	28	5	-4	2	23	-3	17	13
C	8	-3	-18	-3	-33	-1	-5	5	10	28	5	-3	2	23	-4	17	13
D	8	-3	-18	-3	-33	-2	-5	5	10	28	5	-4	2	22	-4	17	13
E	8	-3	-18	-3	-33	-1	-5	5	10	28	5	-4	2	23	-4	17	13
1969–70																	
Solution A	36	17	0	36	0	-20[b]	-27	15	0	36	11	0	19	36	0	23	19
B	36	16	0	36	0	17	0	15	0	36	6	9	18	36	0	-35	17
C	36	17	0	36	0	0	0	15	0	35	10	0	19	32	0	21	19
D	36	19	0	35[b]	0	29[b]	0	15	0	35	-2[b]	17	19	36	0	21	-18
E	36	17	0	36	0	1	0	15	0	36	6	10	19	36	0	24	18
1971–72																	
Solution A	0	0	0	0	0	0	0	0	0	0	0	0	0	0	-33	40	26
B	0	0	0	0	0	0	0	0	0	-9	14	0	0	0	0	-14	25
C	0	0	0	0	0	0	0	0	0	-10	14	0	0	0	0	-15	26
D	0	0	0	0	0	0	0	0	0	-47	5	20	0	0	0	-15	-18
E	0	0	0	0	0	0	0	0	0	-47	5	22	0	0	0	-15	-19

[a] Figures are in billion won.

174

complex in the first period, capacity expansion in sector 6 is cut back to provide part of the financing. In solution B, this reaction in sector 6 helps explain why investment in petrochemicals is best delayed to the second period; in solution D, it helps explain the optimality of the delayed timing for the integrated iron and steel mill. In both solutions, it is best to build up the user facilities of the petrochemical's plant gradually prior to constructing either complex (recall that light manufactures are a major user of petrochemicals). The failure to do this in solution B results in idle capacity that is equal to 60 percent of the total petrochemical capacity in period two. Here we have a clear case of the use of imports to delay the construction of a plant whose costs decrease with size.[29]

Reduction of the growth rate in agriculture. The growth rate of agriculture in the optimal solutions to the two specifications is well above 10 percent per annum. For a better reflection of anticipated trends in agricultural output, two specifications of the model were tried in which agriculture's growth rate was constrained to less than 6 per cent per annum. In the first specification, an exogenous foreign-capital inflow (plus net factor income from abroad) of 180 billion *won* per annum is used (this is similar to the first specification above). The second specification is comparable to the borrowing specification just discussed; the interest rate, r, is 5 percent and the debt limit is 1,080 billion *won*. Higher levels of competitive imports are allowed for both specifications, and the minimum level of per capita consumption growth was reduced to zero.[30]

The limit imposed on the economy's overall growth by the slow expansion of output in one sector can be overcome only through imports of that sector's output or by shifting production away from sectors that use its output. The former requires either greater exports of other sectors' output or more import substitution in the economy as a whole. Because exports are limited in the model, import substitution will be the key element in the process. Table 7 compares some details of the optimal solutions for the specifications in which agricultural growth is not limited with those in which it is. In the latter two solutions, the growth rate of the economy is

---

[29] With all else remaining the same in the specification of the model, increasing the rate of interest on foreign borrowing, r, to 20 percent produces no shift in the optimal timing of investment in petrochemicals nor in the integrated steel mill. However, with r at 0.05, halving the debt limit gives rise to an optimal pattern in which the petrochemical plant is built in period one and the iron and steel mill in period two. In this case, excess capacity plays a greater role in accommodating investment in the complexes, and the paths of total supply in the various sectors display greater dependence upon the timing of investment in the complexes. The size of the optimal plant is not very sensitive to the interest rate on foreign capital. See Westphal (86: chap. 7).

[30] Both specifications use the total sources terminal growth constraint with a post-terminal growth rate of 8 percent. Furthermore, to reduce the number of parameter changes, ϕ_i is set to 1.12. For both, $\rho = 0.00$ and $\omega = 0.25$.

176   II. PLANNING MODELS

TABLE 7. SOLUTIONS FOR REDUCED AGRICULTURAL GROWTH RATE

	Foreign capital inflow specification			
	Exogenous		Endogenous	
Period of investment				
Petrochemicals	n.p.	2	2	1
Steel mill	n.p.	n.p.	2	2
Welfare value	23118	20999	21468	20877
Growth rates (per annum)				
Agriculture	11.2%	6.0%	11.2%	6.0%
Gross domestic product	13.8	12.2	13.7	12.1
Consumption	12.4	10.2	10.8	10.1
Total plan investment[a]	2451	2445	2227	2312
Imports minus exports[b]				
1967/68	180	169	161	205
1969/70	149	191	379	164
1971/72	212	180	−71	112
Proportion of investment in total sources				
1967/68	.26	.29	.29	.31
1969/70	.34	.30	.37	.29
1971/72	.22	.25	.18	.21
Sectors	Percent of total value-added by sector (1971/72)			
1	35.0%	27.2%	33.4%	27.4%
2	1.6	2.4	2.2	2.5
3	8.7	8.5	7.9	8.4
4	1.4	2.2	2.1	2.2
5	5.1	5.2	4.9	5.2
6	2.6	2.3	2.1	2.3
7	1.8	1.9	1.8	1.9
8	0.6	1.1	1.7	1.4
9	1.0	1.8	1.7	1.8
10	7.3	7.1	5.2	6.3
11	0.1	0.2	0.1	0.1
12	0.3	0.6	0.5	0.4
13	0.4	1.3	1.1	1.3
14	2.3	3.5	2.5	3.1
15	32.1	33.2	30.8	33.2
16	0.0	1.6	1.5	1.5
17 & 18	0.0	0.0	0.8	1.1

Note: n.p. indicates no plant constructed during plan.
[a] In billion won.
[b] Yearly average, in billion won.

above 12 percent per annum even though agricultural output grows at only 6 percent. The economy adjusts surprisingly well to the constraint on agriculture's growth.

The most notable feature of these solutions is the effect of slower agricultural growth on the optimal timing of investment in the two complexes. For the nonborrowing specification, the construction of a petrochemical complex in the second period is profitable when agriculture's growth is limited, whereas neither complex was profitable if agriculture's growth was unlimited. With the borrowing specification, the construction of the petrochemical complex is moved up to the first period and the construction of the steel mill continues to be deferred to the second period. In both cases, to sustain a high growth rate for the economy as a whole, more and earlier import substitution is needed than was the case when agriculture grew at the same rate as the rest of the economy. The profitability of building the complexes is sensitive not only to the timing of foreign-capital inflows but also to supply conditions in other sectors.

Implications for Korean Development

The borrowing specification best reflects the conditions likely to prevail in Korea over the next six years. Optimal solutions with this specification indicate that both projects are highly profitable. With agriculture's growth unconstrained, the objective value in the solution in which neither complex is constructed is 2.1 percent below the value for the optimal solution. In other words, shifting 6.7 percent of total investment from the traditional to the complex sectors results in an increased total discounted consumption of 2.1 percent.

We have demonstrated that it is profitable to build the plants only if there is—at the same time—a large amount of investment in their using and supplying industries, along with continued investment in the consumption goods industries.[31] This can be accomplished only with careful coordination of investment plans for the various sectors of the economy.

Planning is presently proceeding on the basis of a petrochemical plant with an annual capacity of between 12 billion and 24 billion *won* output and 1-million-ton capacity integrated steel mill.[32] But the solutions to the model (including many not reported here) indicate that, if constructed, the annual capacity of the petrochemical facility should be upward of 50 billion *won* and the annual capacity of the integrated iron and steel mill about $1\frac{1}{2}$ million tons. It also appears that both plants should be built with considerable excess capacity, at least 20 percent of the capacity of each plant should be idle in 1972.

The growth rates obtained in the solutions appear to be unrealistically high, and for this reason the size of the plants constructed in the solutions may well be in excess of the optimal size when factors that would reduce the growth rates to more reasonable levels are included in the analysis. But the large discrepancy between the presently planned and the optimal (as here determined) capacity of the petrochemical plant can be partly

---

[31] Although it has not been argued in detail, this conclusion holds equally well for the specifications in which agriculture's growth is limited.

[32] This was written in June, 1968. In mid-August, plans for a 40 billion *won* (1965 prices) capacity output petrochemical complex were finalized and the project is now under construction. The steel mill is still in the planning stage.

explained by the fact that no reliable intersectoral estimate of the demands for petrochemicals has been made (most estimates to date have been based on international comparisons).[33]

As for the timing of construction, the optimal solution to the borrowing specification suggests that the best course is to invest simultaneously in both facilities if agricultural growth is not constrained. In this solution, however, investment is almost 50 percent of the gross domestic product during the period of construction and the gap between imports and exports exceeds 30 percent of the value of the gross domestic product. It is probably unrealistic to expect that Korea could efficiently absorb so much foreign capital in such a short period.[34] If the plants are not built simultaneously, the petrochemical plant should be built first, because this results in a greater saving of imports per *won* of investment than construction of the integrated steel mill.

The clearest conclusion that emerges from the model is that the optimal timing of investment in the complexes ultimately depends upon the availability and the cost of foreign capital as well as upon the supply conditions in other major sectors. Some of the elements of the cost of foreign capital have been excluded from the model, such as the effect of a large deficit on the future availability of foreign-capital inflows and on the attitudes of international lending agencies. The final decision should be deferred until a more careful examination has been made of all elements of the cost of foreign capital.

IV. CONCLUSION

In order to plan lumpy investments in decreasing cost industries it is necessary to plan investment in the rest of the economy simultaneously. One-sector models of capacity expansion in industries with economies of scale concentrate only on the role of decreasing unit costs to conclude that overinvestment is optimal as a means of lowering average capacity cost.[35]

---

[33] The sectoral projection model does not give direct estimates of demand for petro-chemicals.

[34] If the construction of the plants is spaced over four years rather than over two years and the net foreign-capital inflow over the plan-period is held to 540 billion *won*, investment and foreign-capital inflow during those four years would be 30 and 20 percent of the gross domestic product, respectively.

[35] See Manne (60) for the application to investment planning of single-sector models with scale economies. The application of Manne's model (using the interest rate on foreign borrowing, "*r*", as the interest rate, and using shadow prices only for foreign exchange) to planning investment in the two complexes leads to quite different conclusions from those of our model with respect to timing and scale. The comparison of the two models suggests that the one-sector model is better when investment in a decreasing cost industry requires a much smaller proportion of total investment. See Westphal (86: sec. 7.4).

But multisectoral models are also able to capture the fact that capacity expansion in some decreasing cost industries requires large chunks of investment resources. Investment elsewhere in the economy must adjust to the lumpiness of investment in the decreasing cost industries, and it is largely on the basis of these adjustments that the optimal timing of investment in the complex sectors must be determined. In terms of the traditional means of ranking sectors by comparative production costs, the important fact is that the ranking of sectors in the next period depends upon the investment program carried out in this period.

Whether the economy can successfully accommodate the lumpy investment in decreasing cost industries depends on a number of factors, but the key factor is the timing (and magnitude) of foreign-capital inflows. The issue, however, is not simply whether the timing of foreign-capital inflows is sufficiently flexible to respond to the phasing of the complexes' construction. With little flexibility, the lumpy investment required to build a plant may nevertheless be profitable because, without this import substitution, foreign-exchange supplies in later periods may be insufficient to permit as great an increase in the supplies of other sectoral commodities. This is clearly brought out in the solutions in which the growth potential of agriculture is limited; earlier investment in the complexes is profitable because, as import-substituting investment, it releases foreign exchange —without which neither equally large imports of agricultural goods nor equally rapid growth in other sectors is possible. Thus the profitability of investment in the complexes is also a function of the resource endowment of the country. Because the lumpy investment in the decreasing cost industries is import-substituting investment, it is profitable only if, in its absence, there is insufficient foreign exchange to sustain equally rapid growth of the supplies of other goods and services. If, however, investment resources are at a premium because of the economy's limited ability to save, the high investment cost of these decreasing cost industries may argue against the expansion of their capacity.

The advisability of investing large amounts of capital in the decreasing cost industries is therefore a function of the relative prices of the resources they require and the resources they save, as well as the manner in which investment elsewhere in the economy is timed to accommodate the concentrated use of the investment resources required to provide capacity in these industries.

It should be recognized, of course, that no single planning technique can be used in isolation to formulate rational decisions; each technique fails to take some elements of consequence into account. Various elements are omitted from the Korean model, and the following items should be mentioned.

1. The model makes no allowance for the fact that a plant's capacity never is fully utilized when it first comes on line. There is always a shakedown period during which the staff learns to operate the equipment and the "bugs" are worked out of the plant.

2. The fact that a plant's construction can be phased over time has been neglected. For example, the integrated steel mill could be built in three stages, of 500,000 tons each, with production and capacity advancing in step. The mill's cost would then be only slightly higher than if it were built all at once.

3. Capacity absorption limits or decreasing returns to investment as a whole have not been specified. In large part this is responsible for the high rates of growth of GDP and high investment rates.

4. Exports have been determined exogenously. Rather than build the complexes to *save* foreign exchange, it may be better to expand exports to *obtain* foreign exchange.[36]

These elements, which could be included in the model with minor modifications, were omitted only because of limited computational capacity and the time constraints under which this study was made. Not easily incorporated in this type of model, however, are the details of resource base, technology, and so forth that go into the engineering calculations that produce the precise specifications for a plant's product mix, technological characteristics, and location.

---

[36] Subsequent experiments with exports specified exogenously (but subject to reasonable upper bounds) do not markedly alter the conclusions of this paper regarding timing and scale of investment in the complexes.

Chapter 6 Glossary

Notational Conventions

In general, uppercase Roman letters are reserved for empirically derived structural parameters, lowercase Roman letters for activity variables, and Greek letters for "plan parameters" that do not reflect structural relationships but constraints on economic activity imposed by the planner. The indices s and t which appear where required for clarity, are used to denote time periods. The operator "Δ" is defined so that Δu_t is equal to $u_t - u_{t-1}$.

Activities

x_i	qroduction activity i, $i = 1, \ldots, 19$
m_i	imports of the ith commodity, $i = 1, \ldots, 14, 16, 17$
Δk_i	investment demand for the ith commodity, $i = 1, \ldots, 17$
$\Delta k_{\text{hous.}}$	gross investment in housing
cn_i	private consumption demand for the ith commodity, $i = 1, \ldots, 15$
g_i	government demand for the ith commodity, $i = 1, \ldots, 15$
e_i	exports of the ith commodity, $i = 1 \ldots, 14, 16$
Δc_i	gross increment to capacity in the ith sector, measured in terms of normal yearly full-capacity output, $i = 1, \ldots, 17$
δ_i	integer variable for investment in complex i, $i = 16, 17$
Δs^f	accumulation of foreign-exchange reserves
f	exogenous net foreign-capital inflow plus net factor income from abroad during period
c_i	capacity in sector i, $i = 1, \ldots, 17$
$sl_{eq.}$	slack variable in equation noted in subscript
c_i^*	capacity actually available over a two-year period, $i = 1, \ldots, 17$
b	amount of foreign borrowing
rp	repayment of foreign debt accumulated within the plan period

Structural parameters

A_{ij}^*	Net output $(+)$ or input $(-)$ of commodity i for unit operation of production activity j, $i = 1, \ldots, 17$; $j = 1, \ldots, 19$
P_t	sum of population estimates in years spanned by the period t
S_i^a	intercept coefficient in the consumption demand function for the ith commodity, $i = 1, \ldots, 15$
S_i	marginal propensity to consume the ith sectoral commodity, $i = 1, \ldots, 15$

B_{ij} variable charge input-capacity coefficient for domestically produced goods, $i = 1, \ldots, 15; j = 1, \ldots, 17$

E_i, E_{17}^* stock accumulation coefficient in production sector i, $i = 1, \ldots, 18$ (E_{17}^* is a weighted average of E_{17} and E_{18})

B_i^n variable charge noncompetitive imports-capacity coefficient, $i = 1, \ldots, 17$

B_j^T

$$= \sum_{i=1}^{15} B_{ij} + E_j + B_j^n \text{ for traditional sectors, } j = 1, \ldots, 15$$

$$= \sum_{i=1}^{15} B_{ij} + B_j^n \text{ for complex sectors, } j = 16, 17$$

B_{ij}^a fixed-charge input-capacity coefficient for complex sectors, $i = 1, \ldots, 15; j = 16, 17$

B_i^{na} fixed-charge noncompetitive imports-capacity coefficient for complex sectors, $i = 16, 17$

B_j^{aT}

$$= \sum_{i=1}^{15} B_{ij}^a + B_j^{na} \text{ for complex sectors, } j = 16, 17$$

M_i^n total noncompetitive imports-output coefficient for production sector i, $i = 1, \ldots, 18$

F conversion factor for exports from *won* value in domestic prices to *won* value of foreign exchange

D_i depreciation coefficient for the ith sector's capacity, $i = 1, \ldots, 17$

V_i, V_{17}^* value-added per unit of output in production sector i, $i = 1, \ldots, 18$ (V_{17}^* is a weighted average of V_{17} and V_{18})

Y_i capacity of largest allowable plant that can be constructed in a single period in complex sector i, $i = 16, 17$

$B_{10,\text{hous.}}$ investment demand for construction for housing per unit of consumption

L conformably dimensioned vector of 1s

I conformably dimensioned identity matrix

Plan parameters

μ_i bound on competitive imports in sector i, $i = 1, \ldots, 14$

ϵ minimum allowable growth rate of per capita consumption

σ maximum marginal propensity to save

τ limit to total discounted debt incurred during the plan

r borrowing interest rate for foreign capital

γ target post-terminal growth rate of gross domestic product or total sources (depending upon specification)

ρ discount rate on within-plan consumption in welfare function

ω discount rate on post-plan consumption in welfare function

ϕ_i factor of proportionality in post-terminal capital stock bound

FORMAL APPROACHES TO REGIONAL
PLANNING IN KOREA

Roger D. Norton

I. Introduction

This paper is a progress report on the model-building aspects of a regional planning program under way in Korea.[1] Also, it will culminate in two major plan documents, the Third Five-Year Plan (1961–75) and the Ministry of National Construction's Comprehensive National Construction Plan, both of which contain regional development plans.

In the past two years there have been increasingly frequent expressions of interest in regional planning in government and academic circles in Korea (92). This interest has been due to two related social concerns: the desire to slow the rate of population growth in Seoul and the desire to raise incomes in the lagging regions, whose representatives have been increasingly complaining of economic discrimination. At present, economic activity remains strongly concentrated in Seoul. In 1966, 34 percent of the nation's manufacturing income and 24 percent of gross domestic product originated within the boundaries of Seoul City, which contains 13 percent of the population and less than 1 percent of the land area. Per capita income in Seoul is about two and a half times as great as in the province with the lowest income level.[2] Because agricultural productivity does not vary greatly throughout the country, dispersal of industry has been viewed as the primary need in effecting more equitable regional distribution of income.

The primary aim of the model discussed in this paper is to assess the

I am particularly indebted to Director Kim Hak So of the Korean Ministry of National Construction, Tarik Carim of the United Nations Development Programme, Marshall K. Wood of the National Planning Association, and Hahm Mahn Joon and Lee Kyu Sul of the Bureau of Statistics, who have contributed to this paper in many ways.

[1] The Economic Planning Board and the Ministry of National Construction are joint sponsors of the program, and active support has been given by AID, the United Nations Development Programme, and by various universities in Korea.

[2] These interregional income comparisons are made in current prices, but deflation by interregional price indices alters the picture only slightly, and in the direction of greater regional income inequalities.

types of industries most appropriate for decentralization, the additional costs of various degrees of decentralization, and the infrastructure investment requirements for regional development under various objectives.

II. REGIONAL DEVELOPMENT PROCESSES

Regional investment allocation strategy may be cast in a form analogous to project or sector allocation strategy, and principles for guiding regional investment decisions may be derived from the usual investment criteria. The need for regional investment criteria arises because, in the short run, there is often a conflict between the goals of more equitable regional income distribution and more rapid national growth. In a given situation, regional income disparities may be sufficiently pronounced, relative to the society's preferences, that sharp reallocations of capital are warranted. In such a case, the private marginal productivity of capital invested in the lagging region may be well below its social marginal productivity. The usual rationale for redistribution programs is that they are temporary; economies of scale or externalities of various sorts eventually will arise to increase the private marginal product of capital in the lagging region so that the need for special inducements for capital will diminish.

In this view of regional development strategy the justification for public intervention in the capital market is the same as the justification for infant-industry tariffs. The first questions that arise are: (1) Given a specific regional income distribution goal, how are the precise allocations of investment by region to be determined? (2) How long are special inducements to capital likely to be required? (3) Which types of investment are most appropriate for the lagging regions?

Specific answers to these questions depend on the specific industrial, geographic, and demographic characteristics of the country concerned, but a general framework may be set forth that provides analytic answers and, with appropriate data, numerical answers.

Regions within a country are differentiated in many ways, but, for the purpose of this analysis, Korea's regions are distinguished from one another primarily by the following sets of factors:

1. Endowments of immobile physical factors of production, such as mineral resources, soils suited for growing particular crops, and natural harbors
2. Population in the base period and its urban-rural distribution
3. Transportation costs, which vary among pairs of regions
4. Savings and consumption behavior, which differ between rural and urban areas
5. Base-year productive capacity in each sector and infrastructure facili-

ties. Regional differences in adequacy of infrastructure give rise to differences in the cost of production among regions.

To better visualize the essential aspects of regional development, we can combine these elements into an illustrative dynamic programming model of a closed two-region economy in which, initially, the lagging regions have lower average savings rates and higher aggregate incremental capital-output ratios (due to the need for substantial infrastructure investment). These factors are two of the causes of the observed interregional income inequities. Other causes are related to the size of the regional market, distance from existing major industrial markets, and spatial distribution of immobile factors of production.

It can be shown in this framework that if the savings coefficients and capital-output ratios are fixed over time, the optimal policy requires that investment allocation favor the more "productive" region in all time periods—where the productivity of a region is defined as the ratio of the average savings rate to the capital-output ratio. This, however, is not necessarily the conclusion when the savings and capital-output parameters change over time.

In the course of industrialization a region's population distribution tends to shift toward urban centers as migration takes place. This population shift tends to raise the savings rate if, as in Korea, urban dwellers have significantly higher propensities to save than rural dwellers. At the same time, additional investment in each region tends to remove the most acute deficiencies in infrastructure facilities. Other things being equal, therefore, the capital-output ratio in lagging regions will tend to fall and to come closer to the figure for more advanced regions.

These dynamic factors tend to equalize the productivity of capital in the different regions and to raise the aggregate savings rate in the long run. Thus the need for special regional investment incentives would diminish with time and the national capacity for reinvestment and more rapid growth would be enhanced. If these were the dominant factors at work, temporary regional investment inducements could be justified on grounds of both equity and long-run growth. The optimal policy, therefore depends on the derivatives of the savings rate and capital-output ratio in each region with respect to prior investment, on the upper bounds placed on these parameters, and on the share of investment allocated to the lagging region. The smooth functioning of the productivity-equalizing mechanism may, however, be inhibited by the existence of economies of scale, in conjunction with varying regional populations and market sizes. If the most advanced region has the largest population and existing market, economies of scale will continue to cause a disproportionate share of investment in that region.

III. STRUCTURE OF THE MODEL: SOME
MODEL-BUILDING CONSIDERATIONS

A static linear programming input-output model has been chosen for analyzing multiregional multi-industry investment choices for alternative development policies.[3] It is a model of the process-analysis type; instead of a choice of technologies, a choice of location is offered for each industry.[4] The objective function to be maximized is a linear function of value added in each region.

A series of solutions is conducted under different sets of constraint values in order to explore the trade-off between rapid growth of GNP and more equitable regional distribution of income and to find the most suitable industries for development in each region. The model is designed to make as much use as possible of the data compiled for the Korean sectoral model (see Chapter 5).

Choices of activity location are determined in the model by market locations, resource locations, interregional transportation costs, infrastructure capital costs, water-system capacities,[5] and economies of scale, in accord with standard location theory (see, for example, Isard [41], Lefeber [51, 52], Lösch [55], and Meyer [64]). Market locations are themselves partly endogenous to the model. In a rapidly expanding economy like Korea's, significant changes in location patterns are occurring and partial equilibrium approaches cannot adequately cope with the major alternatives.

Labor and capital are assumed to be mobile among regions and land is assumed to be available in sufficient amounts in all regions. The first assumption is founded on the substantial interregional migration of the last decade, the existence of a system of branch banks that extends to all thirty-two cities, and a network of agricultural banks in every county. As

---

[3] Some of the important developments in the literature related to this kind of model are noted in the following items. Regional input-output projection models have been constructed by Isard, Leontief, Heady and others (41, 54, 37). Locational programming models for single industries were developed by Fox (27), Henderson (38), Heady and others (36, 37), Ghosh (31), Marschak (61), and Vietorisz and Manne (85). A multi-industry programming model of regional investment choices has been presented by Hurter and Moses (40). Process analysis programming models were developed by Bruno (9), Manne (58, 59), and others. Economies of scale and location for single industries have been investigated in Manne (60) and Vietorisz and Manne (85). Finally, economies of scale, location, and interindustry relationships have been combined by Chenery and Westphal (18) with a mixed-integer programming model. Bos (6) also has used a mixed-integer programming model to analyze the development pattern of industrial centers of different sizes.

[4] Agricultural output levels in each region are assumed exogenous to the model.

[5] Because of the generally mountainous terrain of the country, water is sufficiently expensive to transport that it is assumed nontransportable between regions in this model.

for land, Korea has one of the highest population densities in the world, about 300 persons per square kilometer, and the land is being converted from agricultural to industrial and residential uses at a fairly rapid pace. The availability of land for various activities depends on its marginal productivity in such activities, and hence on its rental cost. Full general-equilibrium analysis would allow for parceling out land among different uses according to soil qualities and rents, but both data requirements and time prohibit an attempt to combine this analysis with the other features of the model. It is assumed that within the relevant range of rents, sufficient land is available in each region to support each activity to the sgecified level. The extent to which this assumption is valid will be discovered in the course of a long-term, detailed, and regional physical-planning effort that is now beginning in Korea.

Each productive activity consists of current and capital inputs and an output. Chart 1 is a schematic presentation of the linear programming tableau.

Investment over the plan period is assumed to be a function of the ter-minal year output rather than of the amount of change in output (see Manne [58]). Capital cost parameters and plant lifetime are used to estimate the coefficients of these investment functions. Plan-period require-ments[6] in individual domestic capital goods sectors are listed as rows in the intermediate input portion of the tableau (see Chart 1), and these same capital goods are aggregated in the domestic savings requirement row in the primary resources input section of the tableau. Foreign-capital require-ments are handled in a comparable manner. Over the planning horizon, the assumption of fixed proportions between domestic- and foreign-capital goods is made for each industry. The rate of capacity utilization is assumed not to vary significantly over the relatively long-time horizon.

It has been shown that both the square-root rule and the proportionality assumption for working capital have *a priori* justification in explaining the relation of stock accumulation to gross sales (see Sen [83]). Required stock accumulation, therefore, is viewed as an own-sector input in the pro-duction process of each sector, and the stock requirements are subtracted from the diagonal coefficients of the (I–A) matrix.

There are four potentially scarce resources in the model: domestic savings, foreign exchange, labor, and water for municipal and industrial use.[7] It is doubtful that the labor constraint will be reached in any of the

---

[6] This formulation considerably simplified computation for capital inputs that are included in the same matrix as current inputs, and interactions are not necessary for deriving changes in the vector of outputs that includes capital goods.

[7] Originally, it was intended that port capacity also be limited by region, but data inadequacies and the difficulties of expressing port capacity in *won* terms prohibit this.

CHART 1. SCHEMATIC TABLEAU OF PROGRAMMING PROBLEM, TWO REGIONS

Production		Transporting		Import activities				Exporting		Constraints		
				M^k	M^n	$M^{c,r}$	$M^{c,s}$	E^r	E^s			
$1 - q_i - a_{ij}^r - b_{ij}$	0	-1	$+1$			$+1$	0	-1	0		$\geq$	$\beta_i V^r$
0	$1 - q_i - a_{ij}^s - b_{ij}$	$+1$	-1			0	$+1$	0	-1	γ_j	$\geq$	$\beta_i V^s$
$s^r z_j v_j - z_j q_j - z_j b_{ij}$	$s^s z_j v_j - z_j q_j - z_j b_{ij}$	$s^r v_j^{T*s}$	$s^r v_j^{T*s}$	0	0	0	0	0	0		$\geq$	K^*
n_j^r	n_j^s	n_j^{rs}	n_j^{sr}	0	0	0	0	0	0		$\leq$	L
a_{wj}^r	0	0	0	0	0	0	0	0	0		$\leq$	W^r
0	a_{wj}^s	0	0	0	0	0	0	0	0	$\times$ γ_j	$\leq$	W^s
v_j^r	0	v_j^{rs*}	v_j^{sr*}	0	0	0	0	0	0	γ_j	$\geq$	$\bar{V}^r$
0	v_j^s	v_j^{s*r}	v_j^{s*r}	0	0	0	0	0	0		$\geq$	$\bar{V}^s$
v_j^r	v_j^s	$v_j^{r*s} + v_j^{rs*}$	$v_j^{s*r} + v_j^{sr*}$									maximand

Notes: 1. $+1$ and -1 indicate diagonal matrices with nonzero coefficients taking shown value.
2. $[\gamma_j]$ is the column vector of activity levels.
3. The foreign exchange use row is analogous to the savings row, with imports requiring foreign exchange and exports producing foreign exchange. See text.

190

four regions during the planning period inasmuch as labor is both plentiful and relatively mobile. Water for agricultural purposes is omitted from the Korean input-output tables, no doubt because of difficulties of measurement. However, because agricultural output levels are exogenous to this model, this omission is not serious.[8]

Domestic savings are both produced and consumed within the model. For each region there is a savings row in which the individual cells are composites of (a) positive entries representing the savings from the income generated by each activity and (b) negative entries representing the domestic savings required for capital formation in each activity. Thus, in net terms, a distinction may be made between activities that are savings-incrementing and activities that are savings-decrementing.

Because savings are endogenous, the exogenous limits to the growth rate in the model are (a) the upper bounds imposed on exports and productive activities, (b) the exogenous forecast of foreign exchange earned through transfers and factor earnings from abroad, (c) the capital-output ratios and the initial capacities per sector, (d) the domestic savings rate, (e) terminal year productive capacity in exogenous sectors, and (f) the exogenous supply of labor.[9]

Two methods of handling exports have been considered.[10] One, which has the virtue of computational simplicity, would allocate export demands over regions according to the base-year level of exports from each international port. In the solution, production of the export commodities need not be in the regions with internatioaal ports, but this tends to occur because of interregional transport costs. If, as regional income constraints are raised in successive solutions, it becomes apparent that some export commodities are highly suitable for production in the lagging regions, it may be worthwhile to investigate the possibility of improving the ports in these regions to raise them to international class. In this approach, export demands would be determined exogenously to the model.

The alternative method, which adds many additional activities but no additional equations, specifies the exporting activities for all exportable commodities and for all regions. The output of each activity is foreign exchange and the inputs are the commodities to be exported and some of the port costs, allocated over labor and capital. Then, in the programming

---

[8] Estimates of municipal and industrial water capacities and per capita residential water consumption were made by officials of the Ministry of National Construction.

[9] Under a sufficiently high shadow price of water, it would become profitable to distill sea water; so this constraint is not binding in the long run.

[10] Throughout this paper "exports" and "imports" denote international trade, not interregional trade. Other terms, such as "interregional shipments," are used for the latter.

tableau, foreign exchange would be classified as an intermediate input, and its "final demand" requirement (on the righthand side of the inequality) would be the expected foreign-exchange accumulation minus net foreign transfers and factor earnings from abroad. This method of handling exports is conceptually preferable for it ties permissible import volumes to export performance, and therefore, in part, it ties the rate of capital formation to export performance. It also allows the model more freedom in choosing regional levels of production for export and gives a clearer idea of port requirements. Exports are prevented from exceeding demands on the world market by upper bounds on the exporting levels.[11] This second approach to exports has been chosen.

Imports are generally determined in one of three ways in economy-wide models: (1) through Leontief-type fixed-production input coefficients or fixed ratios of imports to domestic production of the same class of commodities; (2) through make-or-buy choices, with imports represented by separate activities in an optimizing model; or (3) through forecasting equations that may embody both the production input coefficients and parameters for price substitution. A combination of the first two methods is used here. Capital goods imports and noncompetitive noncapital goods imports are determined through fixed-production coefficients, and competitive imports are allowed to enter the basis. Introducing the make-or-buy choice on competitive imports may complicate the regional allocation choice with questions about wise import-substitution policy, but the fixed coefficient or fixed ratio approach runs the risk of introducing substantial errors in import forecasts over a ten-year period.[12]

In the model, all three types of imports are "produced" with inputs of foreign exchange. The net foreign savings available for importing commodities are determined by export performance within the model, by prior forecasts of net factor earnings and transfers from abroad, and by the desired rate of foreign-exchange reserve accumulation. The model's estimate of the volume of imports required in each region gives a good indication of appropriate priorities for port expansion.

Private plus government consumption requirements by region, divided by the terminal average propensity to consume, sum to the regional income constraints. Private and government consumption alike are proportional to regional income. Government consumption by region is assumed to be

---

[11] In this formulation the final-demand constraints for each row read: "Domestic production plus imports, less intermediate use, less exports, is greater than or equal to consumption."

[12] Even for a five-year period, the standard practice is to make high and low assumptions on the rate of import substitution when fixed ratios are used. See, for example, Bergsman and Manne (5) and Chapter 5 above.

proportional to regional local-government expenditures on current account. Initially, the same sectoral breakdown of government consumption will be used in all regions. At present, the only regional differentiation in private consumption elasticities is based on the different urban-rural weights in the different regions.

Economies of scale are incorporated through iteration (Manne [58] uses this technique). If the operation level of activity *j* in a given region is too low to take advantage of substantial economies of scale, activity *j*, in the next solution, will either be suppressed in that region or will be required to meet a minimum production constraint. Comparison of solutions will indicate the optimal choice. An alternative to this procedure is the use of a mixed-integer programming model with fixed capital charges, but it is desirable that the model computation be kept as simple and inexpensive as possible.

For each sector, different activities represent production in each region. With thirty-two productive sectors and four regions, there are at most 128 such activities. Some of the activities are set at zero level *a priori*. Many sectors' outputs by region are specified exogenously, including the primary sectors and mining, cement, petroleum, and steel. Other industries have constraints that specify both minimum and maximum production levels by region. The minimum production levels correspond to actual base-year production. Later, some of these minimum constraints may be selectively removed to explore the consequences of eliminating some of the activities in some regions. Other constraints require that final demands in each region be met or exceeded and that all activities be run at non-negative levels.

There are two transportation activities for moving the output of each sector between every pair of regions. Thus for four regions and thirty-two productive sectors there are, at most, $12 \times 32 = 384$ transporting activities, but the products of several activities are not transported. Inputs to a transporting activity are the product to be delivered and the transportation costs, and the output is the delivered product. This treatment of inter-regional trade has the advantage of not relying on the assumption of fixed interregional trade coefficients; interregional trade patterns are notoriously unstable, and even fairly sophisticated approaches do not yield very accurate predictions.[13]

Employment in man-years is calculated in each solution and wages are entered, along with other value added, in the income row.

[13] See, for example, Leontief and Strout's (54) interesting attempt to predict inter-regional trade. As noted by Marschak (61), intraregional transport must be deducted in establishing the final demand for transport services.

The model is solved for one period only. Terminal year values are calculated by using terminal year final-demand projections and terminal year constraints. The time horizon is ten years, although project lifetimes frequently are longer, but ten-year forecasts of final-demand and resource limitations are sufficiently inaccurate to preclude extending the horizon further. In addition, the real social discount has been measured at about 15 percent per year in Korea, so that spending decisions that will be made more than ten years from now are very substantially discounted in forming present income–expenditure strategies.

Gross national product, rather than consumption, was selected as the maxim and for a number of reasons. For one thing, it is income (and employment), rather than consumption, that policy-makers are trying to adjust more equitably in regional distribution. Also, specification merely of regional consumption constraints would tend to force various interregional shipments in the solution, but this would not necessarily force investment in the lagging regions. This point is illustrated in the first example in Section V below. Finally, consumption targets in this model are corollary to the income targets as a result of having incorporated the savings function and elasticities with respect to total private consumption.

In the solutions, the water constraints, the transportation costs, and the economies of scale will all work in favor of greater concentration of industry in the regions of Seoul and Pusan. The offsetting factors are the regional income constraints, which represent the government's complementary desires to develop the lagging regions and reduce the rate of migration to Seoul. There has been substantial migration to other cities as well.

It is worth noting that this type of model embodies the major principles of regional planning from the point of view of economic geography, as set forth by Prakasa Rao (77). (a) Geographical conditions constrain each region's development through interregional transportation costs, through prior specifications of the location of primary products and input-output relationships, and through the simultaneous solution for all regions and industries. (b) National policies should be taken into account in formulating regional plans through the specification of nationally determined regional income constraints, after assessment has been made of the trade-off between regional income growth and overall GNP growth.

Classical trade theory asks which commodities should be produced—and traded—by each trading partner under constant or diminishing returns to scale, fixed factor endowments, and fixed factor requirements in production. Here, through the use of programming techniques and the input-output table, we are able to permit increasing returns to scale, factor mobility, and changes in aggregate production functions by means of changes in the sectoral composition of output.

IV. Mathematical Formulation of the Model

The equations of the model are as follows; definitions of the symbols are listed in the section that follows the equations.

Regional final demands are met or exceeded:

$$\left. \begin{aligned} &X_j^r(1 - q_j) - \sum_j a_{ij}^r X_j^r - \sum_j b_{ij} X_j^r - \sum_s X_j^{rs} - \sum_s X_j^{sr} \\ &+ M_j^{c,r} + M_j^{n,r} - E_j^r - G_j^r \geq \beta_j^r \bar{V}^r \quad \text{all } j, r; \; i = 1, \ldots, n \end{aligned} \right\} \quad (1)$$

Use of domestic capital goods plus inventory accumulation in all regions does not exceed available domestic savings:

$$\sum_r s^r \left[\sum_j z_j v_j^r X_j^r + \sum_{j,s} v_j^{rs} z_j X_j^{rs} \right] - \sum_{i,j} z_j b_{ij} X_j^r - z_j q_j X_j^r \geq K^* \quad (2)$$

National constraint on labor availability:

$$\sum_{j,r} n_j^r X_j^r + \sum_{j,r,s} n_j^{rs} X_j^{rs} \leq L \quad (3)$$

Regional constraints on resource use (water):

$$\sum_j a_{wj}^r X_j^r \leq W^r \quad \text{all } r \quad (4)$$

(The constraint value is based on total expected municipal and industrial water capacities and on estimated population by region. For each set of regional income constraints there is a set of corresponding population estimates.)

Regional income constraints:

$$\sum_j v_j^r X_j^r + \sum_j v_j^{r*}(X_j^{rs} + X_j^{sr}) = V^r \geq \bar{V}^r \quad (5)$$

Requirement that some activities' products cannot be shipped among regions, for example, services:

$$X_{j^*}^{rs} = 0 \quad \text{some } j^* \quad (6)$$

Objective function:

$$\max \sum_{j,r,s} (v_j X_j^r + v_j^{r*s} X_j^{rs} + v_j^{r*s} X_j^{sr}) \quad (7)$$

(These equations are based in part on the assumption that no income is generated in the exporting and importing activities other than the usual trade margins that are registered in the I–0 table. Capital outlays for port facilities are estimated exogenously on the basis of plan figures and are included in K^*.)

Equations 1 to 7, along with the bounds on the export and production activities, constitute the model proper. The regional savings parameters, s^r, are determined by base-year savings behavior and by the rate of rural-urban migration in each region during the plan period. This relationship may be embodied in the model proper or utilized for supplementary calculations with each set of solutions. The following equations describe urban population, total population, and the average savings rate in each region.

Migration within a region to urban areas:

$$p^{*r}_t = p^{*r}_0(1 + n^*) + \lambda(N^r_t - N^r_0) \tag{8}$$

Average savings rate:

$$s^r_t = s^r_0 + \sigma(p^{*r}_t/p^r_t) \tag{9}$$

Total regional population and interregional migration:

$$p^r_t = p^r_0(1 + n^*) + \mu(N^r_t - N^r_0)/(N_t - N_0) \tag{10}$$

Definitions of variables[14]

X^r_i	output in region r of sector i
a^r_{ij}	ijth input-output coefficient in region r
X^{rs}_i	amount of sector i output transported from region r to region s
$M^{c,r}_i$	competitive import, sector i commodities, region r
$M^{n,r}_i$	noncompetitive import, sector i commodities, region r
C^r_i	private consumption demand
G^r_i	government consumption demand
$\bar{V}_r$	minimum income constraint, region r
β^r_i	coefficient of consumption relative to income, sector i, region r
E^r_i	exports
q_i	ratio of stock accumulation to output, sector i
b_{ij}	capital goods input-output coefficient
z_j	factor for converting terminal year output in sector j to total plan-period output in sector j, based on prior estimates of growth rate in that sector; $z_j = \sum\limits_{i=0}^{t} (1 + r)^{i-t}$, where r is the prior growth rate estimate and t is the number of years in the planning period
s^r	average savings rate in region r, based on the urban-rural population distribution in that region

[14] Superscripts refer to regions and subscripts to sectors.

K^* domestic savings requirements for the planned capital formation in the transport and export and import sectors

n_j^r man-years of labor used per unit of sector j output, region r

n_j^{rs} man-years of labor used per unit of transport of sector j output between region r and region s

L total estimated labor force in the terminal year

a_{wj}^r water input-output coefficient

W^r water capacity, region r

v_j^{r*s} income in region r per unit of transport between regions r and s

v_j income generated per unit of activity j

p_t^{*r} population at time t in region r, urban areas

p_t^r total population at time t in region r

μ coefficient of interregional migration relative to employment change

λ coefficient of intraregional migration

n^* natural increase rate of population, annual, nationwide

N_t^l employment in region r at time t

σ coefficient of the savings rate relative to the population distribution

V. Some Numerical Examples

A Simple Model

The model can perhaps be best introduced through a two-region two-commodity example. For illustrative purposes, the example concerns the allocation of manufacturing activities over two agricultural regions. Thus we want to find the locational pattern that maximizes the total *increments* in income from investment in manufacturing. For simplicity, only new manufacturing income is treated, and, although there are interindustry flows, it is assumed there are no sales between agriculture and manufacturing.

In the example, the scarce resources are defined as capital—and in one region—water. It is assumed that the cost of transporting water between regions is prohibitive. One of the commodities requires water for its production and the other commodity requires relatively large amounts of raw material inputs. Both commodities can be produced in each region, and in addition there is the possibility of transporting either commodity between the regions.[15] To avoid introducing unnecessary complications, it is assumed that the two commodities require equal amounts of capital.

---

[15] To simplify the problem, only the possibility of transporting from the water-rich to the water-scarce region is considered because it is known beforehand that commodity flows will not occur in the opposite direction.

TABLE 1. INPUT-OUTPUT FLOWS IN A 2-REGION EXAMPLE

Activities / Inputs & outputs	Region A A1	Region A A2	Region B B1	Region B B2	AB1	AB2
A1	10	−3			−10	
A2	−5	10				−10
B1			10	−3	10	
B2			−5	10		10
Primary inputs: K	−3	−3	−3	−3	−1	−1
Primary inputs: L	−2	−3	−2	−3		
Primary inputs: W_A		−1				
Primary inputs: W_B				−1		
$y = K + L$	−5	−6	−5	−6	−1	−1

Definitions of symbols:
$A\,i$ = commodity i in region A
$B\,i$ = commodity i in region B
ABi = transportation of i from region A to region B
K = capital
L = labor
W_A = water in region A
W_B = water in region B
y = value added

Commodity 2, however, requires more labor and its production therefore yields more income per unit of output.

These assumptions are presented in Table 1. The regions are labeled A and B and the commodities 1 and 2. The activity that produces commodity 1 in region A is called A1 and the activity that transports commodity 1 from region A to region B is called AB1. Outputs of activities are given a positive sign and inputs a negative sign. Operation of activity A1 produces 10 units of commodity 2 at the unitary level, 3 units of capital, and 2 units of labor.

The roles of the different constraints can be illustrated if they are introduced one by one in a problem whose objective is to maximize total (national) income. The capital constraint is introduced at the level of 50 units. The requirement that neither activity can be run at a negative level also is specified. Because as yet there are no regional final-demand requirements, the optimal solution is:

$$Z_1(\mathrm{A2}) + Z_2(\mathrm{B2})$$

where $Z_1 + Z_2 = \frac{50}{3}$. In other words, because production of commodity 2 is the highest income activity, the income-maximizing solution is to produce it up to a level at which the supply of capital is exhausted.[16] The

[16] Throughout this example "income" will be used to denote manufacturing income; it is assumed that agricultural income is given, and we are concerned with the additional income from manufacturing.

total income in this solution is $16.7 \times 6 = 100$. Varying the regional distribution of income does not affect total income.

If the water limitation of region B is introduced, say at a level of 3 units, it is obvious that Z_2 can be no greater than 3×1 in the solution. This limitation severely constrains the amount of production of commodity 2 in region B, so that if high national income is the goal, most of the income will be generated in region A. Region B will have an income of at most $3 \times 6 = 18$ units, while region A will have at least 82 units of income. To achieve better regional balance, some of commodity B1 would have to be produced and total national income lowered.

This case is illustrated in Figure 1. Activities A2 and B2 are plotted on the axis. Line KK' is the capital constraint and line $W_B W_B$ is the water constraint in region B. (Note that an infinite amount of water is assumed to be available in region A.) Line KK' touches each axis at a 45 degree angle because the capital requirements per unit of output are the same for

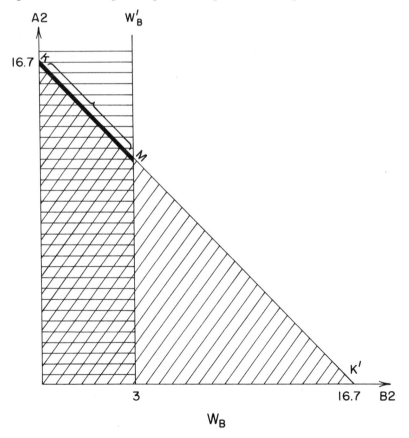

FIGURE 1. OPTIMAL SOLUTION UNDER CAPITAL AND WATER CONSTRAINTS.

the two activities. Any point in the cross-hatched zone is a feasible solution; that is, it does not violate the constraints. An optimal solution is found anywhere along the line MK because the lines of income possibilities also lie at 45 degree angles to the axis and MK is coterminous with the highest income line.

Introduction of the water constraint did not necessarily lower the total attainable income but it severely distorted the regional distribution of income. If, instead of the water constraint, final-demand requirements are introduced, the optimal solution may contain a lower figure for national income. Suppose that 20 units of each commodity are required for consumption in each region (in anticipation of approximately equal income in each region). Then some of commodity 1 must be produced in addition to commodity 2; therefore, with the same capital constraint, the total income cannot be as high. Inspection of the table shows that 4 units of each activity, A1, B1, A2, and B2, will meet the final-demand requirements and at the same time give the highest possible income under the circumstances, which now is 88 instead of 100 (limiting our inspection to integer approximations to the optimum).

If both the final-demand and the water constraints are operable, activity B2 cannot operate at the 4-unit level without violating the water constraint. Thus additional amounts of A2 must be produced for shipment to region B, and since A1 is an input to A2, additional amounts of A1 also are needed. The result cannot be found by simple inspection, but the optimal integer solution is as follows:

A1	:	7.00
A2	:	7.00
B1	:	0.00
B2	:	0.00
AB1	:	2.00
AB2	:	2.00

The maximum national income is further reduced, to 87 in this case, and there is no production in region B. The final-demand constraints are met exactly, no water is used, and 49 of the 50 units of capital are used. Thus in this case the final-demand requirements are the binding constraints. In this solution, region B receives no income from production; so the only income generated in that region is part of the income from the transportation service. If income from interregional transportation is divided evenly between the regions, in this solution region A receives 85 units of income and region B receives 2 units of income.

This striking income disparity results only from the presence of a water constraint in region B and the directive to seek the regional distribution of resources that maximizes national income. If regional populations are even roughly equal, such an income disparity would not be desirable; so additional constraints must be added to ensure minimum regional income goals. Of course, more balanced incomes among regions are achieved only at the expense of lower national income. One of the primary purposes of this model is to assess the trade-off between growth of national income and more equitable regional distribution of income.

The example illustrates the role of the different constraints. Overall capital constraints limit total income and production; water (or other regional resource) constraints limit regional income; final-demand requirements may force interregional commodity shipments but they will not necessarily raise regional incomes; regional income constraints are necessary to bring regional incomes up to minimum desired levels, but there is a cost in terms of lower national income.

Solution of the "dual" to this problem yields shadow prices of all scarce resources that serve as indicators of the most serious bottlenecks in attaining higher national income.

Second Example

The dual is primarily useful for calculating the partial derivatives of the objective function, with respect to the various constraint variables, in order to measure the different bottlenecks to further increases in the objective function. A simpler way to find the major bottlenecks is by calculating the matrix of percentage resource uses per unit of output of each activity (see Masse [62:155–59] and Fox [28]). This procedure is illustrated below.

Suppose the input-output flows and resource constraints are as shown in Table 2. (This example is similar to the previous example, except for some modifications of coefficients and the assumptions that both regions have water constraints and the labor supply is not unlimited.) A glance at

TABLE 2. A SECOND EXAMPLE OF INPUT-OUTPUT FLOWS

Activities

Inputs & outputs	A1	A2	B2	B1	AB1	AB2	R
A1	10	−3			−10		20
A2	−5	10				−10	20
B1			10	−3	10		20
B2			−5	10		10	20
L	2	4	2	4	1	2	60
K	2.5	2	2.5	2	1	1	40
W_A	.5	1					6
W_B			.5	1			4
Y_A	4.5	6			1	1.5	
Y_B			4.5	6	1	1.5	

TABLE 3. MATRIX OF RESOURCE USE MAGNITUDES

	A1	A2	B1	B2	AB1	AB2	R
Case A							
L	.007	.011	.007	.011	.008	.011*	60
K	.014	.008	.014	.008	.013*	.008	40
W_A	.019*	.028*	—	—			6
W_B			.028*	.042*			4
Case B							
L	.007	.011	.007	.011	.008	.011	60
K	.023*	.014	.023	.014	.021*	.014*	24
W_A	.019	.028*	—	—			6
W_B			.028*	.042*			4

Table 2 shows that water is the scarcest resource in all four manufacturing activities but it is not immediately apparent whether labor or capital is the more scarce resource in the transporting activities. The binding constraint for each activity can be found by calculating the supplementary matrix:

$$A_{ij}/R_i \cdot Y_j$$

which shows the percentage of resource i that is used up in the production of one unit of income in activity j. This matrix is shown in Table 3, where the binding resource for each activity is denoted by an asterisk.

In case A, as expected, water is the binding constraint for all four manufacturing activities. In case B, which is the same as case A except that less capital is available, capital becomes the binding constraint in one of the activities in one of the regions. This result is unexpected, for at first glance it is natural to expect the same binding constraint to affect both activities in one region or to affect a given activity in both regions.

A table such as this is very useful for supplying guidance on policy decisions pertaining to regional investment because it shows the factor of production that most seriously inhibits the development of each region. For example, if the binding constraint for most of the activities in a given region were water, a major priority for development of that region would be expansion of its water system. If water systems are very costly to expand in a given region, a wise regional policy may call for emphasizing industries that do not consume large quantities of water.

VI. Uses of the Model

The model is designed to translate rather abstract goals into specific investment strategies—such as more nearly equal regional incomes or more nearly equal regional population growth rates. The model-building effort is based on the premise that investment policy is one of the primary means for meeting regional goals, through the direct allocation of government investment, through the legislated powers of review over proposed foreign-financed private investment projects, and indirectly through inducement of other private investment by the creation of industrial parks and the provision of other social overhead facilities.

Specifically, seven quantitative results can be expected from this type of model.

1. *Costs of decentralization.*   Costs are evaluated for alternative regional development strategies that range from extreme centralization of industrial productive capacity to extreme decentralization. Costs are measured both in terms of capital requirements and the rate of GNP growth, but, since the maximum growth pattern is sought within each strategy, the pattern will be expressed primarily in terms of lower GNP growth.

In an economy in which capital and labor are regionally mobile,[17] purposive decentralization tends to lower overall GNP for two reasons: (1) additional investment must be diverted to building up basic social overhead facilities in the regions to be industrialized, and (2) dispersing industry over several locations may mean failure to take advantage of economies of scale.[18] The rate of trade-off between incomes in the "peripheral" regions and national income depends upon the rapidity of development of each region.

In deriving the trade-offs, regional investment requirements are calculated for each strategy, and these may be compared with past rates of investment by region to estimate the required shift in resource allocation patterns.

2. *Bottleneck resources.*   Shadow prices on scarce resources, such as water-system capacity in each region, indicate the appropriate regional priorities for expansion of these facilities. Hurter and Moses (40) have constructed a regional investment programming model that relies entirely on the shadow prices of capacity in all sectors for indicating investment priorities.

Masse (62) and Fox (28) have provided a relatively simple method for assessing the magnitude of various bottlenecks without computing

---

[17] Mera demonstrates the reduction in efficiency caused by attempting to meet regional income balance goals when regions are unequally endowed with factors of production and these factors are immobile between regions (63).

[18] It is sometimes argued that, in the long run, a degree of decentralization is less costly due to avoidance of excessive urban congestion; that is, due to postponement of the date when external economies are outweighed by external diseconomies in a large urban industrial complex. However, because this point is difficult to test empirically, this model is confined to measuring direct costs in all sectors over a ten-year period.

shadow prices.[19] They calculate the matrix from the initial linear programming tableau:

$$[A_{ij}/R_iY_j] = [r^*_{ji}]$$

which is explained in section V above.

3. *Preferred industrial locations.* An additional question the model treats is the types of industries that are most appropriate for raising incomes in the lagging regions. Several solutions will be conducted under different sets of regional income constraints for the target year. As income constraints are successively raised for the lagging regions, additional industries with positive outputs appear in the solution. Examination of these solutions yields rankings of industries in order of their appropriateness for each region, which in turn indicate the manner in which regional specialization may be expected to develop.[20]

4. *Interregional transportation flows.* A set of interregional shipment volumes will be associated with each solution. Caution must be exercised in interpreting net sectoral flows at such an aggregative level, because, in actuality, gross interregional flows for a single two-digit sector usually are much larger than the net flows.

5. *Social overhead requirements.* Each solution will contain an estimate of regional investment requirements in social overhead facilities and an estimate of electric power demand in each region. This result is of primary importance for implementation of the desired pattern of regional development.

6. *Interregional migration.* By applying either constant aggregate employment–output ratios or migration equations to the regional income estimates in each solution, an estimate of interregional migration under each set of income constraints will be derived.

7. *Criteria for project selection.* The shadow prices on scarce resources and on regional income targets can be used in regional project-appraisal criteria and in a more disaggregative projection-programming model. In the case of investment criteria, the income to be generated in different regions can be assigned different values as a means of implementing the government's desire to develop lagging regions. In the same calculations, regionally scarce resources should be assigned shadow prices from the model solution.

VII. CONCLUSION

In less developed countries, where market size often is the constraining factor in the growth of particular industries, economies of scale can inhibit

---

[19] Fox attributes this technique to F. V. Waugh.

[20] Even in a country as small as Korea, transportation costs are sufficiently high to force regional specialization.

decentralization of plant locations. Nevertheless, the relatively rapid economic and demographic expansion of the leading urban center(s) tends to create wide income disparities among regions and consequent demands for more equitable distribution of the fruits of development.

Assessment of the trade-off between regional income growth and national development involves interindustry relationships as well as interregional relationships. In Korea at present, the scope for change in the industrial character of the regions is so great that partial equilibrium analyses are inappropriate. Programming techniques are suitable for this type of problem, but introduction of the regional dimension threatens to make the problem unwieldy because of its size. A one-period linear programming framework has been found appropriate for keeping the analysis manageable, even though rapid and differential changes in sector locations are expected beyond the planning horizon.

On the demographic side of the model, the rate of creation of manufacturing jobs appears to be a significant determinant of the rate of migration to particular cities. This finding gives further normative force to the model, for the explosive growth of the capital city may be slowed by appropriate investment allocation policies.

CHAPTER 7 APPENDIX

Definition of Regions

I. *Introduction.* The formulation and implementation of a national regional plan and related local regional plans must be based on a set of regions designated for planning purposes. Any set of regional boundaries, however carefully drawn, will contain some arbitrary and unsatisfactory features, but the establishment of regions is an unavoidable part of formulating and administering programs on a spatial basis.

This appendix describes the spatial entities—regions—that form the basis for data collection efforts and regional analysis now being conducted. It reflects the effort of many individuals, over a period of a year and a half, to define an appropriate spatial framework in which different types of regional development studies could be coordinated and regional development plans could be executed.[1] Coordination has been a primary concern, for the practical value of regional studies and plans is sharply reduced if they are carried out on the basis of noncomparable regions.

II. *Basic considerations and criteria.* Two major questions have determined the general nature of this regional framework. The first question concerned the extent to which existing administrative boundaries could be utilized for planning regions. All contributors agreed that the following two factors compel the use of administrative boundaries as much as possible: (1) the overriding consideration that a plan must be implemented if the desired patterns are to be achieved in actuality, and (2) the fact that many existing data are available on the basis of administrative boundaries. In particular, the *gun* (county) and the city are the basic units of tabulation

---

[1] The main contributors to this effort have been Marshall K. Wood, Nam Young Woo, Roger Norton, Lee Kee Jung, Kim Hak So, Tarik Carim, Lee Han Soon, Choi Sang Chul, Kim Ui Won, Jin Byung Ho, Hong Sung Chull, Cha Byung Kwon, and Pak Ha Ryong. Helpful comments were made by Wooh Youn-Hwi, Lee Hee Il, Rhee Ki Jun, Lane Holdcroft, Moon Pal Young, and John Kling, staff members of the Ministry of Home Affairs, and by the planning officials of Cholla Namdo, Cholla Pukto, Chungchong Namdo, and Ulsan City. Reference has been made to many prior studies, some of which are listed in the Bibliography.

for many surveys, such as the population census and the industrial census.[2]

On the other hand, it can be said that administrative boundaries are not immutable, and regional development planning takes a 10- to 15-year perspective. In fact, there has already been considerable study of possible changes in the existing administrative districts in Korea; so the possibility of significant boundary changes within five to ten years is fairly high. It also has been pointed out that since regional development plans involve physical interventions, such as roads, irrigation systems, and factories, these plans can always be interpreted and published on the basis of administrative districts, even if they are formulated on the basis of other regions.

The second, and more difficult, major question was: To the extent that administrative boundaries are not entirely followed, what criteria should be used in defining regions? Since the primary purpose of regional planning is the creation of sound economic-development plans for the different regions in the country, economic criteria generally dominate the decisions, although geographic, demographic, and social factors must also be taken into account. The appropriate criteria follow from the major types of problems for planners and administrators:[3] the rational location of new industrial plants, the establishment of priorities among the various social overhead projects (such as road construction and port expansion), and the need to plan for the rapid growth of urban areas throughout the nation. For both of these general classes of problems, regions must be defined so that each region contains at least one relatively large city.[4] The first problem, location of industry and infrastructure, can be approached efficiently with a set of regions that are defined on the basis of transportation flows around the various urban centers and that highlight the different fresh-water endowments of each area. Even with a relatively decentralized pattern of industrial location, most major industrial plants will be located in cities. Therefore each region should embrace at least one relatively large city, and the surrounding agricultural or mineral-resources hinterlands, so that local transportation flows become intraregional. Also, each region's urban center(s) should be a potential industrial growth center.

In drawing boundaries around the cities, economic *integration* is the

---

[2] There are 139 counties in Korea, and 32 cities are administratively parallel to and independent of the counties. Cities are defined as urban agglomerations of more than 50,000 people. The average county had about 140,000 people in 1966.

[3] "There is no unique and universally applicable definition of a region and the definition must depend on the purpose at hand" (Lefeber [51]).

[4] Most regions will have at least one urban center, but some regions will have more than one large city and thus will have an urban "axis" or "triangle" instead of an "urban center."

primary criterion.[5] Application of the integration criterion means that each *gun* should be grouped with the major city its residents most frequently communicate with and travel to. Origin-and-destination studies are necessary to make the boundaries of such regions precise (121), and likely future transportation patterns should be taken into account.[6]

The regions defined on the basis of integration around major urban centers also are quite appropriate for the other major planning problem, that of adequately preparing for the continuing urban explosion. For this problem, however, the regions may be smaller.[7]

It is clear that regions of different size are needed for different planning purposes, and therefore a hierarchy of regions has been defined by application of the polarization criterion on different levels.

III. *Drawing spatial boundaries.* The solution adopted in drawing geographic planning boundaries in Korea combines the "administrative unit" criterion and the "integration-polarization" criterion. The final solution contains the following elements:

1. The *gun* (and the city) was adopted as the basic spatial building block, and in no instance were the *gun* boundaries crossed in drawing regional boundaries.

2. The nine provinces were adopted as a set of planning regions because no change in their boundaries is likely to occur in the near future and because the provinces may become channels of implementation of regional development programs.

3. Five supraprovincial "programming" regions were designated on the basis of economic market areas and watersheds.[8] These regions closely

---

[5] This concept is similar to the "market area" concept used by Lösch in his pioneering work on location theory (55: esp. pp. 103–220). See also the excerpt "The Nature of Economic Regions," reprinted in Friedmann and Alonso (29).

[6] Major new transportation projects would significantly alter origin-destination patterns; therefore present transportation flows may not be as relevant as anticipated —or desired—future flows.

[7] Regions that are derived from the criterion of integration around urban centers may be called polarized regions. As an alternative criterion, homogeneity within a region is sometimes suggested. For planning purposes, however, this criterion generally has been superseded by integration (polarization). While homogeneity may offer a suitable rule for defining regions for specialized surveys, it is not adequate for overall economic and physical analyses of regions, in which many different characteristics must be studied. It is significant that, about a decade ago, the United States Census Bureau used the integration criterion in redesigning its census districts, which formerly had been delineated on the basis of homogeneity.

Another operational way of stating the criterion is that the regional boundaries should be drawn so that, for a given number of regions, intraregional transportation flows are maximized and interregional flows are minimized.

[8] The term "programming region" is taken from J. R. Boudeville (7). For most calculations, the five regions are aggregated to four by grouping the island of Cheju Do with one of the mainland regions.

follow geographic and historic divisions, in addition to indicating the major market areas. They are aggregations of *guns*, and their boundaries for the most part follow existing provincial boundaries. In a country of Korea's size, five regions are sufficient for formulation of the basic development strategies.

4. Eighteen comprehensive smaller regions have been designated on the basis of major urban centers. Each region includes an urban pole (or "axis" or "triangle" if more than one city is included) and the surrounding agricultural hinterland, and thus is a truly "polarized" region in Boudeville's terminology. The eighteen regions can be aggregated to the programming regions and, with minor adjustments, to the provinces themselves.

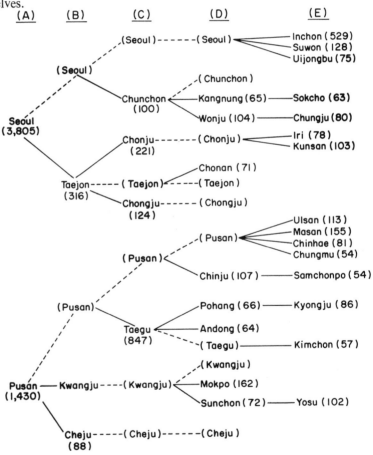

FIGURE A–1. ECONOMIC POLARIZATION AND SCHEME OF CITIES IN KOREA.*
* 1966 city populations are indicated in parentheses (in thousands).

TABLE A-1. SOME BASIC STATISTICS OF PROGRAMMING REGIONS[a]

Region	1966 region population	Area (sq. km.)	1966 pop. density (persons/ sq. km.)	1966 mining and manufacturing production (mill. won)	1965 rice production (mill. tons)	Central city and 1966 population	
1. Northern	9,223,377	30,935	298.2	219,350	602,719	Seoul	3,805,261
2. Kum River	6,216,537	20,268	306.7	49,146	1,095,885	Taejon	315,830
3. Southwestern	4,344,967	13,327	326.0	22,456	654,983	Kwangju	404,459
4. Naktong River	9,086,281	32,118	282.9	152,260	1,141,407	Pusan	1,429,726
5. Cheju Do	336,694	1,830	184.0	1,557	6,530	Cheju	87,569
Total	29,207,856	98,478	296.6	444,769	3,501,524		

[a] Totals may not add precisely to published national totals, due to rounding errors.

211

This procedure results in the polarization of urban centers, as in Figure A–1. Column *A* represents the simplest regionalization, that between Seoul and Pusan. Column *B* shows the main cities of the five programming regions, and column *C* contains the provincial capitals. The cities in column *D* are the chief cities in each of the eighteen regions, and column E lists the other cities in Korea. Some salient characteristics of the programming regions are displayed in Table A–1.

Interestingly enough, this procedure yields a set of polarized regions that are virtually identical with the major watershed districts. This reinforces the usefulness of these regions, for water is a primary resource. For mineral and soil resources, interregional differences in endowments can be readily measured with any set of boundaries, but for water resources, when one region is upriver from another, it is difficult to measure separate regional endowments.

A DYNAMIC NONLINEAR PLANNING
MODEL FOR KOREA

David A. Kendrick and
Lance J. Taylor

I. Introduction

This paper is a report on the construction and solution of a nonlinear medium-term planning model. The specification in this form permitted the inclusion of nonlinear welfare and production functions. This, in turn, provided a better opportunity than is possible with the usual linear programming models for studying the trade-offs between total consumption and savings, among various commodities in total consumption, and between capital and labor inputs in production.

Korean data were used; however, because the work with nonlinear models is just beginning, our results are presented for illustrative purposes only and not to draw substantial conclusions with respect to Korean development. Because it is demonstrated here that it is feasible to solve multisectoral nonlinear planning models and because nonlinear production functions are now being estimated in many countries, it is anticipated that models of this type will someday be used in actual planning situations.

During recent years, economists have formulated and solved a number of dynamic multisectoral planning models in the form of linear programs, namely, Bruno (9), Eckaus and Parikh (23), and Chakravarty and Lefeber (13). Although most of these studies have used linear production and welfare relations, some have employed piecewise linear segments to make linear approximations to nonlinear functions, for example, Adelman and Sparrow (1), Barr and Manne (4), and Carter (11).

This paper discusses a set of numerical experiments that uses a dynamic multisectoral planning model with nonlinear welfare and production relationships. In finding optimal solutions to this planning problem, we employed computational techniques that have been developed in recent

Our research has been financed in part by the Project for Quantitative Research in Economic Development at Harvard University under a grant from the Agency for International Development and in part by the Harvard Institute for Economic Research under a grant from the National Science Foundation. We are indebted to Rod Dobell, Hollis Chenery, Louis Lefeber, Thomas Vietorisz, J. A. Mirrlees, and Arthur Bryson for comments and suggestions and to Andy Szasz for programming assistance.

years by control theorists. Inasmuch as we have reported elsewhere (46) on our numerical methods,[1] we will concentrate in this paper on the formulation and interpretation of the solutions to a four-sector model of the Korean economy.

In Sections II and III we develop the four-sector model and provide numerical values for the parameters. In Section IV we discuss the solution method. Section V is an analysis of the results obtained from a number of numerical experiments with the model. Finally, Section V discusses some of the advantages and disadvantages in the use of control-theory models for development planning.

II. THE MODEL

The basic structure of the model maximizes a welfare function over a thirty-year period, subject to constraints in the form of distribution relations, production functions, absorptive capacity functions, foreign-exchange constraints, and initial and terminal capital stock and foreign debt constraints. The four sectors are (1) agriculture and mining, (2) heavy industry, (3) light industry, and (4) services.

Welfare Function

In a number of linear programming models (e.g., Bruno [9]), the welfare function has been specified in something like the following form:

$$\xi = \sum_{i=1}^{N} (1 + z)^{-i} \sum_{j=1}^{4} c_{ji} \tag{1}$$

z = discount rate
i = time-period index
j = sector index
c = consumption.

The maximand is the discounted sum over time of each year's total consumption. Each c_{ji} has usually been constrained by a linearized income elasticity formula to bear a relationship to $\sum_{j} c_{ji}$, the total consumption in period i.

---

[1] See also Bryson and Ho (10), who give a complete survey of solution methods for optimal control problems that have been proposed to date. Other techniques for solving planning models with various types of nonlinearities have been employed by Chenery and Uzawa (17), Frisch (30), Chakravarty (12), Johansen and Lindhold (44), Mirrlees (65), Stoleru (84), Radner (72, 73), and Radner and Friedman (74).

We have adopted a superficially different but actually similar welfare function:

$$\xi = \sum_{i=1}^{N} (1 + z)^{-i} \sum_{j=1}^{4} a_j c_{ji}{}^{b_i} \qquad 0 \leq b_j \leq 1 \tag{2}$$

$$a_j \geq 0$$

Students of consumption theory will see that the inner sum is merely Houthakker's "direct addilog" utility function (39).

Apart from the time consideration, maximization of a welfare function of the form 2, subject to the constraint,

$$\sum_j c_{ji} = y_i \tag{2a}$$

where y_i is total consumption expenditure in time period i, yields a demand function of the form:

$$c_{ji} = \left[\frac{a_j b_j y_i}{\pi} \right]^{\frac{1}{1-b_j}} \tag{3}$$

with the equation interaction term π determined as the unique solution of the equation:

$$\sum_j \left[\frac{a_j b_j}{\pi} \right]^{\frac{1}{1-b_j}} \left[y_i \right]^{\frac{b_j}{1-b_j}} = 1 \tag{4}$$

To obtain an expression for the income elasticities, we begin by taking the derivative of 3 to obtain:

$$\frac{dc_{ji}}{dy_i} = \frac{1}{1 - b_j} c_{ji} \left[\frac{1}{y_i} - \frac{1}{\pi} \frac{d\pi}{dy_i} \right] \tag{4a}$$

By taking the total derivative of 4 in terms of $d\pi$ and dy_i and solving the resulting expression, we obtain:

$$\frac{d\pi}{dy_i} = \frac{\pi}{y_i} \frac{\displaystyle\sum_j \frac{b_j}{1 - b_j} c_{ji}}{\displaystyle\sum_j \frac{1}{1 - b_j} c_{ji}} \tag{4b}$$

which, on substitution into 4a, yields:

$$E_{c_{ji}/y_i} = \frac{y_i}{c_{ji}} \frac{dc_{ji}}{dy_i} = \frac{1}{1 - b_j} \left[1 - \frac{\displaystyle\sum_j \frac{b_j}{1 - b_j} c_{ji}}{\displaystyle\sum_j \frac{1}{1 - b_j} c_{jn}} \right] \tag{5}$$

By appropriate choice of our a_j and b_j, we can specify initial demand levels and income elasticities. The model will choose optimal consumption levels over time in line with its own generated prices but still roughly in line with the income elasticities in 5.

We chose the parameters a and b, as in Table 1.[2] Table 2 gives the implied consumption shares and income elasticities on the assumption of no price changes. The consumption discount rate, z, was set at 3 percent per year.

Distribution Relations

The distribution relations are of the standard input-output type:

$$q + Dq + m = Aq + B\delta + e + c \qquad (6)$$

q = vector of output levels
δ = vector of investment levels
m = vector of untied imports
e = vector of exports
c = vector of consumption levels
D = diagonal matrix of marginal propensities to import for production
A = input-output matrix
B = capital coefficient matrix.[3]

The basic data sources for the A and B matrices are the eighteen-sector input-output and capital-output matrices used by Larry Westphal in his integer programming study of economies of scale in Korean manufacturing.[4] We aggregated these eighteen sectors to four sectors, using

---

[2] The data tables are in the Appendix to this paper. We are most grateful to David Cole and Larry Westphal for providing us with most of our data as well as with a number of helpful suggestions on the formulation of the model. Since our primary concern in this research was to determine the feasibility of solving multisectoral nonlinear planning models and to learn a little about the characteristics of such models, we ask the reader's tolerance when we seem a bit cavalier with the data.

[3] We assume that the top and bottom rows of B consist of zero elements; that is, that the agriculture and mining sector and the services sector provide negligible amounts of inputs to capital formation. Actually, this assumption is also an empirical result. We aggregated an eighteen-sector Korean input-output B matrix to get our matrix. Only five of the eighteen sectors actually produce capital goods, and these were all aggregated into our heavy and light industry sectors. Note that we assume fixed proportions of light and heavy industrial goods in making up each sector's capital stock. A more accurate specification of the production process would allow substitution between these two types of capital goods. A similar assumption is made with respect to intermediate goods, through our use of the Leontief A matrix. Although this could also be replaced by production functions that permit substitution, it could add greatly to the computations to do so.

[4] Westphal's sources are 43-sector matrices, put together by him and based on the work of Marshall Wood and the Bank of Korea for the year 1965 (see Westphal [86]).

Westphal's data on 1965–66 flows and sectoral capacity levels. The aggregation scheme is given in Table 3, and Tables 4 and 5 give the a_{ij} and b_{ij} coefficients respectively. (The latter two tables also list noncompetitive import requirements per unit of sectoral output and investment.)

Production Functions

In line with recent empirical work, we assume that the production functions are the constant elasticity of substitution type:[5]

$$q_{ji} = \tau_j(1 + \nu_j)^i[\beta_j k_{ji}^{-\rho_i} + (1 - \beta_j)\ell_{ji}^{-\rho_i}]^{-\frac{1}{\rho_i}} \qquad (7)$$

q = output
τ = efficiency parameter
ν = rate of technical progress
β = distribution parameter
k = capital input
ℓ = labor input
$\rho = \dfrac{1}{\sigma_j} - 1$, where σ_j is the elasticity of substitution for the *j*th sector.

The parameters of the CES production functions are given in Table 6. We have assumed a relatively high elasticity of substitution in the agriculture-mining sector and a relatively low elasticity in the services sector. Also, we have assumed lower rates of technical change in services and light manufacturing than in the other sectors. The efficiency parameters were computed from the production functions by using the base-year (1965) labor force, capital stock, and output (see Table 7), along with the assumed values of the other parameters.

Employment Constraint

The labor constraint implied by a neoclassical assumption of full employment is:

$$\sum_{j=1}^{4} \ell_{ji} = \ell_i \qquad (8)$$

where ℓ_i is the exogenously given total labor force in period *i*. In the calculations, the labor-force growth rate, *r*, was set at 2 percent per year.

---

[5] We use the constant returns to scale form of the CES function. The specification of diminishing returns would add no essential complication but the increasing returns specification would make the problem non-convex.

Absorptive Capacity Constraints

Again in keeping with the linear programming tradition, we built absorptive capacity constraints into the model by assuming capital (or capacity) accumulation equations of the form:

$$k_{j,i+1} = k_{ji} + g_j(\delta_{ji'} k_{ji}) \qquad \text{all } i, j \qquad (9)$$

where k_{ji} is the capital stock in sector j at time i, δ_{ji} is an activity representing the total resources devoted to investment in that sector at that time, and $g_j(\delta_{ji'} k_{ji})$ is a function imposing decreasing returns to investment in creating new capacity. To avoid the possibility of unrealistic decumulations in capital stock, we impose the constraints:

$$\delta_{ji} \geq 0 \qquad \text{all } i, j \qquad (10)$$

The functions $g_j(\delta_{ji'} k_{ji})$, which appear in 9,[6] are of the form:

$$g_j(\delta_{ji'}k_{ji}) = \Delta k_{ji} = \mu_j k_{ji}\left\{ 1 - \left[1 + \frac{\epsilon_j \, \delta_{ji}}{\mu_j \, k_{ji}}\right]^{-\frac{1}{\epsilon_j}}\right\} \qquad (11)$$

$$\epsilon_j \geq -1 \qquad \mu_j \geq 0$$

The assumption behind this specification is simply that as the increase in capacity, Δk, approaches some fraction μ of existing capacity k, investment, δ, becomes less and less effective in increasing Δk. Thus $\dfrac{d(\Delta k)}{d\delta} =$ a decreasing function of δ, or, in a convenient functional form:

$$\frac{d(\Delta k)}{d\delta} = \left(1 - \frac{\Delta k/k}{\mu}\right)^{1+\epsilon} \qquad \begin{matrix} 0 < \mu \\ -1 \leq \epsilon \end{matrix} \qquad (12)$$

The parameter ϵ has been introduced to indicate how rapidly the decrease in investment efficiency occurs. The differential equation 12 can be solved to give Δk in terms of δ and k:

$$\frac{\Delta k}{k} = \mu\left\{1 - \left[1 + \frac{\epsilon}{\mu}\frac{\delta}{k}\right]^{-\frac{1}{\epsilon}}\right\} \qquad (13)$$

Note that $\epsilon = -1$ means that $\Delta k = \delta$, so that a linear relationship holds between change in capacity and investment (although there is still an implied upper bound of μ on $\Delta k/k$). For $-1 < \epsilon < 0$, $\Delta k/k$ is a concave and monotonically increasing function of δ/k until $\Delta k/k = \mu$, at which point the function in (10) becomes complex-valued.

For $\epsilon = 0$ we have $\underset{k}{\Delta k} = \mu[1 - e^{\delta/\mu k}]$, which increases asymptotically

---

[6] This function was suggested by Robert Dorfman for a different model but we have adopted it for use here. Although Sam Bowles and Louis Lefeber have suggested that an absorptive capacity relationship should include educated or highly skilled labor as one of the inputs, and we are in agreement, we have not implemented this suggestion in the present model.

to μ. In general, when $\epsilon \geq = 0$, this sort of behavior occurs; so there are both diminishing returns and an absolute upper bound μ on $\Delta k/k$ that is approached when $\delta/k \to \infty$.

For our initial analysis, we set ϵ equal to 0.5 and imposed upper bounds on absorptive capacity in the sectors as follows:

Sector	Capacity Constraint μ
1	0.275
2	0.35
3	0.30
4	0.35

Thus we have assumed that capacity expansion is relatively difficult in agriculture, less difficult in light industry, and relatively easy in heavy industry and services. The actual relationships between δ/k (the sectoral investment rate) and $\Delta k/k$ (increase in capacity) for our parameter choices are shown in Figure 1.

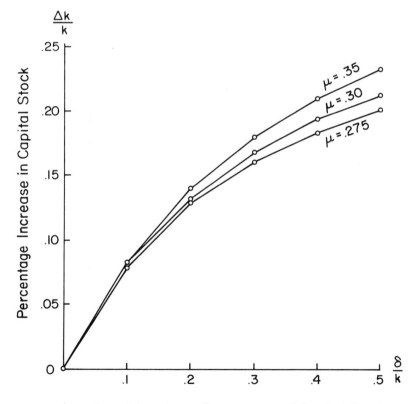

Investment Input as a Percentage of Capital Stock

FIGURE 1. ABSORPTIVE CAPACITY FUNCTION.

Exports, Imports, and Foreign Debt

In the interest of minimizing the number of control variables in the model, we specified sectoral exports exogenously:[7]

$$e_{ji} \text{ given}, \quad \text{all } i, j \tag{14}$$

Also in the interest of simplicity, we allowed no untied imports in sectors 1 (primary production) and 4 (services):

$$m_{1j} = m_{4j} = 0 \quad \text{all } i \tag{15}$$

Using the given export paths and all the different kinds of imports, we can write a foreign debt "accumulation equation" of the form:

$$\gamma_{i+1} = (1 + \theta)\gamma_i + \sum_{j=1}^{4} (d_{jj}g_{ji} - e_{ij} + \pi_j\delta_{ji} + m_{ji}) \tag{16}$$

$\gamma_i = $ foreign debt
$\theta = $ interest rate on foreign debt
$d_{jj} = $ elements of D, that is, marginal propensities to import for production
$\pi_j = $ marginal differential propensity to import for capital formation.

We know initial foreign debt and we can constrain terminal debt to a given level:

$$\gamma_1 \text{ known}, \quad \bar{\gamma}_{N+1} \text{ chosen} \tag{17}$$

but we have no explicit constraints on the level of debt at any intermediate time period.[8]

The export projections, shown in Table 8, were made as follows. A base-year GNP (1965) of \$3.4 billion was used, with assumed GNP growth rates of 8 percent in the first ten years and 7 percent thereafter. Next, total exports were projected by assuming that (1) they would increase linearly

[7] We could, in principle, make exports endogenous to the model, but to have done this we would have required estimates of price elasticities to use in convex functions relating foreign-exchange earnings to volume exports.

[8] Thus we are solving an "isoperimetric" problem with respect to foreign debt, specifying a given *change* in debt (from γ_1 to γ_{N+1}) and letting the model optimally allocate this change over time. (An analogous problem in the classical calculus of variations is finding the maximum area that can be enclosed by a given length of rope.) Possible alternative treatments of foreign debt are (*a*) using penalty functions to hold debt at any time "close" to some predetermined level or (*b*) putting inequality constraints on the level of debt in each period. The former alternative is computationally feasible, although our debt paths seemed to behave well enough for us not to bother with it. The latter approach, involving state variable inequality constraints, is difficult to handle computationally.

from $8\frac{1}{2}$ percent of GNP in the base year to 15 percent of GNP in the tenth year, (2) this percentage would hold constant at 15 percent over the next ten years, and (3) the percentage would decline linearly from 15 percent to 13 percent over the next ten years. Finally, the export path for each sector was computed from the total export projection by assuming the percentages in Table 9 at years zero, 10, 20, and 30, and linear changes of percentages over each ten-year interval. The rate of interest on foreign debt, θ, was set at 5 percent.

Terminal Conditions

We chose targets for the four terminal capital stocks by specifying growth rates over the period. The results are given in Table 10.

Terminal debt was set at $8 billion, an amount whose interest and amortization payments should be about equal to 20 percent of the country's export earnings in the terminal year.

Structure of the System

The system has five state variables (four k_{ji} and one γ_i) and fourteen control variables (four δ, four c, two m, and four ℓ). However, there are effective only nine controls because constraints 6 and 8 can be used to eliminate the four c and one ℓ_j. To carry this out, let

$$P = I - A + D \tag{18}$$

and let P^j and B^j denote the jth row of P and B respectively. Then 6 can be rewritten:

$$c = Pq - B\delta - e + m \tag{19}$$

and from 8 we have:

$$\ell_{1i} = \ell_i - \ell_{2i} - \ell_{3i} - \ell_{4i} \tag{20}$$

Thus, in summary, the problem is:

$$\max \xi = \sum_{i=1}^{N} (1 + z)^{-i} \left[\sum_{j=1}^{4} a_j c_{ji}^{b_i} \right] \tag{2}$$

subject to:

$$k_{j,i+1} = k_{ji} + g_j(\delta_{ji}, k_{ji}) \quad \text{all } i, j \tag{9}$$

$$\gamma_{i+1} = (1 + \theta)\gamma_i + \sum_{j=1}^{4} (d_{jj}q_{ji} - e_{ji} + \pi_j\delta_{ji} + m_{ji}) \quad \text{all } i \tag{16}$$

$$k_{j1} = \bar{k}_{j1} \quad \text{all } j \tag{21}$$

$$\gamma_1 = \bar{\gamma}_1 \tag{22}$$

$$k_{j,N+1} = \bar{k}_{j,N+1} \quad \text{all } j \tag{23}$$

$$\gamma_{N+1} = \bar{\gamma}_{N+1} \tag{24}$$

with:

$$c_{ji} = P^j q_i - B^j \delta_i - e_{ji} + m_{ji} \qquad (25)$$

$$\ell_{1i} = \ell_i - \ell_{2i} - \ell_{3i} - \ell_{4i} \qquad (20)$$

$$q_{ji} = \tau_j (1 + \nu_j)^i [\beta_j k_{ji}^{-\rho_i} + (1 - \beta_j) \ell_{ji}^{-\rho_i}]^{-\frac{1}{\rho_j}} \qquad (7)$$

and

$$g_{ji} = \mu_j k_{ji} \left\{ 1 - \left[1 + \frac{\epsilon_j \delta_{ji}}{\mu_j k_{ji}} \right]^{-\frac{1}{\epsilon_i}} \right\} \qquad \begin{array}{l} \epsilon_j \geq 1 \\ \mu_j \geq 0 \end{array} \qquad (11)$$

III. Method of Solution[9]

The optimization problem posed by the model is to find the consumption paths[10] for each of the four sectors that maximize the welfare index 2, subject to the capital accumulation constraints 9, the foreign debt accumulation constraints 16, the initial and terminal capital stocks 21 and 23, and the initial and terminal foreign debt constraints 22 and 24.

Our method of solution (discussed in detail in [46]) is as follows. We substitute out the consumption variables, one of the labor force variables, the output variables, and the capacity creation variables, using 25, 20, 7, and 11. We are left with a problem of maximizing a function of the five state variables (the four capital stock and the foreign debt variables) and the nine control variables (three labor force, four investment, and two import variables), subject to the difference equations 9 and 16 and the initial and terminal boundary conditions.

Next, additional terms are added to the performance function 2 to penalize any separation between the actual and the target terminal condition. These penalty functions are quadratic and thus give symmetric penalties.

Arbitrary initial paths for each control variable are calculated as the first step in finding a solution. These values of the control variables and the initial values of the state variables are used to obtain the paths for the state variables by integrating the difference equations 9 and 16 forward. The first-order conditions for a constrained optimum are then used to see if the arbitrary initial (or nominal) path is optimal. If it is not, this information is used in making changes in the control variable paths and the process is repeated. Each time the state variables are integrated forward, the terminal values of these variables are checked against the target values

---

[9] We are indebted to Raman Mehra for a copy of his conjugate gradient program and to Robert Kierr for excellent programming assistance in modifying the program to meet our requirements.

[10] A "path" is formed by the values of a particular variable over the time period of the model.

and the penalties are computed and subtracted from the performance index.[11]

IV. SOME NUMERICAL SOLUTIONS

A limited number of solutions of the model were obtained in order to explore some of its more interesting properties: (1) the sensitivity of the solutions to variations in the terminal capital stocks, (2) the effects on sectoral labor allocations of changes in the production elasticities of substitution, and (3) the variations in the upper bound parameters in the absorptive capacity functions.

We begin by discussing some of the characteristics of a "base" solution and then turn to an analysis of the properties mentioned above. Because our primary interest was in the computational problem itself rather than in this particular model, the solutions we report are indicative of the kinds of results one can obtain rather than an exhaustive analysis of the properties of the model.

A Basic Solution

One of the more interesting problems associated with a formal planning model is the sectoral allocation of investment over time. The optimal phasing of investment is bound to have an important influence on decisions made at the project level, in addition to influencing the growth of other components of final demand. Clearly, optimal investment phasing will depend on a number of interdependent factors, including the initial sectoral capital stocks, import and export possibilities, the relative weights given different consumption bundles in the welfare function, and the terminal capital stock targets. One of the main purposes of a general-equilibrium model such as ours is to take account of many of the interrelationships of these factors and to indicate to the planner which of these are critical.

Figure 2 shows the investment activity levels for the basic solution of the model.[12] The solution is characterized by relatively high levels of investment in the early years in the services and agriculture-mining sectors, which decline between years 5 and 10 as investment in heavy industry swings up from an initially low level. Given the particular parameter values we chose in the production functions, these results would suggest a relative oversupply of capital in the heavy industry sector at time zero, although one should not overrate this supposition inasmuch as the parameter choices could not be based on estimated production functions.

[11] The application of these techniques to a simple one-sector model is explained in (45).
[12] The rather uneven character of the paths (see Figure 2) would become smooth if we decreased the plot interval from five years to one or two years.

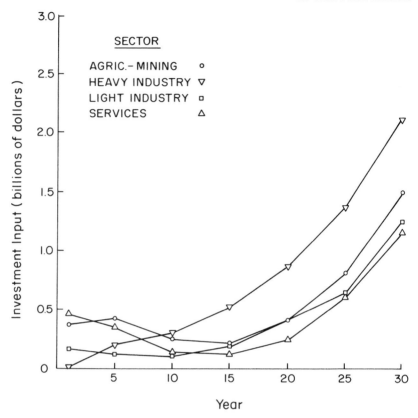

FIGURE 2. BASE SOLUTION—INVESTMENT INPUT BY SECTOR.

Figure 3 shows the consumption paths for the basic solution. These paths reflect the investment pattern, particularly in the heavy industry sector, where consumption falls off as that sector's investment increases between years 5 and 10.[13] The consumption paths in sectors 1 and 3 are quite sensitive to the terminal capital stock targets. In year 30, consumption of goods from sector 1 *decreases* by a factor of more than 25 percent when all the over-the-period capital stock growth rates are reduced by $1\frac{1}{2}$ percent (see below for details), but terminal consumption from capital-producing sector 3 *increases* by about 20 percent. The other two sectoral consumption paths are little affected by these changes in terminal

---

[13] A consumption decline, even though it is confined to one of four sectors, may not be a desirable "optimal" policy, although there is no reason why a decline should be unlikely when the welfare function depends only on *levels* of consumption. Inclusion of rates-of-change terms in the welfare function—to reward consumption increases and penalize decreases—would make decreases less likely to occur.

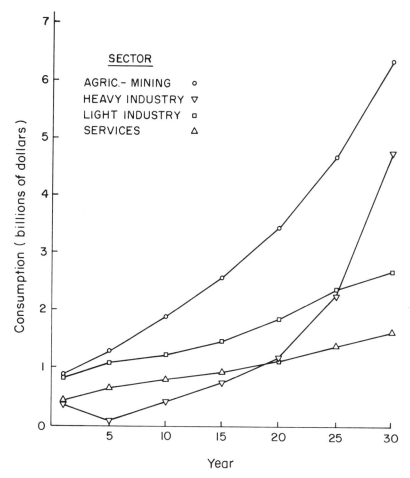

FIGURE 3. BASE SOLUTION—CONSUMPTION PATHS.

capital stock targets, except that in the early years of the planning period sector 2 consumption in the low-terminal-target solution benefits from an inflow of untied imports that is drastically reduced in the basic solution.

Figure 4 shows two measures of total savings and investment in the basic solution. The broken line represents the domestic investment rate (total final product from domestic sources devoted to investment as a share of GNP) while the solid line shows the standard GNP savings rate, taking account of foreign-trade flows. The savings rate begins at a rather low level and increases steadily to year 20 as an initial rise in foreign debt (see the top line of Figure 7) levels off. The initial debt increase finances the high domestic investment rate at the beginning of the planning period,

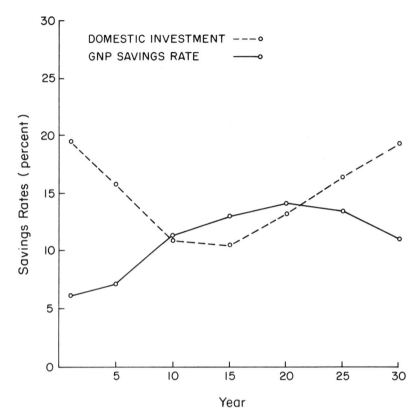

FIGURE 4. BASE SOLUTION—SAVINGS RATES.

as does another debt increase (or burst of dissaving in GNP terms) toward the end of the thirty-year plan.

Figure 5 shows the labor inputs by sector. As might be expected, the labor input for heavy industry grows more rapidly than that for other sectors. Somewhat more surprising are the continued absolute increases in the primary labor force and the slow growth of labor force in the light industry sector. Unlike the consumption paths in these two sectors, the labor force allocations are not significantly affected by a decrease in the terminal capital stock targets.

Figure 6 shows the capital-labor ratios for the four sectors over the time period covered by the model—and rather striking changes in these ratios even over short periods of time. Within the period of the first four years covered by the model, the ratios change by 38, 21, 14, and 66 percent respectively for the four sectors. Because the capital stocks are forced by the terminal conditions to grow over the entire period (but not in any particular subinterval of the period) at a rate greater than that of the labor

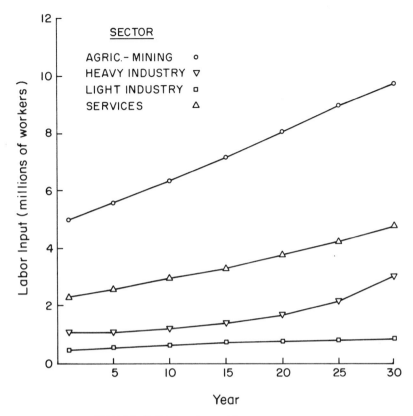

FIGURE 5. BASE SOLUTION—LABOR INPUT BY SECTOR.

force, this is not a surprising result. However, it shows very clearly that one should be careful in employing constant capital-labor ratios in any model in which the rate of growth of capital stock is substantially higher than the rate of growth of the labor force.

It is well known from economic theory that certain types of closed-economy neoclassical models exhibit "turnpike" behavior in the sense that, for most of a sufficiently long planning period, they will be in a balanced growth state, with resource allocations approximately equal to those prevailing asymptotically in an infinite horizon plan (79). On the basis of this theorem, one might expect that the initial stages of a sufficiently long plan would be quite insensitive to terminal conditions. In some previously reported experiments with one-sector closed-economy models (45) we found this type of behavior; in a model with a fifty-year planning horizon the first twenty years of the plan were essentially unaffected by a wide range of terminal conditions.

The more complex model of this paper also displays the hypothesized

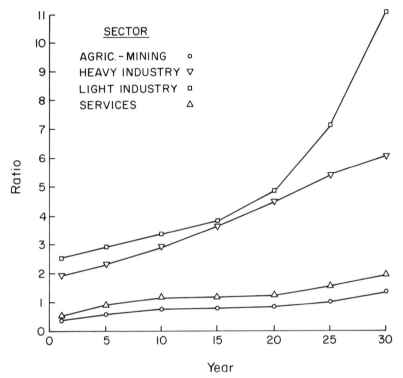

Year

FIGURE 6. BASE SOLUTION—SECTORAL CAPITAL LABOR RATIOS.
The values of μ, τ, and σ used for this calculation were:
$\mu = .275, .35, .30, .35$
$\tau = 6.5, 7.5, 7.0, 7.0$
$\sigma = 1.20, .90, .90, .60$

stability properties, but to a more limited extent, as Figures 7 and 8 illustrate.

Figure 7a shows capital stock accumulation paths for sector 1. We see that for the two lower terminal stocks (which were calculated with thirty-year capital stock growth rates of 5 percent and the basic solution's $6\frac{1}{2}$ percent) the first ten to fifteen years of the plan are largely independent of the terminal conditions. For the high terminal stock (based on a 7 percent growth rate), the accumulation path differs greatly from the other two. In Figure 7b, by contrast, the first ten years of the plan for sector 4 are unaffected by terminal stock targets.[14]

Figure 8, which shows Korea's foreign debt paths, helps explain this

[14] The growth rates used to calculate the target were $5\frac{1}{2}$ percent, 7 percent (basic solution), and $7\frac{1}{2}$ percent.

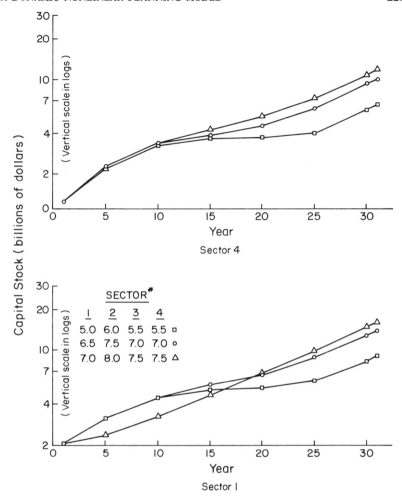

FIGURE 7. CAPITAL STOCK PATHS WITH VARIOUS TARGET CAPITAL STOCKS.
* Growth rate used in calculating capital stock targets.

contrasting behavior. As it turns out, sectors 1 and 4, respectively, have relatively high and low foreign-exchange components in investment (i.e., π_1 [from Table 3] takes the value of 0.63 in equation 16 while π_4 is only 0.10). It can be seen from Figure 8 that, as the terminal stock targets are increased, total foreign debt over the planning period is reduced, even becoming negative during the middle years of the high-target plan. The mechanism by which the reduction of debt between the low-target and the medium-target plan takes place involves the untied imports, m_{2i} and m_{3i} (see equation 16). These imports are drastically reduced between

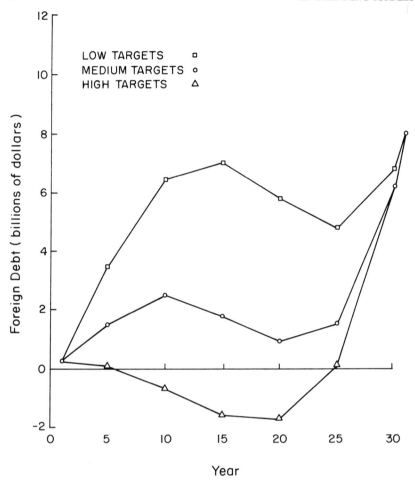

FIGURE 8. FOREIGN DEBT PATHS WITH VARIOUS TARGET CAPITAL STOCKS.

the two lower target solutions.[15] In the high-target solution these "slack" import variables are forced to zero, and other adjustments must be made to hold terminal debt to the required level of 8.0 (billion dollars). As it turns out, investment in sectors with a high import component in capital formation is deferred, which results in the anomaly displayed in Figure 7a. The initial accumulation pattern in sector 4 (Figure 7b) is not significantly affected by the target increase, again because the import coefficient, π_4, is relatively small.

[15] The decline in untied imports between the low-target and basic solutions allows the consumption increases in sectors 2 and 3 that were mentioned in the discussion of Figure 3.

One might conjecture that if more slack were built into the debt constraint (e.g., by the inclusion of activities that allow import substitution and/or export promotion), the initial phases of an optimal plan would be independent of a wider range of terminal capital stocks. In any event, the examples we have given here demonstrate that insensitivity to terminal capital stocks is not a universal characteristic of open-economy models.

Varying Elasticities of Substitution

Conjectures vary on the importance of differential elasticities of substitution in influencing the economic growth process. On the aggregate level, Nelson (as summarized by Nerlove [67]) has shown that when capital and labor are growing at roughly equal rates, changes in the aggregate elasticity of substitution will have little influence on the overall growth rate. In a disaggregated analysis, however, Arrow *et al.* (3) point out that differences in elasticities of substitution among industries will have significant effects on sectoral allocations of capital and labor—and ultimately on the aggregate elasticity of substitution. In particular, high elasticities in the primary sector and lower elasticities in the secondary and tertiary sectors are a means of explaining the well-known shift of labor from the former toward the latter sector.

Using our four-sector laboratory, we made some partial tests of these hypotheses (especially the latter one) by varying sectoral elasticities of substitution *while at the same time recalculating the efficiency parameters* (τ_j in equation 7) *to bring initial outputs in line with those of Korea in 1965-66.* Given this means of normalizing our three-parameter production functions to fit three pieces of data (initial capital stocks, labor forces, and gross production levels), we calculated optimal solutions to the model under the conditions shown in Table 11.

In our first three solutions, sectoral labor forces were essentially unchanged, although there were some shifts in the time phasing of investment. There were major labor force shifts only in solution *d*, where the elasticity of substitution in primary production was raised by more than a factor of two. In this case, labor in the primary sector decreased by 0.6 million workers in the terminal year, representing a shift of about 3 percent of the total labor force of 18 million. In terms of the conventional GNP aggregate, the growth rate in solution *a* during the thirty-year plan was 6.7 percent, and 6.8 percent in solution *d*. Again, the effects of changing substitution elasticities were relatively minor.

How well these preliminary results would stand up under further experimentation is, needless to say, open to question. In particular, shifts of the elasticities of substitution in connection with different welfare functions and/or different normalizations for the efficiency parameter might have more significant effects. It appears, however, that further experimentation along the lines suggested here would provide a partial answer to the empirical questions about the relevance of the elasticity of substitution to actual planning exercises.

Varying Parameter of Absorptive Capacity Function

Because we know relatively little about the parameters of our absorptive capacity functions—particularly the μ parameters that represented the upper bounds on the percentage rates of change of the capital stocks— we were hopeful that the solution would not be too sensitive to variations in these parameters. And this was the case in the range of variation we tested.

We made two runs of variants on the base solution. In the first run we increased each of the upper bound parameters by 10 percentage points over the base-solution levels. Then, in a second run, we decreased them by 10 percentage points. The resulting change was primarily one of speeding up the timing of investment as the upper bound parameters were raised. This is as might be expected inasmuch as large investment was made relatively more efficient by increasing the upper bounds.

V. Conclusions

The purpose of this study was to determine whether it is now feasible to find numerical solutions for dynamic nonlinear multisectoral planning models. Our conclusion is that, with existing algorithms and second-generation computers (of the IBM 7094 vintage), it is feasible to solve models that have four and more sectors. With third-generation computers (of the IBM 360 vintage), a computer language more efficient than the one we used, and existing algorithms, it should be feasible to solve models with ten and more sectors.

Because most development planners have employed linear programming models in the past, a few comments about the comparative advantages of control-theory models are in order.

1. Disaggregation into a rather large number of time periods can be done at relatively less cost in control-theory models than in linear programming models. The reason for this is that the addition of more time periods only adds to the number of difference-equation integration steps in the control-theory formulation; in the linear programming formulation more constraints are required.[16]

2. Adding state and control variables in a control-theory model seems to increase computation time *per iteration* in a roughly linear fashion;

---

[16] The time required to solve a linear program increases roughly as the cube of the number of constraints.

but it is not possible to conduct precise experiments on the matter. Each additional state variable means one additional difference equation must be integrated forward and backward in time, and an extra control variable entails the evaluation of as many partial derivatives at each time step as there are state variables. The relative computation times of these operations depend in great measure on how closely the additional variables are integrated with the rest of the model. This integration factor is also the most important determinant of how many additional iterations in a gradient method the new variables require.

3. In control-theory models, inequality constraints on the control variables are easier to incorporate into the solution techniques than are inequality constraints on the state variables. However, inequality constraints are generally more troublesome in control-theory problems than in linear programming problems. Of course this situation is mitigated by the fact that models specified with nonlinear functions require fewer inequality constraints than linear models.

4. Time lags of more than one period in the investment process can be incorporated into control-theory models by a standard technique for transforming nth order linear difference equations into systems of the first order. The same procedure could be followed if it were deemed appropriate to include arguments for the rate of change of consumption in the welfare index.[17]

5. Although it would be worthwhile to compare numerical control-theory methods for solving nonlinear planning models with other methods for solving nonlinear programming problems, we have not yet accumulated enough experience to make such comparisons.[18]

---

[17] See Brioschi and Rossi (8) for a model with rate of change of consumption in the performance index (and n. 13 above).

[18] R. Bove is presently solving a nonlinear model by the Wilson (87) algorithm. This work, which is part of a Ph.D thesis, is currently in preparation in the Economics Department of Harvard University under the supervision of Robert Dorfman and Hollis Chenery. However, we have not yet been able to make comparisons of computational efficiency on equivalent models.

CHAPTER 8 APPENDIX

The Data Used in the Model

TABLE A-1. WELFARE FUNCTION PARAMETERS

Sector	a	b
1	.48	.85
2	.33	.90
3	.345	.91
4	.3925	.87

TABLE A-2. CONSUMPTION SHARES AND INCOME ELASTICITIES IMPLIED
BY TABLE 1 PARAMETERS

Income	Shares				Elasticities			
50	.482	.099	.219	.200	.816	1.223	1.359	.941
100	.420	.114	.276	.190	.787	1.181	1.312	.908
150	.384	.122	.312	.182	.771	1.157	1.285	.890
200	.359	.127	.338	.176	.760	1.140	1.267	.877
250	.340	.131	.358	.171	.752	1.128	1.253	.867
300	.325	.134	.374	.167	.745	1.118	1.242	.860
350	.312	.136	.388	.163	.740	1.109	1.233	.853
400	.301	.138	.400	.160	.735	1.102	1.225	.848
450	.292	.140	.411	.157	.731	1.097	1.218	.844
500	.284	.141	.420	.155	.728	1.091	1.213	.839

TABLE A-3. AGGREGATION TO FOUR SECTORS

Sector 1—"Primary production"
    Agriculture, Forestry, Fishing, Coal and other minerals
Sector 2—"Heavy industry"
    Fiber spinning; Lumber and plywood; Paper products; Rubber products; Chemicals, chemical fertilizers; Petroleum products; Cement, other ceramic, clay; Stone; Glass; Iron, steel (through ingot), steel products; Finished metal products; Nonferrous metals; Machinery; Transportation equipment; Building maintenance; Construction; Electricity; Water; Commercial; Transportation; Stores; Scrap.
Sector 3—"Light industry"
    Processed food, Beverages, Textiles, Printing, Publishing, Leather, Wood products, Miscellaneous manufactures.
Sector 4—"Services"
    Banking, Insurance, Real estate, Trade margins, Other services.

235

TABLE A–4.   INPUT-OUTPUT COEFFICIENTS

Sector	1	2	3	4
1	.100	.090	.170	.010
2	.090	.330	.240	.120
3	.040	.020	.120	.050
4	.030	.090	.090	.080
Imports	.0008	.090	.030	.004

TABLE A–5.   CAPITAL COEFFICIENTS

Sector	1	2	3	4
2	.6908	1.3109	.1769	.1500
3	.001	.0199	.0022	.0000

TABLE A–6.   PRODUCTION FUNCTION PARAMETERS

Sector	Elasticity of substitution σ	Distribution β	Technical progress ν	Efficiency τ	Initial labor force (million workers)
1	1.20	.35	.03	.41	5.10
2	.90	.30	.035	1.26	.84
3	.90	.25	.025	1.89	.36
4	.60	.20	.025	.47	2.30

TABLE A–7.   CAPACITY AND OUTPUT LEVELS (1965)
(*in billions of U.S. dollars*)

Sector	Capacity	Gross output
1	2.02	1.53
2	2.13	1.38
3	1.26	.91
4	1.27	.94

TABLE A–8.   EXPORT LEVELS BY SECTOR
(*in billions of U.S. dollars*)

	Sector			
Year	1	2	3	4
1	.06	.04	.11	.13
5	.09	.07	.22	.21
10	.11	.14	.42	.30
15	.12	.31	.69	.42
20	.12	.54	.97	.54
25	.15	.97	1.19	.67
30	.20	1.62	1.42	.81

TABLE A–9. PERCENTAGE OF TOTAL EXPORTS IN EACH SECTOR

	Sector			
Year	1	2	3	4
0	.20	.10	.30	.40
10	.10	.15	.45	.30
20	.05	.25	.45	.25
30	.05	.40	.35	.20

TABLE A–10. TERMINAL CAPITAL STOCKS

Sector	Final stock	Growth rate
1	14.2	6.5 (%)
2	20.0	7.5
3	10.2	7.0
4	10.3	7.0

TABLE A–11. VARYING ELASTICITIES OF SUBSTITUTION

	Sector			
Solution	1	2	3	4
a	1.2	0.9	0.9	0.6
b	1.2	1.3	0.5	0.6
c	0.1	0.9	0.9	3.0
d	3.0	0.9	0.9	0.1

Part **III**

PLAN IMPLEMENTATION

Chapter 9

PROJECT SELECTION AND EVALUATION:
FORMULATION OF AN INVESTMENT PROGRAM

Lee Hee Il

The investment program, as a selected set of investment projects, constitutes the basic core of a development plan and determines the direction of the plan. In Korea, three basic steps were used to formulate the investment program for the Second Five-Year Plan.

1. Estimates of investment requirements by sector of manufacturing were made with the sectoral model.

2. Planned investment projects, solicited from the government and private sectors, were given preliminary evaluation to ensure their technical and economical feasibility.

3. Reconciliation of the investment requirements and the planned projects in each sector was carried out by a detailed scrutiny of the projects that eliminated some projects (whose plans exceeded the requirements) and solicited additional projects for sectors in which insufficient investment had been submitted.

I. Estimates of Investment Requirements

The first of the three conceptual phases in formulating the plan's project program was forecasting the demands for capacity expansion in each sector over the next five years (one of the main uses of the sectoral model that is discussed in Chapter 5). When the individual project proposals for the Second Five-Year Plan were initially solicited, the sectoral model had not been completed; therefore the demand forecasts it generated were used only in evaluating the proposals and not for generating projects.[1]

II. Soliciting and Preliminary Evaluation of Planned Projects

The second stage involved soliciting projects and making a preliminary evaluation of each project's technical and economic feasibility. The technical review included a comparison of proposed project processes (now in use in Korea and elsewhere), a compilation of the likely unit production

---

[1] In the development of the Third Five-Year Plan, the sectoral model will also be used to indicate the most urgently needed projects.

costs, and a preliminary judgment on the availability of the necessary raw materials. The economic review includes a study of prospective demand conditions and relative potential project performance.

Performance criteria are the rate of return, employment effects, balance-of-payments effects, and contribution to the growth of GNP. Industry ratios were developed for this purpose, at the 43-sector level, from censuses, industry profiles, and input-output data. Industry demand, projected by analysis of interindustry demand, is based on target projections of exports, private and government consumption, import-substitution rates, and some programmed investments. In addition, the size of a proposed plant is considered from the viewpoint of economic efficiency. Lumpy investments may have to be postponed a few years until demand is sufficient to justify a plant of the minimum, economically viable size.

In general, there was considerable feedback between the sectoral analysis and the individual project studies throughout the planning process. Preliminary efforts to gather project proposals were made before any industry demand forecasts were available, but the crudity of the data necessitated extensive revisions while demand forecasts were being made with the sectoral model. Subsequently, additional project proposals were solicited from private sectors in which the sectoral model forecasts indicated demand would materialize, but insufficient project proposals had been submitted. Since the bulk of investment activities during the plan period are to be carried out by private entrepreneurs, the Economic Planning Board asked all the affected ministries, private firms, and other industrial associations to prepare project proposals in a uniform application schedule, whose contents can be summarized as follows.

1. Brief description of the project proposal
2. Overall demand-and-supply projection of the goods to be produced
3. Production schedule by year
4. Intermediate inputs of domestic and foreign goods and services
5. Balance-of-payments effects
6. Major capital materials inputs
7. Employment schedule during construction period and in normal operation year, by labor categories
8. Estimated cost accountings
9. Money flowsheet by source of funds
10. Value added in normal operation year.

From the schedules submitted, the planning agency formulated a tentative investment program, consisting of about 200 candidate projects and requiring about 955 billion *won* in investment, for more extensive screening.

In August, 1965, the first project-appraisal team was formed, consisting of approximately thirty specialists, economists, engineers, and technicians from the government, private firms, academic circles, and private research institutes. Its function was to review, reorganize, and supplement the previously submitted project data to provide a basis for ranking projects by their technical, economic, commercial, and financial feasibility. The team checked the completeness and consistency of project application data but made no modifications or adjustments of projected proposals. It also produced preliminary policy guidelines for major industries during the plan period. Only projects in the primary and the manufacturing sectors were appraised because extensive analyses of investment needs in transport and electric power had already been carried out.

III. DETAILED SCRUTINY OF PROJECTS

Detailed scrutiny of the plans was made by the industry committees, the successors to the project appraisal teams, which had a coordinating committee and ten specialist subcommittees.[2] Each subcommittee was responsible for the following duties:

1. Verifying the accuracy of the basic data on proposed projects and ensuring that sufficient data became available to compute the required criterion ratios and capital coefficients. The project application forms (prepared by the planning agency in the first stage) were completely revised and the data were transcribed into the "project summary table."

2. Commenting on the proper scale of the project, choice of technology, extent of foreign markets, and any other factors that would facilitate determining whether a project merits further consideration or requires modification.

3. Suggesting new projects or redesigning projects in order to meet production capacity requirements for the sector or to improve the prospective return from the proposed projects.

4. Preparing the industry profiles, which were based on detailed analyses of about 200 recently built, or proposed, manufacturing plants. The industry profiles were designed to improve the accuracy and reliability of sectoral model projections.[3] Heavy emphasis was placed on capital requirement material input and full-capacity output figures.[4] Adjustments were

---

[2] The subcommittees worked in ten areas: (1) processed food and beverages, (2) fibers and textiles, (3) wood, paper, rubber, and leather, (4) chemicals, (5) cement and ceramics, (6) petrochemicals, (7) iron, steel, nonferrous metal, and metal products, (8) nonelectric machinery, (9) electric machinery and miscellaneous, and (10) mining.

[3] Before the profiles were made, the only basis for the sectoral model projections was the 1963 input-output table, adjusted to 1965 prices. To make the model projections, it was necessary to construct a capital coefficients table from anticipated input-output coefficients for industries with rapidly changing technology.

[4] The capital data derived from the profiles was aggregated to capital coefficients at the sectoral level by calculating weighted averages, initially by the use of weights

made in input-output coefficients for sectors in which drastic changes were expected to arise during the plan period (e.g., synthetic fibers, fertilizer, iron and steel). (In the meantime, a team was organized to survey initial capacity and rate of utilization data for use in the sectoral model.)

The investment program did not depend entirely on the demand projections of the sectoral model but was cross-checked by the industry committees, which were encouraged to criticize the overall sectoral model projections and to find the sources of problems in terms of the using sectors. The committee members were encouraged to examine the rows and columns in the input-output table of projected interindustry flows and locate errors. The committees' findings were then incorporated into revised sectoral model projections, usually by reestimating raw material requirements. Each project, thus refined and screened, was cumulated by sector and was rechecked with the investment requirements derived from the sectoral model.

Counterparts to the industry committees were formed for the primary and tertiary sectors. An agricultural working group made detailed studies of investment requirements and growth prospects in each agricultural sector. Special working groups were established to make recommendations for housing and education, and, as mentioned, detailed studies had already been made of electric power and transportation. However, because investment in agriculture and social overhead was exogenous to the sectoral model, it was not formally subjected to the overall consistency test applied to the mining and the manufacturing investment program. Steps are being taken to make virtually all sectors endogenous for the Third Plan's projections.

IV. INVESTMENT CRITERIA AND THEIR APPLICATION

In order to expedite development and maximize growth, the establishment of rational investment criteria is essential to ensure the rational allocation of available resources among sectors and the selection of projects that will contribute most to development. In appraising each project in the various sectors of the economy, economic, technical, and financial feasibility were considered.

The economic criteria for project appraisal were:

1. Suitability with respect to the planned increase in capacity for the appropriate sector

---

that were proportional to output. Later, the coefficients were reweighted and the weights became the expected changes in output, derived from both the sectoral model projections and the estimates made by the subsector specialists on the industry committees.

2. Rate of return on a particular project compared with return on other projects in the same sector

3. Other appropriate criteria, such as value added per unit of investment, balance-of-payments effects, employment per unit of output, etc.[5]

The criteria were applied somewhat differently in each sector, and three classifications of sectors were developed. (1) Growth sectors are the subsectors among agriculture, fishery, mining, and manufacturing that have good potential for growth. (2) Supporting sectors are the sectors that will be needed to support the growth sectors, including electric power, transportation, and other similar sectors. (3) "Other sectors"— sectors that have only indirect relationships to the growth sectors: health, sanitation, housing, education, etc.

The criteria of rate of return on investment, balance of payments, value added, and employment effects were applied to projects only in the growth sectors. In the supporting sectors, technical and economic feasibility studies and benefit-cost analyses were carried out to assure the selection of sound projects and to obviate the generation of problems in the supporting and growth sectors.[6]

The primary criterion in manufacturing, in addition to sectoral demand forecasts, was the annual rate of return on investment, which is a measure of the present value of revenues less expenses per unit of investment cost per year. In these calculations, separate rankings of projects were made on the basis of 15 percent and 26 percent discount rates. It was found that the rankings did not vary much with these two rates. Shadow prices of primary resources were not used because it was felt that in 1965 the exchange rate was fairly realistic and the wage rate approximately in line with the opportunity cost of labor.

[5] The rate of return was defined as the net present lifetime benefit of the investment divided by the gross discounted cost of the investment. Net lifetime benefit of the investment was estimated as total annual revenue minus annual expenditure and depreciation. Gross cost of investment was total annual investment discounted to present value.
The balance-of-payments criteria were total value of exports plus the value of import substitution minus foreign-currency expenditure divided by total investment. Employment effects were calculated as labor requirements during normal operation in man-years divided by total investment. The value-added criterion was value added (gross revenue minus cost of intermediate goods and services) divided by total investment.
[6] Different criteria were applied to projects in "other sectors." Briefly, these were: Electricity: rate of return on investment and the demand for electricity; housing: degree of contribution to the elimination of the housing shortage; multi-purpose dam: benefit-cost ratio; communication: per capita mail posted–telephone supply ratio; urban public works, including water and sewage works; health; and education: degree of urbanization, demand for industrial water, contribution to family planning and public health, and productivity effects.

Although investment criteria are useful in selecting the most productive projects among a number of candidates, they do not give adequate guidance for deciding on the selection of a single-candidate project. The problem is most acute in the appraisal of recently submitted projects that are to be financed by foreign capital and must be acted upon immediately. Thus it was necessary to establish a minimum standard for each sector and for each criterion with which a single-candidate project could be compared. Generally, these standards were the average for the existing firms in each sector.

Small-scale private projects were not examined in detail by the planning authority in order to avoid delaying implementation of the plan. Instead, the estimated levels of investment in various industries were used as partial guides to the various financing institutions that decided on individual loan applications.

Because it was impossible to apply the criteria uniformly, projects in each sector were given A, B, and C ratings. Group A projects—the highest-priority projects—must be implemented during the plan period in order to attain the plan targets. Projects in group B have the nature of continuous programs in which investment can be reduced or deferred without seriously impairing the plan targets. Group C projects are those that will not have a direct impact on the achievement of the plan targets and that can be dropped if the economic and financial situation warrants. Group A accounted for 89 percent of total investment and groups B and C accounted for 7 percent and 4 percent respectively. Table 1 gives a detailed breakdown of the rankings.

A major emphasis of the five-year plan was self-sufficiency in food grains. In agriculture, accordingly, priority was given to projects that would most increase productivity. Research groups were organized to estimate the yield increase from land-improvement projects, to project demand for agricultural products, and to estimate capital-output ratios in agriculture. First, these groups established the basis to be used in determining the priority of each investment and they calculated the internal rate of return of every major project in agriculture, forestry, and fishing. Second, they analyzed grain-production estimates and grain demand-and-supply projections for 1971. Third, demands for the main agricultural products, other than grain, were predicted. Fourth, the annual increment of farming expenditure required to bring about the projected increase in farm production was estimated and the relationship between land required and land available in 1971 was investigated. Finally, the allocation of investment over all agricultural sectors was decided. The minimum acceptable internal rate of return in agriculture was set at 15 percent in view of the real returns experienced in the manufacturing sectors.

TABLE 1. INVESTMENT PRIORITY SUMMARY

		Total requirement			Priority as percent of total[a]		
		Domestic mill. *won*	Foreign thous. $	Total mill. *won*	A	B	C
Agriculture, forestry, & fishery		107,288	129,286	141,598	86	9	5
	Agriculture	83,619	34,499	92,773	87	10	3
	Forestry	17,472	100	17,499	94	6	—
	Fishery	6,197	94,687	31,326	76	11	13
Mining & manufacturing		56,803	493,325	187,732	83	11	6
	Mining	12,360	19,244	17,467	98	1	1
	Manufacturing	44,443	474,081	170,265	82	12	6
Social overhead capital & other services		333,570	457,174	454,903	92	5	3
	Housing	74,614	906	74,854	99	—	1
	Urban development	34,587	52,461	48,510	83	12	5
	Electric power	38,549	151,452	78,744	100	—	—
	Communications	52,841	23,669	59,123	85	8	7
	Transportation	92,310	217,242	149,966	93	5	2
	Health & welfare	8,670	663	8,846	90	5	5
	Tourism	4,360	8,000	6,483	97	—	3
	Education	24,877	—	24,877	80	10	10
	Survey	2,762	2,781	3,500	100	—	—
Others		107,620	257,804	176,043			
	Other agriculture, forestry, & fisheries	18,340	—	18,340			
	Other mining	61,786	194,015	113,278			
	Other manufacturing	27,494	63,789	44,425			
Total (excludes development of scientific technology)		605,281	1,337,589	960,276			

[a] Respective amounts of each priority category.

247

One of the major criteria applied to evaluating agricultural investment was the internal rate of return. Because it is difficult to separate capital costs from current costs in agriculture, the benefit-cost ratio was used as the basis of the internal rate of return calculations.[7] In these calculations, project costs included all the resources and services used directly for development and expansion, regardless of the source of funds; interest and annual repayment of loans, however, were excluded. Operating and managerial costs included the value of all the resources and services used, whether the enterprise was operated by the government or by the private sector.

The electric power program was based partly on the survey made by the Electric Power Industry Survey Team in 1965 (organized under the auspices of US/AID) and partly on the Korean Electric Company's demand projections (made jointly with the EPB). The major policy directives for the power industry during the plan period were to provide the capacity to meet the projected power demand (with a suitable amount of reserve capability), to maintain the minimum system-operating cost (with an appropriate combination of peak- and base-power plants), to modernize and standardize the distribution and transmission system, and to promote balanced regional development by means of rural electrification.

Because the survey team's power demand projection of 4,446 GWH in 1971 appears to be too low in view of the recent trends in GNP growth rates, it was increased to 6,230 GWH for 1971. This figure was confirmed by the sectoral model demand projections, but it is now apparent that 1971 demand will considerably exceed it.[8] The projections had not forecast the great increase in power intensity of production processes that occurred after power rationing was lifted. The survey team's recommendations for plant construction, emphasizing the rate of return on capital, were generally accepted, with adjustments of generating capacity needs and construction timing schedules. The team emphasized the need that rural electrification provide a stimulus to the general economy by creating a market for consumer goods and by reducing operating costs in various

[7] Other conditions being equal, the project that has a higher anticipated rate of return on investment would be more desirable than the project with a lower anticipated rate of return.

[8] For the forecast of power demand, customers were classified by lighting, small power (under 500 KW), large power (over 500 KW), and agricultural power requirements. The load demands for the lighting and small power categories were estimated by a least squares regression equation between the electrical energy consumption and various economic factors. The built-up-projection method, which cumulates demand from existing and anticipated large users, and regression equations were applied to forecast large power and agricultural power demand. Finally, total load demand was obtained by adding up these estimated values of demand for all the service categories.

agricultural and commercial undertakings, and that it fulfill its far-reaching social and political implications.

Project programming in the transportation sector was based on the preliminary report prepared by the Transportation Survey Team of the International Bank for Reconstruction and Development.[9] The survey, which covered all modes of transport, was prepared with the following considerations:

1. The economic development of the country and the volumes of traffic such development will generate, including estimates of the levels and location of future industrial, mining, and agricultural production, and population growth.

2. The allocation of traffic to the most economic transport mode.

3. The specific investments required to ensure adequate transport capacity for the estimated traffic. The investment plan clearly indicated priorities and time phasing; for example, it listed roads according to their economic importance and the time they should be constructed. In order to relate the 1967–71 investment plan properly with investments in prior years, it included estimates of commitments and expenditures in 1966.

4. Measures to minimize the need for new investments through increased utilization of existing capacity, such as improvements in operating methods (including the closing of uneconomic railway lines), road maintenance, taxation, traffic regulation, organizational arrangements, management and administration, rate and fare policies, user charges, the location of new economic activities, transport coordination, etc.

5. The financing of the plan; for example, the extent to which internally generated funds or user charges are estimated to become available, the requirements for budgetary contributions, the foreign-exchange costs, etc. For this purpose, the plan included estimates of revenues and expenditures, cash flow, and balance sheets—annually for 1966–71—for the railway and for other appropriate agencies.

In the education sector, emphasis was placed on meeting the classroom requirements of a compulsory education program. The problem of classroom shortage is serious, and all primary school classes operate on at least a three-shift basis. Moreover, the rapid annual increase in school-age children critically compounds the classroom-shortage problem. Priority therefore was given to the construction and repair of classrooms, but, because of resource limitations, the plan targeted two-shift rather than

---

[9] The team was formed at the request of the Korean government, in cooperation with the IBRD, to conduct an integrated transportation survey and to recommend detailed transport investment requirements for the plan period.

one-shift operation of all primary schools by 1971. It was assumed that 95 percent of school-age children will be enrolled.

In the housing sector, the growing requirements for urban and rural areas were estimated by using data for population and household increase and for the number of dwellings that must be rebuilt. The estimates were based on the assumption of a GNP growth rate of 7 percent during the plan period, with the ratio of investment in housing relative to GNP increasing from 1.8 percent in 1964 to 3.0 percent by 1971. If we assume a gradual decline to a 2 percent population growth rate by 1971, it is possible to develop estimates of the number of dwelling units required to maintain a constant level of adequate housing. The housing required for the plan period was estimated on the assumption there would be no change in the quality of housing, either in terms of availability or increased space. This estimate, which is only a reflection of the minimum investment required to prevent housing deterioration, does not appear excessive in view of other estimates that would improve or rebuild inadequate housing units (tents, huts, market shift vessels) as well as buildings not intended as dwelling units (schools, factories, warehouses, and churches). These factors were incorporated in the later stages, when total investment requirements were adjusted.

Communications, a government sector, has an independent accounting system, and therefore, in the formulation of an investment program, the principle of nonaffection was applied. Thus project selection was carried out within the sector's financial availability, with emphasis on the expansion of telephone line-systems.

V. IMPLEMENTATION OF THE PROJECT PROGRAM

Because the economy grows rapidly, the environment for investment changes rapidly. In this sense, the investment program of the Second Five-Year Plan is simply a set of development targets to be achieved, but not necessarily in five years. As the five-year plan unfolds, unforeseen conditions inevitably require continuing reassessment of the investment program to ensure that it remains appropriate to the nation's overall goals. This reassessment process has already begun, with the formulation of the annual overall resources budget and the establishment of an investment coordination and a project development committee.

The overall resources budget, an annual program, is designed to facilitate effective implementation of the Second Five-Year Plan by making adjustments for changing conditions at home and abroad. It covers the following major topics:

1. Analysis of current economic conditions and trends in the plan year.

2. Establishment of the objectives for the plan year.

3. Development of specific policy measures in order to attain the established objectives in the plan year.

4. Provisions for the major content and the size of the government's fiscal budget, sectoral investment programs (including the private sector), major indicators and trends in the monetary sector, demand-and-supply programs for major commodities, foreign capital imports, price policy, and other activities in the private sector. It outlines the preceding year's economic activities for the benefit of the general public and various organizations (including government agencies).

The overall resources budget is prepared in two stages: a preliminary overall resources budget (prepared in February or March of the preceding year in order to guide the preparation of the government's annual fiscal budget) and the final version (completed around midyear, just before the government budget is prepared). The final version provides a general framework as well as direction for the various programs of the government, including the fiscal budget.

An investment coordination committee, consisting of representatives of the planning agency and the appropriate ministries, was established to prepare and to adjust the annual investment program. The committee performs the following functions:

1. It recommends to the planning agency the level and composition of total public and private investment, based on its analysis of the preliminary overall resources budget, progress reports of recent development, proposals from the various ministries and the working committees for project development, and—especially—on evidence of trends in the "unplanned" category of private-sector investments.

2. It recommends the initiation of feasibility studies by the appropriate ministries or agencies on the basis of projected resource availability and the findings in 1 above.

3. It recommends the incentive measures necessary to induce private investment, both foreign and domestic, in needed projects and sectors, as well as the measures designed to discourage undesirable forms of investment, and it suggests the criteria for selective credit extension.

The temporary industry committees were transformed into permanent investment coordination committees and working committees for project development. Primary responsibility for the formulation of project proposals remains with the respective ministries, but the WCPDs suggest areas in which to formulate projects. These committees also review project proposals and feasibility studies.

For the Third Plan—along with the macro and financial model devel-

opment—the following models are being developed to assist with investment programming: (1) a 109-sector version of the sectoral model (discussed in Chapter 5), (2) a mixed integer programming model for assessing
the proper timing and scale of projects in key sectors (see Chapter 6), and
(3) a regional optimizing model that is based on input-output tables (see
Chapter 7). Formulation of a project program always depends heavily on
individual project-selection procedures, but such procedures alone are
short-sighted and cannot consider such factors as the growth of market
demand (determined partly by interindustry relations), economies of scale,
and the need for overcoming regional income inequities. These models
should help incorporate these considerations into the project program.

1965 KOREAN PROFILE
(End-of-year prices)

Sector Code	
Profile No.	78
270 No.	32300
109 No.	55
43 No.	22

Type of Industry ___ PVC Resin ___
Date of Preparation ___ March 16, 1966 ___
Source of Data ___ EPB ___

I. Full Capacity Output by Product

(Practical maximum production under normal working conditions with obsolete machines excluded)

Product	Quantity	Unit Price	Value
A. PVC Resin	6,600 mill. tons	110,000	726,000,000
B. Caustic soda	5,280 "	25,000	132,000,000
.	.	.	.
.	.	.	.
.	.	.	.

G. Total 858,000,000
H. Basis for computing capacity: hours/day __24__, days/month __30__,
month/year __11__

II. Total Production in 1969

A. For domestic market (producer's price)

Product	Quantity Produced	Unit Price	Value
1. PVC resin	6,600 mill. tons	110,000	726,000,000
2. Caustic soda	5,280 "	25,000	132,000,000
.	.	.	.
.	.	.	.
.	.	.	.
6.			

253

B. For export (*won* value; F.O.B. prices; exchange rate of 270:1)
1. _____   _____   _____   _____
.
.
.
5. _____   _____   _____   _____

C. Total value of production   858,000,000

III. Capital Requirements

	Value	Ratio to Full Capacity Output
A. Building construction (excluding land), machinery installation, installation of electrical and water systems, and other installation	300,000,000	0.34965
B. Machinery and equipment		
1. Imported machinery (including technical training cost, C.I.F. prices, but excluding inland handling costs)	*won* 972,000,000 $ 3,570,000	1.13286
2. Domestic non-electrical machinery	40,000,000	0.04662
3. Domestic electrical machinery	10,000,000	0.01165
4. Office machines (typewriter, calculator, etc.)	1,000,000	0.00116
C. Transportation equipment	8,000,000	0.00932
D. Cost of handling imported and domestic machinery (moving it from port to construction site)	30,000,000	0.03496
E. Cost of office furniture	3,000,000	0.00349
F. Total	1,364,000,000	1.58974

IV. Raw Materials
(intermediate inputs)

	Quantity	Value	Ratio to Total Production
A. Domestic raw materials (including packing materials)			
1. Limestone	18,500 mill. tons	9,250,000	0.01078
2. Anthracite	7,320 "	18,300,000	0.02133
3. Salts	9,650 "	38,800,000	0.04522

4. Packing materials   264,000 bags   10,560,000   0.01231

    .   .   .   .

8. Sub-total   76,910,000   0.08964

B. Imported raw materials (*won* value or dollar; C.I.F. prices; exchange rate of 270:1; excluding handling costs and all tariffs and taxes)

   1. Chemicals (organic)   8,100,000   0.00944
   2.   "   (inorganic)   9,450,000   0.01101

   .   .   .

   8. Sub-total   17,550,000   0.02045

C. Handling costs, tariffs and   4,000,000   0.00466
   taxes on imported raw materials

D. Spare parts, work supplies,
   maintenance material costs   30,000,000   0.03497
   1. Spare parts   10,000,000   0.01166
   2. Work supplies   5,000,000   0.00583
   3. Maintenance materials   15,000,000   0.01748

E. Office supplies   2,500,000   0.00291

F. Total   130,960,000   0.15263

V. Labor Cost

	Annual Average Number (Man-years)	Ratio to Capital Req.	Wages and Salaries	Ratio to Total Production
A. Managerial and office	80	0.01642	22,400,000	0.02610
B. Engineers and technicians	100	0.02565	35,000,000	0.04079
C. Workers (direct labor)	320	0.03284	44,800,000	0.05221
D. Total	500	0.07492	102,200,000	0.11911

VI. Other Input Costs

	Quantity	Value	Ratio to Total Production
1. Electric power	57,750,000 KWH	173,250,000	0.20192
2. Water, sanitary	3,000,000 mill. tons	6,000,000	0.00699
3. Fuel	50,000 "	2,500,000	0.00291

4. Communication	1,000,000	0.00117
5. Storage and transport service purchases	2,000,000	0.00233
6. Insurance and banking services	2,500,000	0.00291
7. Other services	1,000,000	0.00116
a. Business services (advertising, legal, travelling and others)	(500,000)	(0.00058)
b. Repair services	(500,000)	(0.00058)
8. Indirect taxes (business activity, property, automobile, commodity taxes)	30,000,000	0.03497
9. Other value added	311,590,000	0.36316
a. Interest (excluding principal repayments)	(58,320,000)	(0.06797)
b. Rental payments	(1,000,000)	(0.00116)
c. Welfare and pension funds	(10,000,000)	(0.01165)
d. Sales commission	(8,000,000)	(0.00932)
e. Profits (equals income tax + dividend + retained earnings + reserve funds other than depreciation fund)	(234,270,000)	(0.27304)
10. Miscellaneous costs		
11. Depreciation	95,000,000	0.11072
12. Total	624,840,000	0.72825
VII. Total Input Cost (total of IV, V, VI)	858,000,000	1.00000

Chapter 10

STABILIZING AN ECONOMY:
THE KOREAN EXPERIENCE

S. Kanesa-Thasan

South Korea's success in recent years in curbing inflation and achieving a high rate of economic growth has attracted considerable international interest, particularly as a possible model for other developing countries. This paper analyzes the financial stabilization policies implemented by the Korean authorities after 1963, together with the implications of these policies, and with particular emphasis on a number of special factors that contributed to Korea's success but may not necessarily be present in other developing countries.

This paper consists of four parts. The first part outlines the economic situation prior to 1964 and highlights the changes that have occurred since that time. The second, and main, part analyzes the policies that were followed in each major financial policy area. The third part lists the major "exogenous factors" that contributed to the success of the stabilization policies. The last part is a brief concluding section.

I. BACKGROUND

Korea experienced chronic inflation for almost two decades following the division of the country in 1948 and the economic disruption caused later by the Korean War. Although attempts were made to check the inflation, the results were limited and transitory, and during this period the economy was substantially supported by foreign aid, principally from the United States of America. Between 1953 and 1963, for example, such aid paid for almost 60 percent of the total imports, and between 1963 and 1967 the counterpart funds generated by foreign aid constituted almost 41 percent of the government's total budgetary revenue. Although considerable progress was made during this period toward rebuilding the country's infrastructure and resettling the postwar refugee population, even the large inflow of foreign assistance could not cope with the pressing demands for resources for social and economic reconstruction and for national defense. The government, therefore, continuously resorted to inflationary finance.

The inflationary situation worsened markedly between 1961 and 1963.[1] Korea's military regime, which had seized the government in mid-1961, attempted to accelerate the pace of capital formation and lessen the country's dependence on foreign aid by means of a very high rate of monetary expansion.[2] External assets started to decline rapidly, moderating the increase in the money supply. In 1963 its balance-of-payments position became so weak that Korea's earnings of foreign exchange accounted for only 26 percent of its total imports, and foreign-exchange reserves declined to their lowest level since 1956. Faced with a serious balance-of-payments situation, the authorities adopted a very complex exchange system that included a network of multiple currency features and extremely severe quantitative restrictions on imports. Thus the full effects of the monetary expansion between 1961 and 1963 were felt in an acute deterioration in the price situation in late 1963 and early 1964, which was aggravated by a poor harvest in 1963.

In late 1963 the newly elected government of President Park Chung Hee initiated a strong anti-inflationary financial program. At the same time, the First Five-Year Development Plan was scaled down and maximum priority was placed on the development of exports as a leading growth sector. The primary policy emphasis during the years immediately after 1963 was on curbing monetary expansion and expanding the role of the price system to achieve a more efficient resource allocation. Once a substantial measure of success in the anti-inflationary effort was achieved, the government was able to pay increased attention to its own development program, particularly in the context of the Second Five-Year Plan (1967–71).

In fact, the original growth target of 7.0 percent in the government's First Five-Year Plan (1962–66) was exceeded; and an annual 10 percent growth rate is targeted in the Revised Second Five-Year Plan (1967–71).[3]

---

[1] During 1953–63 the increase in the money supply and wholesale prices averaged 38 percent and 21 percent (respectively) a year. The annual rate of increase in consumer prices averaged 23 percent and ranged between 3 and 68 percent.

[2] Between mid-1961 and September, 1962, total bank credit increased by 65 percent and the money supply increased by 60 percent, despite the blocking in quasi-monetary accounts of a substantial amount of bank deposits as part of the monetary reform of June, 1962.

[3] The gross investment–GNP ratio rose from 13.0 percent in 1962 to 20.3 percent in 1967 and the domestic savings–GNP ratio rose from 2.2 percent to 11.7 percent. The public sector–savings ratio rose from negative 1.4 percent to 3.6 percent and the private savings ratio to GNP from 3.6 percent to 8.1 percent. On the other hand, the ratio of public sector investment to total investment declined. The foreign savings–GNP ratio declined from 11.2 percent to 8.6 percent; the ratio of "foreign savings" to gross capital formation declined too, from 83 percent to 42 percent, and so did the ratio of grants to total foreign aid. Annual foreign-exchange earnings more than tripled between 1963 and 1967 and foreign-exchange reserves more than doubled.

During 1964–67 the Korean economy grew at an annual rate of 9.4 percent, and the increase in wholesale prices was limited to an annual rate of 7.0 percent after mid-1964. Rapid economic growth took place in all sectors of the economy, but the most impressive gain was in industrial production and exports, which increased at an annual rate of 16 percent and 39 percent respectively.

II. FINANCIAL STABILIZATION POLICIES

Annual Stabilization Programs

Measures for stabilizing the economy were implemented in stages in the form of comprehensive annual stabilization programs. Since March, 1965, the stabilization programs have been supported by standby arrangements with the International Monetary Fund, under which no drawings have thus far been made. The annual programs set quantitative ceilings for each major sector's financial operations and broadly delineated the necessary supporting policies. With the initiation of the Second Five-Year Plan in 1967, the Korean authorities introduced the technique of "annual over-all resources budgets," which reset the plan target for each year, project annual supply and demand for principal commodities, foreign exchange, domestic liquidity, etc., and indicate the supporting financial and other policies to be followed during the year. Among the most important policy tools which are closely linked to the annual overall resources budget is the Government's fiscal budget for that year.

The three principal elements of the annual financial programs have been (1) the maintenance of overall balance in fiscal sector cash operations, (2) credit restraint and the promotion of domestic savings, and (3) a balance-of-payments policy that emphasizes export growth, capital inflow, the establishment of a realistic exchange rate, and the progressive liberalization of exchange payments—along with greater reliance on import tariffs. These measures were directed not only at reducing the gap between aggregate monetary demand and available supplies (so that the general price increase would be reduced) but also toward enlarging the role of the market system in determining the relative prices of goods and services (so that a better allocation of resources would be realized). In 1963 an extensive system of direct controls and open (or concealed) subsidies resulted in distortions of the pricing system, but in most sectors the price distortions and the related direct controls have now been either eliminated or greatly reduced. The most important changes in this context were a sharp increase in interest rates and a progressive shift from credit rationing to indirect monetary controls; the adoption of flexible and realistic pricing policies for public enterprises and the elimination of direct price controls; the adoption of a unitary floating exchange rate, and the progressive dismantling of direct restrictions on foreign-exchange transactions.

Fiscal Balance

The first major step in 1963 toward stabilizing the economy was aimed at removing the overall fiscal deficit, which had become the major source of inflation in the immediately preceding years,[4] principally by effecting temporary cuts in the government's capital and administrative expenditures.[5] The expansion in current expenditures was also kept down effectively. This was made possible because wages of government employees were not raised despite an almost 60 percent rise in the consumer price index in 1963 and 1964 and because the limited amount of built-in increases in welfare and other expenditures were linked to the price level.

No major changes were made in the tax structure in 1963 or 1964 except the introduction of the "special customs duty," which absorbed 70 to 90 percent of the difference between the "total cost" of imported commodities and the domestic market price. The tax was designed to collect as government revenue the bulk of the profits that would otherwise have accrued to importers of restricted commodities.

The overall cash deficits of the government were almost eliminated by 1964. In subsequent years the government more than counterbalanced the rapid rise in its expenditures by effecting sharp increases in its domestic tax receipts and in the earnings of public enterprises. Between 1964 and 1967 current expenditures of the government in the general budget rose by 150 percent.[6] The rise in revenue, however, was much larger, and an expanding surplus was generated in the general budget to help finance the government's development outlays. The increase in the charges of public enterprises and their improved operational efficiency also provided a surplus for financing a substantial part of their own capital expenditures, through special budget accounts. In addition, foreign borrowing became increasingly important as a source of finance for capital expenditures through special accounts.[7]

---

[4] During 1961 and 1962, net central bank credit extended to the government constituted about 80 percent of the increase in the money supply.

[5] Capital expenditure in the general budget was lowered by 18 percent in 1963 and a further 20 percent retrenchment was made in 1964 despite the increase in import costs consequent on the exchange rate devaluation in that year.

[6] This rise was due for the most part to the special increases of 30 percent a year in wages of public officials effective from 1965, to compensate for the serious loss in their real income incurred in the previous years.

[7] It is noteworthy that despite the rapid increase in government current and capital expenditures, the ratio of total government expenditures to GNP was 13.9 percent in 1967, well below the 23.5 percent in 1962, and the share of government capital formation in the national total declined from about 60 percent in 1962 to about 30 percent in 1967.

Since 1964 there has been a spectacular 245 percent increase in internal tax receipts, due for the most part to improved tax administration, which has been achieved mainly through the new office of National Taxation and by an increase in the number of tax offices and officials and the introduction of speedy techniques of assessment and collection.[8] An important factor in this success was the strong personal support given to the tax drive by President Park. Some tax changes, consisting of upward adjustments in indirect taxes, were made in 1965. Since the main thrust was in improved tax administration, it was perhaps natural that indirect tax revenues expanded less rapidly than direct taxes, where evasion was greater. Despite the sharp increase in tax revenue in recent years, the ratio of tax revenue (including monopoly profits) to the GNP was only 10.3 percent in 1967, compared with 6.0 percent in 1964.

In 1968 the government adopted a large-scale reform of the internal tax and tariff structure. The direct tax structure has been made more progressive and the level and coverage of indirect taxes have been raised. The corporate tax system has been changed, favoring open corporations and establishing an integrated scheme of incentives for preferred investment. The tariff system has also been made administratively flexible and the rate structure rationalized in regard to its revenue producing and protective functions. As a result of continued tax efforts, the tax revenue–GNP ratio is to be stepped up to 14.3 percent of GNP by 1971, during the Second Five-Year Plan period. According to the 1968 overall resources budget, government savings should increase more rapidly than private domestic savings during the balance of the plan period.

Foreign aid, in the form of local-currency counterpart funds generated by U.S. aid, was for many years an important source of budgetary revenue. In recent years, however, the level of counterpart fund receipts in the annual budget has declined, despite the devaluation of the *won* by more than 50 percent since 1963. While the accrual of counterpart funds generated by U.S./AID in the general budget has declined, foreign borrowing for financial capital expenditures through special budget accounts has sharply increased in the 1968 budget. In addition, the counterpart funds generated by grants under the Japanese-Korean treaty are expected to be of some importance in financing capital outlays through special accounts.

While public enterprises have been reformed to operate on a nearly commercial basis and the payment of direct fiscal subsidies (to exporters and the like) has been eliminated, the government has not yet been fully able to apply market pricing policies in its grain-procurement scheme. The government purchases grain for the use of the armed forces and public

---

[8] A description of the government's efforts in this direction is given in the Annex on Tax Reform to the Report of the IBRD Mission Report on Korea of January, 1968.

institutions to prevent undue fluctuations in prices between the harvest season, to improve the terms of trade of the farming sector vis-à-vis the expanding nonfarming sector, and to narrow the difference between per capita incomes in the two sectors.[9] The procurement price theoretically takes into account the changes in farmers' consumer prices, the cost of grain production (particularly the cost of fertilizer and credit inputs), and agricultural productivity, but inadequate consideration appears to have been given the latter.[10]

The government has in general been successful in resisting pressures to increase the total amount of grains purchased, thereby limiting the cash requirements for the program.[11] By selling the purchased grain on a cost-plus basis, it has avoided incurring a loss as a fiscal charge. The Grain Management Special Account has therefore been managed, for the most part, with the surplus from the general budget with recourse to bank credit limited mostly to the grain procurement season.

Credit Policy

Prior to 1964 the government used a complex system of "credit rationing," consisting primarily of quarterly loan ceilings and selective credit allocation. Loan priority schemes and preferential interest rates were supported by other devices, such as advance deposit requirements against imports and quotas on central-bank rediscounts. This system proved ineffective because preferential terms were extended to many sectors, an increasing amount of bank credit was permitted outside the credit ceilings, and there was no effective check on the final use of the bank credit.

After 1964 a firmer policy of credit restraint placed all bank credit under the loan ceilings and cut back the rate of credit expansion to the private sector, despite the increased demand for credit after the devaluation of May, 1964. Credit ceilings continued to be the prime means of credit control until October, 1965. Throughout 1964 and 1965, increasing use also was made of variable reserve requirements and quotas on central-bank rediscounts to check the credit potential of commercial banks.

The shift toward indirect credit controls permitted the authorities more

---

[9] According to the IBRD Mission report of January, 1968, per capita income in the farm sector, which advanced more rapidly than nonfarm income between 1959 and 1964, has been rising less rapidly since 1965. Between 1959 and 1967 per capita farm income (at market prices) increased almost fivefold while nonfarm income rose almost fourfold.

[10] The grain-management scheme, integrated with the official fertilizer distribution and agricultural credit schemes handled by the NACF (National Agricultural Credit Foundation), has probably made a substantial contribution to the increase in grain production in recent years.

[11] The government purchases only about 10 percent of the grain produced.

flexibility in monetary policy. There was a rapid increase in time deposits after the interest-rate reform of October, 1965, and in 1966–67 there was an increase in foreign-exchange reserves. New monetary techniques were necessary to offset the resulting increase in bank liquidity. The minimum reserve requirements on deposits were raised several times in 1965 and 1966, and between October, 1966, and April, 1967, a marginal reserve requirement was set at 50 percent. Other techniques used to check credit expansion were the issue of central-bank bonds and short-term treasury bonds to commercial banks and the requirement that commercial banks maintain interest-earning blocked deposits with the central bank in excess of the required reserves against deposits.

Because of the investment boom in recent years and particularly the need for domestic funds to match the large inflow of foreign capital, the demand for bank credit has remained very high. The authorities have attempted to regulate the growth in the primary liquidity of the central bank and the money multiplier so that the final increase in the money supply will be contained within the limits of the stabilization program. Although the central bank's claims on the fiscal sector and the banking system was reduced somewhat in 1966 and 1967, the residual increase in commercial bank liquidity caused by the external surplus was large enough to enable them to expand their credit at an annual rate of around 66 percent. As a result of this rapid credit expansion and the continued external surplus, total money supply increased at an annual rate of 36 percent during 1966 and 1967, despite a 103 percent increase in quasi-monetary deposits. The relative low rate of price increases recorded, despite the large credit expansion, is largely due to the rapidly expanding demand for money and quasi-money holdings, to the increased inflow of imports, and possibly to lags in the price impact. The demand for total domestic liquidity (money supply plus quasi-monetary deposits) has risen in response to the growth in real GNP at 9.7 percent per annum and increasing monetization of the economy and confidence in price stability.[12] The pattern of liquid balance holdings has also changed with the high interest rate structure; the ratio of time and savings deposits to total liquidity has risen steadily from 40 percent in September, 1965, to 57 percent at the end of 1967.

Unless further deceleration of price increase is achieved, however, it is unlikely that the present rate of growth in imports can be sustained or that the demand for liquidity can continue to increase as rapidly as in the

---

[12] The ratio of total domestic liquidity to the gross national product at market prices has risen from 9.2 percent in 1964 to 18.1 percent in 1967 after having declined from a 13.8 percent level in 1962.

past two years of exceptionally high economic growth. The pace of monetary expansion must be curtailed if the progress thus far made toward financial stabilization is not to be impaired. The current year's stabilization program therefore provides for a tightening of credit restraints and restrictions on the build-up of short-term foreign liabilities, which has been largely responsible for the accumulation of foreign-exchange reserves in 1967.

Interest-Rate Reform

Undoubtedly the most significant change effected in monetary policy was the interest-rate reform introduced in October, 1965. The general level of interest rates was sharply increased to reflect the true scarcity value of capital, to encourage savers by providing an adequately attractive "real" interest rate (i.e., the nominal interest rate adjusted for the rate of price increase), and to help the shift in credit policy from quantitative rationing toward indirect regulation. The interest-rate reform was also intended to serve as a clear-cut demonstration of the government's determination to curb inflation. Other objectives were to attract funds from the "curb market" into the banking system in order to strengthen the influence of the monetary authorities and to promote the use of owned capital (in preference to borrowed capital) by the business sector. The standard loan rate of banking institutions was raised from 14 percent per annum to 26 percent per annum, and the interest rates paid on time and savings deposits were raised by a roughly corresponding margin. The interest rates on deposits with maturities of three months, six months, twelve months, and eighteen months (and longer) were raised to 1.5 percent, 2.0 percent, 2.2 percent, and 2.5 percent per month respectively. However, even the new rates were lower than the rates that prevailed in the "curb market," which usually were 4 to 5 percent per month.

The increase in banks' time and savings deposits was most spectacular immediately after the change, presumably because a substantial amount of money was transferred to the banking system from the curb market. In the quarter following the interest-rate reform, bank deposits increased by 47 percent. An annual increase rate of 103 percent has been sustained since; however, a part of this increase reflects the interest credited to deposit accounts. A recent study indicates that the large increase in the monetary savings was derived mainly from individuals and private households. On the basis of multiple regression analysis relating domestic savings after 1965 at three levels (household savings, gross private savings, and gross domestic savings) to real income, to changes in inventories, and to the real rate of interest, the study also establishes a very strong correlation between the real deposit rate of interest and household savings. In the case of gross private savings and gross domestic savings, however, the addition of the real deposit rate as an explanatory variable produces very little improvement in the regression results.[13]

The interest-rate reform has been very successful in promoting monetary savings, but the application of the high loan rates of interest has been restricted by a wide range of preferential loan rates of interest. Although the standard lending rate of commercial banks was raised to 26 percent per annum, approximately one-third of total commercial bank credit was extended at preferential rates, mostly for increasing exports or for the import of raw materials by export industries. Since the preferential rates applicable to export industry range between 6 and 7 percent per annum, the weighted average of the lending rate of commercial banks has been estimated at about 18 to 20 percent per annum. Moreover, specialized financial institutions (like the Korean Reconstruction Bank, the Medium Industry Bank, the National Agricultural Cooperatives Federation), which receive a substantial part of their resources through budgetary transfer, have extended loans of a volume two to three times that of commercial banks in recent years, and a substantial part of this has been at preferential rates. With the government's approval, the standard loan rate did not apply to loans obtained from private and official foreign sources. The relatively stable exchange rate that has prevailed since 1966 has reduced exchange risks and, together with the restrictive internal credit, has encouraged increased foreign borrowing. As a result, the average interest cost of all borrowed funds was undoubtedly far below the standard loan rate of banks; and with the continued increase in prices, the real cost of borrowed funds was further reduced. Moreover, with the increased availability of bank credit, partly consequent on the rise in time and savings deposits, business enterprises have been able to reduce their dependence on the curb market. Because the prevailing interest rates in the curb market were substantially higher than even the new standard loan rates of banks, this switch helped restrain the increase in their interest costs that resulted from the interest-rate reform.

The demand for bank credit, therefore, remained very strong under the stimulus of the rapid economic expansion.[14] Another reason for the sus-

[13] Kwang Suk Kim. "An Appraisal of the High Interest Strategy of Korea" (unpublished) May 1968, Center for Development Economics, Williams College, Massachusetts.

[14] The *real* rate of return on capital in Korea has been estimated by Edward Shaw in "Financial Patterns and Policies in Korea" (USOM — Korea, April 1967) as being around 15 percent. According to Bank of Korea statistics (*Monthly Statistical Review*) the ratio of net profits to total capital in manufacturing industry was about 8 percent in 1965 and remained stable in 1966.

tained large demand for loan finance, despite the high loan rates of interest, is the nature of the corporate tax system. Interest paid on borrowed funds is allowed as cost in determining profits subject to tax at a corporate tax rate of around 40 percent, whereas interest income—for example, on time and savings deposits—is subject to tax at only around 10 percent. This system therefore further reduced the effective cost of borrowed funds and offered a strong incentive to enterprises to make maximum use of loans and to deposit their own funds in time and savings deposit accounts with banks. Alternatively, entrepreneurs have an incentive to employ their own funds in the enterprise in the form of loans at high interest rates to the enterprise rather than as equity capital.

The narrowed difference between the deposit rate structure and the effective loan rates imposed a severe strain on the profit position of commercial banks.[15] This strain was not felt initially because of the preponderance of demand deposits (on which no interest is payable) in the deposit structure and the relatively low level of reserve ratios applied to deposits. However, the continued rise in the ratio of time and savings deposits to total deposits and the successive increases in the reserve requirements made in order to control bank liquidity generated by the external surplus increased the stress on bank profits. The monetary authorities therefore supported bank profits principally by the payment of interest on commercial bank special deposits required to be maintained with the central bank, and on issues of central bank bonds, the rate was 5 percent and 10 percent respectively. In addition, beginning in October, 1967, the government issued short-term treasury bills with an interest rate of 18 percent per annum, impounding the proceeds in a deposit account with the central bank.

The disparity between—on the one hand—the standard loan rate of banks and, on the other hand, preferential loan rates and the foreign interest rates, resulted in a *de facto* system of credit rationing that has subjected financial institutions and the government departments approving foreign loans to severe pressure from potential borrowers. When the interest rate reform was introduced in 1965, the Korean authorities intended to progressively reduce the disparities between the domestic loan rates and to lower very gradually the general level of interest rates as financial stability was more firmly established, as had been done in Taiwan. In April, 1968, the Korean authorities took steps to simplify the structure of deposit rates of interest and to lower their general level slightly. The

---

[15] As is to be expected in a country which has experienced prolonged inflation, the amount of income yielding financial assets (e.g., government bonds, bank debentures) outstanding was quite small, and trading in such securities even more limited. Therefore the interest rate reform did not result in significant capital loss by holders of such assets.

loan rates of interest, however, were not reduced, thereby providing some direct relief to the hard-pressed profit position of banks. By the time the interest-rate structure is "normalized," it is hoped a structural change will have occurred in the financial asset-holding habits of the population and a high rate of personal savings will be sustained.

Balance-of-Payments

The impressive change in Korea's balance-of-payments since 1963 has been associated with a sharp increase in the export of goods and services and in the inflow of private and government capital, mostly in the form of project loans.[16] Exports have risen since 1963 at a fairly steady rate, about 40 percent a year, and the increase has covered a wide range of light-industry products (e.g., textiles, clothing and footwear, veneer sheets and plywood, and electrical appliances). In 1963, exports of manufactured goods (SITC categories 5 to 8) were 45 percent of total exports, and 62 percent in 1967. Approximately 82 percent of Korea's exports went to industrial countries in 1967.

Imports have increased at an average annual rate of 37 percent during 1965–67, after a decline in 1964. The bulk of the increase in imports since 1965 has been in industrial raw materials, semiprocessed or intermediate goods and machinery, and equipment for industry.

The ability of the Korean economy to effect a rapid expansion in imports contrasts with the experience of other developing countries that have attempted stabilization programs. Although Korea's exports also have grown rapidly, and their ratio to imports has increased in recent years, it is unlikely that Korea would have been so successful without the large increase in invisible receipts (due to a fortuitous factor like Vietnam) and capital inflow. In addition, Korea has made almost no foreign-debt service payments in recent years because almost all the foreign aid it received in previous years was in the form of grants. As a result, imports could fully match the increase in exchange earnings and gross capital inflow. In con-

---

[16] Between 1963 and 1967, exports increased from $87 million to $320 million and invisible earnings (largely from sales to the U.N. command in Korea and exchange remittances of Koreans abroad, particularly Vietnam), from $89 million to $323 million. Total imports (f.o.b.) rose from $497 million to $909 million and invisible payments from $82 million to $155 million. Private transfers and total loan-capital inflow increased from about $52 million and $95 million in 1963 to $91 million and $299 million, respectively, in 1967. In contrast, official grants-in-aid from the United States declined from $206 million to $97 million; but grants from Japan (under the treaty signed between Japan and Korea in October, 1965) amounted to $37 million in 1967. In 1967, foreign-exchange holdings increased by $111 million, compared with a decline of $37 million in 1963. Total foreign-exchange earnings from Vietnam in 1967 were around $130 million, including the remittances of Korean soldiers and technicians and U.S. offshore procurements connected with Vietnam.

trast, most developing countries that have experienced prolonged inflation have accumulated a substantial foreign-debt service burden, which has limited the flow of imported goods and services. A second important difference is the fact that Korea has not experienced a serious erosion of import capability through an adverse movement in external terms of trade, which results from a decline in the price of many primary products.[17]

Devaluation and the Fluctuating Exchange Rate

The development of export- and import-substituting industry as the leading growth sector in the Korean economy has involved policies to make the economy more "open" by allowing the exchange rate to reflect the supply and demand for foreign-exchange and by progressively dismantling quantitative controls on foreign-exchange transactions. Prior to 1964 the overvalued exchange rate did not provide an adequate incentive to produce for export, and the domestic market was too small to provide an adequate base for expanded and efficient production. The tight import restrictions on raw materials imposed an additional constraint, even resulting in an underutilization of the existing infrastructure and industrial capacity.

In May, 1964, as part of the government's overall financial stabilization program, the exchange rate was devalued approximately 50 percent (from 130 to 255 *won* to 1 U.S. dollar). Simultaneously, all existing multiple-exchange rate devices (e.g., cash subsidies for exports and barter and export-import linking arrangements) were eliminated and quantitative import restrictions were relaxed (particularly for industrial raw materials) from the extremely tight controls of 1963.[18] In addition, the import tariff system has been strengthened by the introduction of the special customs duty in January, 1964, to restrict the demand for imports, curtail importers' profits on restricted import items, and increase government revenue.

The devaluation of the *won* had a direct, favorable effect on the fiscal situation by sustaining the counterpart fund receipts—despite a drop of $67 million in foreign grants in 1963–64—and by increasing the revenue from general and special import duties. Devaluation also increased the demand for bank credit and the liquidity position of the banking system and the public, not only because of the increase in foreign-exchange holdings, which occurred subsequently, but because the monetary authorities

[17] According to the Bank of Korea's statistical review, Korea's index of terms of trade has in fact improved, from 100 in 1963 to 115 in 1967, with the structural change in foreign trade.

[18] Export-import linking in the form of marketable rights to import specified commodities was eliminated. An indirect linking of exports and imports was continued in the preference given exporters in the issuance of import licenses, which, of course, were not transferable.

converted the outstanding export-import rights at the old rate (i.e., the import rights against export proceeds already sold to the monetary authorities). Despite the 50 percent devaluation, however, the wholesale price index of imported goods rose only 13 percent in the following three months, presumably because the market prices of imported goods had already been adjusted upward because of the tight import restrictions and the *de facto* depreciation under the previous multiple-currency system. The dishoarding of imported goods that followed the liberalization of imports of industrial raw materials,[19] the favorable grain crops, and the special customs duty that was added as a deterrent to profiteering on restricted imports, all helped restrain the price increase. Also, the anti-inflationary measures and the improved harvest of 1964 temporarily reduced imports. Major declines also were registered in manufactured goods (reflecting the tighter import restrictions in late 1963) and in machinery and equipment (reflecting the temporary decline in the level of real capital formation in 1964).

In March, 1965, a "floating exchange rate system" was introduced in the form of an exchange-certificate market. A recipient of foreign exchange could obtain exchange certificates from an authorized bank or could sell the foreign exchange to the bank for *won* at the daily buying rate posted by the Bank of Korea.[20] Exchange certificates were required for all exchange payments except government payments and payments of less than $50. The market price of exchange certificates was to be freely determined and was to serve as the guide for the eventual establishment of a fixed exchange parity for the *won*. The Bank of Korea's intervention was to be limited to preventing excessive short-term fluctuations, and, to ensure this, the posted rates had to be within 2 percent of the average certificate market rate of the previous day, unless exceptions were approved by the Minister of Finance. A limit also was placed on the decline that might occur during the year in the net foreign-exchange holdings of the Bank of Korea. As a precaution against speculative hoarding of exchange certificates, the certificates' validity period was limited to fifteen days. The high-interest rate structure, adopted in September, 1965, was an additional deterrent to speculative holdings of certificates.

The exchange-certificate rate depreciated from 255 *won* per U.S. dollar to 270 and 275 *won* per U.S. dollar by mid-1965, where it has since remained—with only minor fluctuations that reflect the strengthened balance-of-payments position. With the relative stability of the certificate rate and the high interest rates, an increasing proportion of foreign-

[19] Korean data on inventory investment (at 1965 prices) show that inventories of imported raw materials were reduced by 4.6 billion *won* in 1964, following an increase of 10.3 billion *won* in 1962 and 1963.

[20] Exchange certificates were not issued against PL 480 aid nor exchange bought from the U.N. command; the Bank of Korea's posted rates applied to these transactions.

exchange earnings tended to be sold directly for *won* rather than against exchange certificates, thereby limiting the volume of certificate transactions in the market. In 1966 and 1967, therefore, the validity period of certificates was extended to forty-five days, commercial banks were authorized to operate as certificate dealers (holding certificates as part of their exchange positions) in addition to their previous function as certificate brokers, and the spread between the posted buying and selling rates of the Bank of Korea was widened, offering a direct incentive for an exporter to obtain exchange certificates and for an importer to purchase certificates in the market rather than at the quoted Bank of Korea rates. With the adoption of these measures, the turnover in the exchange-certificate market increased markedly; certificates were obtained against almost 90 percent of the export earnings.

There has been criticism from exporters of the relative stability of the exchange rate despite the rise in domestic prices and wages since mid-1965. This criticism, however, has been relatively subdued—partly, perhaps, because the productivity of the export industries has been increasing as a result of the heavy investment in new facilities and the higher utilization rate of installed capacity. In addition, increased export volume has led to substantial economies. Another reason is the high import content in export products and the increasing amount of foreign-exchange liabilities incurred by export manufacturers to finance the import of machinery and equipment. Almost all the medium- and long-term foreign loans obtained by the private sector are denominated in foreign exchange. Therefore the major pressure from the export sector has been to step up other export incentives, such as special credit facilities at concessional rates of interest, tax remissions, and favored treatment in the licensing of raw material imports for export production and in advance-deposit requirements against imports. Although the structure of direct export incentives has remained more or less the same since the exchange reform of 1964, interest-rate reforms and higher corporate tax rates have widened the preferential margin of interest and tax rates applicable to the export sector. The continuing rise in domestic prices, while the exchange rate has remained relatively stable also has increased the advantage to exporters. Export industries have received the highest priority in the government's allocation of foreign borrowings and "foreign-exchange loans" from Korea's foreign-exchange reserves for the financing of imports of machinery and equipment.[21]

[21] The system of "foreign-exchange loans" was initiated in 1967 with the intention of discouraging the build-up of foreign borrowings (often on nationally disadvantageous terms), at a time when official exchange reserves were rising rapidly. These loans are extended at interest rates comparable to foreign rates and are repayable in foreign-exchange.

The relative stability of the floating exchange rate since mid-1965 is due to the abnormally high level of invisible earnings (connected with Vietnam and the large capital inflow) and to the operation of quantitative restrictions on imports and export incentive measures. As some of these influences diminish, the exchange rate should become more responsive to movements in domestic prices and wages. This factor, and the need for further progress toward domestic price stability and import liberalization, have encouraged the Korean authorities to consider establishing a fixed par-value prematurely. The authorities have already taken steps to tighten the approval process for short-term foreign borrowings, but the pressure of external borrowing will be reduced only as the domestic interest-rate structure is progressively lowered.

Liberalization of Imports

In late 1963 the import control system was made so restrictive that the automatic approval system was completely suspended, and later was limited to final users of industrial raw materials. The first phase of import liberalization, effected in 1964, permitted a somewhat freer flow of raw materials and contributed to a gain in industrial production. Also, it greatly reduced the need to maintain large, costly inventories of such materials. The scope of import liberalization was gradually widened, to include items manufactured in Korea and to help stabilize their domestic prices and improve the efficiency of domestic industry. Import liberalization, supported by the overall financial stabilization program, attempted to curb the rise in domestic demand and prices. By the first half of 1967, about 87 percent of the imports programmed against Korean foreign exchange (as distinguished from foreign aid) was in the automatic approval category (as against 30 percent in 1964), but for the most part the automatic approval list still covered capital and intermediate goods.

In August, 1967, a "negative list system" was adopted exclusively for the items that are subject to import restriction; all other items are eligible for automatic import approval. Previously, only items that were eligible for import either automatically or by prior approval were listed, which made a wide range of "unclassified" items ineligible for import. At the same time, the government announced its intention to eliminate import restrictions completely—for balance-of-payments reasons, in a three-stage operation—after a reform of the tariff system was effected. The first two stages were implemented in August, 1967, and January, 1968. In December, 1967, the tariff system was made more administratively flexible and was restructured on a more rational basis. Imports were broadly divided into "protected" and "revenue" items. In principle, nonprotected items will be subject to a uniform tariff rate, with exemptions for machinery and raw materials. Protective tariffs will be determined on an individual-commodity basis that considers a product's domestically added value, the cost difference between domestic and international products, and the product's degree of essentiality.

The import liberalization has to some extent been responsible for the large increase in imports after 1966. Most of this increase, however, has been in the form of raw materials, intermediate goods, and equipment inputs for the expanding industrial sector, and has been substantially supported by the inflow of short-, medium-, and long-term foreign loans. Import liberalization for finished consumer goods has not been extensive. Moreover, the Ministry of Commerce and Industry seems to exercise considerable indirect influence over imports through a system of registering qualified importers and through its many informal contacts with business enterprises (which in many cases operate both as exporters and importers).[22] The import restrictions on consumer goods have operated as a restraint on the consumption of nonessential imports and as a powerful protectionist measure. As a parallel device for restricting consumption of Korean products, the government makes extensive use of commodity and other indirect internal taxes, which also reduces the protective effects of import restrictions.

In any event, because many consumer product industries are producing not only for the domestic market but also for export, their productivity has steadily improved with the expanding markets and the large-scale modernization programs achieved through new investment. The government's intention is to switch to tariffs for protective purposes so that the extent of the protection given to industry will become open and more measurable.

Inflow of Foreign Private Capital

A very important factor in Korea's economic success in recent years has been the enlarged inflow of foreign capital, particularly private loans, and the ability of the Korean economy to "absorb" the capital inflow effectively.[23] The main reasons for the rapid increase in private-capital

---

[22] Also, the classification of import items under the new "negative list system" appears to be incomplete; the ministry apparently has not determined the status of many items that were unclassified under the previous system.

[23] The total of committed and outstanding medium- and long-term private loans increased from $129 million at the end of 1963 to $458 million at the end of 1967; by the end of 1967, total import arrivals against such committed loans amounted to $304 million. The total of committed and outstanding short-term import credits increased from $58 million at the end of 1966 to $240 million at the end of 1967; on an import arrival basis, the amount outstanding at the end of 1967 was $148 million. The total of committed official loans outstanding at the end of 1967 was $430 million and the total for import arrivals was $246 million.

inflow were the normalization of relations between Korea and Japan, the promotional efforts of the Korean authorities and of the governments of the principal lending countries, the high interest-rate structure within Korea, and increased international confidence in the Korean economy. Approximately half of the committed medium- and long-term private loans has been negotiated from Japan.

Of the promotional measures implemented by the Korean authorities, the most important are (1) a repayment guarantee, liberally extended by the government to private loans (almost 95 percent of all outstanding medium- and long-term private loans have a government guarantee); (2) considerable advance work by the Economic Planning Ministry on the feasibility of projects, interindustry linkages, and—in particular— the availability of satisfactory infrastructure facilities; and (3) the liberal terms offered to equity capital vis-à-vis tax treatment, transfer of profits and capital, and majority capital holdings (particularly after the revision of the Foreign Investment Law in 1966). In addition, intervention by the government is kept to a minimum once approval is granted a project and its associated foreign loan, provided satisfactory progress is shown in the execution of the project.

The confidence shown by foreigners in providing increasing amounts of capital is related largely to the close involvement of their governments (mainly Japan and the United States), the still relatively low external debt-service burden (which amounted to only 5 percent of total foreign-exchange receipts in 1967), and the generally satisfactory performance of the projects financed with the foreign capital. The remarkable capability shown by the construction industry in Korea in completing industrial projects, the relatively satisfactory availability thus far of infrastructure facilities and the technicians and managers needed to operate the projects, and the quick adaptability and discipline of Korean labor have helped sustain the inflow of private capital. An additional attraction in the case of equity capital has been the low wage structure in Korea. The inflow of equity capital has thus far been relatively small, but the changes in the Foreign Investment Law and the demonstrated momentum of economic progress in Korea have recently generated even greater interest among foreign investors.

III. Exogenous Factors

The results achieved by the government's economic policies are largely due to favorable environmental factors in Korea, and nine of the most important factors can be identified as follows.

1. Korea was not subject to disruptive internal tensions, such as racial, religious, or language divisions. Moreover, the existence of a hostile

regime in North Korea has been a unifying factor and has provided its own impetus toward economic growth. The Korean government has frequently stressed the point that rapid economic development should precede, and would promote, the eventual unification of Korea.

2. Korea has been strategically important in international geopolitics, a fact that has been largely responsible for the inflow of foreign aid.

3. Korea has had stable political leadership and clear-cut economic programs and policies. Its highly centralized political system invests enormous power in the hands of its president, who has attached primary importance to the government's economic program and has shown a high degree of personal involvement in its implementation. Political opposition to the government has been relatively weak and ineffective, particularly in its criticism of the government's economic policies, whose emphasis on rapid economic modernization and national self-reliance have had great public appeal. It is also significant that, unlike many other developing countries, the Korean government has not had to face strong pressures to expand public welfare expenditures.

4. There has been an absence of powerful pressure groups—for example, trade unions—who felt their economic interests were threatened by the government's anti-inflationary program. Further, with the rapid gain in domestic production after the introduction of the anti-inflationary program and with the continued large supply of goods financed by foreign loans and aid, no important section of the population (except government officials) at any time suffered even a temporary loss of real income of any significant magnitude. Government officials, who experienced a serious erosion of buying power or real wages, fully supported the government's anti-inflationary program even though their salaries were not increased to keep pace with the rise in prices.

5. Public confidence was generated in the government because of the early and impressive results of its economic program, and this confidence was felt in all sectors of the population, which benefited in various degrees. Although concentration of ownership of new industries and heavy reliance on indirect taxation is producing an unequal distribution of the expanding income, there is as yet relatively little evidence of the provocative and ostentatious consumption by the richer classes and government officials that is seen in many other developing countries.

6. There has been an emergence of young, pragmatic, career-minded economic administrators, who enjoy considerable prestige within the government bureaucracy and with the public.[24]

---

[24] It is perhaps significant that most senior officials of the rank of bureau directors in the economic ministries are in their thirties. It is also noteworthy that the range of offices available to career officials has been increased, giving more stability to the bureaucratic system.

7. There has been a rapid growth of a dynamic entrepreneurial class that has proved itself capable of constructing and managing large-scale industrial enterprises and competing successfully in international markets. Significantly, a large proportion of the foreign aid negotiated by the government is channeled directly into the private sector and produces a relatively quick expansion in investment and production.

8. Because of the pervasiveness of educational facilities, a relatively large supply of labor possessing many of the skills needed to build an expanding industrial society has been available.

9. The government has followed a policy of population control in recent years. The population growth rate has declined from 2.7 percent in 1962 to 2.4 percent in 1967, and is projected to decline to 2.0 percent in 1971, by the end of the Second Five-Year Plan.

The successful organization and management of the five-year development plans—particularly the generally balanced structure of the expanding investment programs—also can be regarded as an important "exogenous factor" that has contributed to the success of the stabilization policies. In this context, three aspects of the plans are especially noteworthy. The first aspect is the long-standing emphasis the government has placed on increased agricultural production. It is significant that Korea is one of the few densely populated developing countries in which agricultural production has increased faster than population.[25] The second aspect is the anticipated need for developing infrastructure facilities, which provided the base for the rapid industrial expansion of recent years. Because industrial production has grown at a faster pace than had been envisaged under the development plans, a shortage of infrastructure facilities is possible and may require larger investment in this sector than was envisaged in the Second Five-Year Plan. The third aspect is the very strong export orientation given to industrial development.

IV. CONCLUSION

The crucial elements in Korea's anti-inflationary financial program can be identified as follows. In the fiscal area, the government strove to increase the internal tax revenue and to implement a realistic pricing policy for public enterprises. In monetary policy, the government instituted the interest-rate reform and developed indirect monetary control techniques. In balance-of-payments policy, the government implemented a wide range of measures—including the fluctuating exchange rate, liberalization of import controls, and reform of the tariff system—that were directed toward the progressive opening up of the Korean economy.

[25] An institutional factor that made this possible was the land-reform program implemented in 1946.

It is apparent, however, that Korea's economic success was due not so much to the novelty of her financial policies as to the fact that generally they were implemented in a balanced and sustained manner. This was possible largely because of the particular social, political, and institutional factors that prevail in Korea.

The second key feature was the rapid increase, since 1964, in the supply of goods and services from domestic industry and agriculture, and imports. This, in turn, was due mainly to the reserve of infrastructure facilities, industrial labor, and underutilized industrial capacity that was available for immediate exploitation, plus the increased import of intermediate and capital goods. The increase in agricultural output was the result of policies that emphasized agricultural productivity over a number of years, and to some extent of such chance elements as favorable crop conditions. The large expansion in imports was supported largely by the inflow of foreign grants and loans and by the increase in foreign-exchange earnings associated with the Vietnam war.

The third important feature was the very rapid increase in the demand for monetary and quasi-money balances as a function of the increase in the real national product, the strengthened confidence in price stability, and the high interest-rate structure. It must be noted that the price inflation experienced by Korea was not of the extreme type, which has completely undermined public confidence in the monetary system. Therefore it was not necessary for the Korean authorities to impose extreme financial stringency upon the economy—except very briefly, during the initial stages of the stabilization program in 1963–64—thus avoiding the disruption of production and distribution that has been experienced by many other countries.

Rapid expansion of bank- and foreign-credit financed imports in 1966 and 1967, however, raises the prospect of deviation from the relative economic realism Korean authorities have displayed in recent years, which can only too easily cause an intensification of inflationary pressures. A growing tendency toward overoptimism about the capabilities of the economy, the pace of economic growth that may be achieved, and the accumulation of external debt perhaps makes this more than a theoretical possibility, particularly in light of renewed pressures for greater expenditure on defense.

KOREA'S USE OF FOREIGN
AND DOMESTIC RESOURCES:
A CROSS-COUNTRY COMPARISON

Alan M. Strout

Korea's growth in the past few years has been remarkable, as everyone knows by now, but the skeptic may wish to raise two specific questions. How well has Korea performed relative to other developing countries during the same period? And how well has Korea utilized the available foreign aid and other external resources?

The first question can be answered, at least in a conventional manner, by reference to the usual growth indicators. Table 1 presents recent data for a 32-country less developed countries (LDC) sample of GNP and export growth rates, gross capital-output ratios, and observed marginal savings rates. In only one case does Korea rank first in this sample (export growth in the most recent of the two periods covered), but in every case Korea is within the upper quartile of good performers.[1] Particularly noteworthy is its high score on export growth, which for the 1963–65 to 1965–67 period came to 44 percent per year (including goods and services).

It is also of interest that the median LDC in the same sample (between the two periods examined) improved both its GNP and its export growth rate but did not improve its capital productivity or its savings mobilization. The median gross capital-output ratio rose from 2.79 to 3.16 and the marginal savings–GNP ratio fell from 0.19 to 0.16. The 32-country weighted average was even worse: the marginal savings rate fell from 21 to 12 percent—a singularly poor performance record (about which more will be said later).

The performance indicators shown in Table 1, however, are relatively superficial and say little about the use of external resources. To explore this latter question, two models are proposed: one to relate investment

---

[1] The composition of the 32-country sample was determined solely by the countries for which AID maintains current national accounts records extending back seven or more years. The subperiods analyzed are 1961–63 to 1963–65 and 1963–65 to 1965–67, except where the lack of 1967 estimates made it necessary to use three-year averages, beginning with 1960. These subperiods are hereafter referred to as period 1 and period 2, respectively.

TABLE 1. INDICATORS OF ECONOMIC PERFORMANCE—KOREA AND AVERAGE LDC

	32-country sample[a]				
	Weighted average	Median	Upper quartile	Range	Korea
Period 1 (1961-63 to 1963-65[b])					
GNP growth rate (%)	5.0	5.1	6.6	2.6 –10.3	7.6
Export growth rate (%)	7.0	8.3	13.5	0.1 –23.5	18.2
Gross capital-output ratio	3.50	2.79	2.39	8.19– 1.80	1.86
Marginal saving ratio	0.21	0.19	0.31	−0.24– 0.52	0.31
Period 2 (1963-65 to 1965-67[b])					
GNP growth rate (%)	4.9	5.3	6.9	0.3 –11.5	9.8
Export growth rate (%)	6.8	9.1	12.5	−1.5 –43.6	43.6
Gross capital-output ratio	3.63	3.16	2.49	38.6 – 1.46	1.59
Marginal savings ratio	0.12	0.16	0.31	−0.35– 1.71	0.34

Source: Table A1.
[a] Central America (Costa Rica, El Salvador, Guatemala, Honduras, and Nicaragua) treated as one country.
[b] Lack of 1967 data made it necessary to define period 1 as 1960-62 to 1962-64 and period 2 as 1962-64 to 1964-66 for ten of the thirty-two countries.

growth to foreign capital flows and the other to relate the observed capital-output ratios (or the output-capital ratio) to imports.

INVESTMENT GROWTH MODEL

The basic proposition of this model is that a country's gross new investment is made up of *potential* domestic savings plus some fraction of net foreign-capital inflows (foreign savings). When a country's growth is constrained by available foreign resources, the fraction that goes to increased domestic investment will be close to 1.0. When there are fairly plentiful foreign resources but the country suffers from shortages of domestic savings, some of the foreign resources will be redundant (from the viewpoint of increasing domestic investment) and the fraction will be less than 1.0. Thus by definition:

$$I_t = \bar{S}_t + F_t^s = S_t + F_t \qquad (1)$$

I = gross investment
$\bar{S}$ = potential national savings, *ex ante*
S = realized national savings, *ex post*
F^s = *ex ante* investment–savings gap
F = realized net foreign-capital inflows (imports minus exports, goods, and services), *ex post*
t = subscript denoting a particular year.

Hence:

$$I_t = \bar{S}_t + \gamma_t F_t \tag{2}$$

γ = proportion of foreign capital used for domestic investment = F^s/F. The assumption is also made that:

$$\bar{S}_t = \bar{S}_t - 1 + \alpha'(V_t - V_t - 1) \tag{3}$$

V = GNP
α' = marginal potential savings–GNP ratio.

Note also that in "two-gap" terminology the fraction γ is equal to the ratio between the savings gap, F^s, and the actual capital inflow.[2] When the savings gap is "dominant" ($F^s > F^m$ [where F^m equals the import or foreign trade gap]), γ is 1.0 and potential savings are equal to observed savings. (Observed savings are almost inevitably computed for LDCs as the difference between observed capital formation and net foreign-capital inflows, or $S_t = I_t - F_t$). When, however, the import (or trade) gap dominates the savings gap, observed savings will be less than potential savings because $\gamma_t < 1.0$.

Substituting equation 3 in equation 2 and expressing the result in terms of change over time, we have:

$$\Delta I = \alpha' \Delta V + \gamma_{t+1} F_{t+1} - \gamma_t F_t \tag{4}$$

$\Delta I = I_{t+1} - I_t$, etc.

Equation 4, in turn, can be reduced to:

$$\Delta I = \alpha' \Delta V + \gamma^* \Delta F \tag{5}$$

γ^* is a weighted average of γ_{t+1} and γ_t.

Although γ_t can theoretically only take values of 0 to 1, γ^* can take almost any value, depending upon γ_{t+1}, γ_t, F_{t+1} and F_t.

Empirical evidence for this model is found in the 32-country data mentioned above. In nineteen countries the marginal foreign-capital–GNP ratio ($\Delta F/\Delta V$) increased between the two subperiods. In fifteen countries the coefficient of new capital formation ($\Delta I/\Delta V$) also increased between these two periods, as would be expected from equation 5. Conversely, the marginal foreign-capital coefficients fell in the remaining thirteen cases, and in all but two instances (the Dominican Republic and Jordan) decreasing foreign capital was accompanied by relative decreases in new capital formation.

Although the proposed model appears reasonable, its use for cross-

---

[2] For a treatment of the two-gap approach to growth analysis, see (16).

section analysis is limited to defining an "average" relationship because of the considerable (and fully anticipated) country-to-country variation in marginal savings ratios and dominant-resource constraints on growth. For example, when it is applied to the 32-country sample[3] we find:

	Estimated α'	Estimated γ^*	$\bar{R}^2$
Period 1			
32 observations	.22	.60	.50
	(9.0)	(5.7)	
Period 2			
32 observations	.21	.99	.31
	(3.2)	(3.9)	
31 observations	.17	.36	.15
	(5.2)	(2.5)	
Pooled data			
64 observations	.22	.81	.33
	(6.3)	(5.7)	
63 observations[a]	.19	.48	.31
	(9.5)	(5.4)	

Note: t-ratios are in parentheses.

[a] Dominican Republic omitted because low GNP growth (ΔV) in period 2 results in very high values of $\Delta I/\Delta V$ and $\Delta F/\Delta V$ and a disproportionate weight in the regression calculations.

In neither period is the formal statistical fit very good. For the pooled data, except for a particularly aberrant observation, the model "explains" only one-third of the observed intercountry variation in $\Delta I/\Delta V$. The values of the parameters appear reasonable, however, and they may be used in a normative fashion to represent average attainment for the principal aid-receiving LDCs. Thus the "potential" marginal savings rate for the average LDC appears to be about 20 percent, with some decline registered between the two periods. On the margin, the LDCs in the sample appear to have increased gross investment by amounts roughly equal to 50 percent of their increased foreign-resource inflows.

The most interesting aspect of the results is the increase in the unexplained variance in $\Delta I/\Delta V$ (decline in the model's goodness-of-fit) between the two periods. The relative change in foreign capital ($\Delta F/\Delta V$) showed a distinct relationship with the relative change in investment ($\Delta I/\Delta V$) during the years 1961–63 to 1963–65 but little if any relationship in the years 1963–65 to 1965–67. This result was not the fault of one or two observa-

[3] The estimate derived from the deflated form of equation 5, is

(5') $\dfrac{\Delta I}{\Delta V} = \alpha' + \gamma^* \dfrac{\Delta F}{\Delta V} + \mu$, where Δ represents the change over a particular sub-period (e.g., 1961 + 62 + 63 to 1963 + 64 + 65) and μ is the error term.

tions but of a generally random investment–foreign capital pattern for a large number of countries. The explanation seems to be that a considerable increase occurred between the two periods in the variability of foreign-resource availability. The variance of relative foreign-capital inflows (as measured by $\Delta F/\Delta V$) increased by a small amount, but export earnings were more variable. The increased variability of foreign-exchange availability, in turn, led to a substantial (more than 60 percent) increase in the variance of relative imports. As a consequence, there apparently was some increase in underutilized foreign capital (from the viewpoint of LDC capital formation) and a wider range of values for γ^*.

Korea's performance against this general background was quite good. Average LDC capital formation during 1963–65 to 1965–67 was slightly less than might have been expected on the bases of available foreign capital and average LDC behavior (63-observation pooled data) over the longer 1961–67 period (see Table 2). The median LDC in our sample, however, increased its investment about as expected. Upper quartile performance showed an actual ratio of $\Delta I/\Delta V$, about 0.12 above the expected value. The Korean record was better than this: the actual ratio of $\Delta I/\Delta V$ was 0.39 while the ratio calculated from the parameters found for the

TABLE 2.   GROWTH OF CAPITAL AND CHANGE IN CAPITAL PRODUCTIVITY—
KOREA AND AVERAGE LDC

	32-country sample			
	Weighted average	Median	Upper quartile	Korea
Rate of growth of capital $\left(\dfrac{\Delta I_2}{\Delta V_2} - \dfrac{\Delta I_1}{\Delta V_1}\right)$	$-.02$	$.02$	$.12$	$.14$
Difference between actual and estimated investment increase, period 2 $\left(\dfrac{\Delta I_2 - \Delta \hat{I}_2}{\Delta V_2}\right)$, where $\dfrac{\Delta \hat{I}}{\Delta V} = .19 + .48\dfrac{\Delta F}{\Delta V}$	$-.04$	$.01$	$.12$	$.18$
Change in output-capital ratio $\left(\dfrac{\Delta V_2}{I_1} - \dfrac{\Delta V_1}{I_0}\right)$	$-.01$	$-.02$	$.06$	$.09$
Difference between actual and estimated output-capital ratio, period 2 $\left(\dfrac{\Delta V_2 - \Delta \hat{V}_2}{I_1}\right)$, where $\dfrac{\Delta \hat{V}}{I} = .23 + 1.08\dfrac{\Delta M}{I}$	$-.03$	$.00$	$.04$	$-.09$

63-observation pooled sample (shown above and based upon the rather small increase in net foreign capital registered during the period) was only 0.21.

In terms of the relationship between investment growth and net foreign capital, the Korean record has been fairly consistent over time. Equation 5, applied to time-series data for Korea, gives the following:

$$\frac{\Delta I}{\Delta V} = 0.29 + 1.0 \frac{\Delta F}{\Delta V} \tag{6}$$

$$\Delta I_0 = \sum_{60}^{61} I_t - \sum_{57}^{58} I_t$$

$$\Delta I_1 = \sum_{61}^{62} I_t - \sum_{58}^{59} I_t, \text{ etc.}$$

This equation explains about 95 percent of the period-to-period variation in Korea's $\Delta I/\Delta V$. It implies a fairly stable marginal savings rate of about 29 percent and foreign-capital productivity (from the viewpoint of domestic-capital formation) of close to 1.0, the theoretical maximum.

Capital Productivity Model

Once new capital is in place, the extent of its use depends upon demand-and-supply factors. We know that supply conditions, and particularly foreign-exchange bottlenecks, are important in a number of developing countries. This factor can be incorporated in a capital productivity model in which an increase in GNP in one period is related to the capital stock installed in the previous period *and* to the foreign exchange (imports) available in the current period. Thus:

$$\Delta V = aI_t + b\Delta M_v \tag{7}$$

$\Delta V = V_{t+1} - V_t$

$\Delta M = M_{t+1} - M_t$, and M_v equals imports of goods and services used for domestic production (as opposed to those for direct consumption or for direct capital investment)

$a =$ the reciprocal of the incremental gross capital-output ratio = the output-capital ratio

$b =$ the reciprocal of the marginal import coefficient for general domestic production.

In practice, it is difficult to measure M_v, and I will assume that (*a*) the increase in consumption of imports is generally inconsequential, (*b*) imports of investment goods bear a direct relationship to the increase in domestic investment, and (c) the rate of increase in new investment will tend to be constant. Thus:

(a) $\Delta M_c = 0$, where c represents direct consumption imports
(b) $\Delta M_i = c\Delta I$, where i represents direct investment goods
(c) $\Delta I = dI$.

Imports of intermediate goods may be related to total imports as follows:

$$\Delta M_v = \Delta M - \Delta M_c - \Delta M_i \tag{8}$$

Substituting assumptions a through c, we have: $\Delta M_v = \Delta M - cdI$; and introducing this into equation 7 gives:

$$\Delta V = a^*I_t + b\Delta M, \quad \text{where} \quad a^* = (a - bcd) \tag{9}$$

Dividing through by I_t gives us an expression for the conventional gross incremental output-capital ratio:

$$\frac{\Delta V}{I_t} = a^* + b\frac{\Delta M}{I_t} + \mu \tag{10}$$

As was true for the investment growth model, the capital productivity model seems at least roughly descriptive of the real world. Between the two periods examined, seventeen sample countries registered relative increases in imports per unit of GNP. For twelve of these countries the gross output-capital ratio $(\Delta V/I)$ also increased. This rough correlation was higher in the negative direction: thirteen of the fifteen countries where relative imports decreased also were characterized by declines in the incremental output-capital ratio.

The statistical goodness-of-fit of equation 10 in describing the real world is not exceptional when it is applied on a cross-section basis, but the model can nevertheless be used as a simple description of an "average" relationship. For the 32-country sample, we have:

	Estimated a*	Estimated b	$\overline{R^2}$
Period 1			
32 observations	.27	.88	.34
	(9.6)	(4.1)	
Period 2			
32 observations	.19	1.29	.63
	(6.7)	(7.4)	
31 observations[a]	.19	1.25	.60
	(6.5)	(6.7)	
Pooled data			
64 observations	.22	1.12	.51
	(11.4)	(8.2)	
63 observations[a]	.23	1.08	.48
	(11.3)	(7.7)	

Note: t-ratios in parentheses.
[a] Excluding Dominican Republic in period 2.

There is little stability in the sample's average parameter values between the two periods. Import availability, judging by the values of b, seems to have been more important as a contributor to GNP growth in the second period; and the implicit gross capital-output ratio, with no import increase (as approximated by $1/a^*$) also increased—from approximately 3.70 to approximately 5.30.

A significantly better statistical fit is obtained by adding two variables that have been found important in explaining intercountry differences in capital-output ratios. The first, $\Delta V/V$, is a measure of the GNP growth rate. It captures the fact that the gross (but not necessarily the net) capital-output ratio tends to decrease as the GNP growth rate increases. The second variable, V/N, or GNP per capita, reflects the tendency (observed by Kuznets) for the net capital-output ratio to be low for low per capita income countries and to rise severalfold for higher-income countries (presumably as social overhead investment becomes relatively more important).[4]

Thus the new model becomes:

$$\frac{\Delta V}{I_t} = e + b\frac{\Delta M}{I_t} + f\frac{\Delta V}{V_t} + g\frac{V_t}{N_t} + \mu \tag{11}$$

$\Delta V = V_{t+1} - V_t$

$\frac{\Delta V}{V_t}$ = annual average GNP increase divided by initial GNP

V_t/N_t = GNP per capita in dollars.

The values found for these parameters (t ratios again shown in parentheses) are:

Estimated coefficient values

	e	b	f	g	$\overline{R^2}$
Period 1					
32 observations	.13	.45	4.19	−.00018	.78
	(4.1)	(3.3)	(7.5)	(4.4)	
Period 2					
32 observations	.06	.54	4.34	−.00011	.90
	(2.6)	(4.4)	(9.0)	(3.1)	
31 observations[a]	.06	.54	4.37	−.00011	.89
	(2.3)	(4.3)	(8.7)	(3.1)	
Pooled data					
64 observations	.09	.49	4.32	−.00014	.86
	(5.0)	(5.4)	(12.0)	(5.5)	
63 observations[a]	.10	.48	4.31	−.00014	.84
	(4.3)	(5.3)	(11.7)	(5.4)	

[a] Excluding Dominican Republic in period 2.

[4] A capital-output ratio model that uses these two variables was derived in Alan Strout, "Savings, Imports, and Capital Productivity" (unpublished paper presented to

For this form of the capital-productivity model there is greater period-to-period coefficient similarity. The contribution of import availability to GNP growth (the coefficient b) is reduced to half of that in the earlier formulation, but again there is an increase in its value between the two periods. The coefficient f becomes the most important explanation factor of capital productivity (its partial $\bar{r}^2$ for the 63-observation sample is 0.69, compared to 0.31 for b and 0.32 for g); it says that for a 5 percent increase in GNP, the output-capital ratio can be expected to increase by an absolute value of about 0.22.[5] (0.05 $\times$ 4.31 = 0.22; for the 63-observation sample the mean value of $\Delta V/I$ is 0.35.) Increasing GNP per capita, on the other hand, will tend to *reduce* the capital-productivity ratio by about 0.014 for each \$100 per capita GNP increase.

The Korean relationship between capital productivity and imports appears to be about the same as for the average LDC (based on cross-country data). The Korean overall output-capital ratio has been increasing, and has more than doubled between 1957–61 and 1963–67. More than two-thirds of this increase, however, appears to be associated with a fast rate of GNP growth rather than with the increased availability of non-capital imports.

For the period 1957–67, a function of the following form fits the Korean moving average data quite well:

$$\frac{\Delta V_t}{I_t} = 0.18 + 0.60 \frac{\Delta M_{vt}}{I_t} + 4.3 \frac{\Delta V_t}{V_t} \tag{12}$$

$$\Delta V_0 = \frac{1}{3}\left(\sum_{59}^{61} V_t - \sum_{57}^{59} V_t \right)$$

$$\Delta V_1 = \frac{1}{3}\left(\sum_{60}^{62} V_t - \sum_{58}^{60} V_t \right), \text{ etc.}$$

$$I_0 = \frac{2}{3}\sum_{57}^{59} I_t; \quad I_1 = \frac{2}{3}\sum_{58}^{60} I_t; \text{ etc.}$$

the First World Congress of the Econometric Society, Rome, September 14, 1965). The $\bar{R}^2$ for 35 developing countries during the period 1957–62 was found (in the earlier paper [n. 2]) to be 0.727. For the 63-observation sample used in the current study and for the same model, $\bar{R}^2$ equals 0.803. Expressed as an output-capital rather than a capital-output model, the present 63-observation sample gives $\bar{R}^2$ = 0.776. Adding $\Delta M/I$ as an explanatory variable increases $\bar{R}^2$ to a very respectable 0.845 (see below). Cf. J. Vanek and A. H. Studenmund, "Towards a Better Understanding of the Incremental Capital-Output Ratio," *Quarterly Journal of Economics* (August, 1968): 452–64.

[5] Another way of viewing this is to note the large element of LDC capital formation that is not (statistically) related to intercountry growth-rate variations over as short a time period as five years. Thus a higher GNP growth rate, if other conditions are satisfied, can often be achieved with a relatively small increase in capital investment.

M_v = total imports of goods and services minus capital goods imports (SITC 7)

$$M_{v0} = \frac{1}{3} \sum_{57}^{59} M_{vt}; \quad M_{v1} = \frac{1}{3} \sum_{58}^{60} M_{vt}; \text{ etc.}$$

$$V_0 = \frac{1}{3} \sum_{57}^{59} V_t; \quad V_1 = \frac{1}{3} \sum_{58}^{60} V_t; \text{ etc.}$$

Inasmuch as noncapital import goods have accounted for about two-thirds of Korea's increased imports in recent years, the 0.60 coefficient for $\Delta M_v/I$ is roughly equivalent to a coefficient of 0.40 applied to $\Delta M/I$, which in turn is not much less than the pooled cross-country coefficients shown earlier, 0.48 to 0.49. The per capita income coefficient, g in the cross-country model, is not too important quantitatively, and the chief difference between Korea and the average less developed country appears to lie in an initially higher value of the equation's constant term. This comparison is shown quantitatively in Table 3.

TABLE 3.   ESTIMATED CONTRIBUTIONS TO KOREAN OUTPUT-CAPITAL RATIO, 1957–62 AND 1962–67

	Based on Korean time series results			Based on 63 observations cross-country results		
	1957–62	1962–67	Diff.	1957–62	1962–67	Diff.
Constant term	.18	.18	0.00	.10	.10	0.00
Import factor	−.03	.08	.11	−.01	.08	.09
Growth rate factor	.16	.42	.26	.16	.42	.26
Per capita income factor	(n.a.)	(n.a.)	(n.a.)	(negligible)		—
Total (estimated)	.31	.68	.37	.25	.60	.35
(cf. Actual output-capital ratio)	(.31)	(.67)	(.36)	(.31)	(.67)	(.36)
Equivalent estimated capital-output ratio	3.22	1.49	—	4.00	1.67	—

The pooled cross-country results, as applied to the Korean data, underestimate the output-capital ratio in both periods, but the estimated *change* for the period (see column 6 in Table 3) is approximately correct. Both models attribute the largest element in the capital productivity change to the increase in GNP growth rate from 3.7 percent per year in 1957–62 to 9.9 percent in 1962–67.

CONCLUSION

The above analysis, in addition to attesting to Korea's superior economic performance in recent years, quite clearly suggests that this performance has been strongly influenced by an underlying domestic savings constraint.

Marginal savings rates have been high, the country has efficiently employed its net foreign capital in the creation of domestic investment, and capital productivity has increased progressively over the past ten years. These factors are the classical indicators of savings-limited growth. There is additional evidence, too, on the import side. Foreign exchange has for the most part been plentiful, and the direct contribution of imports to GNP growth (as opposed to capital formation) apparently was slightly lower than the average for developing countries.

In these respects Korea provides an interesting contrast to the "average" LDC of our 32-country sample. For this sample, the foreign-trade constraint apparently was much more important than the savings constraint. Only about 60 percent of the net foreign-capital inflow was translated into new domestic investment (1961–63 to 1963–65), and this ratio declined throughout the period as foreign capital became at least relatively more plentiful. Average capital productivity, however, increased. If India (adversely affected by drought) is omitted, the GNP growth rate of the other countries registered a respectable increase, from 5.2 percent in period 1 to 5.6 percent in period 2. The output-capital ratio for the same group of 31 countries increased from 0.30 to 0.32, and the annual growth rate of new capital formation rose from 5.5 percent to 6.3 percent. This improved capital-forming and capital-using performance was accompanied by a sharp rise in the marginal import-GNP ratio, from 0.16 in period 1 to 0.24 in period 2. Although capital formation increased over these seven years, it did not increase as rapidly as net foreign capital. The apparent marginal savings ratio—measured as the difference between observed capital formation and observed foreign-capital inflows rather than as the difference between capital formation and *effectively* used foreign capital (i.e., $\gamma\Delta F$)—consequently fell. More specifically, the average figures were:

	32-country sample		31-country sample (excluding India)	
	Period 1	Period 2	Period 1	Period 2
Output-capital, $\Delta V/I$	.29	.28	.30	.32
Marginal import/marginal output, $\Delta M/\Delta V$	.17	.23	.16	.24
Marginal capital/marginal output, $\Delta I/\Delta V$	.21	.18	.19	.20
Marginal foreign capital/marginal output, $\Delta F/\Delta V$	.00	.05	−.02	.04
Observed marginal savings ratio, $\Delta S/\Delta V$	.21	.13	.21	.16

Korea, in short, was able to generate an unusually high rate of domestic savings and maintain a high rate of capital formation despite the relative decline in net foreign capital (see Table A–2). If Korea had performed in a manner similar to the average LDC (based upon the pooled regression results reported above), Korea's increase in annual gross investment between 1957–59 and 1965–67 would have been only about $276 million rather than the $450 million actually recorded. However, Korea's capital-productivity performance during this period did not differ greatly from that of the average LDC, after allowance is made for differences in growth rate. As shown in Table 3, the Korean output-capital ratio increased from 0.31 in 1957–62 to 0.67 in 1962–67. Using parameters from the pooled regression results, we see that the estimated increase in this ratio would have been from 0.25 to 0.60. Thus Korea's capital productivity was somewhat higher than the LDC average, but its change over the time period was about average, given the available imports and the GNP growth rate.

CHAPTER 11 APPENDIX

TABLE A–1. ECONOMIC PERFORMANCE INDICATORS—SELECTED LDCs—1961-63 TO 1963-65 (PERIOD 1) AND 1963-65 TO 1965-67 (PERIOD 2)*

Region	Country	GNP growth rate (%)[a]		Gross capital output ratio[b]		Observed marginal savings/GNP ratio[c]		Export growth rates (%)[d]	
		Period 1	Period 2	Period 1	Period 2	Period 1	Period 2	Period 1	Period 2
Latin America	Argentina	2.6	4.3	8.19	4.52	.23	.23	7.7	3.0
	Bolivia	5.4	6.0	2.45	2.55	.35	.24	23.5	17.4
	Brazil	3.1	4.2	5.78	3.69	.01	−.04	4.8	6.0
	Central America[f]*	5.9	5.6	2.16	2.48	.15	.13	12.6	13.6
	Chile	4.5	4.7	3.99	3.79	.46	.40	11.0	10.9
	Colombia	4.3	4.5	4.81	4.33	.18	.07	8.5	−0.2
	Dominican Republic	3.6	0.3	2.75[e]	38.6[e]	−.24	1.71	10.9	−1.3
	Ecuador*	4.6	5.1	3.30	2.80	.08	.05	4.9	7.8
	Mexico	7.1	7.1	2.67	2.85	.24	.23	8.0	7.4
	Panama*	8.2	7.7	2.28	2.50	.28	.12	13.9	9.5
	Peru	6.1	5.3	2.87	3.30	.10	.30	9.1	8.8
	Venezuela*	5.0	5.9	4.24	3.81	.22	−.04	.4	−0.9
Africa	Ethiopia	4.6	4.4	2.33	2.57	.14	.12	12.8	6.7
	Ghana	2.8	1.8	4.90	6.83	.21	−.03	.1	−1.0
	Kenya*	6.0	5.3	1.98[e]	2.00[e]	.16	.13	8.3	7.1
	Morocco*	5.2	1.3	2.06	8.93	.15	.84	6.9	6.1
	Tunisia	4.6	2.7	4.87	9.66	.31	.14	2.8	6.3
	Uganda*	4.1	6.2	2.71[e]	1.82[e]	.04	.18	13.1	9.8

290

		(1)	(2)					
Near East and South Asia	Ceylon*	3.1	2.6	4.74	.14	−.13	8.7	.7
	Cyprus*	3.9	4.5	4.18	.36	.54	4.2	10.1
	Greece	7.7	7.7	2.80	.31	.14	10.5	13.2
	India	4.1	1.8	3.76	.20	−.28	6.3	−1.5
	Iran	4.6	7.8	3.31e	.17	.25	15.0	12.7
	Israel	10.3	4.6	2.81	.17	−.35	14.8	12.2
	Jordan*	8.6	9.8	1.80	.04	−.18	15.3	16.5
	Pakistan	6.0	5.4	2.47	.04	−.02	1.7	11.4
	Turkey	5.8	6.8	2.47	.35	.33	8.0	12.0
East Asia	China (Taiwan)	9.3	11.5	1.95	.41	.35	4.9	24.1
	Korea	7.6	9.8	1.86	.31	.34	18.2	43.6
	Malaysia	6.2	6.4	2.79	.06	.28	.5	5.5
	Philippines	4.9	4.7	3.96	.52	.08	14.8	9.5
	Thailand	7.8	7.8	2.49	.39	.32	11.4	17.7
32-country sample	Weighted average	5.0	4.9	3.50	.21	.12	7.0	6.8
	Median	5.1	5.3	2.79	.19	.16	8.3	9.1
	Upper quartile	6.6	6.9	2.39	.31	.31	13.5	12.5

Source: Derived from A.I.D., Statistics and Reports Division data as of May 1968.

Period 1 = 1961-63 to 1963-65 (or 1960-62 to 1962-64 when marked by *).

Period 2 = 1963-65 to 1965-67 (or 1962-64 to 1964-66 when marked by *).

a Compound annual real growth rate based upon 3-year terminal period averages.

b Computed as ratio of gross investment/GNP ratio in base period (e.g., 1961-63) to GNP growth *rate* during following period (e.g., 1961-63 to 1963-65) from columns (1) and (2).

c National savings computed as difference between gross investment and "balance on goods and services," including factor services paid abroad.

d Based upon exports of goods and services from IMF, *Balance of Payments Yearbook*, in most cases.

e Based upon fixed investment only.

f Costa Rica, El Salvador, Guatemala, Honduras, and Nicaragua.

TABLE A–2.   KOREA—THREE-YEAR MOVING SUMS OF PRINCIPAL NATIONAL
ACCOUNTS VARIABLES, 1957–67

($ *million 1966 U.S. dollars*)

Years	GNP (*V*)	Gross invest-ment (*I*)	National savings (*S*)	Goods and services		Net foreign capital (*F*)	Change in stocks (*I*ₛ)
				Imports (*M*)	Exports (*E*)		
1957–59	6,901	883	−43	1,201	275	926	170
58–60	7,178	788	−13	1,114	313	801	73
59–61	7,437	772	84	1,054	366	688	27
60–62	7,684	853	101	1,178	426	752	9
61–63	8,119	1,145	253	1,377	485	892	124
62–64	8,691	1,308	393	1,465	550	915	174
63–65	9,406	1,469	652	1,494	677	817	200
64–66	10,330	1,753	1,015	1,694	956	738	145
65–67	11,337	2,231	1,314	2,274	1,383	891	66
Changes							
59-61 to 57-59	536	−111	127	−147	91	−238	−143
60-62 to 58-60	506	65	114	64	113	−49	−64
61-63 to 59-61	682	373	169	323	119	204	51
62-64 to 60-62	1,007	455	292	287	124	163	50
63-65 to 61-63	1,287	324	399	117	192	−75	20
64-66 to 62-64	1,639	445	622	229	406	−177	−55
65-67 to 63-65	1,931	762	688	780	706	74	−79

Source: A.I.D., Statistics and Reports Division.

GENERAL BIBLIOGRAPHY

GENERAL LITERATURE ON PLANNING

1. Adelman, Irma, and F. T. Sparrow. "Experiments with Linear and Piece-Wise Linear Dynamic Programming Models," in Adelman and Thorbecke (eds.), (2).
2. Adelman, Irma, and Erik Thorbecke (eds.). *The Theory and Design of Economic Development.* The Johns Hopkins Press, Baltimore, 1966.
3. Arrow, K. J., H. B. Chenery, B. S. Minhas, and R. M. Solow. "Capital-Labor Substitution and Economic Efficiency," *Review of Economics and Statistics*, vol. 43, no. 3 (August, 1961): 225–50.
4. Barr, James L., and Alan S. Manne. "Numerical Experiments with a Finite Horizon Planning Model," Research Center in Economic Growth, Memorandum 51, Stanford University, Stanford, California (May, 1966).
5. Bergsman, Joel, and Alan S. Manne. "An Almost Consistent Intertemporal Model for India's Fourth and Fifth Plans," in Adelman and Thorbecke, (eds.), (2).
6. Bos, H. C. *Spatial Dispersion of Economic Activity.* Rotterdam University Press, Rotterdam, 1965.
7. Boudeville, J.-R. *Problems of Regional Economic Planning.* Edinburgh University Press, Edinburgh, 1966.
8. Brioschi, F., and S. Rossi. "The Complementarity of Consumption in the Optimal Savings Problem," *Estratto da Calcolo*, vol. 4, no. 2 (April–June, 1967).
9. Bruno, Michael. "A Programming Model for Israel," in Adelman and Thorbecke, (eds.), (2).
10. Bryson, Arthur E., and Yu-Chi Ho. *Optimization, Estimation, and Control.* Blaisdell Publishing Company, Waltham, Massachusetts, 1968.
11. Carter, Nicholas G. "A New Look at the Sandee Model," in K. Shell (ed.), *Essays on the Theory of Optimal Economic Growth.* The M.I.T. Press, Cambridge, Massachusetts, 1967.
12. Chakravarty, S. "Optimum Saving with a Finite Planning Horizon," *International Economic Review*, 3, no. 3 (September, 1962): 338–55.
13. Chakravarty, S., and Louis Lefeber. "An Optimizing Planning Model," *Economic Weekly* (annual number; February, 1965): 237–52.
14. Chenery, Hollis B., and K. Kretschmer. "Resource Allocation for Economic Development," *Econometrica*, 24, no. 4 (October, 1956): 365–400.
15. Chenery, Hollis B., and Arthur MacEwan. "Optimal Patterns of Growth and Aid: The Case of Pakistan," in Adelman and Thorbecke (eds.) (2).
16. Chenery, Hollis B., and A. M. Strout. "Foreign Assistance and Economic Development," *American Economic Review*, 56 (September, 1966): 679–733.
17. Chenery, Hollis B., and Hirofumi Uzawa. "Nonlinear Programming in Economic Development," in K. J. Arrow, L. Hurwicz, and H. Uzawa

(eds.), *Studies in Linear and Nonlinear Programming*. Stanford University Press, Stanford, California, 1958.

18. Chenery, Hollis B., and Larry E. Westphal. "Economics of Scale and Investment Over Time," Project for Quantitative Research in Economic Development, Memorandum 16 (revised), Center for International Affairs, Harvard University, Cambridge, Massachusetts (1967).

19. Dantzig, George B. *Linear Programming and Extensions*. Princeton University Press, Princeton, New Jersey, 1963.

20. Davis, Ronald E., David A. Kendrick, and Martin Weitzman. "A Branch and Bound Algorithm for Zero-One Mixed Integer Programming Problems," Project for Quantitative Research in Economic Development, Memorandum 69, Center for International Affairs, Harvard University, Cambridge, Massachusetts (1967).

21. Dobell, A. R., and Y. C. Ho. "Optimal Investment Policy: An Example of a Control Problem in Economic Theory," *IEEE Transactions on Automatic Control*, vol. AC–12, no. 1 (February, 1967): 4–14.

22. Dorfman, Robert, Paul A. Samuelson, and Robert Solow. *Linear Programming and Economic Analysis*. McGraw-Hill Book Company, New York, 1958.

23. Eckaus, R. S., and Kirit Parikh. *Planning for Growth: Multisectoral Intertemporal Models Applied to India*. M.I.T. Press, Cambridge, Massachusetts, 1968.

24. Eckaus, R. S., and Louis Lefeber. "Planning in India," a paper prepared for a conference on economic planning (November 27–28, 1964) sponsored by Universities–National Bureau Committee for Economic Research in Princeton, New Jersey.

25. Fletcher, R., and M. J. D. Powell. "A Rapidly Convergent Descent Method for Minimization," *Computer Journal*, 6 (1963): 163–68.

26. Fletcher, R., and C. M. Reeves. "Function Minimization by Conjugate Gradients," *Computer Journal* (July, 1964).

27. Fox, K. A. "A Spatial Equilibrium Model of the Livestock-Feed Economy in the United States," *Econometrica* (October, 1963): 547–66.

28. Fox, K. A. "Comment," in Adelman and Thorbecke (eds.), (2).

29. Friedmann, John, and William Alonso. *Regional Development and Planning*. The M.I.T. Press, Cambridge, Massachusetts, 1964.

30. Frisch, R. "A Survey of Types of Economic Forecasting and Programming and a Brief Description of the Oslo Channel Model," Institute of Economics Memorandum, University of Oslo (May, 1961).

31. Ghosh, A. *Efficiency in Location and Interregional Flows: The Indian Cement Industry during the Five-Year Plans, 1950–59*. North-Holland Publishing Company, Amsterdam, 1965.

32. Haldi, John. "Economies of Scale in Economic Development," Stanford Project for Quantitative Research in Economic Development, Memorandum E–7, Stanford, California (1960).

33. Haldi, John, and David Whitcomb. "Economies of Scale in Industrial Plants," *Journal of Political Economy*, 75 (August, 1967): 373–85.

34. Halkin, H. "A Maximum Principle of the Pontryagin Type for Systems Described by Nonlinear Difference Equations," *SIAM Journal on Control*, 4, no. 1 (February, 1966): 90–111.

35. Harbison, Frederick, and Charles A. Myers. *Education, Manpower and Economic Growth*. McGraw-Hill Book Company, New York, 1964.
36. Heady, Earl O., and Alvin C. Egbert. "Spatial Programming Models to Specify Surplus Grain Producing Areas," in Manne and Markowitz, (ed.) (56).
37. Heady, Earl O., Narindar S. Randhawa, and Melvin D. Skold. "Programming Models for the Planning of the Agricultural Sector," in Adelman and Thorbecke (eds.), (2).
38. Henderson, J. M. *The Efficiency of the Coal Industry*. Harvard University Press, Cambridge, Massachusetts, 1958.
39. Houthakker, H. "A Note on Self-Dual Preferences," *Econometrica* (October, 1965): 797–801.
40. Hurter, Arthur P., Jr., and Leon N. Moses. "Regional Investment and Interregional Programming," *Regional Science Association Papers*, 13 (1964): 105–11.
41. Isard, Walter. *Location and Space-Economy*. The M.I.T. Press, Cambridge, Massachusetts, 1956.
42. Isard, Walter, and Eugene Smolensky. "Application of Input-Output Techniques to Regional Science," in Tibor Barna (ed.), *Structural Interdependence and Economic Development*. Macmillan & Co., London, 1963.
43. Jacoby, Neil H. *U.S. Aid to Taiwan*. Frederick A. Praeger, New York, 1966.
44. Johansen, L. (assisted by T. Lindhold). "Savings and Growth in Long Term Programming Models: Numerical Examples with a Nonlinear Objective Function," Oslo Institute of Economics, Memorandum (August, 1964).
45. Kendrick, D. A., and Lance J. Taylor. "Numerical Methods and Nonlinear Optimizing Models for Economic Planning," Project for Quantitative Research in Economic Development, Report 65, Center for International Affairs, Harvard University, Cambridge, Massachusetts (November, 1967). Forthcoming in Hollis Chenery (ed.), *Studies in Development Planning*.
46. Kendrick, D. A., and Lance J. Taylor. "Numerical Solution for Nonlinear Planning Models," Project for Quantitative Research in Economic Development, Report 98, Center for International Affairs, Harvard University, Cambridge, Massachusetts (May, 1968). Accepted for publication (subject to revision) by *Econometrica*.
47. Koopmans, T. "On the Concept of Optimal Economic Growth," in Salviucci *et al.*, *The Econometric Approach to Development Planning*. North-Holland Publishing Company, Amsterdam, and Rand McNally & Company, 1966.
48. Korea University (Asiatic Research Center). *International Conference on the Problems of Modernization in Asia*. Reports of June 28–July 7, 1965. 1966. (Mimeo.).
49. Lasdon, E. S., S. K. Mitter, and A. D. Warren. "The Conjugate Gradient Method for Optimal Control Problems," *IEEE Transactions on Automatic Control*, AC–12, no. 2 (April, 1967): 132–38.
50. Lefeber, Louis. "General Equilibrium Analysis of Production, Transporta-

tion and the Choice of Industrial Location," *Papers and Proceedings of the Regional Science Association*, 4 (1958): 77–86.

51. Lefeber, Louis. *Location and Regional Planning*. Center of Planning and Economic Research, Athens, 1966.

52. Lefeber, Louis. "Regional Allocation of Resources in India," in P.N. Rosenstein-Rodan (ed.), *Pricing and Fiscal Policies*. George Allen and Unwin, London, 1964.

53. Leontief, Wassily, and others. *Studies in the Structure of the American Economy*. Oxford University Press, New York, 1953.

54. Leontief, Wassily, and Alan Strout. "Multiregional Input-Output Analysis," in Tibor Barna (ed.), *Structural Interdependence and Economic Development*. Macmillan & Co., London, 1963.

55. Lösch, August. *The Economics of Location*. Yale University Press, New Haven, Connecticut, 1954.

56. Manne, Alan S., and Harry M. Markowitz. *Studies in Process Analysis*. John Wiley & Sons, New York, 1963.

57. Manne, Alan S. "Key Sectors of the Mexican Economy," in Manne and Markowitz (eds.) (56).

58. Manne, Alan S. "Key Sectors of the Mexican Economy, 1962–72," in Adelman and Thorbecke (eds.), (2).

59. Manne, Alan S. *Investments for Capacity Expansion*. George Allen and Unwin, London, 1966.

60. Manne, Alan S. (ed.). *Investments for Capacity Expansion: Size, Location and Time Phasing*. The M.I.T. Press, Cambridge, Massachusetts, 1967.

61. Marschak, Thomas A. "A Spatial Model of U.S. Petroleum Refining," in Manne and Markowitz (eds.)(56).

62. Masse, Pierre. *Optimal Investment Decisions*. Prentice-Hall, Englewood Cliffs, New Jersey, 1962.

63. Mera, Koichi. "Tradeoff between Aggregate Efficiency and Interregional Equity: A Static Analysis," *Quarterly Journal of Economics* (November, 1967): 658–74.

64. Meyer, J. R. "Regional Economics: A Survey," in American Economic Association and Royal Economic Society, *Surveys of Economic Theory, II*. Macmillan, New York, 1967.

65. Mirrlees, J. A. "Optimum Growth when Technology Is Changing," *Review of Economic Studies*, 34(1), no. 97 (January, 1967): 95–124.

66. National Planning Association. "PARM Interregional," draft of report to the Office of Emergency Planning, Executive Office of the President Washington, D.C., 1967.

67. Nerlove, Marc. "Recent Empirical Studies of the CES and Related Production Functions," in Murray Brown (ed.), *The Theory and Empirical Analysis of Production*. National Bureau of Economic Research, Washington, D.C. 1967.

68. Norton, Roger D., and Kee Jung Lee. "The Korean Input-Output Planning Model," paper presented to the Second Far Eastern Meeting of the Econometric Society, Tokyo, July 1, 1967.

69. Norton, Roger D. "The Spatial Framework of Development Planning in Korea," USOM/Korea (April, 1968). Memorandum.

70. Nugent, Jeffrey B. *Programming the Optimal Development of the Greek Economy, 1954–1961*. 2 vols. Research Monograph Series No. 15. Center of Planning and Economic Research, Athens, 1966.

71. Ohkawa, Kazushi, and Henry Rosovsky. "The Role of Agriculture in Modern Japanese Economic Development," *Economic Development and Cultural Change*, 9, no. 1, pt. 2 (October, 1960): 43–67.

72. Radner, Roy. *Notes on the Theory of Economic Planning*. Center of Planning and Economic Research, Athens, 1963.

73. Radner, Roy. "Optimal Growth in a Linear-Logarithmic Economy," *Internation Economic Review*, 7, no. 1 (January, 1966): 1–33.

74. Radner, Roy, and S. Friedman. "An Algorithm for Dynamic Programming of Economic Growth," Center for Research in Management Science, Working Paper 99, University of California, Berkeley, California (1967).

75. Ramseyer, Charles F. "Comparative Investment Costs for Different Steel-making Processes," in *A Study of the Iron and Steel Industry in Latin America, vol. 2: Proceedings of the Export Working Group Held at Bogota, Columbia*. E/CN.12/293/Rev. 1, 1954: 316–27.

76. Ranis, Gustav. "The Financing of Japanese Economic Development," *Economic History Review*, 2d ser., 11, no. 3 (April, 1959): 440–54.

77. Rao, V. L. S. Prakasa. *Regional Planning* (No. 20 in the Indian Statistical Series). Asia Publishing House, London, 1963.

78. Rosenberg, Nathan. "Capital Goods, Technology, and Economic Growth," *Oxford Economic Papers*, new ser., 15, no. 3 (November, 1963): 217–27.

79. Samuelson, P. A. "A Catenary Turnpike Theorem Involving Consumption and the Golden Rule," *American Economic Review*, 55, no. 3 (June, 1965): 486–96.

80. Samuelson, P. A., and Robert M. Solow. "A Complete Capital Model Involving Heterogeneous Capital Goods," *Quarterly Journal of Economics*, 7, no. 4 (November, 1956): 537–62.

81. Scitovsky, Tibor. "Growth—Balanced or Unbalanced?" in Moses Abramovitz (ed.), *The Allocation of Economic Resources*. Stanford University Press, Stanford, California, 1959.

82. Scitovsky, Tibor. "Two Concepts of External Economies," *Journal of Political Economy*, 62 (April, 1954): 143–51.

83. Sen, A. K. "Working Capital in the Indian Economy: A Conceptual Framework and Some Estimates," in P.N. Rosenstein-Rodan (ed.), *Pricing and Fiscal Policies*, George Allen and Unwin, London, 1964.

84. Stoleru, L. G. "An Optimal Policy for Economic Growth," *Econometrica*, 33, no. 2 (April, 1965): 321–84.

85. Vietorisz, Thomas, and Alan S. Manne. "Chemical Processes, Plant Location, and Economies of Scale," in Manne and Markowitz (eds.), (56).

86. Westphal, Larry Edward. "A Dynamic Multi-Sectoral Programming Model Featuring Economies of Scale," Ph.D. dissertation, Harvard University, 1968.

87. Wilson, R. B. A, "Simplicial Algorithm for Concave Programming," Ph.D. dissertation, Harvard University Graduate School of Business Administration, Boston, 1963.

LITERATURE ON KOREA

88. Adelman, Irma. "Macro Planning Model for Korea," USOM/K (July 12, 1965). Memorandum.

89. Adelman, Irma. "A Growth Model for Korea," USOM/K (September, 1965). Memorandum.

90. Adelman, Irma. "A Resource and Material Balance Model for Sectoral Planning in Korea," USOM/K (October 14 and 27, 1965). Memorandum.

91. Cazell, Gabriel F. "Report on Economic Indicators in Korea (Preliminary)," Surveys and Research Corporation mimeo. (December 1, 1961).

92. Han, Kee Chun. "A Study of Inter-Industry Relations in Korea" (September, 1966 [mimeo.]).

93. International Agricultural Resource Research Institute (Jae Suh Koo). *A Study of Regional Characteristics of Korean Agriculture.* Korea University, College of Agriculture, Seoul, 1967.

94. Kim, Byong-Kuk. *Central Banking Experiment in a Developing Economy: Case Study of Korea* (Korean Studies Series Vol. 12). The Korean Research Center, Seoul, 1965.

95. Kim Hak So, Tarik Carim, and Roger Norton. "Toward Development of Regional Planning Activities in Korea" (November, 1967 [mimeo.]).

96. Koh, Byung-Chul (ed.). *Aspects of Administrative Development in South Korea.* The Korea Research and Publication Company, Kalamazoo, Michigan, 1967.

97. Korean Development Association. *A Study of Regional Planning by Using Regional Input-Output Models.* Seoul, 1967.

98. Kuznets, Paul. "Population, Education, and Labor Force in Korea—A Preliminary Survey" (March, 1967 [mimeo.]).

99. Lee, Han Soon. Regions in Korea, Kyunghee University, Seoul (July, 1967 [mimeo.]).

100. Lee, Kyu Sul. *Population Pressure and Its Effects on Korean Farm Households.* Bureau of Statistics, Economic Planning Board, Seoul, 1967.

101. Lewis, J. P. *Reconstructions and Development in South Korea* (Planning Pamphlet 94). National Planning Agency, Washington, D.C., December, 1955.

102. McKinnon, Ronald I. "Tariffs and Commodity Tax Reform in Korea: Some Specific Suggestions," Report prepared for USOM/K (July, 1967 [mimeo.]).

103. McKinnon, Ronald I. "Reaction to Draft 'Negative List'," Report prepared for USOM/K (1967) (mimeo.).

104. Musgrave, R. A. "Revenue Policy for Korea's Economic Development" (Nathan Economic Advisory Group mimeo.) (September 27, 1965).

105. Politics and Economics Research Institute of Korea. *The Structural Analysis of Local Government Finances and Policy Recommendations* (with a statistical appendix "Provincial Income Estimates and Local Government Revenue and Expenditure [in Korea]"). Seoul, 1966.

106. Regional Planning Work Group. "Report on Regional Planning Field Trip," USOM/K (September, 1967 [mimeo.]).

107. Sam Boo Business Promotion Company. *National Boundary Planning Report.* Ministry of National Construction, Seoul, 1965 (in Korean).

108. Wolf, Charles, Jr. "Economic Planning in Korea," *Asian Survey*, 2, no. 10 (December, 1962): 22–28.

109. Wood, M. K., and R. D. Norton. "Economic Regions in Korea," USOM/K (February, 1968 [mimeo.]).

KOREAN STATISTICS

110. Republic of Korea, Economic Planning Board. *Economic Survey, 1967.* Seoul, December 1967.
111. Republic of Korea, EPB. *Korea Statistical Yearbook, 1967.* Seoul, August 1967.
112. Republic of Korea, EPB. *Overall Resources Budget: 1967 (Second Five-Year Economic Development Plan, 1967–1971).* Seoul, January 1967.
113. Republic of Korea, EPB. *Overall Resources Budget: 1968 (Second Five-Year Economic Development Plan, 1967–1971).* Seoul, August 1967.
114. Republic of Korea, EPB. *1960 Population and Housing Census of Korea, Vol. 1: Complete Tabulation Report.* Seoul, November 1963.
115. Republic of Korea, EPB. *First Five-Year Economic Development Plan (1962–1966)* (adjusted version). Seoul, March 1964.
116. Republic of Korea, EPB. *The Economically Active Population Survey (No. 4) 1965.* Seoul, May 1966.
117. Republic of Korea, EPB. *The Korean Sectoral Plan, 1967–1971.* Seoul, 1966.
118. Republic of Korea, EPB and Korean Reconstruction Bank. *Report on Mining and Manufacturing Census, 1966.* Seoul, 1967.
119. Republic of Korea, Ministry of Agriculture and Forestry. *Yearbook of Agriculture and Forestry Statistics, 1966.* Seoul, September 1966.
120. Republic of Korea, Ministry of Education. *Statistic Yearbook of Education, 1967.* Seoul, November 1967.
121. Republic of Korea, Ministry of National Construction. *Traffic Survey on Major Roads.* Seoul, 1966.
122. Republic of Korea, Ministry of Reconstruction. *Economic Survey, 1959.* Seoul, November 1959.
123. Republic of Korea, Prime Minister's Office of Planning and Coordination. *Evaluation Report on the First Five-Year Economic Plan (1962–1966)* (written by Evaluation Faculty). Seoul, 1967 (in Korean).
124. Republic of Korea. *Summary of the First Five-Year Economic Plan, 1962–66.* Seoul, January 1962.
125. Republic of Korea, Ministry of Transport. *Korea Transportation Survey.* Seoul, 1967.
126. Government of the Republic of Korea. *Second Five-Year Economic Development Plan, 1967–1971.* Seoul, July 1966.
127. Government of the Republic of Korea. *The Second Five-Year Plan for Development of Science and Technology, 1967–1971.* Seoul, July 1966.
128. Republic of Korea, Bank of Korea. *Monthly Statistical Review,* 21, no. 7 (July, 1967) (in Korean).
129. Republic of Korea, BOK. *Monthly Statistical Review,* vol. 22, no. 2 (February, 1968).
130. Republic of Korea, BOK. *Description of the 1963 Input-Output Tables, 1965.* Seoul, 1965.
131. Republic of Korea, BOK. *Input-Output Analysis for the Korean Economy, 1963, and 1966.* Seoul, 1966.
132. Republic of Korea, BOK. *The Interindustry Relations Study for the Korean Economy, 1960, and 1964.* Seoul, 1964.
133. United Nations, Economic Commission for Asia and the Far East. *Economic Survey of Asia and the Far East, 1966.* Bangkok, 1967.

134. United Nations, Food and Agriculture Organization. *Production Yearbook, 1965.* Rome, 1966.
135. United Nations, Korean Reconstruction Agency. *An Economic Programme for Korean Reconstruction.* New York, 1954.
136. United States Operations Mission to Korea, Rural Development Division. "Revised Foodgrain Production and Consumption for 1962–64, and Projections to 1971" (December, 1965 [mimeo.]).

INDEX

Absorptive capacity function: in nonlinear model, 218–19, 232
Adelman, Irma, 14n, 19, 109n, 140, 156n, 213
Africa: economic performance in, 290
Agency for International Development, 13–14, 45
Agriculture: criteria for project appraisal in, 246–48; expansion plans for, 26; and food consumption expenditures, 48, 82, 93; good crop years, 52, 59, 269; grain-management scheme, 261–62; gross fixed investment in, 83–84, 92; impact of price changes, 99–100; importance of, 55; incomes of farmers, 58; increased production in, 275; investment in, 7–8, 20, 24, 35, 45, 83–84; policies in, 27–28; poor crop years, 4, 48, 53, 59; priorities in, 247; production function of, 80–81, 91; reduced growth rate in, 175–77; and self-sufficiency in grains, 41, 42, 45, 57–59. *See also* Grains
Alternative planning strategies: in econometric model, 100–5; in mixed integer model, 164–77; in sectoral model, 130
Aluminum refining plant, 21, 117
Annual financial programs, 259
Argentina: economic performance in, 290
Asia: economic performance in, 291
Attitudes toward Second Plan, 36–37
Auerbach, Kay, 109n

Balance-of-payments: changes in, 267–68; constraint in econometric model, 90; constraint in sectoral model, 111, 114–15; and project appraisal, 245n; projections for, 43
Bank of Korea, 17, 44n, 54, 61, 116, 135, 136, 216n, 269–70
Banking: and interest-rate reform, 5, 264–67; monetary policies, 62, 262–63
Barr, J. L., 213
Bergsman, J., 192n
Bolivia: economic performance in, 290
Borrowing: foreign (*see* Foreign capital); by government, 61
Boudeville, J. R., 209n, 210
Bove, R., 233n
Bowles, S., 218n
Brazil: economic performance in, 290
Brioschi, F., 233n
Bruno, M., 147, 188n, 213, 214
Bryson, A., 213n, 214n
Budgets: construction of, 9; Overall Resource Budgets, 12, 39n, 53, 54, 56–57, 77, 78, 132, 133, 250–51, 259

Capacity: expansion with foreign-capital inflows, 166–75; expansion in nonlinear model, 218–19, 236; increases in mining and manufacturing, 113–14; measurements of, 119–21; rates of utilization of, 121; related to output, 110, 114
Capital: coefficients in sectoral model, 114, 117–19, 120; estimated requirements for, 42; from foreign investors (*see* Foreign capital); output-capital ratio, 81, 282–86, 290; ratio to labor in nonlinear model,

226–27, 228; requirements for foreign capital, 102–5; scarceness of, 62
Capital goods: ratio to consumer goods, 25–26
Capitalism, guided, 41, 42n, 50n
Carim, Tarik, 185n, 207n
Carter, N. G., 213
Cement making, 18
Central America: economic performance in, 290
Ceylon: economic performance in, 291
Cha, Byung Kwon, 207n
Chakravarty, S., 213, 214n
Chang Key Young, 56
Chenery, H., 61n, 78, 145n, 146, 147, 157, 188n, 213n, 214n, 233n
Chile: economic performance in, 290
China: economic performance in, 291
Choi, Sang Chul, 207n
Christ, C. F., 128n
Cities: definition of, 208n; population of, 210
Coal mining. *See* Mining
Cole, D., 53, 145, 166n, 216n
Colombia: economic performance in, 290
Commerce and Industry Ministry, 28, 57n
Committees: industry, 9, 14, 116–17, 118–19, 130, 243
Communications: criteria for project appraisal, 245n, 250; priorities in, 247
Communism: threat of, 3
Computer model, 140
Construction industry: capability of, 273; growth of, 52; labor-intensive methods in, 17
Consumer goods: ratio to capital goods, 25–26
Consumption: in First Five-Year Plan, 41–42; of food, 82, 93; government share of, 55, 83, 93, 125, 192–93; nonfood, 83, 93; in nonlinear model, 224–25; and output per capita, 68; private, 82–83, 93; projections of, 123–26; rural behavior in, 125, 126; by type of purchaser, 71; urban behavior in, 125, 126
Controls: governmental, 5
Corruption: sources of, 5, 51
Costs: of decentralization, 203; of sectors, comparative, 165, 166
Cottage industries, 121
Counties: number of, 208n
Credit: policies in, 262–64; responses to increases in, 95–97, 99; restriction in, 62
Currency. *See* Monetary policies
Cyprus: economic performance in, 291

Dam project, 245n
Dantzig, G. B., 147n
Davis, R. E., 147
Decentralization of industry, 7, 27–28, 185–212
Defense budget, 45
Demand. *See* Supply and demand
Dembowski, D., 109
Democratic institutions, 4
Deposits: and interest-rate reform, 264–67; responses to increase in, 95–97, 99

301

129; final-demand projections in, 123–27; gestation lags in, 114, 121; impact on investment program, 131–32; implementation of, 128–31; import-input ratios in, 122–23; input-output coefficients in, 116–17, 135–38, 139; labor input coefficients in, 122, 123; mathematical foundation of, 113–16; parameters in, 116–23; predictive ability of, 127–34; process of solution, 112; production functions, 80–82, 91; rates of utilization in, 121; reformulation of, 138–40; relationship of output to capacity, 110, 114; savings-investment constraint in, 111, 115; and sequential programming system, 138–43; structure of, 110–12; total use: total availability equalities in, 110, 113
Selection and evaluation of projects, 241–56
Self-sufficiency: as goal, 15, 24, 26, 41, 42, 45, 54, 57–59, 246
Sen, A. K., 189
Sequential economic programming, 138–43
Services: gross fixed investment in, 85, 92; production function for, 82, 91
Shaw, E. S., 14n, 78, 95, 265n
Skilled workers: quality of, 60
Smuggling: inverted, 63n
Social overhead: gross fixed investment in, 85, 92; priorities in, 247; production function for, 81, 91; and regional development, 204
Sparrow, F. T., 156n, 213
Stabilization of economy, 257–76; annual programs for, 259; background of, 257–59; and balance-of-payments, 267–68; and credit policy, 262–64; and exchange rate, 268–71; exogenous factors in, 273–75; fiscal balance in, 260–62; and import liberalization, 269, 271–72; inflow of foreign private capital in, 272–73; and interest-rate reform, 5, 264–67; policies in, 5, 12, 51, 53, 61, 259–73
Steel mill, 7, 8, 18, 21, 29, 43, 53, 131; planning of investment in, 146–78
Stoleru, L. G., 214n
Stone, R. N., 136
Strategies in development planning, 21–32
Strout, A., 14n, 61n, 109n, 127n, 193n, 284n
Structural equations: estimation of, 79–88
Studenmund, A. H., 285n
Students: political activities of, 4, 5, 17
Supply and demand: in mixed integer model, 153–55; relationships in, 5, 6, 20, 44
Supreme Council for National Reconstruction, 13, 17, 18, 34

Szasz, A., 213n

Taiwan: economic performance in, 291
Target growth rates. See Growth rates
Taxes. See Revenues
Technology. See Science and technology
Thailand: economic performance in, 291
Third Five-Year Plan, 7
Three-Year Plan: export and import targets in, 25–26; impact of, 33; policies in, 12, 16, 17, 22; target growth rate in, 22
Time deposits: responses to increase in, 95–97, 99
Tourism: priorities in, 247
Trade balance: improvement of, 16, 17
Transportation: criteria for project appraisal, 249; growth of, 52; investments in, 18, 35, 43; priorities in, 247; and regional planning, 193, 204; study of, 14
Tunisia: economic performance in, 290
Turkey: economic performance in, 291

Uganda: economic performance in, 290
Unbalanced growth strategy, 26, 45
Unemployment: and construction projects, 17; estimates of, 55; levels of, 59
United Nations Korean Reconstruction Agency, 11, 13, 15
United States: assistance from, 4, 13, 23, 257, 261
Urban centers: in regional planning, 208–12
Urban consumption behavior, 125, 126
Urban development: priorities in, 247
Utilities. See Power industries
Utilization of capacity: rates of, 121
Uzawa, H., 214n

Vanek, J., 285n
Venezuela: economic performance in, 290
Vietnam: remittances from, 61, 267, 271
Vietorisz, T., 188n, 213n

Water supply, 191n, 197, 203
Waugh, F. V., 204n
Weather conditions: and agriculture production, 80–81
Weitzman, M., 147
Welfare function: in nonlinear model, 214–16, 235
Westphal, L., 147, 148n, 178n, 188n, 216
Whitcomb, D., 147n
Wolf, C., 23n, 26, 32n, 44n
Wood, M. K., 109n, 185n, 207n, 216n
Wooh, Youn Hwi, 109n, 207n
World Bank, 14, 23–24, 28n, 35

THE JOHNS HOPKINS PRESS
Designed by Arlene J. Sheer
Composed in Times Roman text and display
by Monotype Composition Company
Printed on 50-lb. Perkins and Squier R
by Universal Lithographers, Inc.
Bound in Columbia Riverside Vellum
by L. H. Jenkins Co., Inc.